Empedocles : The Extant Fragments

EMPEDOCLES
THE EXTANT FRAGMENTS

Edited with Introduction,
Commentary, Concordance and
New Bibliography by

M.R. Wright

Bristol Classical Press

The cover illustration shows the temple to Concordia,
built in the fifth century BC and still standing,
in the outskirts of Empedocles' home town of Acragas, the modern Agrigento.

First published in 1981 by Yale University Press

Second edition published in 1995 by
Bristol Classical Press
an imprint of
Gerald Duckworth & Co. Ltd
61 Frith Street
London W1D 3JL
e-mail: inquiries@duckworth-publishers.co.uk
Website: www.ducknet.co.uk

Reprinted 2001

A catalogue record for this book is available
from the British Library

ISBN 1-85399-482-0

Printed in Great Britain by
Antony Rowe Ltd, Eastbourne

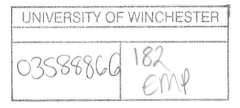

Contents

III. *TRANSLATION AND COMMENTARY*

Note to the Second Edition

Since the first edition of *Empedocles* the study of the Presocratics and of this author in particular has flourished, with many selections of fragments and translations appearing in Europe and North America. The controversy about Empedocles' cosmology and the phases involved, which previously dominated the scholarship, has more recently given way to agreement with the position adopted in the earlier edition, and many of the details concerning the ordering of the fragments first put forward there have been similarly accepted, although some dispute has arisen over whether one or two poems are involved. I think the arguments for two separate but related poems addressed to different audiences in different settings still hold, but the issue does not affect the underlying theory in any substantial way. My main concern has always been to establish Empedocles as a serious thinker in the mainstream of Presocratic philosophy rather than an oddity on its fringe, and most of the scholarship on the author over the past decade has provided welcome confirmation of this. I am content to have been instrumental in winning increased respect for Empedocles, and I am very grateful that this paperback edition will allow a wider readership to become more closely acquainted with his ideas and his poetry.

M.R. Wright
Lampeter 1995

Acknowledgment

It is a pleasure to give credit to those who have assisted this work at different stages, to Professor G. E. L. Owen, Professor P. H. J. Lloyd-Jones, the Center for Hellenic Studies and its director, Professor B. M. W. Knox, to Mr. E. L. Hussey, Professor A. P. D. Mourelatos, Ms. Sharon Slodki, and *in primis* Dr. Moorhead Wright.

I. Introduction

1. Life and Writings

DATING EMPEDOCLES' LIFE

Empedocles' dates are uncertain. Apollodorus sets his *floruit* in the 84th Olympiad (444–440 B.C.), but as this period connects with the foundation of Thurii in 444 B.C., which Empedocles was said to have visited soon after it was established, the notice is suspect.[1] According to the chronology of Eusebius, Empedocles was becoming known together with Parmenides in the 81st Olympiad (456–452 B.C.), and with Democritus in the 86th Olympiad (436–432 B.C.). Aulus Gellius puts the *floruit* of Empedocles' philosophical activity between the defeat of the Fabii at Cremera (477 B.C.) and the establishment of the Decemvirate (451 B.C.).[2] On the authority of Neanthes, Diogenes relates that when there were signs of the beginning of a tyranny in Acragas, Empedocles persuaded the people to put an end to their rivalries and to adopt a democratic form of government. This would have taken place some time after the expulsion of Thrasydaeus, the last tyrant of Acragas, in 472 B.C.[3] No more can be concluded from these accounts than that Empedocles' working life covered a period between 477 and 432 B.C.

Aristotle states that Empedocles was younger than Anaxagoras, and according to Theophrastus Empedocles was born not long after Anax-

---

1. Apollodorus ap. D.L. 8.52, 74; Glaucus of Rhegium quoted by Apollodorus on the visit to Thurii ap. D.L. 8.52; cf. the mechanical dating of Xenophanes, Parmenides, and Zeno in connection with the foundation of Elea in 540 B.C.: D.L. 9.20, 23, 29, and of Protagoras with Thurii: D.L. 9.50, 56.

2. Eusebius *Chron.* Ol. 81, 86; Gellius *Noct. Att.* 17.21.14.

3. Neanthes ap. D.L. 8.72; for the expulsion of Thrasydaeus by Syracuse and the establishment of democracy at Acragas cf. Diodorus Siculus 11.53.

agoras.[4] If the date of Anaxagoras' birth is accepted as ca. 500 B.C.,[5] then 495–490 is a possible range for that of Empedocles. And this in turn agrees with the remark of Apollodorus that Empedocles could not have fought with Syracuse against the Athenians (in 415 B.C.), as some suppose, because he would then have been dead or a very old man.[6]

Further support for this dating of Empedocles' birth comes from his connection with the Eleatics. He is said by Theophrastus to have admired Parmenides and to have imitated him in his poems.[7] This need not mean that Empedocles was personally acquainted with Parmenides, and Theophrastus here finds common ground in the fact that they both wrote in hexameters. But Empedocles gave careful consideration to the work of Parmenides, and his own theory is in part a later reply to it. According to Alcidamas, Empedocles was a pupil of Parmenides at the same time as Zeno was, and in the *Suda* Melissus, Empedocles, and Zeno are contemporaries.[8] The approximate dates of Parmenides and Zeno can be calculated from Plato's *Parmenides*, where Parmenides is said to have been about sixty-five years old and Zeno nearly forty when they met the young Socrates in Athens.[9] Since Socrates' death at seventy was in 399 B.C., if he is taken to have been approximately twenty years old at the time of this meeting, Parmenides' birth would be ca. 515 B.C., and Zeno's ca. 490 B.C.; this would fit well with the hypothesis that Empedocles was born between 495 and 490 B.C. However, the reliability of Alcidamas' account as given by Diogenes is vitiated by the addition that, after hearing Parmenides, Empedocles became the pupil of both Anaxagoras and Pythagoras, imitating the former in his physiology and the latter in the dignity of his life and demeanor.[10] The affectation of character and dress

4. Aristotle *Metaph.* 984a11; Theophrastus ap. Simplicius *in Phys.* 25.19.

5. Cf. Apollodorus and Demetrius of Phalerum ap. D.L. 2.7; on Anaxagoras' chronology generally cf. A. E. Taylor *CQ* 1917, pp. 81–87; J. S. Morrison *CQ* 1941, p. 5, n. 2, J. A. Davison *CQ* 1953, pp. 39–45; W. K. C. Guthrie *History of Greek Philosophy* vol. 2, pp. 322–23; D. O'Brien *JHS* 1968, pp. 93–113.

6. Apollodorus ap. D.L .8.52; cf. F. Jacoby *Apollodors Chronik* p. 273.

7. Theophrastus ap. D.L. 8.55, and cf. Simplicius loc. cit., who adds that Empedocles was even more a follower of the Pythagoreans; for Empedocles as a favored pupil of Parmenides cf. also Porphyry ap. *Suda* s.v. Empedoklēs.

8. Alcidamas ap. D.L. 8.56; *Suda* s.v. Melētos. Melissus' work, however, is probably later, for DK 30 B7(3) and B8 look like a reply to Empedocles; cf. Guthrie *HGP* vol. 2, pp. 115–16.

9. Plato *Parmenides* 127b.

10. F. M. Cleve, *The Giants of Pre-Sophistic Greek Philosophy* vol. 2, pp. 332–33, accepts Alcidamas' report in its entirety but can do so only by following G.F. Unger in putting

that Empedocles is said to have adopted is also attributed to the influence of Anaximander.[11]

Other teachers assigned to Empedocles may be discounted. Hermippus, for example, asserts that Empedocles followed not Parmenides but Xenophanes and spent part of his life with him. In the *Suda* Archytas is given as the teacher of Empedocles. Timaeus reports that Empedocles was a pupil of Pythagoras and was expelled, like Plato, for *logoklopia*. Neanthes agrees with this, with the correction that Empedocles was a pupil not of Pythagoras but of some unknown Pythagorean; he adds that no reliance should be placed on the letter attributed to Telauges, which claims that Hippasus and Brontinus taught Empedocles. A further dubious tradition makes Empedocles the pupil of this Telauges.[12]

Empedocles is also said to have been the teacher of Gorgias.[13] If this is correct it would suggest that Empedocles was older than Gorgias by at least ten years. Gorgias' birth is generally agreed to be ca. 483 B.C.,[14] and so an earlier date in the period 495–490 B.C. would be appropriate for Empedocles. Even if the teacher-pupil relationship is based mainly on a passage from Plato's *Meno*, where a theory of pores and effluences derived from Empedocles is attributed to Gorgias, Empedocles' seniority is still presupposed.[15]

According to Aristotle, as quoted by Apollodorus, Empedocles died at the age of sixty. This notice is more reliable than the evidence for the variants of seventy-seven and one hundred and nine years. The first comes from the same source as the dubious account of Empedocles' death as the result of a broken thigh, and the second is an obvious confusion with the age of Gorgias at his death.[16] From an assessment of the available

---

Empedocles' birth back to 521 B.C. Even on this unwarranted assumption Empedocles could not have attended courses by Anaxagoras *and* Pythagoras after hearing Parmenides.

11. Diodorus of Ephesus ap. D.L. 8.70.

12. Hermippus ap. D.L. 8.56; *Suda* s.v. Archytas; Timaeus and Neanthes ap. D.L. 8.54–55; Telauges as Empedocles' teacher: D.L. 8.43, Eusebius *PE* 10.15; on the hexameter line supposedly addressed by Empedocles to Telauges cf. below, n. 94.

13. Satyrus ap. D.L. 8.58; cf. Quintilian 3.1.8, Olympiodorus *Plat. Gorg. proem.* 9, *Suda* s.v. Gorgias, Empedoklēs.

14. Cf. [Plut.] *Vit. X orat.* 832f, and the discussion by E. Wellmann, *PW* s.v. Gorgias (8).

15. Plato *Meno* 76c, and cf. Empedocles as the founder of rhetoric: D.L. 8.57, Sextus Empiricus *adv. math.* 7.6.

16. Aristotle (and Heraclides if Sturz's emendation is accepted) ap. D.L. 8.52, 74; Neanthes ap. D.L. 8.73, and cf. J. Bidez *La Biographie d'Empédocle* p. 64; for 109 years for Empedocles and Gorgias cf. D.L. 8.74, 58.

testimony, therefore, it may be concluded that Empedocles' dates are approximately 494–434 B.C.

POLITICS, RHETORIC, AND MEDICINE

Empedocles was a native of Acragas, son of Meton and grandson of Empedocles. The family was said to have been wealthy and distinguished, and this is borne out by the grandfather's victory in horse racing at Olympia in 496 B.C.[17] It is reported that Empedocles himself was rich and that from his resources he provided dowries and maintained a train of attendants, but such details are most probably elaborations of his own words in fragment 102(112).[18] Empedocles is credited with a brother, Callicratides, a sister, a son, and a daughter, and, by the daughter, a grandson who was also called Empedocles.[19]

Most authorities give Meton as the name of Empedocles' father, but in the letter of Telauges it is said to be Archinomos; according to Satyrus the father was Exaenetos, and Empedocles had a son of the same name. The *Suda* has Meton, with Archinomos and Exaenetos as alternatives.[20] Karsten suggests that Archinomos was a *cognomen magistratus* of Meton and was later mistakenly assumed to be the name of Empedocles' father.[21] As for the second variant, an Exaenetos of Acragas won an Olympic victory for the *stadion* in the 91st and 92nd Olympiads (416 and 412 B.C.), and a double confusion seems to have arisen. First, Empedocles was mistaken for his grandfather as a victor in horse racing, and second, the later victory of Exaenetos in running was attributed to the son of Empedocles. Moreover, the confusion of Empedocles with his grandfather, Empedocles the Olympic victor, is likely to have been the basis of another tradition, that Empedocles went to Olympia and, because of fragment 118(128), that he there sacrificed an ox made of honey and barley meal.[22]

---

17. Empedocles, son of Meton: Timaeus, Hermippus, Hippobotus, Apollodorus ap. D.L. 8.51, Aetius 1.3.20; Empedocles' grandfather of the same name: Timaeus, Hippobotus; horse training: Heraclides Ponticus; Olympian victory (71st Ol.): Aristotle (quoted by Eratosthenes), Apollodorus; his fame: Timaeus, Hermippus; cf. D.L. 8.51–52.

18. Cf. D.L. 8.73.

19. Cf. Favorinus, Satyrus, Aristotle, Hieronymus ap. D.L. 8.53, 57; *Suda* s.v. Empedoklēs (2).

20. D.L. 8.53, *Suda* s.v. Empedoklēs.

21. S. Karsten *Empedoclis Agrigentini carmina reliquiae* p. 4, n. 5.

22. Exaenetos' victories: Diodorus Siculus 12.82.1, 13.34.1, 82.7; the victory of the

Empedocles was a favorite subject for the detailed elaboration of the Hellenistic biographers, and very little of the evidence for his life that comes from this source can be considered reliable. It does seem, however, that Empedocles played some part in the political activities of Acragas. Theron died in 473 B.C.; his period of power had proved beneficial and popular, and he was awarded a hero's honors after his death. He was succeeded by his son Thrasydaeus, a violent and lawless tyrant, who within a year was driven from Acragas by Syracusan troops under Hieron and later condemned to death. Peace and democracy were restored to Acragas, but there was still much tension, and ten years later civil strife broke out in all the Sicilian democracies.[23] It is credible that a family of wealth and standing, as that of Empedocles was said to be, would be involved in these changes in the city. Many of the details of this involvement come from Timaeus; his statements are carefully reported from the original book by Diogenes, and his information on Sicilian politics may preserve an authentic tradition.[24] Two facts, however, throw some suspicion on the importance of Empedocles' role in politics. The first is that Diodorus does not mention Empedocles at all in his Sicilian history apart from quoting a line from fragment 102(112) to illustrate the hospitality of Acragas;[25] the second is that Timaeus does report a deal of nonsense about Empedocles, and it is difficult to estimate his reliability on any one point.[26]

After the death of Empedocles' father, according to Neanthes, signs of tyranny became noticeable in Acragas; Empedocles then himself persuaded the people to put an end to their seditions and to observe political equality.[27] His prodemocratic outlook is preserved in a fragment of Aristotle, φησὶ δ' αὐτὸν καὶ 'Αριστοτέλης ἐλεύθερον γεγονέναι καὶ

Exaenetos who was said to be Empedocles' son was in wrestling according to Satyrus, and according to Heraclides Lembus, in running: D.L. 8.53; for Empedocles as victor, and for the bloodless sacrifices cf. Athenaeus 1.3, *Suda* s.v. Athēnaios, D.L. 8.53, Philostratus *Vit. Ap.*1.1.2, Eustathius *ad Od.* 1454.20; Karsten, *EAcr* p. 5, suggests that Exaenetos was the name of the great-grandfather and of the uncle of Empedocles.

23. Diodorus Siculus 11.53.1–5, 72.1–2, and cf. E. A. Freeman *The History of Sicily from the Earliest Times* vol. 2, p. 345.

24. E.g., Diogenes quotes from books 15, 9, 18, 11, and 12 of the *Histories* of Timaeus at 8.51,54,60,66; cf. F. Susemihl *Geschichte der Griechischen Litteratur* vol. 1, p. 571, n. 258.

25. Diodorus Siculus 13.83.1.

26. Cf. Timaeus on Empedocles as a pupil of Pythagoras, and the anecdote of the skins: D.L. 8.54,60; Timaeus is called γραοσυλλέκτρια, *Suda* s.v.; cf. Plutarch *Nic.* 1.2–4, Diodorus Siculus 13.90.6.

27. Neanthes ap. D.L. 8.72.

πάσης ἀρχῆς ἀλλότριον, and this is elaborated in Xanthus to a refusal of the kingship.[28]

Diogenes quotes three incidents from Timaeus which show that Empedocles was actively democratic.[29] The first, which is said to mark the beginning of Empedocles' political career, is a curious tale of his prosecuting two state officials for signs of incipient tyranny in their domineering manner to their guests. The guests had been kept waiting, and when the wine was finally brought they were ordered either to drink it or to have it poured over their heads.[30] In the second story the physician Acron petitioned the *Boulē* for some land for a memorial to his father. Empedocles, speaking περὶ ἰσότητος, caused the petition to be rejected. Empedocles' third action was to break up an organization called the "Thousand," three years after it had been established. Nothing is known of this organization; it may have been a formal senate similar to the senate of a thousand at Rhegium or an aristocratic conspiracy or club.[31] A notice of Plutarch that may be referring to this dissolution also shows Empedocles taking measures against leading citizens who had antidemocratic aims.[32] Whatever the truth of these anecdotes, the tradition presents Empedocles as a champion of the people, capable of firm and independent action. The contrast between the character he revealed in political life and the proud attitude he adopted in his poetry was remarked on.[33]

In a fragment of the *Sophist* preserved in Diogenes, Aristotle states that Empedocles invented rhetoric. Satyrus too calls Empedocles ῥήτωρ ἄριστος, but the only evidence given in support of this is that Gorgias was his pupil.[34] In the reports of Empedocles' political activity two speeches on equality are mentioned, one in reply to Acron's request, and

28. Aristotle and Xanthus ap. D.L. 8.63; cf. a similar refusal reported of Heraclitus: D.L. 9.6.

29. D.L. 8.64–66.

30. T. S. Brown, *Timaeus of Tauromenium* p. 52, suggests that the story presents a caricature of Empedocles, originating perhaps in one of the comedy writers, and not to be taken seriously.

31. Cf. Freeman *History of Sicily* vol. 2, pp. 349, 560; also Xenophanes fr. 3 and, on the Assembly at Mytilene, D. Page *Sappho and Alcaeus* p. 178.

32. Plut. *adv. Col.* 1126b: 'Ε. δὲ τούς τε πρώτους τῶν πολιτῶν ὑβρίζοντας καὶ διαφοροῦντας τὰ κοινὰ ἐξήλεγξε.

33. Timaeus ap. D. L. 8.66; cf. Empedocles' comment on the luxurious life at Acragas, quoted below, n. 36, and Favorinus' description of Empedocles' own dress and retinue, D.L. 8.63 and 73, but these details in Favorinus are almost certainly a later elaboration.

34. Aristotle ap. D.L. 8.57; Satyrus ap. D.L. 8.58; cf. D.L. 9.25, Sextus Empiricus *adv. math.* 7.6, *Suda* s.v. Zeno, Quintilian 3.1.8.

the other against tyranny, given after the death of Meton. Yet neither of them should be accepted unconditionally, for the first serves to introduce an epigram that is almost certainly spurious, and the second rests only on the dubious authority of Neanthes.[35] If, however, Empedocles did work for democracy, and with some success, persuasive oratory may have contributed to this success; nevertheless, no quotation from any work in prose by Empedocles is extant,[36] and there is no means of assessing his competence as a rhetorician.

It is also difficult to come to a decision about Empedocles' medical skill: was he a genuine healer or a charlatan? The tradition is elaborate and confused, and it is well to start from Empedocles' own words. The fragments contain several observations of an elementary character on anatomy and physiology, and not necessarily presupposing professional knowledge. The functions of seeing and breathing, for example, are explained analogically by the ordinary mechanism of the lantern and the clepsydra. The structure of bone is represented by a simple ratio of four parts fire to two each of earth and water. The alignment of the male to the warm (and left) side of the womb, and of the female to the cold (and right), seems more an arbitrary disagreement with Parmenides than a medical observation.[37] Further information is supplied by the doxographers about Empedocles' accounts of nourishment, growth, sleep, and death, as well as such details as the cause of tears and sweat, and the composition of nails and sinews; according to one authority Empedocles also had an explanation for some mental disorders.[38] But these accounts, like that of sensation by means of pores and effluences, need not be the result of deduction from clinical experience; the conclusions could equally well have been reached by reasoning from a physical theory that aimed to be all-embracing.

Empedocles seems to have had a particular interest in embryology,

35. περὶ ἰσότητος διαλεχθείς D.L. 8.65; εἶτα τὸν ᾿Ε. πεῖσαι τοὺς ᾿Ακραγαντίνους παύσασθαι μὲν τῶν στάσεων, ἰσότητα δὲ πολιτικὴν ἀσκεῖν D.L. 8.72. For the epigram cf. below, n. 94; for an assessment of Neanthes' merits as a historian cf. Jacoby, F. Gr. H. IIa, pp. 144–45, and on his bias and powers of invention, Bidez Biographie pp. 65–67.

36. With the possible exception of Empedocles' comment on the luxury at Acragas, from Timaeus at D.L. 8.63: ᾿Ακραγαντίνοι τρυφῶσι μὲν ὡς αὔριον ἀποθανούμενοι, οἰκίας δὲ κατασκευάζονται ὡς πάντα τὸν χρόνον βιωσόμενοι.

37. Frs. 88(84), 91(100), 48(96), 57(65), 58(67); and cf. Aristotle Part. An. 648a25–31; G. E. R. Lloyd (JHS 1964, p. 102) suggests that male and warm were related as intrinsically superior to female and cold.

38. Aetius 5.27.1, Soranus Gynaec. 1.57 (DK 31 A79); Aetius 5.24.2, 25.4, 22.1; Caelius Aurel. Morb. chron. 1.5 (DK 31 A98).

but this is in the Presocratic tradition, for the subject was also treated by Parmenides (in the *Doxa*), and by Anaxagoras and Diogenes of Apollonia. Some dates Empedocles gives in this connection are quite precise. It may have been from observation that he decided that the development of the fetus began on the thirty-sixth day and was completed on the forty-ninth day, and that the milk was formed on the tenth day of the eighth month.[39] Yet the correlation of nine and seven month births with the earlier cosmic days of nine and seven months' duration suggests that Empedocles was attempting to find a connection between the development of man and the growth of the world, rather than putting forward a medical theory based on personal practice.[40]

In a well-known fragment, doctors are set with prophets, minstrels, and leaders as belonging to the highest stage of human life; it is probable that Empedocles considered the four careers to be united in himself. Obviously he would be ὑμνοπόλος and πρόμος, and he claims that in the towns people flocked to him in thousands, expecting of him both prophecies and cures.[41] Moreover, Empedocles promises Pausanias that he will learn of φάρμακα κακῶν and, what was obviously thought to be unattainable, defense against old age and restoration to life.[42] But Empedocles' words on healing are ambiguous, for the φάρμακα κακῶν could be a genuine cure or a more dubious remedy,[43] and the εὐηκὴς βάξις ἐπὶ νούσων παντοίων, medical advice or an incantation.

There is a report from Satyrus that quotes Gorgias as saying ὡς αὐτὸς παρείη τῷ Ἐμπεδοκλεῖ γοητεύοντι.[44] The expression is not complimentary, and Diels has tried to show that it could not have been used by Gorgias of Empedocles but that it probably came from a dialogue of Alcidamas.[45] However, no such dialogue is known, and Gorgias may well have been present at the type of scene described in fragment 102(112) and have regarded the proceedings with some suspicion. Philostratus gives

39. Aetius 5.21.1 and fr. 59(68); cf. Aetius 5.15.3.

40. Aetius 5.18.1.

41. Frs. 132(146), 102(112).10–11; and cf. the commentary on ἰατρόμαντις under fr. 132(146).

42. Cf. Empedocles' fr. 101(111).1–2, 9: γήραος ἄλκαρ πεύσῃ . . . ἄξεις δ᾽ ἐξ Ἀΐδαο καταφθιμένου μένος ἀνδρός and *Hom. Hym. Apoll.* 192–93: οὐδὲ δύνανται / εὑρεμέναι θανάτοιό τ᾽ ἄκος καὶ γήραος ἄλκαρ.

43. *Suda* s.v. ἄπνους introduces fr. 101(111) with ἦν δὲ οὗτος καὶ γόης, cf. Plato *Symp.* 203d of Eros, δεινὸς γόης καὶ φαρμακεὺς καὶ σοφιστής, *Crat.* 405a–b, and the definitions in *Suda* s.v. γοητεία.

44. Satyrus ap. D.L. 8.59.

45. Diels, "Gorgias und E.," *SPAW* 1884, p. 344, n. 1.

Empedocles, Pythagoras, and Democritus as ὁμιλήσαντες μάγοις (in the standard tradition of philosophers learning their wisdom from travels in Egypt and the East) but adds that they did not practice the *technē* of the magi.[46] On the other side the three names are given by Celsus as the most famous of those skilled in the art of medicine; according to Satyrus Empedocles was a physician and rhetorician, and Galen speaks of Philistion, Empedocles, Pausanias, and their ἑταῖροι as Italian physicians.[47] Heraclides Ponticus also claimed that Empedocles was a physician and prophet, but this claim is based admittedly on Empedocles' address to the people of Acragas.[48]

Four beneficial actions are recorded of Empedocles, on the border line between medical and magical cure. The authority for them is questionable, and they are usually regarded as elaborations on Empedocles' own words. First, it is said that Empedocles allayed a young man's murderous rage against his host, Anchitos, with a soothing melody on the lyre, and that the young man afterward became Empedocles' most famous pupil.[49] There may be some confusion here between this person and Pausanias, son of Anchitos, to whom Empedocles addresses his physical poem, and also an attempt to link Empedocles with the Pythagoreans, for Pythagoras too was said to have been able to soothe affections of soul and body with music.[50]

Second, there are various versions of Empedocles' control of the winds, which brought him the epithets ἀλεξάνεμος and κωλυσανέμας. The simplest account is in Plutarch and Clement.[51] A powerful wind was blowing onto the plain of Acragas through a mountain cleft, bringing diseases and making the women barren. Empedocles checked the wind by blocking the cleft. Timaeus and the *Suda* give the additional detail of Empedocles ordering the skins of flayed asses to be hung stretched on the headlands to act as a windbreak. In Philostratus Empedocles is said to have stopped a storm cloud from overwhelming the people of Acragas.[52] The

---

46. Philostratus *Vit. Ap.* 1.2, and cf. Pliny *HN* 30.2.9.

47. Celsus *proem.* 2.11 (DK 68 B300.10); Satyrus ap. D.L. 8.58; Galen *meth. med.* 1.1 (10.6K), and cf. *Suda* s.v. Parmenides.

48. Heraclides Ponticus ap. D.L. 8.61 with fr. 102(112).

49. Iamblichus *Vit. Pyth.* 113.

50. Porphyry *Vit. Pyth.* 30 and cf. 32–33, Cicero *Tusc.* 4.3; but cf. also Plato *Charmides* 157b, *Laws* 802–03, and R. C. Lodge *Plato's Theory of Education*, especially pp. 166, 299.

51. Plutarch *curios.* 515c, *adv. Col.* 1126b; Clement *Strom.* 6.3.30, and cf. Eustathius *ad Od.* 1645.43, Porphyry *Vit. Pyth.* 29, Iamblichus *Vit. Pyth.* 135.

52. Timaeus ap. D.L. 8.60, *Suda* s.v. apnous and Empedoklēs; Philostratus *Vit. Ap.* 8.7.8.

detail of the asses' skins is perhaps derived from Homer's portrait of Aeolus and goes against Empedocles' warning on the treatment of animals. The incidents are clearly invented as a background to Empedocles' promise to Pausanias that he will be able to check the force of harmful winds.[53]

Empedocles is also said to have cleared Selinus of a plague caused by an evil stench from the river, which was killing the citizens and affecting childbirth. At his own expense he drew off channels from two neighboring rivers, and so sweetened the water and stopped the plague.[54] Three coins dated ca. 466–415 B.C. clearly refer to deliverance from a plague connected with the river Selinus, but it is impossible to say whether Empedocles himself was instrumental in the cure or if his name was introduced later.[55] Diodorus of Ephesus, who is the source of the story of Empedocles' action here, is not mentioned anywhere else by Diogenes, and he cannot be dated except insofar as his account of Empedocles' death is included with that of Hermippus and Hippobotus among those rejected by Timaeus. Diodorus states that, after Empedocles eradicated the plague, the people of Selinus rose from a feast when he appeared and worshiped him as a god; to confirm their belief he leaped into the fire.[56] These details, together with the mention of Empedocles' emulation of Anaximander's dress and deportment, throw doubt on Diodorus' authority. It can only be said that there are coins indicating a plague at Selinus in Empedocles' lifetime, and near his town of Acragas; the diversion of the rivers seems a sensible remedy, and Empedocles had the wealth to carry it out. The incident is not so obviously based on fragment 101(111) as is that of the wind checking, and it could well be true. Later it was attached rather carelessly to the tradition of Empedocles' leap into Etna.

The fourth story concerns a woman in a trance and is first found in Heraclides Ponticus. He relates that Empedocles revived a woman who had been for thirty days without sign of breathing or pulse (ἄπνους καὶ ἄσφυκτος); Empedocles revealed the facts of the case to Pausanias, and among the people he became famous for having sent a dead woman away alive. Hermippus gives the name of the woman as Pantheia and adds that

53. Empedocles fr. 101(111). 3–4, Homer *Od.* 10. 19–22.

54. Diodorus of Ephesus ap. D.L. 8.70.

55. For a description of the coins and a discussion of their interpretation cf. B. V. Head *Historia Numorum* p. 168; Karsten *EAcr* pp. 22–23; Guthrie *HGP* vol. 2, p. 133, n. 2; A. H. Lloyd, "The Coin Types of Selinus and the Legend of Empedocles," *NC* 1935, pp. 73–93.

56. D.L. 8.70.

the doctors had despaired of reviving her.[57] Heraclides' writings were known to both Pliny and Galen, who give further details, but without mentioning Empedocles. According to Pliny a woman had been *exanimis* for seven days, and the cause was *conversio volvae*;[58] in Galen she is said to have resembled a corpse, except for some breath at the center of the body.[59] If these accounts are taken together with Empedocles' interest in respiration and embryology, and his theory that sleep is the partial and death the complete chilling of the warmth in the blood,[60] the incident can be made plausible: Empedocles explained to Pausanias the confirmation of his physical theory and showed how the warmth could be fully restored, but to the people he appeared to have performed a miracle. Nevertheless, it is likely that Heraclides invented the tale, or at least made concrete a vague legend of Empedocles raising the dead, which in turn originated from the line ἄξεις δ' ἐξ 'Αίδαο καταφθιμένου μένος ἀνδρός.[61] The incident is combined with the leap into Etna, and Timaeus rejected the whole as a fabrication, calling Heraclides παραδοξολόγος.[62]

Any medical pretensions of Empedocles come under fire from the author of *Ancient Medicine*, who considers Empedocles' work, together with the physical speculations of all previous philosophers and doctors, to be irrelevant to medicine. The treatise is a deliberate attempt to divorce medicine from philosophy and is substantiated by a claim that medicine alone, if conducted along the right lines, would lead to an understanding of natural philosophy. It is directed against the methods of transferring philosophy to medicine, which was already an established *technē*, founded on observation, experiment, and rule.[63] Empedocles is no doubt singled out for attack because he is a well-known example of a philosopher attempting to base medicine and physics on similar principles.[64]

Empedocles may, however, be exonerated from the attack of the author of *Sacred Disease*.[65] In that work there is a violent denunciation of

---

57. From the Περὶ Νόσων of Heraclides: D.L. 8.60, 61; 67; cf. *Suda* s.v. apnous; Hermippus ap. D.L. 8.69.

58. Pliny *HN* 7.52.

59. Galen *de loc. aff.* 6.5 (8.415K).

60. Aetius 5.24.2: 'Ε. τὸν μὲν ὕπνον καταφύξει τοῦ ἐν τῷ αἵματι θερμοῦ συμμέτρῳ γίνεσθαι, τῇ δὲ παντελεῖ θάνατον.

61. Empedocles fr. 101(111).9.

62. Timaeus ap. D.L. 8.72; for the *pueriles fabulae* of Heraclides cf. Cicero *ND* 1.13.34, Plutarch *Camillus* 22.3.

63. Cf. *VM* 1-2, 15, 20.

64. Cf. Festugière ed. *VM* p. 58, n. 69, Jaeger *Paedeia* vol. 3, p. 296, n. 40 on *VM* 20.

65. *Morb. Sacr.* 2.1-32, and cf. the attacks on superstition *Aer.* 22.

those who claim to cure the sick καθαρμοὺς προσφέροντες καὶ ἐπαοιδάς. Such charlatans are represented as saying that they can bring down the moon, cause eclipses of the sun, bring rain or fine weather, and make the earth barren at will. They attach diseases in an absurd way to deities, making no prayers or sacrifices but prescribing cleansing with blood; and there are various taboos, especially connected with food and washing with water. Despite the mention of *katharmoi* and power over the weather, it may be argued that no reference to Empedocles is implied since he is against all bloodshed, approves of sacrifice of a bloodless kind, and recommends purificatory ablution.[66] The taboos and food prohibitions in the account in *Sacred Disease* suggest a base form of Pythagoreanism, but this cannot be established.

Empedocles' position with regard to medicine can now be summarized. His views on physiology and anatomy may to some extent have been conclusions based on observation, and a place was found for them in his physical theory. This theory aimed to be all-inclusive, extending from the structure of the cosmos to the simplest forms of life, but Empedocles also had an interest in some of the details for their own sake. None, however, presupposes specialized medical knowledge. Although Empedocles ranked healing as one of the four highest careers, promised remedies, and was expected to provide them, it need not be assumed that he practiced medicine as a *technē*. The place he was later given in the history of medicine as a doctor of repute is probably due to the direct influence his physical theories had on medical science.[67] On the other hand, Empedocles can be cleared of charges of wizardry. His promises are explicable as the power that is expected to come from knowledge of natural forces, and the requests of the people may have arisen from exaggerated hopes based on these promises, combined with the confidence Empedocles' popularity and assurance inspired. It is impossible to know whether gratitude for specific benefactions was involved or not.

---

66. Cf. Empedocles frs. 107(115), 118(128), 129(143).

67. E.g., for birth and death as the mixing and separating of elements cf. *Reg.* I 4, *Aph.* 3.7, *Nat. Hom.* 3–4; for health, temperament, and intelligence depending on their balance and proportion cf. *Reg.* I 4, *Aer.* 24, *Anon. Lond.* 20; for their connection with cosmic forces cf. *Aer.* 1, *Nat. Hom.* 7, *Aph.* 3.3, *Reg.* I 2, and with the humors of the body cf. chap. 2, n. 28. For the development of Empedocles' theory of pores and effluences as an explanation of nutrition, respiration, and cognition cf. *Reg.* I 23, *Anon. Lond.* 26, 34; cf. further W. H. S. Jones *Philosophy and Medicine in Ancient Greece* pp. 10–13, and J. Jouanna, "Présence d'E. dans la Collection Hippocratique," *BAGB* 1961, pp. 452–63.

THE MANNER OF EMPEDOCLES' DEATH

The remaining details of Empedocles' activities which are recorded in the biographers connect with the accounts of his death and may be assessed with them. Some of the many widely different versions of the way in which he died may be dismissed immediately as mere guesswork by unreliable authorities. Demetrius of Troezen, for example, states that Empedocles hanged himself; Favorinus, that he fell from a carriage while traveling to Messene, broke his thigh, and died from the resulting illness; the letter of Telauges, that, when an old man, he lost his balance on board ship and was drowned.[68] More important, since it was later accepted as the true version, is the leap into Etna. The story is first found in Heraclides Ponticus.[69] After the cure of the ἄπνους, Empedocles is said to have offered sacrifice with some friends near the field of Peisianax. He stayed at the table after the others had retired but at daybreak was missing. Someone claimed to have seen a brilliant light and to have heard a voice calling aloud to Empedocles in the night. Pausanias asked the people to start a search but later stopped them, for events εὐχῆς ἄξια had happened, and Empedocles was now to be honored as a god. The voice from the sky and the bright light, combined with the sudden disappearance, indicate an apotheosis, but from Timaeus' objections to Heraclides' account it seems that Heraclides explained the disappearance by saying that Empedocles had leapt into the crater.[70]

Further elaborations are found in later authors. Hermippus gives the number of those present at the sacrifice as eighty. According to Hippobotus, Empedocles jumped into the crater in order to confirm the report that he had become a god; as evidence for this, one of his sandals was found, which was claimed to have been thrown up by the volcano. Diodorus of Ephesus sets the scene not at Acragas but at Selinus, where the people at a feast rose and revered Empedocles as a god, and in confirmation of this he leaped into the fire.[71] From the second century B.C. on, the leap into Etna superseded all other accounts of Empedocles' death. It is found, for example, in Horace and Ovid; Lucian, mocking the story of the volcano and the sandals, suggests that Empedocles was

---

68. Demetrius and Telauges ap. D.L. 8.74; Favorinus (or perhaps the authority here is Neanthes, cf. Bidez *Biographie* p. 64) ap. D.L. 8.73.

69. Heraclides ap. D.L. 8.67–68, 71–72.

70. Timaeus ap. D.L. 8.71.

71. Hermippus, Hippobotus ap. D.L. 8.69; Diodorus ap. D.L. 8.70.

driven to suicide by melancholy, a humor first attributed to him in the Aristotelian *Problems*.[72] Empedocles' death in Etna is found also in Claudian, and it provided the Christian fathers with material for sermons on the follies of claiming to be a god.[73]

Nevertheless, this version of Empedocles' death may be discounted. First there are the objections that Timaeus brings against Heraclides' account.[74] Peisianax was a citizen of Syracuse and had no land at Acragas, so the feast could not have taken place by his field; Pausanias did not set up any shrine or statue to Empedocles as a god, although, being a rich man, he could easily have done so;[75] Empedocles had nothing to say about craters in his poems; and, in short, this is a typical invention of Heraclides. Second, there is the disagreement about the location. Acragas, Selinus, and Syracuse are the various places given for Empedocles' last hours, and in addition Favorinus claims that Empedocles' tomb was in Megara. The later elaborations, such as the increase in the number of people present and the discovery of the sandal, are obvious fictions. According to fragment 107(115) the daimon is cast into fire from earth, and this would be sufficient basis for a story of Empedocles leaping into fire after a life on earth. Finally, because of the geography of Mount Etna it would have been extremely difficult for anyone to cover the distance to the foot of the mountain, to make the climb of over ten thousand feet, and then to survive the intense heat long enough to approach the mouth of the crater.[76]

Timaeus claims that Empedocles left Sicily permanently for the Peloponnese. Elsewhere it is said that while Empedocles was absent from Acragas the descendants of his political enemies opposed his return.[77]

---

72. Horace *Ars P.* 464-66, Ovid *Ibis* 597-98, Lucian *Dial Mort.* 6.20.4, *Fug.* 2, [Arist.] *probl.* 953a27.

73. Cf. Claudian *Paneg. Theod.* 72, Tertullian *De Anim.* 32; Lactantius *Div. Inst.* 3.18, Gregory *Ad Nem.* 281, and others quoted by Bidez *Biographie* p. 96.

74. Timaeus ap. D.L. 8.71.

75. Hippobotus (D.L. 8.72) counters this objection, however, with the assertion that there were two statues of Empedocles, one at Acragas showing him veiled, and another, unveiled, which was removed to Rome.

76. Cf. Strabo's detailed description of Etna, and his demonstration of the impossibility either for Empedocles to have leaped into the crater or for a sandal to have been thrown up by the fire (6.2.8). Etna is about seventy miles from Acragas and a hundred from Selinus.

77. D.L. 8.67: τοῦ Ἀκράγαντος ⟨ἀπ⟩οικιζομένου, ἀντέστησαν αὐτοῦ τῇ καθόδῳ οἱ τῶν ἐχθρῶν ἀπόγονοι, so reads Bignone *BPEC* 1941, p. 106, and for the participle cf. Sophocles *OT* 998; τοῦ Ἀκράγαντος οἰκ⟨τ⟩ιζομένου, printed by H. S. Long, O.C.T.

Little is known of his travels abroad apart from the visit to Thurii and, from his own words, his tour of prosperous towns.[78] Timaeus reports that he made a memorable impression at Olympia, but reasons have already been given for suspecting the accounts of his victory and offerings there.[79] According to the *Suda*, Empedocles was in Athens at the same time as Acron, but this seems unlikely. Acron was known as a physician in Acragas and it would be assumed that he worked there with Empedocles. He is said to have practiced at Athens during the plague, and so a story that Empedocles accompanied him could easily have been started, especially if the version of Empedocles' cure of the plague at Selinus were known. But the date is too late, the story has no support elsewhere, and according to Timaeus, Empedocles' attitude to Acron was unsympathetic.[80]

Most probably, therefore, Timaeus is correct in saying that the manner of Empedocles' death was unknown. It is likely that Empedocles did travel in Sicily and southern Italy, and perhaps crossed to the Peloponnese. His political activities could well have made him unpopular with a section of the community at Acragas, so that his return was prevented, but nothing further was told of the end of his life. The biographers would not accept such a lacuna and invented ways in which Empedocles might have died; the most dramatic and popular, and in keeping with his poems, was the suicide on Etna.[81]

WORKS ATTRIBUTED TO EMPEDOCLES

On the authority of Aristotle, Diogenes states that Empedocles wrote tragedies, political works, a *Ξέρξου διάβασις*, and a *Προοίμιον εἰς Ἀπόλλωνα*.[82] He adds that Hieronymus claimed to have met with forty-three of the tragedies, and Neanthes with seven which Empedocles had written in his youth, but that Heraclides (Lembus) maintained that these tragedies were the work of some other writer. Since their authorship is thus disputed and there is no further trace of tragedies by Empedocles,

---

1964, and translated by R. D. Hicks, Loeb 1925, "when Agrigentum came to regret him," can hardly be right.

78. D.L. 8.52, Empedocles fr. 102(112).7.

79. Timaeus ap. D.L. 8.66.

80. Cf. *Suda* s.v. Akrōn, Plutarch *de Is. et Os.* 383d, Pliny *HN* 29.4, D.L. 8.65.

81. Cf. the versions of the deaths of Heraclitus and Diogenes of Apollonia: D.L. 9.3–4, 6.76–77.

82. D.L. 8.57.

they need not be taken into consideration here.[83] The political writings attributed to Empedocles may also be dismissed. The only hint of works of this kind is the mention of two speeches περὶ ἰσότητος which are attributed to him. If they were delivered, then versions of them may have appeared later, but the speeches are suspect, and no quotation from any prose work by Empedocles is known.[84]

The Persian work has some support in the manuscripts of the *Problemata*, where fragment 49(34) is quoted as ἐν τοῖς Περσικοῖς. This fragment is also quoted in the manuscripts of the *Meteorologica* of Aristotle as ἐν τοῖς Φυσικοῖς, with the exception of the excellent manuscript *E* which reads Περσικοῖς.[85] Because the context in the *Problemata* and the *Meteorologica* connects the fragment with the mixing of dry and wet ingredients, it could have come from a simile in the physical poem or from a description of the preparation of food on campaign. However, the story, reported by Diogenes on the authority of Aristotle,[86] of a sister or daughter of Empedocles deliberately burning the work because it was unfinished, shows that there was little or no trace of a *diabasis* by Empedocles in the fourth century. Since there is no other quotation attributed to such a work, and no mention of it elsewhere, it can be discounted as a possible source for the extant fragments.

The *Prooimion* to Apollo is more interesting. According to Ammonius,[87] Empedocles rejected the traditional anthropomorphic *mythoi* of the gods and substituted, particularly in the case of Apollo, a *logos* which he thought more fitting. The use of such a method is supported by Menander, who testifies that Empedocles, like Parmenides, made use of ὕμνοι φυσιολογικοί.[88] Menander gives as one example a hymn to Apollo, which was in fact an account of the *physis* of the sun. If the *Prooimion* existed it may similarly have been couched in allegorical terms, but a separate work on Apollo by Empedocles is not otherwise known. The tale of the accidental destruction of the *Prooimion* makes its existence also suspect.[89]

---

83. According to the *Suda* s.v. Empedoklēs (2), Empedocles' grandson was a tragedian, and his tragedies numbered about twenty-four.

84. Cf. D.L. 8.65,72.

85. [Arist.] *probl.* 929b16–17, *Mete.* 382a1; cf. also Alexander *in Mete.* 199.4–7, Olympiodorus *Mete.* 297.18–19, Empedocles fr. 48(96).4, and the commentary on fr. 49(34).

86. D.L. 8.57.

87. Ammonius *in Int.* 249.1–11.

88. Menander Rhetor 1.2.2, 5.2 (DK 31 A23); he gives as another example the representation of Hera as air and Zeus as heat; cf. the commentary on fr. 7(6).

89. Cf. D.L. 8.57.

This set of four groups of writings allotted to Empedocles in Diogenes need not therefore be considered in an ordering of the fragments. No direct quotation is extant which comes indubitably from any one of them, and even if these works are accepted as authentic because Diogenes claims Aristotle as his authority, the evidence tells against their survival into the fourth century. Karsten suggests that Empedocles may well have written on all four subjects in his youth because they are themes likely to appeal to a prolific writer of Empedocles' temperament and wide interests, but the suggestion can be no more than speculation.[90]

There is no reliable evidence that Empedocles composed epigrams, or that any of the extant fragments are assigned to such writings. The epigrams attributed to Empedocles by Diogenes are almost certainly spurious. The first, on Pausanias, looks suspiciously like an elaboration of the ninth line of fragment 101(111); moreover, it is attributed to Simonides in the *Anthology*.[91] In addition, the authorship of the second epigram, a punning couplet on Acron, is disputed. Simonides is also credited with this couplet, and the first four words appear anonymously in Eustathius. An alternative to the second line was known.[92] There is also an isolated hexameter verse addressed to Telauges, which is referred to Empedocles by Hippobotus.[93] It seems possible that this fragment originated with the later tradition which assigned to Pythagoras a son called Telauges and then attempted to establish Empedocles as a successor of Pythagoras by citing this Telauges as his teacher.[94] No other extant writer before Diogenes attributes epigrams to Empedocles.

In addition, Diogenes credits Empedocles with an Ἰατρικὸς λόγος of approximately six hundred lines, and Ἰατρικὰ καταλογάδην are attributed to him in the *Suda*.[95] Pliny states that Empedocles and Hippocrates give an explanation in various places of the way in which some epidemics can be alleviated by lighting fires;[96] this too suggests that Empedocles wrote a medical work. Some editors have accepted such a

---

90. Karsten *EAcr* pp. 63–67.

91. DK 31 B156 from D.L. 8.61, *Anth. Gr.* 7.508.

92. DK 31 B157 from D.L. 8.65, and cf. *Suda* s.v. Akrōn, Eustathius *ad Od.* 1634.12.

93. DK 31 B155 from D.L. 8.43.

94. Telauges is not in the list of Pythagoreans in Iamblichus *Vit. Pyth.* 267 (although he does appear in par. 146 and Porphyry *Vit. Pyth.* 4); nor is he in the Pythagorean notices of Aristotle, Aristoxenus, or Dicaearchus, which suggests that the verse was introduced in the later embroidery on Pythagoras' life.

95. D.L. 8.77, *Suda* s.v. Empedoklēs.

96. Pliny *HN* 36.69.202.

work by Empedocles composed in verse and were confident enough to print fragment 101(111) as ἐκ τῶν Ἰατρικῶν.[97] Nevertheless it has been shown that the evidence for Empedocles having specialized medical knowledge or skill is not definitive.[98] The tradition that he wrote on medicine may have developed for the same reasons as and along with his reputation as a doctor. There was the influence that his work had on subsequent medical theory, the elaborations of his own words and the anecdotes which they gave rise to, as well as the attack directed against him in *Ancient Medicine*. But a separate medical work was unknown, for example, to Aristotle[99] and his commentators, and to Plutarch and Sextus Empiricus. Moreover, no quotation from such a work is given in any of the authorities for Empedocles, and so this title also has not been taken into account in ordering the fragments.

The evidence for a physical poem by Empedocles is indisputable. The work is listed by Diogenes and the *Suda* under the title Περὶ Φύσεως,[100] and various quotations, expressly said to come from it as Περὶ Φύσεως or τὰ Φυσικά, are given by Simplicius, Aetius, and Tzetzes.[101] In addition, a poem with the heading οἱ Καθαρμοί is known to Diogenes; he and Theon Smyrnaeus give fragments that they say are from the *Katharmoi*, and Hippolytus lists part of the subject matter of such a work.[102] That there were genuine writings of Empedocles known by these two titles need not therefore be doubted, although the titles themselves may not have been his own.[103]

According to Diogenes the *Physics* and the *Katharmoi* add up to about five thousand lines, and in the *Suda* the *Physics* is said to be in two books and to total approximately two thousand lines. But the best *Suda* manuscripts, *A* and *F*, lack the relevant passage on the number of books, the first editors printed βιβλία γ̄,[104] and the Codex Marcianus has βιβλία δ̄.

---

97. E.g., Karsten *EAcr* p. 148, F. G. A. Mullach *Fragmenta Philosophorum Graecorum* vol. 3, p. 14.

98. Cf. above, pp. 9–14.

99. Karsten, however, suggests (*EAcr* p. 71) that there is a reference to an Ἰατρικόν by Empedocles at Aristotle *Poet.* 1447b16–20.

100. D.L. 8.77, *Suda* s.v. Empedoklēs.

101. Simplicius *in Phys.* 32.1, 157.27, 300.20, 331.10, 381.29; Aetius 1.30.1; Tzetzes *ex. Il.* 53.20.

102. D.L. 8.54, Theo Sm. 104.1, Hippolytus *RH* 7.30.3–4; cf. also D.L. 8.63 on the recitation of the *Katharmoi* at Olympia.

103. See chap. 5.

104. Surely with some MSS. support; they are unlikely to have been misled by Tzetzes as the first edition of the *Chiliades* was produced later; cf. the discussions by Diels *SPAW* 1898, p. 398, and C. Horna *WS* 1930, pp. 6–7.

Three books for the *Physics* is supported by Tzetzes, who quotes from the first and third.[105] Diels, however, argues that Tzetzes understood the *Katharmoi* as the third book of the *Physics*, and accordingly he prints B 134 with the *Katharmoi* fragments. Yet Tzetzes also quotes from the first book of the *Physics*, and the assumption that he read the *Katharmoi* as the third book of the same work is unwarranted. The confusion is more likely to be in the *Suda*, but in any case the division into books would not have been definitive, or indeed Empedocles' own.

Two books for the *Katharmoi* are now attested.[106] The length of the work as a whole, however, is in dispute, for if Diogenes' figure of πεντα- κισχίλια for the two poems combined is taken together with the *Suda* total of two thousand lines for the *Physics*, the *Katharmoi* would be three thousand lines long. Diogenes or his source is probably exaggerating,[107] and a thousand could well have been a round number for the lines of a book, even if the exact total was much less. On the Homeric model, three books of the *Physics* and two of the *Katharmoi* could average five to six hundred lines each, giving a total of two and a half to three thousand.[108]

This means that the fragments comprise sixteen to twenty percent of the total.[109] Since Empedocles admittedly repeats himself,[110] and there are no important theories reliably attributed to him that are not to some extent illustrated by the remaining fragments, a nucleus of the original is available for a reasonably confident reconstruction of the main points of Empedocles' work.

---

105. Fr. 7(6) from the first book of the *Physics*: Tzetzes *ex. Il.* 53.20; fr. 97(134) from the third book: *Chil.* 7.514.

106. παρὰ μέντοι 'Ε. ἐν β' καθαρμῶν ἐστιν εὑρέσθαι ἐκτεταμένον τὸ α. . . . The fragment is published by H. Hunger: "Palimpsest-Fragmente aus Herodians 'Καθολικὴ Προσῳδία'," *Byz. Jarh.* 1967, p. 5; cf. also M. L. West *Maia* 1968, p. 199, and F. Lasserre *MH* 1969, p. 82, and below on fr. 152.

107. Cf. the large number of lines Diogenes allocates to the various works of Epimenides, including a *Theogony* and *Curetes* of ἔπη πεντακισχίλια, D.L. 1.111.

108. The *Iliad* averages 654 lines a book and the *Odyssey* 505 lines. Diels suggested πάντα τρισχίλια for πεντακισχίλια, *SPAW* 1898, p. 398.

109. Four hundred and fifty lines and ten phrases are extant.

110. Cf. fr. 17(25), and the repetitions of fr. 8(17).7–8, 10–13 at fr. 16(26).5–6, 9–12.

2. Physics

EARTH, AIR, FIRE, AND WATER

Basic to Empedocles' philosophy is the assumption of four eternally existing "roots," the arrangement and rearrangement of which account for all *genesis* and *olethros*, and for the particular and changing characteristics of *thnēta*. At their first appearance in the *Physics* these roots are given the names of gods and goddesses, but there is no attempt to establish a technical or even consistent vocabulary for any of them. They are variously designated by the terms fire, air, earth, and water, by the names of divinities, and by their most obvious manifestations in the physical world. Empedocles' use of different expressions for the same root is recognized by Aristotle, and explained by Simplicius in these words: ἐπάγει ἑκάστου τῶν εἰρημένων τὸν χαρακτῆρα, τὸ μὲν πῦρ ἥλιον καλῶν, τὸν δὲ ἀέρα αὐγὴν καὶ οὐρανόν, τὸ δὲ ὕδωρ ὄμβρον καὶ θάλασσαν.[1] The terminology is set out in the table below.

In calling his roots by divine names Empedocles is showing that they are the new gods; he sets them up as worthy, because of their eternal and unchanging nature, of the respect and wonder with which the Olympians were traditionally viewed. It is said to have been his aim to replace the traditional myths with a more seemly *logos* about the gods,[2] and in this he is in line with the work of Xenophanes, Heraclitus, and Parmenides. Empedocles' description of the individual *timai* of the roots and their equality of power recalls directly Homer's language on the equality of

---

1. Aristotle *GC* 315a10–11; Simplicius *in Phys.* 159.10–12, and cf. *in Phys.* 32.3–4.
2. Menander Rhetor 1.2.2, 5.2 (DK 31 A23), Ammonius *in Int.* 249. 1–21.

Terms used by Empedocles for the four roots

Fragment	fire	air	water	earth
7(6).2–3	Ζεύς	"Ηρη*	Νῆστις	Ἀϊδωνεύς
8(17).18	πῦρ	ἀήρ	ὕδωρ	γαῖα
14(21).3–6	ἠέλιος	αὐγή	ὄμβρος	αἶα
25(22).2	ἠλέκτωρ	οὐρανός	θάλασσα	χθών
27(38).1–4	ἥλιος*	ἀήρ, αἰθήρ*	πόντος	γαῖα
53(62).4–6	πῦρ	(εἶδος)*	ὕδωρ	χθών
60(71).2	ἠέλιος	αἰθήρ	ὕδωρ	γαῖα
77(109).1–2	πῦρ	αἰθήρ	ὕδωρ	γαῖα
83(98).1–2	"Ηφαιστος	αἰθήρ	ὄμβρος	χθών
107(115).9–11	ἠέλιος	αἰθήρ	πόντος	χθών, γαῖα
19/21(27).1–2	ἠέλιος		θάλασσα	αἶα
31(37).1	(πῦρ)	αἰθήρ		χθών
48(96).1–3	"Ηφαιστος		Νῆστις	χθών
62(73).1–2	πῦρ		ὄμβρος	χθών
30(54).1		αἰθήρ		χθών
33(39).1		αἰθήρ		γῆ
84(85).1	φλόξ			γαῖα
88(84).7,9–10	πῦρ		ὕδωρ	
13(9).1		αἰθήρ		
64(78).2		ἀήρ		
69(76).3				χθών
91(100).5,7,18,24		αἰθήρ		
91(100).11,15,21			ὕδωρ	
91(100).12,18			ὄμβρος	
91(100).13		ἀήρ		

Note: For the placing of words marked by an asterisk cf. the commentary on the relevant fragments.

privilege and allotment of power enjoyed by Zeus, Poseidon, and Hades.[3]

Empedocles also calls the elemental fire ἥλιος and the root of water ὄμβρος and πόντος. His general identification of the four roots with the great visible masses of earth, air, fire, and water is in accord with his own admonition that the evidence provided by the different senses is a basis for understanding.[4] The observable earth, sky, sun, and sea are at one with the four roots, and the various terms for each root are interchange-

3. Cf. fr. 8(17). 27–29 and Homer *Il.* 15.187–93, 209, and also fr. 51(59).1.
4. Cf. fr. 5(3). 5–8.

able, because the present manifestation of the roots as world masses reveals their eternal characteristics as the basic material for *thnēta*.[5]

On two occasions Aristotle states that Empedocles posited four basic roots but treated them as if they were only two, opposing fire to air, earth, and water.[6] Support for this statement is found in the extant fragments and in the doxography. Philoponus gives as one reason for the contrast the fact that fire is hot and the other three cold,[7] but this is too superficial. In Empedocles' cosmogony and biology fire is κινητική,[8] acting on the other elements in various ways. For example, at the beginning of the formation of this world, air was the first root to be separated out, but fire then hardened part of the air into the surrounding crystal.[9] The moon is said to be air that was cut off by fire and also hardened.[10] The motion of the hemispheres round the earth started as a result of the pressure exerted by the accumulation of fire in one of them, and the first inclination of the poles was due to the air yielding to the force of the sun.[11] Empedocles' fragment 62(73) describes Kypris, in the formation of *thnēta*, giving the mixture of earth and water to fire to harden, and in another fragment the surprisingly large proportion of fire used to make up bone may have been required to account for its hardness.[12] Another obvious example of the hardening property of fire is in the theory of the solidification of salt.[13] And also of interest is the account of reflections in mirrors, in which the

---

5. Cf. fr. 25(22).1–3

    ἄρθμια μὲν γὰρ ταῦτα ἑαυτῶν πάντα μέρεσσιν,
    ἠλέκτωρ τε χθών τε καὶ οὐρανὸς ἠδὲ θάλασσα,
    ὅσσα φιν ἐν θνητοῖσιν ἀποπλαχθέντα πέφυκεν

and the description of the fire in the eye as ὠγύγιον πῦρ, fr. 88(84).7. H. Cherniss (*Aristotle's Criticism of Presocratic Philosophy* p. 372) accuses Aristotle of misapprehension and prejudice in identifying Empedocles' roots with the visible masses of earth, air, fire, and water, but Aristotle's commentary is supported by Empedocles' own words here.

6. Aristotle *GC* 330b20–21, *Metaph.* 985b1–3, and cf. Alexander *in Metaph.* 34.6–10.

7. Philoponus *in GC* 227.21–23, and cf. Asclepius *in Metaph.* 33.4–5.

8. Cf. Aristotle *Metaph.* 984b6–8, which W. D. Ross, in his commentary on the passage, refers to Empedocles.

9. Aetius 2.11.2.

10. [Plut.] *Strom.* ap. Eusebium *PE* 1.8.10 (DK 31 A30).

11. [Plut.] loc. cit., Aetius 2.8.2.

12. Empedocles fr. 48(96); Simplicius (*in de An.* 68.11–12) says that the large amount of fire gives bone its dry, white character, but hardness could well be an additional result.

13. Empedocles fr. 45(56); cf. also the petrifaction caused by heat, [Arist.] *probl.* 937a14–16, and the effects of fire working in the earth, Seneca *Q Nat.* 3.24.1, Plutarch *de prim. frig.* 953e.

parts of the root of fire that are in the composition of the mirror are said to "set" the ἀπορροιαί from the object into the observed reflection.[14]

In addition to these various ways of acting on other elements, fire by itself is a powerful force. It is the upward thrusting of the fire in the earth that caused the genesis of the οὐλοφυεῖς τύποι, and the growth of trees was first due to the same cause, for they were pushed up by the heat in the earth.[15] Fire also exerts force in the form of the heat that thrusts air out of the body when the embryo takes its first breath; and the fragments contain the notice that the characteristic physical strength of men is a result of their having been conceived in the warmer part of the womb.[16] A final indication of the importance of fire in Empedoclean theory is the essential part it plays in the preservation of life. Sleep results from the partial separation of the fiery element from the body, and the complete separation brings about the death of both σῶμα and ψυχή.[17]

These examples show that, although Empedocles was careful at the beginning of the *Physics* to make clear the balanced equality of privilege and power held by the four roots, in working out the details of the physical scheme he saw in fire a solidifying agency capable of working on the other roots either individually or in combination, as well as a power responsible for the genesis of plants and animals, and necessary for the preservation of life.[18]

It is sometimes assumed that Empedocles took over the four basic opposites of hot, cold, wet, and dry from the Milesians and made them the substances of his four roots.[19] Such an exclusive tetrad of opposites cannot, however, be attributed to Anaximander or Anaximenes on the extant evidence. In the surviving fragment of Anaximander, *dikē* and *tisis* could refer to the law governing any number of perceptible oppositions, although hot, cold, wet, and dry may have been the most obvious. At the genesis of the world, according to Anaximander's scheme, there seems to have been a mutual reaction between fire and the air, or mist,

14. Aetius 4.14.1.

15. Empedocles fr. 53(62), Aetius 5.26.4.

16. Aetius 4.22.1, Empedocles fr. 58(67), contradicting Parmenides on this point, cf. Aristotle *Part. An.* 648a25–31.

17. Aetius 5.24.2 and 25.4.

18. Whether or not there is Heraclitean influence here, there was a later conflation of Empedocles with Heraclitus and the Stoics as assuming ἐκπύρωσις and a divine νοερὸν πῦρ, cf. Hippolytus *RH* 1.3.1 (DK 31 A31), Clement *Strom.* 5.14.103.6.

19. Cf. J. Burnet *Early Greek Philosophy* p. 228; G. S. Kirk and J. E. Raven *The Presocratic Philosophers* pp. 119, 329; Guthrie *HGP* vol. 2, p. 142.

around the earth, this being explained in the terms of the doxographical tradition as the product of τὸ ἐκ τοῦ ἀιδίου γόνιμον θερμοῦ τε καὶ ψυχ-ροῦ.[20] Similarly, in the accounts of Anaximenes' cosmogony, the opposition of hot and cold is likely to have been a later interpretation of the way in which fire, cloud, water, earth, and stones were produced by the thinning and thickening of air.[21] Nor is the view that four opposites were already standardized in the earlier Presocratics adequately supported by fragment 126 of Heraclitus: τὰ ψυχρὰ θέρεται, θερμὸν ψύχεται, ὑγρὸν αὐαίνεται, καρφαλέον νοτίζεται. Heraclitus is giving four obvious and balanced examples of the successive changes of opposites in general into each other, and in other fragments the tensions of further opposites are supposed.[22]

Empedocles himself does not use four opposites exclusively; in characterizing his roots he introduces bright and dark as well as hot and cold.[23] Aristotle states that Empedocles assigned *diaphorai* to the roots, but the only examples he gives are of the sun as white and hot, of water as cold and dark, and of earth as heavy and hard.[24] Empedocles may have described in greater detail the *ēthos* of each root, including those obvious characteristics that played a prominent part in the Milesian cosmologies, but, whether or not he did do so, the economical theory of just four roots, whose combinations can account for the observed differences in phenomena, is apparently Empedocles' own.

The limiting of basic opposites to four and their correlation to the roots is first found in medicine. Alcmaeon worked on the assumption of an indefinite number of opposites,[25] but it was Empedocles' theory that the medical writers later took over and adapted to a fixed number of powers, and then of humors, in the body. Philistion in a simple way listed four *ideai* of the body, relating hot to fire, cold to air, dry to earth, and moist to water. In the Hippocratic *Nature of Man* the four opposites were brought

20. [Plut.] *Strom.* 2 (DK 12 A10); cf. Aristotle *Phys.* 187a20, Simplicius *in Phys.* 24.17–25 (where the reference to the four elements is an obvious anachronism) and 150.22-25; the pairs wet and dry or hot and cold are suggested in Plato *Soph.* 242d. C. H. Kahn, *Anaximander and the Origins of Greek Cosmogony,* posits eight opposites for the Milesians—hot, dry, bright, and rare vs. cold, moist, dark, and dense, cf. pp. 159–62.

21. Hippolytus *RH* 1.7.3 (DK 13 A7).

22. Cf. Heraclitus frs. 57, 62, 67, 88, 111, and G. S. Kirk *Heraclitus, The Cosmic Fragments* pp. 150–54.

23. Empedocles fr. 14(21). 3,5, and cf. fr. 75(90).

24. Aristotle *GC* 314b20 (from Empedocles fr. 14(21).3,5) and 315a10–11.

25. Cf. Alcmaeon ap. Aristotle *Metaph.* 986a31–34, Aetius 5.30.1, and also (Hippocrates) *VM* 14.

into line with the humors, and with the seasons of the year, in the following scheme:

winter (cold and wet)	:	phlegm
spring (wet and hot)	:	blood
summer (hot and dry)	:	yellow bile
autumn (dry and cold)	:	black bile.[26]

The next step, which may have originated with Diocles,[27] was to bring in the elements by connecting air and cold with phlegm, water and wet with blood, fire and hot with yellow bile, and earth and dry with black bile. This scheme of elements and humors, with the more subtle pairing of opposites established by Aristotle, became the standard formula.[28]

Empedocles therefore probably did not arrive at his theory of four roots by adapting an already recognized tetrad of opposites, although he did contribute to the subsequent formulae of elements based on the opposites of hot, cold, wet, and dry. It is also doubtful whether he simply conflated previous views on the basic constituents of the world. On two occasions Aristotle denies that any of the physicists posited earth as an *arché*; it was Empedocles who added earth to water, fire, and air, which already had their several supporters. But elsewhere Empedocles is said to have added water to fire, earth, and air, whereas in the *Physics* each of the four elements is assumed to have had its champion.[29] In these passages Aristotle is adopting the historian's point of view, but it is unlikely that Empedocles worked in this way, and the different versions given by Aristotle indicate that Empedocles was not so formal. It may have been that he acted as he instructed Pausanias to do,[30] and looked about him. In a coastal town like Acragas one could clearly see land, water as sea and rain, the air (which Empedocles could show to be just as corporeal and forceful as water), and fire—in the sky as the sun, and coming from the volcanic earth. There was no obvious fifth mass, nor could any of these four be dispensed with.[31] Earth, air, fire, and water

---

26. Philistion ap. *Anon. Lond.* 20.24; *Nat. Hom.* 7.

27. Cf. M. Wellmann *Die Fragmente der Sikelischen Arzte, Intr.* pp. 74–93, and Diocles fr. 8, p. 119.

28. Cf. Aristotle *GC* 329b6–330a29, and H. E. Sigerist *History of Medicine* vol. 2, pp. 318–25. There is a simpler version in (Hippocrates) *Carn.* 2, with *aithēr* as hot, earth as cold and dry, air as hot and wet, and (water) as wet and thick; cf. Kahn *Anaximander* p. 127.

29. Aristotle *De An.* 405b8, *Metaph.* 989a6–9, *GC* 329a3, *Phys.* 193a22; cf. also *Nat. Hom.* 1.

30. Cf. fr. 14(21).1–6.

31. Cf. fr. 8(17).30; Theophrastus seems first to have pointed out that fire could not be

were remarked as distinct, balanced, and individually characterized; Empedocles argued that together they comprise all that there is, and he constructed the world from them.

The epic tradition, however, may have had some influence. In the Homeric *dasmos* the divisions are sky, sea, and ζόφος ἠερόεις, with earth and Olympus common to all; the areas of earth, sky, and sea appear again as the first workings by Hephaistos on Achilles' shield. Earth and sky, together with Styx, make up the form of the oath of the gods, and such an oath is used in Homer and in the *Homeric Hymn to Apollo* to confirm the assignment of a divine province.[32] Hesiod in the *Theogony* gives the genesis of the gods from earth, sky, sea, and dark night. But he also transfers the epithet δνοφερός to earth, and Tartarus ἠερόεις replaces night, the formula then being:

$$\dots \gamma \tilde{\eta} \varsigma \ \delta \nu o \phi \epsilon \rho \tilde{\eta} \varsigma \ \kappa \alpha \grave{\iota} \ T \alpha \rho \tau \acute{\alpha} \rho o \upsilon \ \mathring{\eta} \epsilon \rho \acute{o} \epsilon \nu \tau o \varsigma,$$
$$\pi \acute{o} \nu \tau o \upsilon \ \tau' \ \mathring{\alpha} \tau \rho \upsilon \gamma \acute{\epsilon} \tau o \iota o \ \kappa \alpha \grave{\iota} \ o \mathring{\upsilon} \rho \alpha \nu o \tilde{\upsilon} \ \mathring{\alpha} \sigma \tau \epsilon \rho \acute{o} \epsilon \nu \tau o \varsigma.[33]$$

The order of the generation of these masses is clear. After Chaos there arose earth and misty Tartarus. The first child of earth was sky, and later she brought forth sea without *philotēs*.[34] Nevertheless, as Kahn has argued, a careful consideration of these epic terms shows that the classic theory could not have developed directly out of them. The *ouranos* is not fire, and *aēr* not air but mist.[35]

There are also some relevant points in the earlier physical theories. According to the doxographers, Anaximander thought that the first living creatures came from warmed earth and water.[36] For Anaximenes wind and stones are listed equally with earth, air, fire, and water, and he says that from all of these everything else arises.[37] The expression, however, is vague, as are Xenophanes' statements that all things begin and end in earth, that they are composed of earth and water, and that men

---

a primary body equal with the other three, because fuel is necessary for its survival, cf. *Ign.* 4.

32. Homer *Il.* 15.187–93, 209, 18.483; the oath of Hera: Homer *Il.* 15.36–37; of Leto: *Hom. Hym. Apoll.* 3.84–86; cf. Pindar *Ol.* 7.55, and F. M. Cornford *From Religion to Philosophy* pp. 22–24.

33. Hesiod *Theog.* 106–07, 736–37, 807–08, and cf. 847.

34. Hesiod *Theog.* 116–33.

35. Kahn *Anaximander* p. 152.

36. Censorinus 4.7, Aetius 5.19.4, Plutarch *quaest. con.* 730e (DK 12 A30); cf. in Hesiod the creation of Pandora from earth and water, *Erga* 60–64, *Theog.* 571–72.

37. Anaximenes ap. Simplicius *in Phys.* 24.26–31, and cf. Hippolytus *RH* 1.7.1–3.

have their generation from earth and water.[38] Heraclitus perhaps supposed that man is in some way made up of fire, water, and earth, which separate at death, but this is not a direct anticipation of Empedocles' assertion that individuals come into existence as the result of an arrangement of a fixed number of basic things.[39]

The first occurrence of elements in this sense seems to be in Parmenides' *Doxa*, the κόσμος ἐπέων ἀπατηλός, in the positing of universal fire and night. The *Doxa* presents these two as the constituent elements in all things: πᾶν πλέον ἐστὶν ὁμοῦ φάεος καὶ νυκτὸς ἀφάντου.[40] Further, the equality and independence attributed to fire and night in the *Doxa* in the words ἴσοι ἀμφότεροι and ἑωυτῷ πάντοσε τωὐτόν, τῷ δ' ἑτέρῳ μὴ τωὐτόν are found in Empedocles' description of the roots: ταῦτα γὰρ ἴσά τε πάντα . . . πάρα δ' ἦθος ἑκάστῳ.[41]

There can be no doubt that Empedocles was aware of Parmenides' work and that it was a major influence in shaping his own physics. More important than the *Doxa* were the conclusions of Parmenides' *Alëtheia*, some of which Empedocles assumed as basic postulates for his theory of roots, and others he adapted or modified. Primarily Empedocles was persuaded by the arguments of Parmenides that denied μὴ ὄν, and he seized on the first deduction from this, that there is no *genesis* or *olethros*, for these entail nonexistence. What exists cannot be added to[42] or subtracted from in any way;[43] birth and death, coming to be and passing away, are names used by men mistakenly, for they do not describe what is true.[44]

From here Empedocles began to reason independently of Parmenides. Nothing can be added to or taken from what exists, but what exists, in Empedocles' theory, is not unique but comprises four "things"—the four roots. These are within the range of the senses, and the perceptible world is reinstated. But after assuming these four roots, Empedocles then conceded, καὶ πρὸς τοῖς οὐδ' †ἄρ τι† ἐπιγίγνεται οὐδ' ἀπολήγει, in deference to Parmenides' assertion, οὐδὲν γὰρ ἢ ἔστιν ἢ ἔσται ἄλλο

38. Xenophanes frs. 27, 29, 33.
39. Cf. Heraclitus frs. 31, 36.
40. Parmenides fr. 9.3.
41. Parmenides frs. 9.4, 8.57–58, Empedocles fr. 8(17). 27–28.
42. Parmenides fr. 8.7: πῇ πόθεν αὐξηθέν; Empedocles fr. 8(17.32): τοῦτο δ' ἐπαυξήσειε τὸ πᾶν τί κε, καὶ πόθεν ἐλθόν;
43. Parmenides fr. 8.19: πῶς δ' ἂν ἔπειτ' ἀπόλοιτο ἐόν; Empedocles fr. 8(17).33: πῇ δέ κε κἠξαπόλοιτο; fr. 9(12).2: καί τ' ἐὸν ἐξαπόλεσθαι ἀνήνυστον; and cf. fr. 104(11).2–3.
44. Parmenides fr. 8.38–39, and cf. frs. 8.53, 9.1; Empedocles frs. 12(8).4, 13(9).5.

πάρεξ τοῦ ἐόντος.⁴⁵ The Eleatic argument for self-consistency, moreover, was given a new application. Each root has its particular ἦθος and τιμή, and the roots are ἠνεκὲς αἰὲν ὁμοῖα; left to themselves they reach each to its like (πρὸς ὁμοῖον ἱκέσθαι), as does τὸ ἐόν for Parmenides (ἱκνεῖσθαι εἰς ὁμόν).⁴⁶

In denying spatial discontinuity Parmenides claimed that there cannot be more of what exists in one place than in another, τὸ γὰρ οὔτε τι μεῖζον / οὔτε τι βαιότερον πελέναι χρεόν ἐστι τῇ ἢ τῇ, nor can μὴ ὄν intervene and prevent what is from reaching its like. Empedocles reinterpreted these points first by asserting that the roots occupy all the available place, τῶνδ' οὐδὲν ἐρῆμον, and then by equating μὴ ὄν with kenon. Thus there is no empty place to interrupt or alter the consistency of the roots: οὐδέ τι τοῦ παντὸς κενεὸν πέλει οὐδὲ περισσόν.⁴⁷ In sum, Empedocles attributed to his four roots the spatial and temporal continuity, the changelessness, and the homogeneity of Parmenides' ὄν. Taking this as his starting point he then set out to explain everything perceptible to the senses as an arrangement of parts of these roots, in which the proportion of the parts accounts for the perceived characteristics.

LOVE AND STRIFE

In addition to the four roots Empedocles assumes the existence of Love and Strife. Like the roots these are divine and eternally existing,⁴⁸ and they act on the roots, Love bringing them into a unity and Strife separating them. But Love is described as ἠπιόφρων and θεμερῶπις, her names are Joy and Aphrodite, and by her agency men φίλα φρονέουσι καὶ ἄρθμια ἔργα τελοῦσι. Strife on the other hand is οὐλόμενον, λυγρόν, μαινόμενον, and is also known as Δῆρις αἱματόεσσα.⁴⁹

In the first book of the Metaphysics Aristotle observes that Empedocles is trying to say that Love is the cause of good, and Strife of evil.⁵⁰ Later he assumes that this is Empedocles' theory, first when he criticizes Empedocles for supposing that evil, that is, Strife, is indestructible (which

45. Parmenides fr. 8.36–37, Empedocles fr. 8(17).30.

46. Parmenides fr. 8.46–47; Empedocles frs. 8(17).28,35; 53(62).6.

47. Parmenides fr. 8.44–45; Empedocles frs. 8(17).33, 10(13); and cf. 9(12).3.

48. Fr. 11(16).

49. Cf. frs. 8(17).23–24, 47(35).13, 116(122).2, and Plutarch de Is. et Os. 370d–e; also frs. 8(17).19, 77(109).3, 25(22).8, 107(115).14, 116(122).2, and the κακαὶ ἔριδες of 26(20).4.

50. Aristotle Metaph. 985a4–10, and cf. 988a14–16.

is contrary to Aristotle's own view), and second when he compares Empedocles and Anaxagoras with the Magi, since it is true of them all that τὸ γεννῆσαν πρῶτον ἄριστον τιθέασι.[51] Related to Empedocles' *Physics* this would mean that Love is good insofar as she is the efficient cause of good, her agency resulting in a desirable state of affairs, whereas the consequences of the working of Strife are deplorable, although inevitable. A similar contrast is made by Plutarch when he states, 'Εμπεδ- οκλῆς δὲ τὴν μὲν ἀγαθουργὸν ἀρχὴν φιλότητα καὶ φιλίαν (καλεῖ) . . . τὴν δὲ χείρονα νεῖκος οὐλόμενον.[52]

Aristotle further complains that according to Empedocles' scheme Love and Strife are equally destructive *aitiai*, for there is a destruction both when the many are brought into one by Love and when Strife separates the many from one. This gives Aristotle reason to criticize Empedocles' lack of economy in positing two motive causes when one could do the work of both.[53] There is, however, a fundamental difference between the two destructions. The *phthora* caused by Strife brings about the disintegration of ὁ εὐδαιμονέστατος θεός, which is the unity of all things in the sphere, but that of Love is a necessary step toward the harmonious reunion.[54] In Empedocles' theory both Love and Strife are needed to account for the recurring generations. As Aristotle himself observes, if Strife did not exist all things would be one,[55] and if there were no principle of Love the roots would be in a state of permanent separation. It is the antagonism of two opposed principles as each fights[56] for control over the roots during the times of transition of power that gives rise to the world of *thnēta*.

Empedocles was led to posit his theory of Love and Strife as cosmic forces from the observed fact that these have the greatest influence on the behavior of men, causing them to approach each other and act together in friendship or shun and destroy each other in enmity.[57] The line of reasoning is similar to that which argued for the existence of the four roots and their characteristics from the visible world masses of earth,

51. *Metaph.* 1075b6–7, 1091b8–12, and for Aristotle's theory of evil cf. *Metaph.* 1051a17–21.

52. Plutarch *de Is. et Os.* 370d–e, and cf. Alexander *in Metaph.* 63.8–11.

53. Aristotle *Metaph.* 1000a26–b12, 985a21–29.

54. Cf. Philoponus *in GC* 264.30: 'Ε. θεὸν καλῶν τὸν σφαῖρον, τὴν μὲν φιλίαν ἐπαινεῖ ὡς αἴτιον τούτου τῇ πάντων συγκρίσει, τὸ δὲ νεῖκος ψέγει ὡς διακριτικὸν τοῦ θεοῦ.

55. Aristotle *Metaph.* 1000b1–2.

56. Cf. Aristotle *GC* 315a16–17.

57. Cf. Aristotle *Phys.* 252a27–31.

sea, sun, and sky. The consistency in the action of Love and Strife at all stages of the cycle, from the vast cosmic movements to the individual events in human life, is shown in the extant fragments. In the great sweep of the universal view the roots are described:

ἄλλοτε μὲν φιλότητι συνερχόμεν' εἰς ἓν ἅπαντα,
ἄλλοτε δ' αὖ δίχ' ἕκαστα φορεύμενα νείκεος ἔχθει.

When the roots are beginning to mix and *thnēta* to be formed the language is similar:

ἐν δὲ κότῳ διάμορφα καὶ ἄνδιχα πάντα πέλονται,
σὺν δ' ἔβη ἐν φιλότητι καὶ ἀλλήλοισι ποθεῖται.

And this tallies with the descriptions of love and hate in individuals.[58] The study of human behavior enables one to understand the nature of the cosmic principles.

Parmenides had argued that, as there is no *genesis* or *olethros*, what is is held fast by the bonds of Anankē. Empedocles claims that his roots are ἀκίνητοι, but only insofar as the character of each is invariable and the rotation of the roots from unity to separation, and from separation to unity, is unalterable and unending.[59] At the time of change determined by the oath, the roots begin to move from one state to the other, and so they commence the production of ἔθνεα μυρία θνητῶν.[60] It is Love and Strife that Empedocles gives as the cause of this change and as the reply to Parmenides' denial of *kinēsis*. Like the roots, these principles have continuous existence in time,[61] and control them alternately. The Eleatic language for the spatial uniformity of what is—μέσσοθεν ἰσοπαλὲς πάντῃ . . . οἱ γὰρ πάντοθεν ἶσον—is taken over by Empedocles for this extension of Love and Strife over the roots. Philotēs is for them ἴση μῆκός τε πλάτος τε and Neikos ἀτάλαντον ἁπάντῃ.[62]

This does not, however, imply, as is generally assumed,[63] that Love and Strife are as material as the roots. ἀτάλαντον ἁπάντῃ, the descrip-

---

58. Cf. frs. 8(17).7-8, 14(21). 7-8, 26(20). 1-5, 25(22). 1-9.
59. Fr. 8(17). 9-13, and cf. the commentary on these lines.
60. Cf. frs. 23(30), 47(35).16-17, 14(21).6-14, 16(26).3-7.
61. Cf. fr. 11(16).1-2.
62. Parmenides fr. 8.44, 49; Empedocles fr. 8(17).19,20.
63. E.g., by Burnet *EGP* p. 232: "The fragments leave no room for doubt that Love and Strife were thought of as spatial and corporeal"; Kirk-Raven *PP* p. 330: "Empedocles is still unable to imagine any form of existence other than spatial extension, and in consequence Love and Strife are still represented as if they too were material."

tion of Strife, means "matched (to the roots) in every direction," as in
Homer Pylaimenes is ἀτάλαντος Ἄρηΐ, and Odysseus Διὶ μῆτιν ἀτάλαντος, the reference being not to weight but to power.[64] Like Parmenides,
Empedocles is making a point about uniformity and balance, not bulk
and weight.[65] This is brought home when Empedocles tells Pausanias
to look at the sun, sky, sea, and earth, for these are ἐπιμάρτυρα of the
four roots, but insists that the nature of Philotēs cannot be understood by
sitting and looking. Love and Strife do not exist as things in the way that
the roots do—in this case the eyes are useless witnesses, and one must use
nous instead.[66]

In support of the claim that Love and Strife are as corporeal as the
roots, Burnet quotes two passages. One is from Theophrastus,[67] stating
that Empedocles sometimes gave an efficient power to Love and Strife
and sometimes put them on a level with the four roots. But Theophrastus'
distinction is clear. He interprets Love and Strife as having ποιητικὴ
δύναμις, since the roots are brought into one and separated into many by
their agency, but lines 17–20 of fragment 8(17) show that Love and
Strife can also be regarded as ἰσόστοιχα with the roots. This is so insofar
as all six are ungenerated, unchanging, and indestructible,[68] but the
power of Love and Strife can extend over all the roots, for they all come
into unity under Love and are separated by Strife.

The second passage is a notice of Aristotle to the effect that Empedocles, ἀτόπως, posits Love both as moving cause and, because it is part of
the mixture, as material cause.[69] Generally, when Aristotle is discussing
Empedocles' theory, he represents the four roots as predecessors of what

64. Homer *Il.* 5.576, 2.169.

65. Cf. G. E. L. Owen *CQ* 1960, p. 99, on Parmenides fr. 8.43.

66. Cf. Empedocles frs. 14(21).1, 8(17).21–26. D. O'Brien, *CQ* 1967, pp. 36–37, *ECC*
pp. 138–39, assumes from fr. 8 (17).19-20 that Love is a solid sphere and Strife a hollow
one, i.e., "an even spherical layer surrounding Love." But ἀτάλαντος ἀπάντῃ as a description of a *hollow* sphere cannot be deduced from comparisons with a shield (Homer
Il. 12.294), Prometheus' liver (Hesiod *Theog.* 524), and Parmenides' line, fr. 8.49. And if
Love is a *solid* sphere, not equal to all the elements taken together (p. 36), what place is
there for the elements, and how is ἐν τοῖσιν to be explained? In any case O'Brien (p. 36,
n.6) admits the possibility that fr. 8(17).19-20 means that Strife is everywhere equal,
and Love equal in length and breadth, to all the elements taken together.

67. Burnet loc. cit., Theophrastus *Phys. Dox.* fr. 3 (Diels *Doxographi Graeci* p. 478); cf.
Aristotle *GC* 314a16-17.

68. Simplicius, *in Phys.* 159.6-8, includes Love and Strife in Empedocles fr. 8(17).27
because they are without beginning and end in time.

69. Aristotle *Metaph.* 1075b3.

he would call material cause, and Love and Strife as among the first recognitions of efficient cause.[70] And his suggestion that Love might be the *logos* of the different mixtures of the roots in the formation of the body also shows that he viewed Love as basically different in function from the corporeal elements.[71] However, on occasion he is inclined to argue that, since Love is the cause of all things coming into one, it could be said to be unity. This unity is the *archē* from which the world has its genesis, and so Love might be viewed as τὸ ὑποκείμενον.[72] Therefore in saying that Love is a part of the mixture Aristotle need not be interpreted as meaning that it is a material part in exactly the same way as fire, air, earth, and water. He may have had in mind Empedocles' phrase καὶ φιλότης ἐν τοῖσιν.[73] Love is "in" the roots in that it is the power which draws them together, in contrast with Strife, which is pushing and holding them apart. Fire could never be "in" water in the same way that Love is "in" both fire and water when they are united.[74]

If this interpretation is correct then Love and Strife are to be viewed as powers with expanding and contracting areas of application, and difficulties concerned with the question of where Love and Strife "go" during the times of the diminution of their respective *timai* become irrelevant. Strife takes up less place as its power subsides, in that less and less of the root masses are held apart. Conversely, Love takes up more place insofar as more and more parts of roots are brought together and mingle further. Love and Strife are manifest in the pattern of balance and movement of the roots, and they are contained within the same limits as them.

MIXING AND SEPARATING

The type of mixture that the roots form in their unitings and separatings presents some difficulties. First, how are earth, air, fire, and water com-

---

70. E.g., Aristotle *Phys.* 189a24-26, *GC* 314a16-17, 333b22-24, *Metaph.* 988a33-34.

71. Aristotle *De An.* 408a23-24.

72. Cf. *Metaph.* 996a7-8, 1001a12-14, 1053b15-16, and also *Metaph.* 1069b21-22, *GC* 315a19-21.

73. Fr. 8(17).20.

74. Cf. Alexander *in Metaph.* 62.15-16: τὸ γοῦν νεῖκος καὶ ἡ φιλία στοιχεῖα μὲν κατ' 'Ε. καὶ ἐν τοῖς στοιχείοις, ἀλλ' οὐχ ὡς ὕλη, and 224.8-10, 718. 8-15; also Aristotle's discussion of the different ways in which "in" is used, *Phys.* 210a14-24. The suggestion put forward here does not preclude the fact that Empedocles, like Parmenides, still had to make use of material terms, e.g., φιλότητος ὁρμή, fr. 47(35).13.

pletely one in the sphere? Aristotle links this part of Empedocles' scheme
with Anaximander's *apeiron* and Anaxagoras' theory of the original
state of the cosmos.[75] The three assume a stage of some kind of mixture,
where elements or opposites are undifferentiated, followed by a stage
of separating out which makes them distinct. Elsewhere, in suggesting
a way in which precedent might be found for his own theory of poten-
tiality and actuality in change, Aristotle proposes that these "mixtures"
would be better expressed as ἦν ὁμοῦ πάντα δυνάμει, ἐνεργείᾳ δ'οὔ.[76]
The process of separating out of opposed substances is the common
feature of the three systems. "Mixture" is used loosely for the stage preceding the separation, for, from Aristotle's point of view, there must have
been some sense in which the ingredients were in existence before the
separating, and the best way of putting it would be to say that they existed
potentially.

In the *De Generatione et Corruptione*, however, Aristotle shows that
Empedocles' denial of generation and destruction for the roots is incompatible with their uniting.[77] When the roots are brought into one they
each lose their individual characteristics,[78] but Empedocles was not aware
that this uniting involves their virtual destruction. Aristotle's argument
runs as follows. The *diaphorai* of the roots come into existence when Strife
breaks up the one; sun white and hot, and earth heavy and hard, then
become discernible. The roots are only distinguishable now by their
diaphorai, and since the *diaphorai* come into existence they can also be
taken away. Consequently the roots are destroyed into the one and generated from it, and so they are generated from each other; this is inconsistent with Empedocles' basic assumption that the roots are ungenerated
and indestructible.[79]

Philoponus restates Aristotle's argument in more dogmatic terms.[80]
He says that the sphere under Love is ἄποιος and ἀδιάφορον σῶμα καὶ

75. Aristotle *Phys.* 187a20–26.

76. Aristotle *Metaph.* 1069b21–23, and on the sense and punctuation here, cf. W. D.
Ross *Aristotle's Metaphysics* vol. 2, pp. 350–52.

77. Aristotle *GC* 315a4–19.

78. Cf. Empedocles fr. 21(27).1, and Eudemus' comment, Simplicius *in Phys.* 1183.2.

79. Cf. Aristotle's comment on ἴσα τε πάντα fr. 8(17).27 at *GC* 333a16–29: if the
phrase means that the roots are comparable in amount a common unit of measure
would be supposed, and if in power, a common faculty; in either case the roots could
change into each other. For Aristotle's assumption that the roots for Empedocles are
absolutely basic (*contra* Cherniss *ACPP* p. 96, n. 405) cf. *Cael.* 305b1–3, *GC* 333a16–18,
Metaph. 1000b18–20.

80. Philoponus *in GC* 19.3–20.4.

ὁμοειδὲς αὐτὸ ἑαυτῷ, with none of the roots individualized. However, if the roots have their own characteristics, so that for example a part of fire but of none of the other elements occupies a given place, then the sphere is not *adiaphoros*; if on the other hand the roots are not individually characterized in their union in the sphere, then they change into each other. Such arguments suggest that Empedocles wanted to say both that the roots are individual and immortal and that in the sphere under Love there is a mingling of minute particles of the component roots such that no one root could in any part be picked out as distinct from another. Later it was recognized that one of these two assumptions would have to be sacrificed, for Empedocles' conditions would mean in effect that the union of all things would be a complete fusion.[81]

Aristotle, then, may still legitimately[82] classify Empedocles as both monist and pluralist.[83] The one is elemental in being prior to the now recognizable distinction of earth, air, fire, and water caused by the action of Strife, the many are elemental and πρότερα τὴν φύσιν[84] in that the one comes into existence derivatively, as a result of the combining of the roots. The processes eternally alternate,[85] and Empedocles' scheme may be viewed as monistic or pluralistic according to the particular stage of the theory under consideration.

Second, there is the question of the nature of the parts of the roots into which Strife breaks up the mixture under Love. As a result of Strife's working, each root gradually becomes distinct, and the process continues until the elements are separated and Strife is dominant. Aristotle describes the Empedoclean theory of a separating out of one element from another as an apparent rather than an actual *genesis*, as if from a vessel and not an underlying ὕλη. It is "a process of excretion from a body of what was in it all the time, so that it involves no change of anything."[86] A further elaboration of this process is given by Philoponus, who compares

81. Cf., for example, the medical theory of *pepsis*, which is a complete fusion with no particular *dynamis* perceptible, *VM* 19, and Galen's contrast of a fusion of elements for Hippocrates with their "touching" in Empedocles' theory, *Hipp. nat. hom.* 15.49K (DK 31 A43).

82. Despite the criticisms by Cherniss, *ACPP* pp. 36, 51, 110. The point made here and in the two preceding paragraphs on the roots in the sphere was first put forward in my thesis, "An Interpretation of Empedocles" (Oxford, 1963) pp. 147-49; J. Longrigg's article "Roots," *CR* 1967, pp. 1-4, is based on this.

83. Cf. Aristotle *Phys.* 187a21-22, *GC* 315a19-24.

84. Cf. *GC* 315a25, 333b21.

85. Cf. Aristotle *Phys.* 187a24.

86. Aristotle *Cael.* 305b1-5, trans. J. L. Stocks.

the squeezing of the roots from each other to the shooting out of fruit pips from between the fingers.[87] This suggests that one root is pushed out from another in small parts, which would be built up into other bodies.

The small size of the parts of the roots is confirmed by two notices of Aetius. The first gives Empedocles' assumption of θραύσματα ἐλάχιστα οἱονεὶ στοιχεῖα πρὸ τῶν στοιχείων ὁμοιομερῆ, and according to the second, Ἐμπεδοκλῆς δὲ ἐκ μικροτέρων ὄγκων τὰ στοιχεῖα συγκρίνει, ἅπερ ἐστιν ἐλάχιστα καὶ οἱονεὶ στοιχεῖα στοιχείων.[88] The mention of elements may be derived in Aetius from Aristotle's criticism of Empedocles in the De Generatione et Corruptione and the contrast with the Timaeus,[89] but the notion of minuteness occurs again in Galen's comparison of the parts of the roots to the fine powder resulting from the grinding down of various metals.[90] The small size may be accepted as authentic Empedoclean theory, for there is a similar assumption of extreme smallness of parts in the description of the pores and membranes of the nose and eye, and of extreme fineness in that of the ἀπορροαί which are universally given off.[91]

The small parts of roots are not, however, to be viewed as atomic; this point is brought out by Aristotle in the De Caelo,[92] where, in tabulating the possible analyses of elements he says that the process will be either infinite or finite. If it is finite the last member of the division will be either atomic or, as Empedocles seems to have intended, διαιρετὸν μὲν οὐ μέντοι διαιρεθησόμενον οὐδέποτε. A contrast is then drawn between this theory and that of the atomists. Simplicius' commentary enlarges on this notice of Aristotle.[93] He represents the Empedoclean elements as διαιρετά; they do not change into each other and they are indestructible, but not in the same way as the atoms of Democritus, for the division of the elements in Empedocles' theory never reaches to an undivided last member. Philoponus has a similar mention of nonatomic stoicheia for Empedocles.[94] These reports use Aristotelian terminology, but they show that Empedocles' theory was distinguished from that of the atomists; his roots are to

87. Philoponus in Phys. 88.11–23.

88. Aetius 1.13.1, 1.17.3.

89. Aristotle GC 325b23–24.

90. Galen Hipp. nat. hom. 15.32K (DK 31 A34).

91. Cf. frs. 91(100).3–4, 88(84).7–8, 73(89); and Theophrastus Sens. 7; Aristotle describes the kinds of tastes in water, according to Empedocles, as ἀναίσθητα διὰ μικρότητα, Sens. 441a3–6.

92. Aristotle Cael. 305a1–6.

93. Simplicius in Cael. 628.6–13.

94. Philoponus in GC 24.26–29.

be viewed as capable of being broken into very small, but nonatomic, "bits."

Third, these small parts of the different roots are put together by Love to form an organism, yet it is clear that they do not lose their identity in the process. Aristotle infers such a compound mixture as the basis of Empedocles' theory of the constitution of the bodily parts in the words ἀνάγκη γὰρ σύνθεσιν εἶναι καθάπερ ἐκ πλίνθων καὶ λίθων τεῖχος, καὶ τὸ μῖγμα δὲ τοῦτο ἐκ σῳζομένων μὲν ἔσται τῶν στοιχείων, κατὰ μικρὰ δὲ παρ' ἄλληλα συγκειμένων, οὕτω δὴ σὰρξ καὶ τῶν ἄλλων ἕκαστον.[95] The individual organism is a synthesis of the component "bits" of roots which touch but do not fuse. Similarly, in the comparison previously mentioned, Galen speaks of a body built up of elements as like a powder composed of different metals finely ground, and elsewhere he contrasts this "side by side touching" with the Hippocratic fusion of elements. Notices in Aetius and Alexander are in the same tradition.[96]

Empedocles himself perhaps did not use the figure given by Aristotle of bricks and stones lying side by side to form a wall, but the important simile which he does introduce is evidence that the interpretation by Aristotle and the commentators of the way the elements are built up into *thnēta* is in the main correct. In fragment 15(23) Empedocles shows how it is possible for only four roots to make up the countless variety of *thnēta* observable in the world by alterations in the proportions of the constituent parts, illustrating the method from the technique of a painter with his *pharmaka*. The painter, using only a few basic colors but in different proportions and various arrangements, is able to reproduce likenesses of all things.

Now the mixing of colors of which Empedocles is speaking in the simile is almost certainly not a blending to produce further shades but the setting of pigments of one color side by side with those of another in an arrangement to give the effect of a familiar object. From the scanty evidence available it seems that, through most of the fifth century, painters limited themselves to black, white, red ochre, and yellow ochre, eschewing blue and the greens and violets that could be made from mixtures.[97] According to Pliny this was the case, and Apelles in the fourth century was still working with only four colors, more exotic ones being rare and expen-

---

95. Aristotle *GC* 334a27-31.

96. Cf. Galen *Hipp. nat. hom.* 15.32, 49K (DK 31 A34, 43) and above, n. 81. Aetius 1.24.2, Alexander *in Metaph.* 359.17-21.

97. Cf. M. Robertson *Greek Painting* p. 96; for a light blue wash on panels, cf. p. 13.

sive.[98] If a different shade was needed, a coat of one color was put on top of a coat of another, rather than the two being mixed, and the extant pigment on sculptures indicates that the method was that of "a few flat washes effectively correlated to produce rich and gay compositions."[99]

The general practice, then, in painting was apparently to fill in an outline with a simple color and to achieve the required effect by juxtaposition of the different washes. Accordingly, when the analogy of the painter's colors is applied to the elements, it can be concluded that Empedocles did not see individual organisms as a complete fusion of the constituent roots but as the juxtaposition of small parts of the roots in a pleasing arrangement, a product of Love's craftsmanship.[100] The μίξις τε διάλλαξίς τε μιγέντων and the lines

$$αὐτὰ \ γὰρ \ ἔστιν \ ταῦτα, \ δι' \ ἀλλήλων \ δὲ \ θέοντα$$
$$γίγνεται \ ἀλλοιωπά· \ †τὰ \ γὰρ \ διὰ \ κρῆσις† \ ἀμείβει$$

should similarly be interpreted as referring to the shifting mosaic or "shuffle" of small parts of roots, the arrangements and rearrangements of which produce the variety of thnēta.[101]

Other similes illustrate the way in which parts of the elements are brought together. Whatever the context, Aristotle quotes fragment 49(34), ἄλφιτον ὕδατι κολλήσας . . ., to show how wet and dry ingredients mutually react, each working as a kind of glue on the other.[102] The Homeric simile of fragment 61(33), ὡς δ' ὅτ' ὀπὸς γάλα λευκὸν ἐγόμφ-

---

98. Cf. Pliny NH 35.32.50, 36.92, Cicero Brutus 18.70; the Alexander mosaic reproduces a four-color original, cf. P. Devambez Greek Painting p. 32. Where green appears it was, it seems, not a mixed color but produced from green chalk, so Vitruvius 7.7. Plutarch, glor. Ath. 346a, says that Apollodorus was the first to discover φθορὰ καὶ ἀπόχρωσις σκιᾶς, where φθορά is a technical term for μίξεις τῶν χρωμάτων 725c, 393c, cf. G. Richter Greek Art pp. 275–77. At Plato Tim. 68d only god can blend colors and resolve them. [Arist.] Col. 792a–b deals mostly with black, white, red, and yellow; variations are due to the different proportions of light and shade. For early artists deliberately restricting the number of colors used in order to simplify experiments with form, cf. V. J. Bruno Form and Colour in Greek Painting chap. 6, esp. p. 64.

99. Cf. G. Richter, "Polychromy in Greek Sculpture," AJA 1944, p. 322, and L. F. Hall's reconstruction of sculpture coloring in plates 7–11 of this volume.

100. Cf. frs. 15(23).4–5, 83(98).3–5, 47(35).12–17; cf. also the use of the verb πηγνύναι, "to fit together," as of the work of a carpenter or shipwright: frs. 70(75).1, 78(107).1, 85(86), 106(15).4, and the phrases παντοίαις ἰδέησιν ἀρηρότα 47(35).17, ἀρμονίης κόλλησιν ἀρηρότα 48(96).4, γόμφοις ἀσκήσασα καταστόργοις Ἀφροδίτη 86(87).

101. Frs. 12(8).3, 14(21).13–14; cf. Joachim's commentary on Aristotle GC 334a26–b2.

102. Aristotle Mete. 381b31–382a2; cf. the reference to a hard substance resulting from two soft ingredients, GA 747a34–b6.

INTRODUCTION 40

ωσεν καὶ ἔδησε, is referred by Plutarch to the unifying effect of Philia.[103] Fragment 74(91), on water mingling with wine and resisting oil, is quoted as an illustration of symmetry and asymmetry of πόροι and ναστά[104] and shows Empedocles' interest in the mutual reaction of the components of various types of mixture. The text of fragment 76(93) on the dyeing of linen is in doubt, but from its context in Plutarch Empedocles seems to be giving an example of a fast union resulting from a combination of dissimilar ingredients.[105]

Lastly, whereas Love puts together small parts of roots in tight juxtaposition to form an organism, Strife breaks up combinations; as a result of its agency parts of the same root are drawn toward their like, but their method of union is obscure. In fragment 73(89) Empedocles states that there are ἀπορροαί from all things that have come to be, and the context of this fragment in Plutarch includes earth and sea, which would be roots in an unmixed, or comparatively unmixed, state. Further, according to Theophrastus' account of Empedocles' theory of sense perception, it is said that there are pores in the different roots.[106] Empedocles may therefore have thought that, in their cosmic assembling, parts of the same root come together and fit on the same principle as their coincidence in perception; but the point should not be pressed, and Aristotle found no clear explanation of the process.[107] He does, however, call the increase of each root by its like a *prosthesis* and elsewhere describes the resulting mass as τὸ σωρευόμενον μέγεθος. Alexander also assumes that the root masses are built up under Strife by contact: τῷ γὰρ ἅπτεσθαι ἀλλήλων καὶ ἐπὶ τοῦ νείκους εἴη ἂν ἐν ἑνί.[108]

THE PLAN OF THE *PHYSICS*

The activity of the roots under Love and Strife follows a certain repetitive pattern. That the pattern is repeated is shown by the use of the word κύκλος in the phrases περιπλομένοιο κύκλοιο and κατὰ κύκλον, and it was so understood by Plato and Aristotle.[109] There is an unceasing

---

103. Plutarch *amic. mult.* 95a–b; cf. Homer *Il.* 5.902.

104. Or κοῖλα and πυκνά, Philoponus *in GA* 123.13–20; Aristotle uses κοῖλα and στερεά in a reference to the lines, *GA* 747b6–8.

105. Plutarch *def. or.* 433a–b, and cf. the commentary on this fragment.

106. Plutarch *quaest. nat.* 916d, Theophrastus *Sens.* 7, 12–13.

107. Aristotle *GC* 325b22–23, and cf. *GA* 747b6–10.

108. Aristotle *GC* 333a35–b3, 325b22, Alexander *in Metaph.* 35.21.

109. Empedocles frs. 16(26).1, 8(17).13, 16(16).12; Plato *Soph.* 242d (the gentler

alternation of all the roots coming into one through Love and separating into many through Strife; during each process there is a genesis and a destruction of *thnēta*. The lines are:

δοιὴ δὲ θνητῶν γένεσις, δοιὴ δ' ἀπόλειψις·
τὴν μὲν γὰρ πάντων σύνοδος τίκτει τ' ὀλέκει τε,
ἡ δὲ πάλιν διαφυομένων †θρυφθεῖσα δρεπτή†.
καὶ ταῦτ' ἀλλάσσοντα διαμπερὲς οὐδαμὰ λήγει,
ἄλλοτε μὲν φιλότητι συνερχόμεν' εἰς ἓν ἅπαντα,
ἄλλοτε δ' αὖ δίχ' ἕκαστα φορεύμενα νείκεος ἔχθει.[110]

Between coming into one and separating into many the roots are wholly united in the sphere and completely controlled by Love. Simplicius quotes Eudemus on the lines that describe this state, when the individual characteristics of the roots are not discernible:

ἔνθ' οὔτ' ἠελίοιο διείδεται ὠκέα γυῖα[111]

Three periods can therefore be distinguished: (1) the roots come together under Love, (2) the union of all things results, (3) the roots separate under Strife.

Any attempt to divide one revolution of the κύκλος must face the problem of the possibility of a stage antithetical to that of the sphere under Love, in which the elements are completely separated and Strife has universal control. Despite assertions to the contrary,[112] the sum of

---

Sicilian Muses, in contrast to those of Ionia, suppose that unity and plurality are successive and not simultaneous); Aristotle *Phys.* 187a20–24 (Empedocles is contrasted with Anaxagoras in their theories of separation from mixture: τῷ τὸν μὲν περίοδον ποιεῖν τούτων, τὸν δ' ἅπαξ), and cf. *Metaph.* 985a23–29.

110. Fr. 8(17).3–8; it is hard to see how Solmsen can interpret line 3 here as a destruction of compounds and genesis of the ἕν, and as a corresponding destruction of the ἕν and genesis of compounds (*Phronesis* 1965, p. 140), or Hölscher, as a reference to an individual organism (*Hermes* 1965, pp. 31–32). Fr. 8(17) gives in outline the cosmic pattern of the roots uniting and separating, in each case causing a genesis and destruction of *thnēta*; the application of the universal activity to individual organisms comes later, in frs. 25(22) and 26(20). For the text of fr. 8(17).5 cf. the commentary on the line.

111. Eudemus ap. Simplicius *in Phys.* 1183.28–1184.1 quoting fr. 21(27).

112. E.g., by H. von Arnim *Festschrift Gomperz* pp. 16–27; P. Tannery *Pour l'histoire de la science hellène* p. 319; Cherniss *ACPP* pp. 175, 205; J. Bollack *Empédocle* vol. 1, pp. 108–10; Hölscher and Solmsen loc. cit. In favor are F. Dümmler *Akademika* p. 217; Burnet *EGP* p. 234; F. M. Cornford *Cambridge Ancient History* vol. 4, p. 566; E. L. Minar *Phronesis* 1963, p. 127; Guthrie *HGP* vol. 2, pp. 174–78. C. E. Millerd, *On the Interpretation of Empedocles* pp. 54–55, suggests only two stages, the separating into many and the

the evidence available does incline to the conclusion that Empedocles envisaged a domination of the whole by Strife, following the destruction of a generation of *thnēta*.

First there are Empedocles' own words. He states quite clearly that there is a twofold destruction of *thnēta*: δοιὴ δὲ θνητῶν γένεσις, δοιὴ δ' ἀπόλειψις. He goes on to say that one of these destructions of *thnēta* is caused as the roots separate, and then adds that this separation is the work of Strife, ἄλλοτε δ' αὖ δίχ' ἕκαστα φορεύμενα νείκεος ἔχθει. From fragment 47(35) it is known that when the roots are under the control of Strife they stay unmixed and are not formed into compounds.[113] In other fragments the function of Strife is represented as balancing that of Love.[114] The balance would be disturbed, and the fight an unequal one, if the complete sway that Love enjoys in the perfection of the sphere were not matched by a complementary dominance of Strife.

In the *Physics* Aristotle represents the stages of the complete control of Love and Strife as stages of rest in contrast to the world in motion, when the many are coming into one, and again when the one is separating into many. The references to Empedocles are: ἢ ὡς Ἐμπεδοκλῆς ἐν μέρει κινεῖσθαι καὶ πάλιν ἠρεμεῖν, κινεῖσθαι μὲν ὅταν ἡ φιλία ἐκ πολλῶν ποιῇ τὸ ἓν ἢ τὸ νεῖκος πολλὰ ἐξ ἑνός, ἠρεμεῖν δ' ἐν τοῖς μεταξὺ χρόνοις . . . ὡς τὸ κρατεῖν καὶ κινεῖν ἐν μέρει τὴν φιλίαν καὶ τὸ νεῖκος ὑπάρχει τοῖς πράγμασιν ἐξ ἀνάγκης, ἠρεμεῖν δὲ τὸν μεταξὺ χρόνον.[115] It is doubtful whether von Arnim is correct in seeing a significant distinction between the use of the singular and the plural of χρόνος in these passages of Aristotle. The plural form most obviously refers to both intervals between the two stages of motion, and the singular, to each separate interval. Millerd and Cherniss argue that Aristotle's evidence is worthless here, for they claim that he uses this quotation because he could find nothing better to support a period of rest under Strife. They conclude that he then twisted the meaning of the last line—ταύτῃ δ' αἰὲν ἔασιν ἀκίνητοι κατὰ κύκλον—to make it fit his preconceived theory.[116] Against

---

gathering of the many into one. Cf. also E. Bignone *Empedocle, studio critico*, and the summary by A. A. Long in *The Pre-Socratics*, ed. A. Mourelatos, pp. 397-425.

113. Fr. 8(17).3,5,7; fr. 47(35).8-9, 12-14.

114. E.g., frs. 11(16).1-2, 16(26).5-6, 23(30).2-3, 26(20).2-5.

115. Aristotle *Phys.* 250b26-29 followed by a quotation of Empedocles fr. 8(17).9-13 (repeated fr. 16(26).8-12), and 252a7-10.

116. von Arnim *Fest. Gomperz* p. 16; Millerd *Empedocles* p. 54, Cherniss *ACPP* p. 175, supported by Hölscher loc. cit. p. 12, N. van der Ben *The Proem of Empedocles' Peri Physios* pp. 28-30.

this it may be said that Aristotle is sometimes careless in his use of examples to illustrate the points he is making, and if in this case he uses a quotation concerned with motion to illustrate Empedocles' theory of motion and rest, it cannot be inferred that Empedocles' poem contained no lines describing intervening periods.[117] Aristotle has not misrepresented Empedocles, for he is referring to the rotation of the elements from many to one and from one to many, and to the permanence of this rotation. Since the μεταξὺ χρόνοι are only implied in the first and third stages of the rotation of (many), many to one, (one), one to many, Aristotle's citation of the lines may be criticized on the grounds of inadequacy but not of inaccuracy.[118]

Aristotle supports the interpretation of a separation of elements by Strife, corresponding to their union under Love, in the following: ὅταν μὲν γὰρ εἰς τὰ στοιχεῖα διίστηται τὸ πᾶν ὑπὸ τοῦ νείκους, τό τε πῦρ εἰς ἓν συγκρίνεται καὶ τῶν ἄλλων στοιχείων ἕκαστον· ὅταν δὲ πάλιν ὑπὸ τῆς φιλίας συνίωσιν εἰς τὸ ἕν, ἀναγκαῖον ἐξ ἑκάστου τὰ μόρια διακρίνεσθαι πάλιν.[119] It is also assumed in two of his criticisms of Empedocles. In the first, Aristotle asks how the earth could keep its position when the elements were held apart by Strife, for this could not have been explained by the dinē. The second is the passage where he states that Empedocles omitted the genesis of the cosmos ἐπὶ τῆς φιλότητος, and where he suggests a reason for the omission: οὐ γὰρ ἂν ἠδύνατο συστῆσαι τὸν οὐρανὸν ἐκ κεχωρισμένων (στοιχείων) κατασκευάζων. Elsewhere Aristotle concludes of the ouranos, καὶ οὐ φοβερὸν μή ποτε στῇ, ὃ φοβοῦνται οἱ περὶ φύσεως, and Alexander explains that the reference here is to Empedocles.[120]

Simplicius fills out these remarks of Aristotle. In commenting on the Physics passage he says that in Empedocles' theory change and motion are in one respect eternal but in another there is no change, because, although there is a periodic move from many to one and from one to many, after each move there is a reestablishment of the eidos of the one and the many respectively. Themistius agrees: τὴν γὰρ ἠρεμίαν ἐν τοῖς

---

117. Fr. 21(27) does refer to one of these periods.

118. This seems to be the point of Aristotle's comment following the quotation, Phys. 251a4–5, and was so interpreted by Simplicius, in Phys. 1125.15–24; on the quotation cf. G. A. Seeck Hermes 1967, pp. 30–36.

119. Aristotle Metaph. 985a25–29.

120. Aristotle Cael. 295a30–32, 301a15–18, Metaph. 1050b23–24, Alexander in Metaph. 592.31–32.

μεταξὺ τῶν μεταβολῶν χρόνοις γίνεσθαί φησι.[121] And with reference to the *De Caelo* criticism, Simplicius points out that when the elements are actually separated by Strife there is a different *katastasis* from the present one, which is coming into existence under Strife.[122]

A passage from Aetius mentions the complete domination by Strife, which involves the destruction of the world: Ἐμπεδοκλῆς τὸν κόσμον φθείρεσθαι κατὰ τὴν ἀντεπικράτειαν τοῦ νείκους καὶ τῆς φιλίας.[123] Plutarch also definitely accepts an absolute rule of Strife and refers two lines of Empedocles to this time.[124] In the context of the lines Plutarch elaborates on the state of the elements under Strife's control: οὐ γῆ θερμότητος μετεῖχεν, οὐχ ὕδωρ πνεύματος, οὐκ ἄνω τι τῶν βαρέων οὐ κάτω τι τῶν κούφων, ἀλλ' ἄκρατοι καὶ ἄστοργοι καὶ μονάδες αἱ τῶν ὅλων ἀρχαὶ μὴ προσιέμεναι σύγκρισιν ἑτέρου πρὸς ἕτερον μηδὲ κοινω-νίαν, ἀλλὰ φεύγουσαι καὶ ἀποστρεφόμεναι καὶ φερόμεναι φορὰς ἰδίας καὶ αὐθάδεις . . .[125] Here Plutarch is in agreement with the previous evidence in his account of the destruction of the world, the domination by Strife, and the unmixed state of the roots. Nor need he be contradicting Aristotle's assumption in the *Physics* of ἠρεμία after the roots have sep-arated from one to many. The present participles in the quotation from Plutarch would describe the tendency the elements have to move toward their own kind and away from what is unlike them in each case; this tendency is realized when Strife has control, and all the fire has moved outward, the earth to the center, and the air and water between. This then gives the parallel with the state in the *Timaeus* which Plutarch claims is found after the four kinds have been "winnowed" from their dissimilars into aggregates of like elements, having their particular places before being arranged into a *kosmos*.[126]

There would then be some support for those who suggest that under Strife the roots are arranged in four concentric "layers," with earth surrounded by water, which in turn is enveloped by air, and with fire

---

121. Simplicius *in Phys.* 1125.17–24 on Aristotle *Phys.* 250b23; cf. Simplicius *in Phys.* 1153.27–30, 1183.5–6.

122. Simplicius *in Cael.* 528.9–10 on Aristotle *Cael.* 295a29.

123. Aetius 2.4.8 (Stobaeus).

124. Plutarch *fac. lun.* 926e–f quoting fr. 19(27).1–2.

125. Cf. Proclus *Plat. Parm. Comm.* 849: . . . ἀπὸ δὲ τῆς ἑνώσεως αὐτῶν εἰς πᾶν προελήλυθε σκεδασμοῦ καὶ ἑτερότητος, ἐνταῦθα γὰρ τὸ 'Ε. νεῖκος καὶ ὁ γιγαντικὸς πόλεμος . . ., and Cherniss on Plutarch *fac. lun.* (Loeb) p. 82, n. c.

126. Cf. Plato *Tim.* 53a–b; a "vibration" of the root masses is suggested, as they try to shun each other, but, in the absence of void, cannot do so completely.

beyond that.[127] This follows the Ionian tradition and was carried on through Greek philosophy; its very obviousness may account for the lack of surviving comment on such a pattern for the massed roots in Empedocles' scheme.[128] Simplicius says, however, that the *katastasis* of complete separation is not the one immediately present, and there is evidence for this elsewhere. The roots are not yet totally collected into their aggregates, for fires still burn beneath the earth, there are underground streams, and also compounds of fire and air in the *ouranos*.[129] Last, it is not known for how long Strife, and Love, would have complete control. Fragments 19(27) to 22(29) suggest a certain period in a settled state, but, as in the *Politicus* myth, there may have been only a moment of equilibrium before the motion of the cosmos swung into reverse.[130]

There has been much controversy among modern commentators concerning the place of the present world in Empedocles' scheme. His lines

δοιὴ δὲ θνητῶν γένεσις, δοιὴ δ' ἀπόλειψις·
τὴν μὲν γὰρ πάντων σύνοδος τίκτει τ' ὀλέκει τε,
ἡ δὲ πάλιν διαφυομένων †θρυφθεῖσα δρεπτή†[131]

assert that there is a generation and destruction of *thnēta* as the roots move from many to one, and a second generation and destruction as they separate from one into many. So far as these lines go, the present could be in either transitional stage, but the available evidence inclines to the

127. Cf. Millerd *Empedocles* p. 56; Kirk-Raven *PP* p. 346; Guthrie *HGP* vol. 2, p. 177; O'Brien *CQ* 1967, p. 36, *Empedocles' Cosmic Cycle* p. 350.

128. Cf. Anaximander ap. [Plut.] *Strom.* 2; Plato *Phaedo* 111a and *Tim.* 63d–e; Aristotle *Mete.* 340a19–22, *Cael.* 311a24–29, 313a6–10, and *De An.* 415b28–416a2.

129. Empedocles fr. 32(52), Plutarch *de prim frig.* 953e, Seneca *QNat.* 3.24.1, Aetius 2.11.2, 25.15, and also 1.5.2. The point is made against Solmsen, *Phronesis* 1965, p. 117, who maintains that complete separation has already taken place, cf. Long *Pre-Socratics*, ed. Mourelatos, p. 406.

130. Plato *Pol.* 273a; O'Brien, *CQ* 1967, pp. 29–34, *ECC* pp. 59–69, claims that Aristotle recognizes the unity under Love as the only stage of rest, and that this lasts as long as the other three stages combined. But rest under Strife is not disproved by *Cael.* 301a15–18, which relates only separated elements explicitly to Empedocles, or by 300b27–31, which is a later stage after the reentry of Love. The phrase, *Phys.* 252a31, τὸ δὲ καὶ δι' ἴσων χρόνων δεῖται λόγου τινός refers not to the alternation of rest and movement but to the times (1) of many to one and unity, i.e., of Love, (2) of one to many and separation, i.e., of Strife. The sentence following shows that the criticism is similar to that made at *GC* 334a7–9 and *Metaph.* 1000b12–17.

131. Fr. 8(17).3–5; for the last two words as θρεφθεῖσα διέπτη cf. the commentary on these lines.

conclusion that it is in the period of increasing Strife, when the roots are separating from unity into their respective masses.[132]

Aristotle, querying how the same state of the world can hold under Love, which initiates motion παρὰ φύσιν, and under Strife, whose motion is κατὰ φύσιν, says, ἅμα δὲ καὶ τὸν κόσμον ὁμοίως ἔχειν φησιν ἐπί τε τοῦ νείκους νῦν καὶ πρότερον ἐπὶ τῆς φιλίας.[133] Elsewhere he makes a similar comparison when he relates an incorrect embryological theory to Empedocles' account of isolated parts of animals in the words ὥσπερ τότε ἐν τῇ γῇ ἐπὶ τῆς φιλότητος, οὕτω τούτοις ἐν τῷ σώματι.[134] ἐπὶ τῆς φιλίας, or φιλότητος, does not mean "when Love is in complete control" (which in Empedocles' scheme would be the state described in fragment 21(27).1–3), for he assigns the genesis of the animal parts to the same time. Simplicius' explanation of the phrase, οὐχ ὡς ἐπικρατούσης ἤδη τῆς φιλότητος, ἀλλ᾽ ὡς μελλούσης ἐπικρατεῖν, is more plausible.[135]

Further, it has been seen that Aristotle was inclined to link Empedocles with Anaximander and Anaxagoras for supposing that the generation of this world was a separating out of its constituent parts from some sort of mixture, but this would be unwarranted if Empedocles had believed that the *kosmos* in its present state was generated from the elements after they had been completely separated by Strife.[136] Empedocles did not give an account of the genesis of the *ouranos* ἐπὶ τῆς φιλότητος, and Aristotle suggests that it would have been difficult for him to do so if the elements were already separate. The conclusion then would be that Aristotle understood Empedocles to have posited a stage of many to one under increasing Love, and another of one to many under increasing Strife; some remarks on animal life were included in the account of the first, but a cosmogony was not given, whereas the description of the second, the world as it is now, contained a detailed cosmogony and biology.[137]

132. Cf. Simplicius *in Phys.* 1124.20–22: τὴν μὲν κίνησιν κατὰ τὴν γένεσιν θεωρεῖ τοῦ τε ἑνὸς ἐκ τῶν πολλῶν καὶ τῶν πολλῶν ἐκ τοῦ ἑνός.

133. Aristotle *GC* 334a5–7.

134. Aristotle *GA* 722b25–26.

135. Simplicius *in Cael.* 587.24–25; cf. Aristotle *Cael.* 300b30, *GA* 722b19.

136. Cf. [Plut.] *Strom.* 10 (DK 31 A30): ἐκ πρώτης φησι τῆς τῶν στοιχείων κράσεως ἀποκριθέντα τὸν ἀέρα περιχυθῆναι κύκλῳ.

137. Cf. Aristotle *Cael.* 301a15–19; the greater detail and interest would obviously come with the account of the cosmos as it is now, and the "glaring contradiction" that Solmsen finds (*Phronesis* 1965, p. 130) can perhaps be mitigated along these lines. Hölscher's "weak" interpretation of ὁμοίως ἔχειν at *GC* 334a5–7 (*Hermes* 1965, p. 25) blunts the point of Aristotle's criticism of Empedocles for (1) having like states resulting from

The evidence from Aristotle for the place of the present world in Empedocles' scheme is supported by Simplicius, who has two notices to this effect. One has been previously mentioned, where Aristotle's phrase ὅτε τὰ στοιχεῖα χωρὶς διειστήκει ὑπὸ τοῦ νείκους is explained: ὡς ἄλλην τινὰ κατάστασιν παρὰ τὴν νῦν ἐκείνην λέγων τὴν ὑπὸ τοῦ νείκους γινομένην.[138] The other is the statement that this world is brought about by Strife ὅταν (τὸ νεῖκος) ἐπικρατῇ μὴ τελέως, διὰ τῆς διακρίσεως τὸν κόσμον τοῦτον ποιοῦν.[139] A passage from Theophrastus may be added here, for in criticizing Empedocles' theory of effluences he writes, συμβαίνει δὲ καὶ ἐπὶ τῆς φιλίας ὅλως μὴ εἶναι αἴσθησιν ἢ ἧττον διὰ τὸ συγκρίνεσθαι τότε καὶ μὴ ἀπορρεῖν, showing that a σύγκρισις ἐπὶ τῆς φιλίας is a stage other than the present one.[140]

The paragraph from Aetius which states that according to Empedocles the men of today are as infants compared with men of the past puts the world now in a worse state than previously. And this is borne out by the account of trees, which, with their symmetrical mixture, were the first living things to be produced, before night and day were distinguished and when there was heat in the earth to raise them up.[141] It would seem that Empedocles shared Hesiod's pessimism in seeing the world as it is now degenerating from a better time in the past, and in the scheme of his *Physics* this is because the elements are separating out from one to many under the inevitable increase of the baneful agency of Strife.[142]

Although there is no temporal starting point for the cosmic phases, to be intelligible they would need to have been described in a sequence, allowing for some repetition and recapitulation of points already made. At the beginning of the *Physics* Empedocles lists the four roots as the commencement of his exposition.[143] Throughout, in the fragments dealing

---

opposite motive principles, (2) confusing the issue by introducing chance and natural elemental movement, and (3) not accounting for τὸ πρῶτον κινοῦν.

138. Simplicius *in Cael.* 528.9-10 on Aristotle *Cael.* 295a31, and cf. *in Cael.* 590.19-21, 293.20-23.

139. Simplicius *in Phys.* 1124.3; cf. Alexander ap. Philoponus *in GC.* 268.8-13, Simplicius *in Cael.* 528.21-22.

140. Theophrastus *Sens.* 20; cf. Hippolytus *RH* 7.29.15, Millerd *Empedocles* p. 45.

141. Aetius 5.27.1, 5.26.4.

142. Epiphanius *adv. haer.* 3.19 (*Dox.* 591), κεχώριστο γάρ, φησί, τὸ πρότερον (τὰ στοιχεῖα) νῦν δὲ συνήνωται, ὡς λέγει, φιλωθέντα ἀλλήλοις, seems to be the only passage suggesting that the present is in a world of increasing Love, but the account is very condensed and is perhaps a summary of the work Love is still able to achieve, cf. frs. 8(17).23, 25(22).1-5.

143. Cf. fr. 7(6).1: τέσσαρα γὰρ πάντων ῥιζώματα πρῶτον ἄκουε.

with the cycle, he says first that the roots come from many into one, and then that they separate into many from one.[144] This suggests that Empedocles started from earth, air, fire, and water, and viewed the unity of the sphere as derived from them. The natural movement of the roots is to separate from each other and to gather to their like; the activity of Love is παρὰ φύσιν in that it compels the roots to break up their family connections and combine with one another. That the sphere under Love is derived from the roots, rather than being the logical starting point from which their separation follows, is also shown by Aristotle's notice that Empedocles' four elements are φύσει πρότερα to god.[145]

The plan of the *Physics* is then as follows. First there would be a brief summary of the cosmic history, starting with an outline statement of the roots in separation, of their coming together into the unity of the sphere under Love, and of their breaking up into many from this unity through the agency of Strife. The activity of the principles as we know them is similar to, and an illustration of, their universal functioning. Then in more detail comes the formation of the present world, with references to the sun and moon, and some meteorological phenomena. In his discussion of the genesis of living things, Empedocles goes back to the stage of the progress from many to one and gives a brief account of the creatures that existed at that time;[146] he then continues with a description of life in this world in the process from one to many. He has scope here to develop his biological theories and his explanation of growth, perception, and thought as relevant now. There was a precedent for this method in the poem of Parmenides, where the program of the argument was first summarized and then the various points elaborated.[147]

---

144. Cf. frs. 8(17).1-2, 3-4, 7-10; 16(26).5-6, 8-9.

145. Aristotle *GC* 333b21; for the paradoxical character of Love's activity cf. *GC* 333b27-33.

146. Cf. fr. 47(35).1-2.

147. This ordering of the fragments, starting from the roots rather than the sphere, answers some of Solmsen's objections to a cyclic theory (*Phronesis* 1965, pp. 124-48). The following points may also be made against his argument: (1) one would expect Love's work, that of uniting, to be consistent throughout; (2) it is not Strife's work to create a zoogony, for Strife separates and Love combines; (3) the roots are not yet in a state of complete separation, and so Strife has not yet reached its acme; (4) the mixtures now achieved by Love are in very few cases "perfect," for Love is fighting a losing battle against Strife; (5) Simplicius' quotation of fr. 47(35) does not put it necessarily in the same context, "to wit the present νῦν," as 60(71); (6) a strained sense is given to fr. 8(17).3, cf. above, note 110. Similar objections tell against Hölscher (*Hermes* 1965, pp. 7-35). Cf.

MONSTERS AND MEN

The available evidence tends to show that the present generation of men and women occurs in the period of increasing Strife. The fragments also speak of separate limbs, monstrous formations, and "whole-nature forms," and it remains to consider their place in the cosmic history.

The most important testimony for the separate limbs comes from three notices of Aristotle, all of which quote the first line of fragment 50(57). They are: (1) μίξεις ἐξ ὧν συνίσταται τὰ κατὰ φύσιν συνιστάμενα σώματα, λέγω δ' οἶον ὀστᾶ καὶ σάρκας, καθάπερ Ἐμπεδοκλῆς φησὶ γίνεσθαι ἐπὶ τῆς φιλότητος, λέγει γὰρ ὡς "πολλαὶ μὲν κόρσαι . . ." (2) ὥσπερ γὰρ καὶ μεγάλα ὄντ' ἀδύνατον διεσπασμένα σῴζεσθαι καὶ ἔμψυχα εἶναι, καθάπερ Ἐμπεδοκλῆς γεννᾷ ἐπὶ τῆς φιλότητος, λέγων "ᾗ πολλαὶ μὲν κόρσαι . . ." (3) σύνθεσίς τις ἤδη νοημάτων ὥσπερ ἐν ὄντων, καθάπερ Ἐμπεδοκλῆς ἔφη "ᾗ πολλῶν μὲν κόρσαι ἀναύχενες ἐβλάστησαν," ἔπειτα συντίθεσθαι τῇ φιλίᾳ.[148] These quotations show, first, that the heads, arms, and eyes mentioned in fragment 50(57), although unattached, are ἔμψυχα, composed of bone and flesh and therefore similar to the corresponding parts in the present generation of men and women, and second, that these limbs were generated ἐπὶ τῆς φιλότητος and then put together by Love.

It has been concluded that Aristotle's comparison of the *kosmos* now, ἐπὶ τοῦ νείκους, with the former state ἐπὶ τῆς φιλότητος, taken with lines 3–5 of Empedocles' fragment 8(17), puts the world as it is now in the time of increasing Strife; ἐπὶ τῆς φιλότητος would then be the complementary stage, that generated under the power of increasing Love, when the elements come from many to one. And so Simplicius: ἐπὶ τῆς φιλότητος οὖν ὁ Ἐμπεδοκλῆς ἐκεῖνα εἶπεν, οὐχ ὡς ἐπικρατούσης ἤδη τῆς φιλότητος, ἀλλ' ὡς μελλούσης ἐπικρατεῖν, ἔτι δὲ τὰ ἄμικτα καὶ μονόγυια δηλούσης. Earlier, after quoting lines 10–13 of fragment 47(35), which describe the gradual advance of Love and corresponding retreat of Strife, he had explained, ἐν ταύτῃ οὖν τῇ καταστάσει "μουνομελῆ" ἔτι τὰ γυῖα ἀπὸ τῆς τοῦ νείκους διακρίσεως ὄντα ἐπλανᾶτο τῆς πρὸς ἄλληλα μίξεως ἐφιέμενα.[149]

The monstrous formations mentioned in fragments 140(60) and 52(61) would then come into existence when Love increases her control at the

---

Long loc. cit. p. 412, and van der Ben *Proem* pp. 28–30, who follow Solmsen and Hölscher.

148. Aristotle *Cael.* 300b27–31, *GA* 722b17–20, *De An.* 430a27–30.

149. Aristotle *GC* 334a5–7; Simplicius *in Cael.* 587.24–27, 18–19.

expense of Strife. Simplicius, following Aristotle,[150] explains that the monsters come after the stage of separated limbs, occurring later in the *kosmos* started by the entrance of Love: ὥσπερ Ἐμπεδοκλῆς κατὰ τὴν τῆς φιλίας ἀρχήν φησι γενέσθαι ὡς ἔτυχε μέρη πρῶτον τῶν ζῴων, οἷον κεφαλὰς καὶ χεῖρας καὶ πόδας, ἔπειτα συνιέναι ταῦτα "βουγενῆ ἀνδρόπρῳρα." Moreover, Simplicius says that the further mingling of the elements referred to in fragment 51(59) happens ὅτε τοῦ νείκους ἐπεκράτει λοιπὸν ἡ φιλότης.[151] And it is as a result of this further mingling, and the rising strength of Love, that the limbs combine.

This account by Simplicius is the obvious interpretation of the Aristotelian passages; it is not, however, in agreement with the views of either Alexander or Philoponus. Alexander takes Aristotle's phrase ἐπὶ τῆς φιλότητος to refer to the time when the elements are united under the complete control of Love, which is seen as a μίξεως παράδειγμα. For this he is criticized by Simplicius: πῶς δὲ ἂν εἴη μίξεως σημαντικὸν ἡ "ἀναύχενος κόρση"; for the wandering of the limbs is a disorderly movement and their combinings haphazard. Simplicius continues, μήποτε οὖν οὐκ ἐν τῇ ἐπικρατείᾳ τῆς φιλίας ταῦτα λέγει γενέσθαι ὁ Ἐμπεδοκλῆς, ὡς ἐνόμισεν Ἀλέξανδρος, ἀλλὰ τότε, ὅτε οὔπω τὸ νεῖκος

πᾶν ἐξέστηκεν ἐπ᾽ ἔσχατα τέρματα κύκλου,
ἀλλὰ τὰ μέν τ᾽ ἐνέμιμνε μελέων τὰ δέ τ᾽ ἐξεβεβήκει.[152]

Philoponus also refers the limbs to the sphere, saying that in it were mixed not only the elements but also the parts of animals. The monsters occur ἐν τῇ πρώτῃ διακρίσει τοῦ σφαίρου . . . πρὶν τὸ νεῖκος τελείως ἀπ᾽ ἀλλήλων διακρῖναι τὰ εἴδη. Elsewhere he gives an explanation of ἐπὶ τῆς φιλότητος that is inconsistent with this commentary from the *Physics*. He holds that in Empedocles' account the heads, hands, and other animal parts form combinations on the earth ἐπὶ τῆς φιλότητος, τουτέστιν ἐπὶ τῇ ἥττῃ μὲν τῆς φιλότητος, ἐπικρατείᾳ δὲ τοῦ νείκους.[153] Philoponus' interpretation seems to be that the parts of animals are contained in the sphere; when Strife enters and proceeds to win over the *kosmos* from Love the limbs are then put together. Since Philoponus admits only two states, the sphere and this world, he has to find a place for the monsters in the

---

150. Aristotle *GA* 722b20–21: εἶθ᾽ οὕτως συμφύεσθαί φησιν, *De An.* 430a30: ἔπειτα συντίθεσθαι τῇ φιλίᾳ.

151. Simplicius *in Phys.* 371.33–35, *in Cael.* 587.21.

152. Simplicius *in Cael.* 586.25–587.12, with Empedocles' frs. 50(57) and 47(35).10–11.

153. Philoponus *in Phys.* 314.6–25, *in GA* 28.9–14.

time under Strife. This results in the strained explanation of ἐπὶ τῆς φιλότητος as ἐπὶ τῇ ἥττῃ τῆς φιλότητος.[154]

Simplicius' version is likely to be more reliable than those of Alexander and Philoponus, for he alone of the commentators gives further independent quotations from Empedocles' poem to illustrate his interpretation, and it is likely that he was the only one to work with a text of Empedocles before him.[155] It may therefore be assumed that he is on the whole correct in following Aristotle and that his explanation of a genesis of living but unattached limbs soon after the separation of the elements by Strife, and the combining of these limbs as they seek union with each other under the increasing control of Love, substantially reproduces Empedocles' own theory.

It is not known whether Empedocles gave any account of the genesis of plants ἐπὶ τῆς φιλότητος. According to Aristotle, Empedocles should have been consistent and extended his principle of monstrous combinations of animal parts to plants, with such results as ἀμπελογενῆ ἐλαιό-πρῳρα,[156] but it is not possible to say whether this is an implied objection to any explanation that Empedocles did give concerning the genesis of plant life when Love's power was increasing.[157] The phrase describing the *thnēta* resulting from the gradual encroachment of Love over Strife, ἔθνεα μυρία θνητῶν, παντοίαις ἰδέῃσιν ἀρηρότα, θαῦμα ἰδέσθαι, does not necessarily refer to limbs and monsters. It is similar to Empedocles' wording elsewhere on the great variety of living things—plants, animals, and men—that are seen in the present world.[158]

The notice of Aristotle that the world was in a similar state formerly, ἐπὶ τῆς φιλότητος, as now, ἐπὶ τοῦ νείκους, suggests that there were men and women in the period corresponding to the present one. Fragment 53(62) gives the genesis of men and women from "whole-nature forms" sent up by fire as it was separating, but this does not exclude the possibility that there was a human generation at some other period. In the

154. Philoponus' contrast between the sphere under Love and this world under Strife is due in part to his wish to fit Empedocles' scheme into that of the circles of same and other of the *Timaeus*; cf. Philoponus *in Phys.* 24.12–17.

155. Cf. the index fontium for the lack of independent quotation in Alexander and Philoponus.

156. Plants are, however, included generally in Aetius' account (5.19.5) 'E. τὰς πρώτας γενέσεις τῶν ζῴων καὶ τῶν φυτῶν μηδαμῶς ὁλοκλήρους γενέσθαι, and cf. Simplicius *in Cael.* 586.9–11 quoted below, n. 160, in the context of fr. 47(35).

157. Aristotle *Phys.* 199b10–13, and cf. Philoponus *in Phys.* 319.9–20, Simplicius *in Phys.* 382.25–31.

158. Empedocles fr. 47(35).16–17, and cf. frs. 15(23).5, 107(115).7.

time of the movement from separation to unity Empedocles found a solution to the problem of the existence of legendary figures like the Minotaur and the Centaurs. He set the generation of such a population then, in much the same way as Plato put his ideal statesman in a different stage of his cosmic cycle, as having little relation to the present world.[159] It would, however, also be reasonable to suppose that as Love's power increased better combinations were effected, and that some of the human and animal parts were joined in a more fitting manner, with a result similar to that which Love is still able to achieve. Such a conclusion is actually given by Censorinus, and Simplicius supposes that Empedocles envisaged some normal as well as abnormal combinations of the unattached limbs during the increasing domination of Love.[160]

Monstrous births occurring now are accounted for, not by an ill-fitting union of unattached limbs, but by some defect in the seed or fault in its motion.[161] A survival of monstrous combinations into the present should not be read into a notice of Aristotle criticizing a view that bodily parts are produced by necessity and not by design. Aristotle gives his supposed opponents this conclusion: ὅπου μὲν οὖν ἅπαντα συνέβη ὥσπερ κἂν εἰ ἕνεκά του ἐγίγνετο, ταῦτα μὲν ἐσώθη ἀπὸ τοῦ αὐτομάτου συστάντα ἐπιτηδείως· ὅσα δὲ μὴ οὕτως, ἀπώλετο καὶ ἀπόλλυται, καθάπερ Ἐμπεδοκλῆς λέγει τὰ βουγενῆ ἀνδρόπρῳρα. The βουγενῆ ἀνδρόπρῳρα are added as an illustration of combinations not fit to survive, but this does not mean that the whole context reproduces Empedocles' theory of the rise of the human race. Simplicius, in his commentary here, clarifies the interpretation, for he gives Empedocles' standpoint first and then makes the general application for those who do not recognize a natural teleology.[162]

In the extant fragment that is concerned with the generation of men and women it is said that they were preceded by οὐλοφυεῖς τύποι. These, having a share of water and heat, sprang from the earth, sent up by fire as it tended to reach its like; their limbs were not articulated, and they could not reproduce their kind.[163] The recognizable human forms result from

---

159. Plato Pol. 275a.

160. Censorinus 4.7 (DK 31 A72), Simplicius in Cael. 586.9-11: . . . καὶ ὅλως τὰ τῶν ζῴων μέρη καὶ τῶν φυτῶν καὶ αὐτὰ τὰ ζῷα καὶ τὰ φυτά, ὥσπερ Ἐ. γίνεσθαί φησι ἐπὶ τῆς φιλότητος. Cf. also the commentary on fr. 16(26).

161. Cf. Aetius 5.8.1.

162. Aristotle Phys. 198b29-32, Simplicius in Phys. 371.33-372.11, and cf. O. Hamelin in W. D. Ross Aristotle's Physics p. 528.

163. Empedocles fr. 53(62) quoted by Simplicius in Phys. 381.31.

the further differentiation by Strife of these τύποι,[164] whereby the parts become articulated and sexual reproduction possible. Love continually strives to make the resulting *thnēton* as perfect as the material allows and occasionally gains a striking victory, as in the tongue of the orator or the hand of the craftsman, where the elements are in the appropriate proportions. As Love loses ground, however, such victories become increasingly rare in the persistent battle between the two opposed principles.[165]

It is now possible to interpret Aetius' account of the four generations of living things.[166] The passage is a condensed summary of various forms of life envisaged by Empedocles. It does not give their place in the cosmic scheme and says nothing about the passing away of each kind, nor whether there are one or more occurrences of each generation at the different stages. The order need not be accepted as Aetius gives it, but with the foregoing conclusions no change is necessary.

The first generation is that of the single limbs described in fragment 50(57), and given by Aetius as Ἐμπεδοκλῆς (φησι) τὰς πρώτας γενέσεις τῶν ζῴων καὶ φυτῶν μηδαμῶς ὁλοκλήρους γενέσθαι, ἀσυμφυέσι δὲ τοῖς μορίοις διεζευγμένας. Empedocles' explanation, it has been suggested, began with the elements in separation, sketched their coming into unity under Love, and later returned to this time with the start of the account of ζῷα. At her first entry after the separation of the elements, Love gradually gains sufficient power to fashion individual limbs (which make up this first generation) but cannot overcome the discordant and disruptive activity characteristic of Strife.[167] τὰς δὲ δευτέρας συμφυομένων τῶν μερῶν εἰδωλοφανεῖς—the second generation is the monstrous unions of the separate limbs mentioned in fragments 51(59) and 52(61), which arise as the elements combine more and more but which then pass from the world as Love's power increases and more satisfactory unions are possible.

The next generation, of a different kind, comes after the unity of the elements in the sphere, when they are separating out. Love still has pre-

---

164. Cf. Aristotle *GC* 334a1, διέκρινε τὸ νεῖκος, and Simplicius' setting of fr. 53(62) πρὸ τῆς τῶν ἀνδρείων καὶ γυναικείων σωμάτων διαθρώσεως.

165. Cf. Aristotle *GC* 315a16–17, ἄλλως τε καὶ μαχομένων ἀλλήλοις ἔτι τοῦ νείκους καὶ τῆς φιλίας, and Theophrastus *Sens.* 11.

166. Aetius 5.19.5; cf. Millerd *Empedocles* pp. 57–58, Guthrie *HGP* vol. 2, pp. 200–08, and for a different interpretation, Bollack *Empédocle* vol. 1, pp. 194–207, Minar *Phronesis* 1963, pp. 140–45, Solmsen *Phronesis* 1965, pp. 132–38.

167. Cf. Empedocles frs. 26(20).5, 25(22).6–9.

dominant control, but Strife's work of discrimination and articulation is gaining hold. The manuscripts of Aetius here read τὰς δὲ τρίτας τῶν ἀλληλοφυῶν, followed by τὰς δὲ τετάρτας οὐκέτι ἐκ τῶν ὁμοίων οἷον ἐκ γῆς καὶ ὕδατος, ἀλλὰ δι' ἀλλήλων. The word ἀλληλοφυεῖς seems to convey no more than the (γένεσις) δι' ἀλλήλων in the fourth stage. Such repetition is unlikely in a brief summary, and, as there would otherwise be no mention of the οὐλοφυεῖς τύποι, the editors are no doubt correct in adopting Karsten's emendation of ἀλληλοφυῶν to ὁλοφυῶν.[168] This then gives the two types of generation in the present period—the earlier, of whole-nature forms coming from the earth, and the later, when the earth ceased to generate spontaneously.[169]

The pattern of balance and antithesis may be summarized as follows: (1) There are the elements in separation under the control of Strife. (2) As they begin to come together with the entry and advance of Love, the unattached limbs are formed. (3) These combine in various monstrous unions, except perhaps some which join in a manner fit to survive, giving in this way a generation of men and women. (4) As Strife decreases all life is absorbed with the coming of the elements into one under Love. (5) The entrance of Strife into the mixture causes the roots to separate toward their like, and the whole-nature forms result. (6) These forms, when fully articulated, give the present generation of men and women. They in turn pass away when (1) Strife succeeds once more in holding the elements apart.[170]

The pattern is continuous and self-repeating, and the times of the alternate rise and fall of Love and Strife are fixed according to a "broad oath."[171] Aristotle argues that this explanation is not adequate unless it is supported by examples and analogous instances;[172] it is not sufficient to say "this is the way things are," or, with Democritus, "it happened so

---

168. Cf. Karsten *EAcr* p. 445. ἀλληλοφυῶν is possibly a corruption of ἀλλοφυῶν from the following δι' ἀλλήλων. It might then be argued that ἀλλοφυῶν is similar in meaning to ἀλλογενῶν, which contrasts with the fourth stage and would still be a description of the whole-nature forms. For ὁμοίων Karsten suggests στοιχείων, Reiske οἰκείων, Gomperz ὁμοστοίχων, and Diels ὁμοιομερῶν.

169. Cf. above, n. 164.

170. The "shoots" from which men and women come are ἐννύχιοι, i.e., they sprang up before night and day were distinguished (Aetius 5.26.4). And a day for the first-born generation of men was ten months long; the men of today are as infants compared with them (Aetius 5.27.1, 18.1). This tells against putting separate limbs immediately before the "shoots," or between the οὐλοφυεῖς τύποι and the present generation.

171. Fr. 23(30).3, and also 107 (115).1.

172. Aristotle *Phys.* 252a31–35, *Metaph.* 1000b12–17.

before." Empedocles, however, would hardly have been aware of such a deficiency in his account. His broad oath is very like Parmenides' δεσμοὶ ἀνάγκης, a bond, conceived almost in literal terms, which ensures the invariance of the pattern.[173]

The limits of Love and Strife are reached in the circumference of the sphere that persists throughout,[174] and the denial of *kenon* puts all the movement of the roots within the circumference, as the movement of bodies in a plenum, in a series of minglings and shuffles. Love and Strife, as has been shown, do not take up place in the same way as the roots; their activity is continuous but can expand and contract.

The complete process seems to have been worked out along the following lines. At one time the roots are completely separate under Strife, and Love lies inactive at the circumference; then comes her rise to power, which is initiated by her rush to the center. The relative positions of the two principles here are given in the lines

ἐπεὶ νεῖκος μὲν ἐνέρτατον ἵκετο βένθος
δίνης, ἐν δὲ μέσῃ φιλότης στροφάλιγγι γένηται . . .[175]

Gradually Love consolidates her position, and Strife is slowly pushed back.[176] The interchanges between them cause the rise of a generation of *thnēta*, but toward the circumference there are some parts of roots that are still unmixed, held by Strife μετάρσιον. Love wins the battle, eventually bringing all the elements into one and so generating the θεὸς εὐδαιμονέστατος, in which Strife has no part.[177] But the ideal state comes to an end, and τελειομένοιο χρόνοιο Strife strikes, as Love did, by rushing in to claim the center. This causes the god to be disturbed: πάντα γὰρ ἐξείης πελεμίζετο γυῖα θεοῖο.[178]

Strife then begins the process of separation. First air is drawn out and flows round in a circle. Fire follows air upward, solidifying part of it into the *ouranos* and driving part of it down toward the center. The fire in the hemisphere then causes a rotation, the force of which compresses the

173. Cf. Parmenides fr. 8.26,31, and R. B. Onians *Origins of European Thought* pp. 332, 457 n. 3.

174. κύκλος, used in fr. 47(35).10 of place as in fr. 16(16).1 of time, shows that the round shape continues.

175. Empedocles fr. 47(35).3-4, and cf. the commentary on these lines.

176. ὑπεκπροθεῖν, "to run on ahead," used of Strife, fr. 47(35).12; the metaphor is of an enemy army in retreat, cf. the commentary on the fragment.

177. Cf. Aristotle *Metaph.* 1000b2-4: ὅταν γὰρ συνέλθῃ, τότε δ᾽ ἔσχατον ἵστατο νεῖκος, *GC* 315a6-8, and Simplicius *in Cael.* 529.16-20.

178. Empedocles fr. 24(31).

earth and exudes the water from it.[179] As Strife still held some parts of the roots aloft and unmixed in the complementary generation of *thnēta*, so in the present world it is to be expected that Love has not yet relinquished her hold on the parts of the roots nearest the circumference, but keeps them in their former state. Beyond the *ouranos* but within the sphere some of the original amalgam under Love is still preserved;[180] eventually, in her turn, Love will be driven back ἐπ' ἔσχατα τέρματα κύκλου, until once more she rises to claim her prerogatives.

---

179. Cf. Aetius 2.6.3, [Plut.] *Strom.* 10 (DK 31 A30).

180. Cf. Aetius 1.5.2: 'Ε. δὲ κόσμον μὲν ἕνα, οὐ μέντοι τὸ πᾶν εἶναι τὸν κόσμον, ἀλλ' ὀλίγον τι τοῦ παντὸς μέρος, τὸ δὲ λοιπὸν ἀργὴν ὕλην.

3. *Katharmoi* and *Physics*

COMMON GROUND

The question of the relationship of the *Katharmoi* to the *Physics* is problematic, and it is often thought that the two poems represent incompatible, or even contradictory, positions taken up by Empedocles either simultaneously or successively.[1] In this section it will be argued that the two poems are not irreconcilable, that the theory of the *Katharmoi* is in accord with that of the *Physics*, and that it is supplemented and clarified by the *Physics* on several key points.

It is plain that any interpretation must be based firmly on the fragments themselves. There is very little external evidence that is relevant and trustworthy, and any attempt to tie Empedocles to a particular set of religious cults, beliefs, or practices has no adequate basis. The contexts of the fragments and the comments of ancient authors have to be used with caution. Aristotle, for example, admits that he is puzzled about how

---

1. On "hopeless contradiction" between the poems cf. E. Rohde *Psyche* pp. 382–83, Millerd *Empedocles* pp. 89–94, Burnet *EGP* p. 250, W. Jaeger *The Theology of the Early Greek Philosophers* pp. 132–35, Vlastos *PhilosQ* 1952, p. 121. For the *Physics* as a youthful scientific work, and the *Katharmoi* the product of a later "conversion" to religion, cf. Diels *SPAW* 1898, p. 406, Wilamowitz *SPAW* 1929, p. 655, and for the opposite ordering cf. Bidez *Biographie* pp. 160–71, Kranz *Hermes* 1935, pp. 111–19, and his *Empedokles* passim. Some attempts to reconcile the poems have been made by Bignone *Empedocle* chap. 1; H. S. Long *AJPh* 1949, pp. 142–58; C. H. Kahn *AGPh* 1960, pp. 3–35; Kirk-Raven *PP* pp. 357–61; G. Zuntz *Persephone* p. 269; S. M. Darcus *Phronesis* 1977, pp. 175–90; and an explanation of the daimon in terms of the elements has been put forward by H. Reiche *Empedocles' mixture, Eudoxan astronomy and Aristotle's connate pneuma* pp. 50–54; S. Souilhé *ArchPhilos* 1932, pp. 1–23; H. E. Barnes *CJ* 1967, pp. 18–23. This chapter is a fresh attack on the problem.

Empedocles would define the soul, but although in his arguments he quotes extensively from the *Physics* he does not make use of the *Katharmoi*.[2] This may or may not be deliberate, but it makes for one-sidedness. Some later commentators try to find support in Empedocles for pro-Pythagorean propaganda or skeptical ways of thinking, and others tend to interpret him in Neoplatonic terms. It is best therefore to keep as much as possible to Empedocles' own words, with two caveats: first, that it is uncertain to which of the two poems a number of the fragments should be allocated, and second, that the order of the composition of the poems is not definitely known.[3]

It is appropriate to start with the four roots. When, in fragment 107(115), Empedocles says that the might of *aithēr* pursues the daimon into sea, sea casts him onto earth, earth into sun, and sun again into the eddies of *aithēr*, there can be little doubt that the areas chosen are not arbitrary but are references to the masses of the four elements as given in the *Physics*. There ἥλιος is the most common word for the root of fire, αἰθήρ is the usual term for the root of air, πόντος, θάλασσα, ὄμβρος, and Nestis are interchangeable for water, and earth is obviously γαῖα and χθών in both poems.[4] The character, activity, and primary importance of the four roots are explained in the *Physics*, and in the *Katharmoi* the four appear, under the names familiar from the physical work, as the areas of banishment for the daimon.

The four roots combine in countless ways to give the variety of *thnēta* known in the world. The word Empedocles uses in the *Physics* for the different shapes and kinds of *thnēta* is εἶδος, as for example εἴδη θνητῶν, εἴδεα ποιπνύουσα (of Kypris), and in the simile of the painter, εἴδεα πᾶσιν ἀλίγκια.[5] The same term is found in the *Katharmoi* in παντοῖα εἴδεα θνητῶν, and also εἴδε' ἀμείβων.[6] Moreover, the phrase for the "changing of the paths" of the roots in the *Physics* when the immortal puts on mortal forms, διαλλάξαντα κελεύθους, is given again for the daimons when they too change their paths: μεταλλάσσοντα κελεύθους.[7]

---

2. Cf. Aristotle *De An.* 408a18–24; the only quotations from the *Katharmoi* are at *Poet.* 1457b13–14 (on metaphors) and *Rhet.* 1373b16–17.

3. Cf. chap. 4 and, on the order of composition of the poems, n. 23.

4. Cf. the list of terms for the roots set out above in the second chapter of the introduction.

5. Frs. 60(71).3, 62(73).2, 15(23).5; cf. also ἔθνεα μυρία θνητῶν, fr. 47(35).7.

6. Frs. 107(115).7, 130(125).

7. Frs. 47(35).15, 107(115).8; the change in both cases is from "immortal" to "mortal," but it refers in the *Physics* to separate elements assuming various shapes as they come into unity, and in the *Katharmoi*, to the different forms of life adopted after separation.

Now boy, bush, bird, and fish[8] are obviously examples of the εἴδεα
θνητῶν that the daimon assumes as he goes from one hard way of life to
another, and they are lives in different elements.[9] The passing from one
element to another can therefore be seen as exchanging a life in one element for that in another, under the law of necessity; and when Empedocles says that he has been at some time boy, bush, bird, and fish his
words can be interpreted in the light of fragment 107(115). Empedocles
supposes that, according to necessity and the universal law, coming
under Strife results in birth as *thnēton*; so, finding himself as prophet,
leader, minstrel, and healer at the highest stage of the εἴδεα θνητῶν he
would suppose that the law had run its course in his case. It would be
natural to infer that he had passed through the required births as *thnēta*,
and since this involves different elements in turn, previous lives would be
as bird, fish, plant, and human. This need not imply that Empedocles
remembers being in these states; it is an inference from the law that the
daimon of necessity takes on a variety of forms.

Like the four roots, the Love and Strife of the *Physics* have their place
in the *Katharmoi*, and it is the account of their nature and function in the
physical work that helps in the understanding of their role in the other
poem. In the *Physics* the names for Love are Philotēs, Gēthosunē, Aphrodite, Harmonia, and Kypris, the last two occurring also in the *Katharmoi*.[10] The influence of Kypris, elaborated in fragments 118(128) and
119(130) of the *Katharmoi* as resulting in universal sympathy, tallies with
that of Philia/Kypris in the *Physics*. In addition, her responsibility for
friendly thoughts, given in the *Physics* as one of her characteristics, is
found in the *Katharmoi* in the prevalence of friendly thoughts under her
sway.[11]

As Love, in the *Physics* and in the *Katharmoi*, is the principle of friendship and unity and thus works for good, so Strife is the complementary

8. Cf. fr. 108(117).

9. Aristotle *Mete.* 382a6-8 relates the material of which an animal is made to its
environment. Life in fire is denied here but accepted at *HA* 552b10-17; at *GA* 737a1-5
heat, not fire, is said to be responsible for some forms of life, and fire animals are relegated
to the moon, 761b13-22. On texts relating to lives in different elements cf. A. S. Pease on
Cicero *ND* 2.42, p. 639.

10. Cf. fr. 8(17).24, and for Kypris frs. 62(73).1, 70(75).2, 83(98).3, 87(95).1 from the
Physics and 118(128).3 from the *Katharmoi*; for Harmonia frs. 48(96).4 (and cf. 21(27).2)
and 116(122).2; cf. also Plutarch *de Is. et Os.* 370d: Ἐ δὲ τὴν μὲν ἀγαθουργὸν ἀρχὴν
φιλότητα καὶ φιλίαν πολλάκις, ἔτι δὲ ʽΑρμονίαν καλεῖ θεμερῶπιν.

11. Cf. frs. 25(22).4-5, 119(130).1, 8(17).23 τῇ τε φίλα φρονέουσι, and 119(130).2
φιλοφροσύνη τε δεδήει.

principle of hatred, enmity, and separation. In the *Physics* Neikos is described as οὐλόμενον and λυγρόν, and there is an immediate reminder of this in the first appearance of Neikos in the *Katharmoi* as νεῖκος μαινόμενον.[12] Further, in the *Physics* it is said that bodies "are torn apart by evil strifes," and in the *Katharmoi* the tearing apart of limbs described in fragments 118(128) and 124(137) is to be understood as the work of Strife, when Kypris is no longer in control.[13] The representation of this world as the meadow of Atē, the ἀτερπὴς χῶρος, reinforces the theory of the degenerate age of increasing Strife given in the *Physics*.[14]

The *Physics* also prepares the way for the *Katharmoi* in rejecting traditional mythology and requiring some rethinking of what it means to be a god. Like Xenophanes before him Empedocles combats the notion that god looks like a man, and he denies him head, arms, legs, and genitals. It is the roots that have Olympian names—Zeus, Hera, Hephaistos— and they enjoy the privilege and eternal life generally associated with the Olympians. Similarly, in the *Katharmoi* Homeric and Hesiodic theology is replaced in the lines

> οὐδέ τις ἦν κείνοισιν Ἄρης θεὸς οὐδὲ Κυδοιμός
> οὐδὲ Ζεὺς βασιλεύς, οὐδὲ Κρόνος οὐδὲ Ποσειδῶν,
> ἀλλὰ Κύπρις βασίλεια.[15]

In the *Physics* the four roots and the sphere under Love are truly god, but a place is found for "long-lived gods, highest in honor"; these are made up, in the same way as plant, animal, and human life, from temporary combinations of the roots. The superiority of such gods rests mainly on the fact that the particular arrangement of roots which give them their character lasts for a longer time, before its dissolution, than that of other forms of life. That the θεοὶ τιμῇσι φέριστοι are as much *thnēta* as plant and animal kinds is shown by fragment 14(21), where all things, past, present, and future, are said to come from the roots: "trees sprang from them, and men and women, animals and birds and water-nourished fish, and long-lived gods too, highest in honor."[16]

The θεοὶ τιμῇσι φέριστοι in the *Physics* are last in a list of forms of life appearing as a result of various combinations of the roots, and in the

12. Frs. 8(17).19, 77(109).3, and 107(115).14.

13. Cf. fr. 26(20).4 κακῇσι διατμηθέντ' ἐρίδεσσι. ἔριδες is repeated at fr. 114(124).2 as characterizing the present generation.

14. Fr. 113(121); cf. frs. 112(118), 114(124), 123(145).

15. Fr. 118(128).1–3.

16. Fr. 14(21).9–12, and cf. fr. 15(23).5–8, where the list is repeated.

Katharmoi they are the final and most honorable stage in a series of lives that includes plants and animals. The repetition of the phrase from the *Physics*, and of the same verb, βλαστάνειν, in the *Katharmoi*, would be a reminder of the position held by these gods in the physical poem, where they are represented not as beings totally different from the human race but as having the same origin as men and parts of the same roots in their composition; they are superior only in that there is a longer term to their existence in the same form.[17] Moreover, the θεοὶ τιμῇσι φέριστοι at the end of the series of lives in the *Katharmoi* are almost certainly the δαίμονες μάκαρες of its beginning, and there the phrase of the *Physics*—θεοὶ δολιχαίωνες—that pinpoints the length (but not eternity) of the life of the gods is echoed in the description of the daimons as οἴτε μακραίωνος λελάχασι βίοιο.[18]

This erasing of the dividing line between men and gods, which in the epic tradition was fixed and, except in rare cases, impassable, has two effects. One is to reduce to some extent the status of these gods by showing them superior only in having a longer and happier existence than other forms of life. The second is to raise the status of the life of plants, animals, and humans by recognizing in them a nature like that of the honored gods; but they have a shorter and less fortunate term of existence as particular arrangements of parts of roots. All forms of life have *phronēsis*,[19] and all are subject to the alternating control of Love and Strife. So the theory of the *Physics*, which removes the traditional distinctions between life as god, man, animal, and plant, makes less startling the transition from one to another described in the *Katharmoi* as endured by the daimon.

The *Physics* and the *Katharmoi* break down the division between men and long-lived gods, and between plants and animals and men, and as a corollary to this they question the accepted frontiers of birth and death. At the beginning of the *Physics* Empedocles criticizes others for the narrowness of their outlook: "After observing a small part of life in their lifetime . . . they are convinced only of that which each has experienced . . . yet all boast of finding the whole."[20] These men make rash generalizations about τὸ ὅλον based only on their own experience in this present life; rather, they should view this life not as beginning with birth

17. Cf. frs. 14(21).10 and 132(146).3.
18. Frs. 132(146).3, 107(115).5, 14(21).12, 15(23).8.
19. Cf. frs. 100(110).10 and 81(103).
20. Fr. 1(2).3–6.

and ending with death but as a *meros* of a broader scheme. Fragment
106(15) elaborates on this:

οὐκ ἂν ἀνὴρ τοιαῦτα σοφὸς φρεσὶ μαντεύσαιτο,
ὡς ὄφρα μέν τε βιῶσι, τὸ δὴ βίοτον καλέουσι,
τόφρα μὲν οὖν εἰσίν, καί σφιν πάρα δειλὰ καὶ ἐσθλά,
πρὶν δὲ πάγεν τε βροτοὶ καὶ ⟨ἐπεὶ⟩ λύθεν οὐδὲν ἄρ' εἰσίν.[21]

And in the *Physics* are the supporting (Eleatic) arguments, that nothing
comes from nothing and that what is cannot cease to be.

Since this is so, birth and death must be reinterpreted, and for them
are substituted the mingling and separating of eternally existing roots.
When parts of the roots are arranged in the form of an animal, this is
what men call birth, and when the arrangement is broken up, this is what
is known as death.[22] It therefore comes as no surprise to learn in the
Katharmoi that a man *is* in some way, and meets with good and ill, before
and after his present life; birth is not to be considered as generation from
what did not exist before, nor death the annihilation of that which at present is.

There is one more point of connection between the *Physics* and the
Katharmoi. In fragment 94(105) Empedocles says, αἷμα γὰρ ἀνθρώποις
περικάρδιόν ἐστι νόημα. Theophrastus interprets: διὸ καὶ τῷ αἵματι
μάλιστα φρονεῖν. ἐν τούτῳ γὰρ μάλιστα κεκρᾶσθαι τὰ στοιχεῖα τῶν
μερῶν.[23] In Empedocles' theory, then, blood is of primary importance
because it is the instrument of thinking for man, having its parts in almost equal proportion. The arrangements of the roots that make up
thnēta are due to the activity of Love, and the best arrangements, those
coming most closely to a 1 : 1 ratio of the ingredients, are possible where
Love is least hindered by Strife. When Love had power in the sphere and
Strife was inactive, the roots were perfectly mixed according to this ratio;
the combination of elements that comes nearest in this world of de-
creasing Love to the perfect combination achieved when Love had complete control is found for men in the blood around the heart.

The importance of blood as the instrument of thought and best work
of Aphrodite, as explained in the *Physics*, immediately illuminates the
prohibition against bloodshed set out so forcefully in the *Katharmoi*. This

21. Cf. also fr. 104(11) and chap. 4 for the suggestion that frs. 106(15) and 104(11)
should be allocated to the *Katharmoi*.

22. Fr. 13(9).1–5.

23. Theophrastus *Sens.* 10, and also 11: οἷς δὲ καθ' ἕν τι μόριον ἡ μέση κρᾶσίς
ἐστι, ταύτῃ σοφοὺς ἑκάστους εἶναι.

prohibition is elaborated on three counts. First, the shedding of blood is given as one of the causes for the exile of the daimon from happiness; second, the age of Kypris was characterized by the absence of animal sacrifice; and third, the continued shedding of blood, the φόνος δυσηχής in the name of religion, is represented as grounds for the continuing misery of human life.[24] The traditional Greek awe and horror at the crimes of homicide and cannibalism are reinforced by the reminder from the *Physics* that these are a destruction of the work of Love, and so a "trusting" in Strife.

So far, then, the two poems are not diametrically opposed, and the *Physics* has prepared the way for the *Katharmoi* on several issues. The theory of the four roots helps to explain the exchange of lives of the daimon in air, earth, sea, and sun, and the account of the cosmic activity of Love and Strife is necessary to show how the daimon can come under these powers, and the consequences of this. Moreover, the *Physics* argues that the frontiers of birth and death are unreal and also that traditional theology must be reexamined. Plants, animals, men, and gods have a common origin and nature, and there are no fixed boundaries marking off the kinds of life. Finally, reasons are put forward for the special significance of blood.

CRIME, PUNISHMENT, AND RESPONSIBILITY

Both poems give an alternation between god and man, mortal and immortal. In the *Physics* the elements united under Love are god, when held separate by Strife they are ἀθάνατα, and in the intervening times they take on the forms of θνητά. The daimons in the *Katharmoi* are born as θνητά, and in their turn the πολυφθερεῖς ἄνθρωποι become θεοὶ ἀθάνατοι.[25] But there is a difference. In the *Katharmoi* the alternation of the states of "immortal" and "mortal" takes on a vividly personal tone. Notions of wrongdoing, banishment, and final return to happiness give individual histories to gods and mortals, which at first sight seems hard to square with arrangements and rearrangements of roots.

Empedocles may perhaps have worked out his theory as follows. Before the present state of the world all things were united under Love; this was an ideal state, and our present one is a degeneration from it. In physical terms the roots were perfectly blended, held fast in harmony,

---

24. Cf. frs. 107(115).3, 120(139), 118(128).8-10, 122(136), 123(145), 124(137).
25. Cf. frs. 21(27), 24(31), 47(35).14, 105(113).2, 132-33(146-47), 107(115).7.

and Neikos, the principle of enmity and separation, had no control. For the people of Acragas this would be explained as an age when the daimons were happy. Then, at a fixed time, there came an end to the ideal state. Strife entered the sphere and made the god tremble, the elements began to be separated, and the different forms of life resulted. In the language of the *Katharmoi* Strife gained control of some of the daimons and separated them from their fellows, causing them to be born in different forms of life. That this is the same process viewed in two ways is confirmed by the mention of the oath at the appropriate moment in each poem: in the *Physics* and in the *Katharmoi* the time for the end of the rule of Love, for the rise to power of Strife and the consequent generation of mortal things, is "held secure" by the broad oath of necessity.[26]

In fragment 107(115), however, Empedocles says that a daimon who adopts mortal form has previously, in error, polluted himself, and this is connected, if not explicitly, with the shedding of blood. Slaughter, as has been shown, takes on added significance because of the noetic importance given to blood in the *Physics*, but it is likely that Empedocles related this crime to the daimon because it was traditionally punishable by exile; for it was the law in Athens and Sparta, and a commonplace generally, that the homicide should be banished. There are several examples in Homer of a person leaving the country after killing a man, and Plato in the *Laws* states that this penalty for homicide is a revered and ancient *mythos*.[27] When Empedocles sees that he is living in a world of increasing strife and sorrow, having come from a former happier state, it is natural for him to posit as the cause of such a banishment the crime that in this world brought with it the penalty of exile.[28]

Diels's reading of line 4 of fragment 107(115) is usually accepted. This

26. Cf. frs. 23(30).3, 107(115).2.

27. Cf., for example, Homer *Il.* 13.696, 16.573, 23.85, *Od.* 13.258, 15.272, Xenophon *An.* 4.8.25, Plato *Laws* 865d–e; for homicide laws being unchanged, the oldest, and reverting to Draco, cf. Antiphon 6.2, *Ath. Pol.* 7.1, and Demosthenes 20.158, 23.51, 47.71; cf. further on the Homeric examples G. Glotz *La Solidarité de la Famille* pp. 50–52, and for the tradition covering all Greece G. Calhoun *The Growth of Criminal Law in Ancient Greece* p. 111. For the Greek interest in error in criminal cases cf. D. Daube *Aspects of Roman Law* pp. 147–51.

28. When the distinction between unintentional and intentional homicide came to be made, banishment was generally decreed for the first and was available in the case of the second if the defendant left before the final two speeches of the trial, cf. Glotz, loc. cit., pp. 425–42, D. M. MacDowell *Athenian Homicide Law in the Age of the Orators* pp. 110–29 and especially pp. 177–21 on IG I² 115, and J. W. Jones *Law and Legal Theory of the Greeks* pp. 255–57.

assumes that perjury is a second crime that brings with it the consequences of separation and wandering.[29] But it is the same crime from a
different aspect: the daimon is represented as bringing *miasma* on himself, and in so doing he transgresses the oath that binds him.[30] There may
even be a sense in which murder, perjury, and trust in Strife are the same
event from three points of view. The violence can be thought of as a
breaking of the bond imposed by Love,[31] as well as a manifestation of
acting under the domination of Strife.

There is, moreover, the Hesiodic precedent for punishing perjury,
like bloodshed, with exile. In the *Theogony* it is said that whenever one
of the *athanatoi* swears a false oath by Styx he lies *anapneustos* for a great
year, and then for a further nine years is barred from the company and
feasts of the gods, returning to them in the tenth.[32] Empedocles is almost
certainly influenced by Hesiod here and even adopts some of his phrasing.
Among other similarities, Empedocles' line

$$ἄλλος δ' ἐξ ἄλλου δέχεται, στυγέουσι δὲ πάντες$$

reflects Hesiod's

$$ἄλλος δ' ἐξ ἄλλου δέχεται χαλεπώτερος ἆθλος.^{33}$$

For one of the *athanatoi* to be forced from the company of his fellows for
a time of exile, and eventually to return to them, is basic to Empedocles'
theory of the daimon; borrowing from Hesiod, he gives an act of perjury
as a cause for the exile.

In addition, tragedy in the fifth century provides instances where those
guilty of bloodshed and perjury are thought unacceptable to the elements. Oedipus, for example, is sent indoors by Creon because, convicted
of parricide and incest, he is unwelcome to the sun, and "not earth or

29. E.g., Kirk-Raven *PP* p. 351: "whenever one of these demi-gods . . . has sinfully
defiled his dear limbs with bloodshed, or following Strife has sworn a false oath"; Burnet
EGP p. 222, Guthrie *HGP* vol. 2, p. 251; for other views cf. the commentary on this fragment.

30. Cf. the commentary on the line. This would account for Hippolytus' omission of
line 3 and Plutarch's of line 4. It would be arbitrary to leave one out if the two lines represented genuine alternatives, but not if they are to be understood as two versions of the
same event.

31. Cf. fr. 21(27).2

32. Hesiod *Theog.* 793–806.

33. Cf. fr. 107(115).12 and Hesoid *Theog.* 800; the Hesiodic passage begins at line 782
with ὁππότ' ἔρις καὶ νεῖκος ἐν ἀθανάτοισιν ὄρηται, which again connects perjury with
strife.

holy rain or light" will receive him. In Euripides, Jason is appalled that
Medea should still be looking on sun and earth after murdering her
children. Pylades, in the *Orestes*, takes an oath for earth and radiant day
to reject him if he deserts his friend, and Hippolytus prays that if he is
forsworn in the proclamation of his innocence, taken in the name of Ζεὺς
Ὅρκιος, neither sea nor earth may receive his body.[34]

In Greek legal and poetic tradition, therefore, bloodshed and perjury
can result in exile, and the man who has so acted is abhorrent to the elements. It is in these terms that Empedocles describes the daimon's de-
parture from the company of his like, and his birth in, and rejection by,
one element after another. Yet present-day commentators speak of the
Katharmoi as a theory about "the primal sin and fall of man," concerned
with purification from the taint of original sin and with the subsequent
salvation.[35] This sort of language is of course at variance with the theory
of the *Physics*, and it is a mistaken interpretation of Greek ethics in
Christian terms that distorts Empedocles' way of thinking.

To explain further. Early examples of Greek theory and practice
concerning crime and punishment show the interest to have centered on
the act alone. Once a crime is committed the consequences follow, and
the individual bears the responsibility for what he has done, whether or
not he could have avoided behaving as he did; and he might not have
been able to avoid the act if he had come under the power of a god. In
epic and tragedy a pattern can be traced: divine agency compels a man
to act in a certain way, the deed is done, and the man must then face the
consequences. Further, the "criminal" in such a case does not usually
give divine agency as an excuse for evading the penalties; he recognizes
that he was in the power of forces beyond his control, and he recognizes
with equal clarity that he must make amends.

Some instances of this. The obvious one in Homer is Agamemnon's
apology, where Agamemnon says, concerning his theft of Briseis:

ἀλλ᾽ ἐπεὶ ἀασάμην καί μευ φρένας ἐξέλετο Ζεύς,
ἄψ ἐθέλω ἀρέσαι, δόμεναί τ᾽ ἀπερείσι᾽ ἄποινα.

As Professor Dodds has pointed out, this is not an evasion of responsibil-

---

34. Cf. Sophocles *OT* 1424-28, Euripides *Med.* 1327-28, *Or.* 1086-88, *Hipp.* 1029-31;
in particular the man who has shed blood is repugnant to the sun and sunlight, cf. Euripides *HF* 1231, *IT* 1207, *Or.* 819-22.

35. E.g., Jaeger *TEGP* p. 145; Kirk-Raven *PP* p. 351; Guthrie *HGP* vol. 2, pp. 123
and 251; "the fallen spirits" Kahn *AGPh* 1960, pp. 20-21 and *passim*; Long *CQ* 1966, p.
274.

ity; Agamemnon will pay for his act even though he could not have acted otherwise.[36] Clytemnestra in the *Oresteia* is in a similar position. She claims that it was Alastor in female form who killed her husband; the chorus replies that no one will bear witness that she is *anaitios* of the murder, and she answers, with whatever sincerity, that in consequence she is ready to give up the kingdom. Orestes admits that he killed his mother by order of Apollo, but he accepts the responsibility, not "blaming" the god, since it was his own hand that slew her.[37] Similarly with the Oedipus of Sophocles. Apollo is said to be the cause of the parricide and incest, but Oedipus committed them and is therefore *atheos*. And in the *Coloneus* he gives as his apology:

$$τά \ γ' \ ἔργα \ μου$$
$$πεπονθότ' \ ἐστὶ \ μᾶλλον \ ἢ \ δεδρακότα.^{38}$$

Perjury seems to have worked in much the same way. Hector, in *Iliad* 10, swears a false oath when he promises Dolon the horses of Achilles, even though his intention is to fulfill his promise, and the events preventing its fulfillment are beyond his control; there is really no alternative "true" oath he could have sworn. But Homer's language makes no distinction between this and the intentional false oath; *epiorkon* is the term for unintentional as well as deliberate perjury, and it is adopted by Empedocles.[39]

The case of the epic and tragic heroes helps in the interpretation of Empedocles. They acted in ignorance or as the result of external compulsion, but they are ready to accept personal liability for the inevitable consequences. To quote again from Professor Dodds: "Thyestes and Oedipus are men who violated the most sacred of nature's laws, and thus incurred the most horrible of all pollutions, but they both did so without πονηρία, for they knew not what they did—in Aristotle's quasi-legal terminology it was a ἁμάρτημα and not an ἀδίκημα."[40] ἀμπλακία and ἁμαρτάνειν are words used in the *Katharmoi* in connection with the dai-

36. Homer *Il.* 19.137-38, and cf. the complete commentary on this passage by E. R. Dodds *The Greeks and the Irrational* chap. 1.

37. Cf. Aeschylus *Ag.* 1500, 1505-06, 1569-77, *Eum.* 588-96; also Dodds, loc. cit., pp. 39-40, and H. Lloyd-Jones, "The Guilt of Agamemnon," *CQ* 1962, pp. 187-99.

38. *OT* 1329-34, 1360, *OC* 266-67; cf. B. M. W. Knox *Oedipus at Thebes* pp. 33-38.

39. Cf. Homer *Il.* 10.332 with 3.279, 19.260 and 264.

40. E. R. Dodds, "On Misunderstanding the Oedipus Rex," *GR* 1966, p. 39, and also pp. 43 and 48 on the horror and innocence of Oedipus' acts. "*Hamartēma* does not originate in vice," cf. Daube loc. cit. on Aristotle *Rhet.* 1374b, *EN* 1110b18, 1113b21, 1135a15.

mon.[41] When, therefore, Empedocles states that he came under the power of Strife and suffered as a result he probably should not be taken as meaning that this was a deliberate intention, or that an alternative, such as trust in Love, was available. "Trust in Strife" is a stage in the necessary course of events in much the same way as the curses and oracles "had" to be worked out. Empedocles, like Oedipus and Orestes, sees himself as the individual involved, who accepts the responsibility and suffers the consequences.

There is further help from Plato. The account in the *Timaeus* does not assume that the soul[42] is guilty of an original "sin" that led to its "fall." *Thnēta* are brought into being "so that the whole might be complete," and the souls are necessarily implanted in bodies.[43] The nature of the life subsequently led conditions the next move, whether a return to the "consort star" in which the soul was once temporarily set or to a second and inferior life on earth. But there is no way in which the first incarnation (if the sequence can be thought of as having a starting point) can be chosen or avoided by the soul. Subsequently, because of the material used in its composition, and the use made of the material, the soul may be "a cause of evil to itself."[44]

A similar line is taken in the *Phaedrus* in the account of the series of births: "Hear now the ordinance of necessity. Whatsoever soul has followed in the train of a god and discerned something of truth, shall be kept from sorrow until a new revolution shall begin, and if she can do this always she shall remain always free from hurt. But when she is not able so to follow, and sees none of it, but meeting with some mischance comes to be burdened with a load of forgetfulness and *kakia*, and because of that burden sheds her wings and falls to the earth, then thus runs the law. In her first birth . . ."[45] For Plato, therefore, in these myths it is not the "fault" of the soul but the necessary working of the law (or the will of the

41. Empedocles fr. 107(115).3-4, and cf. the commentary here.

42. Significantly called the δαίμων, a φυτὸν οὐράνιον which has ἐν οὐρανῷ συγγένεια, *Tim.* 90a.

43. *Tim.* 41c, 42a (ὁπότε δὴ σώμασιν ἐμφυτυθεῖεν ἐξ ἀνάγκης . . .).

44. *Tim.* 42b, 42e; cf. R. S. Bluck, "The *Phaedrus* and Reincarnation," *AJP* 1958, pp. 156-64 and especially p. 163.

45. *Phdr.* 248c, trans. Hackforth (with "wrongdoing" for *kakia*). The Greek of the last sentence is: ὅταν δὲ ἀδυνατήσασα ἐπισπέσθαι μὴ ἴδῃ, καί τινι συντυχίᾳ χρησαμένη λήθης τε καὶ κακίας πλησθεῖσα βαρυνθῇ, βαρυνθεῖσα . . . ἐπὶ τὴν γῆν πέσῃ, τότε νόμος . . . Cf. Kahn *AGPh* 1960, p. 25, n. 67 for Empedoclean reminiscences in the *Phaedrus*.

Demiurge) that causes the soul to leave its home and kindred and to take on mortal form.

To summarize: Empedocles views life on earth as an exile from an earlier and more ideal state; in human terms exile results from shedding blood and swearing falsely, and these are given as the acts committed by the daimon, resulting in his present banishment. He has taken on a series of mortal forms and has lived in one element after another, while, like the man who has committed homicide or perjury, he is abhorrent to these elements. Nevertheless, although the daimon has come under the power of Strife and so is said to have "done" a wrong act, this need not imply wrong intention or power of choice on the part of the daimon; Strife "had" to take control.

EMPEDOCLES AS DAIMON

Empedocles gives the account of the wrongdoing and banishment of the daimon as his own personal history. He says that he committed the evil deed of eating (flesh) and became an exile and a wanderer. He wept at being born on earth, and since then he has lived through a number of lives. Now he is poet and prophet, giving a *mythos* that is true, and he goes among the people as an immortal god.[46] What meaning can be given to the *egō* that is used by Empedocles at each stage of the daimonic cycle?

It has been shown that Empedocles' assertion that he has been born as boy, girl, plant, bird, and fish need not imply a personal remembrance of such states but is rather an inference from the universal law ordaining that the daimons be born in all elements as different kinds of *thnēta*.[47] Nevertheless, Empedocles' use of *egō* at each stage of the history of the daimon seems to imply some constant factor, and this would be incompatible with the theory of the complete dispersal at death of the parts of the roots that make up the individual. Yet the daimon would have to be related to the sphere, the four roots, and Love and Strife, since according to the physical poem these are the only things in existence.

46. Cf. frs. 120(139), 107(115).13, 108(117), 112(118), 103(114), 102(112).4.

47. The argument that it would be no punishment to be incarnated in a lowly plant unless one could remember one's former existences (cf. H. S. Long *A Study of the Doctrine of Metempsychosis in Greece from Pythagoras to Plato* p. 105ff.) has little weight. The notion of punishment is misleading here; where there is no choice one cannot accurately speak of punishment for making the wrong choice. Even in myths that did interpret life on earth as a term of punishment for a wrong choice, the draught of Lethe was a necessary preliminary to that life.

In the *Physics* the eternal and unchanging roots are called gods, which, when the time comes round, adopt the form of mortal things. The θεὸς εὐδαιμονέστατος is the union of these roots in a perfect mixture brought about by Love and resulting in holy mind—φρὴν ἱερή. Strife on the other hand breaks up good mixture, separates the roots, and blunts thoughts. In the *Katharmoi*, therefore, one would expect gods to be similarly explicable in terms of the mingling of the roots, the activity of Love and Strife, and the faculty of thought.

Admittedly, Empedocles speaks of hearths and tables, but fragment 135(147) can hardly be taken literally. Throughout Greek and Roman religion the happiness of the soul could be viewed as the enjoyment of a banquet, and the notion that privileged people win admittance to the banquets of the gods is very ancient. Even Plato, who condemned the eternal intoxication he found depicted in Orphic eschatology, allowed a feast to the souls in the *Phaedrus* as they encircled the heavens.[48] "Enlightened minds accepted the old descriptions of joyous feasts only in a figurative sense. A less coarse conception of immortality suffered them to be looked on as symbols or metaphors."[49] So with Empedocles. At the first stages the daimon is said to have been forced from the company of the blessed as the result of pollution and perjury committed under the power of Strife, and at the end the daimon's return to the gods is represented anthropomorphically as a rejoining of the immortals at their feasts.

It is evident that the age of Kypris described in fragments 118(128) and 119(130) is to be taken as an account of the early history of man. The praise given for the bloodless sacrifices that were then customary is the complement of Empedocles' own self-reproach, in which he gives bloodshed and meat eating as the causes of his exile from a happy state. The time when Kypris, not Ares, was revered corresponds, in the cosmic scheme of the *Physics*, to the stage soon after the sphere under Love, when Strife as yet had little control. The gains of Strife marked the beginning of discord; this enmity continues to the present day and is on the increase. It is exemplified in the *Physics* in the tearing apart of limbs, the abstention from which is shown in the *Katharmoi* as a characteristic of Love's influence.[50]

On the theory of the *Katharmoi*, then, before the "trust in Strife" and

48. Cf. *Rep.* 363d, *Phdr.* 247a, also Vergil *Ecl.* 4.63, *Aen.* 6.656–57.

49. F. Cumont *After Life in Roman Paganism* p. 206; cf. also pp. 204–05 and the discussion in his *Astrology and Religion among the Greeks and Romans* pp. 109–10; for the persistence of the allegory of the feasts of the gods into Stoic eschatology cf. Epictetus *Ench.* xv.

50. Cf. frs. 118(128).9–10 and 26(20).4–5.

the daimon's consequent appearance in this world, he was in the company of the gods and under the control of Love. In the language of the *Physics* this is the state of the sphere when the many are brought into one, and the god that is holy mind results. The daimons, or gods, of the *Katharmoi* therefore would have an affinity to the divine mind, and so they are, or have, intelligence. And this intelligence would be of the highest, because the daimons are at the top of the scale of living things, all of which are said to have a share of νόημα.[51]

Now for men, according to fragment 94(105), νόημα is the blood around the heart. This suggests that the intelligence which the daimon has or is connects with the heart-blood, and indeed Cicero and Macrobius state that Empedocles identified the soul with blood.[52] Nevertheless Plutarch unambiguously asserts that the daimon is not blood, and this is obvious, for blood is seen to disintegrate with the rest of the body at death.[53]

If the daimon then has or is intelligence and is not blood, he must be intelligence without blood, and that Empedocles did envisage intelligence without blood is shown by the line πάντα γὰρ ἴσθι φρόνησιν ἔχειν καὶ νώματος αἶσαν. There is thinking at a higher and at a lower level than that of man.[54] At the lowest level each root has a primitive form of νόημα, where no mixing with other roots is involved. A piece of fire, for example, is capable of thinking fire in that it is aware of another piece of fire and will tend toward it when not brought into a mixture with parts of other roots by Love.[55] At the highest level of thinking there is holy mind—φρὴν ἱερή—where perfection is achieved by the constituent roots being so exactly mingled that there is no variance in the thought. And this is in contrast to blood, which, although approaching perfection, is still sub-

---

51. Cf. frs. 81(103), 78(107), and 100(110).10.

52. Cicero *Tusc.* 1.19, Macrobius *Somn. Scip.* 1.14.20, and cf. Aetius 4.5.8.

53. Plutarch *exil.* 607d.

54. Cf. Sextus *adv. math.* 8.286: (ʼΕ.) πάντα ἠξίου λογικὰ τυγχάνειν καὶ οὐ ζῷα μόνον ἀλλὰ καὶ φυτὰ ῥητῶς γράφων . . . seq. fr. 100(110).10. Aetius 4.5.12: Παρμενίδης καὶ ʼΕ . . . ταὐτὸν νοῦν καὶ ψυχήν, καθ' οὓς οὐδὲν ἂν εἴη ζῷον ἄλογον κυρίως, Aristotle *De An.* 404b12 on each of the elements being soul, and Philoponus *in de An.* 489.29–31. All things—animals, plants, and elements—give off emanations (Plutarch *quaest. nat.* 916d on fr. 73(89).1) and have pores (Philoponus *in GA* 123.13 on fr. 74(91).1), so that αἴσθησις and φρόνησις converge, and at any particular point in the range it would be impossible to distinguish between them; this in part accounts for the standard Peripatetic complaint that Empedocles identified perception and thought, and in particular for Theophrastus' query (*Sens.* 12): τί διοίσει τὰ ἔμψυχα πρὸς τὸ αἰσθάνεσθαι τῶν ἄλλων;

55. Cf. fr. 53(62).6: τοὺς μὲν πῦρ ἀνέπεμπε θέλον πρὸς ὁμοῖον ἱκέσθαι.

ject to changes of temperature and other variations. For men blood is intelligence, the best mixture they have in their constitution, but Empedocles, as it seems, is οὐκέτι θνητός.[56]

Empedocles' theory of thinking is relevant here, and its interpretation is best begun with Parmenides. According to Parmenides' *Doxa*, taken with Theophrastus' commentary,[57] it is by means of the constituent elements within men that the like elements outside are perceived and known. Further, perception and thought in men are similar, in the proportion of their parts, to the object that is perceived or thought. But Parmenides worked with only two principles, light and night. For him the light and dark forms that are in the composition of our frames think respectively the light and darkness in the world—in separation, as in the case of the corpse, which knows only darkness, and in varying compounds. Thinking is dependent on the mixture of the two forms in the body at any one time; as the mixture that gives the thinking changes, so does the quality of the thought, as well as the range of symmetrical contact with the external world.[58]

Empedocles follows and develops this part of Parmenides' *Doxa* in several ways. Primarily, the physical basis of cognition is clarified. Thought, with which the daimon has been shown to be connected, is explicable in terms of the four roots; in Aristotelian terminology it is σωματικόν, and the act of thinking is a form of contact.[59] The nature of the contact, which is between the constituent part of the body and its like in the external world, is brought out in the following lines:

γαίῃ μὲν γὰρ γαῖαν ὀπώπαμεν, ὕδατι δ' ὕδωρ,
αἰθέρι δ' αἰθέρα δῖον, ἀτὰρ πυρὶ πῦρ ἀίδηλον,
στοργὴν δὲ στοργῇ, νεῖκος δέ τε νείκεϊ λυγρῷ.
ἐκ τούτων ⟨ὡς⟩ πάντα πεπήγασιν ἁρμοσθέντα
καὶ τούτοις φρονέουσι . . . [60]

It is clear that Empedocles supposed that the attraction of, and perception by, like for like covered the whole range of the forms of life. Each of the roots has a "soul," that is, it is capable of a rudimentary sensation

56. Cf. frs. 102(112).4–5, 105(113).2.

57. Parmenides fr. 16 and Theophrastus *Sens.* 3–4.

58. On this interpretation cf. W. J. Verdenius *Parmenides* pp. 6–19, and G. Vlastos, "Parmenides' Theory of Knowledge," *TAPA* 1946, pp. 66–74.

59. Cf. Aristotle *De An.* 427a26–27, Philoponus *in de An.* 489.27–31.

60. Frs. 77(109) and 78(107), which are surely consecutive, cf. Theophrastus *Sens.* 10.

of a simple unit of its own kind; plants and animals are more complex and have correspondingly more complex perceptions. Man is composed of parts of the four roots, and in his heart-blood he has a particularly good mixture of them, so that he is able both to perceive simples and to think compounds. Beyond this is the perfect mixture, which too is capable of assimilation to its like—the process of highest (and purest) thought.[61]

Further, and significantly, Aristotle quotes two fragments of Empedocles alongside Parmenides' fragment 16. The first states that "man's wisdom grows according to what is present," and the second, that "insofar as (men) have changed in their nature, so far changed thoughts are always present to them."[62] So it may be assumed that Empedocles, like Parmenides, believed that the mixture of the bodily components reflects or represents whatever is thought about in the external world, and that the continual physical changes in the structure of the body alter the character of the thinking.[63] But Empedocles brought out the corollary that the thought can be confused or dulled according to the state of the mixture and the intention of the thinker, or correspondingly made purer.

Empedocles, however, says that he is superior to man, and in him therefore there is present a mixture of elements, corresponding to that of φρὴν ἱερή, which is perfect and invariant, no longer subject to the changes undergone by the heart-blood, its closest equivalent in man.[64] Empedocles expects to survive death and to rejoin the immortals who are his fellows and the god to which he is akin; and it is this compound that would be the surviving Empedocles.

The perfect *phronēsis*, which survives death and which is a complete blending of the component parts of roots, would have no visible character. The notion of a characterless and unvarying perfect mixture, given in

61. On the range of perception cf. the references given above in n. 54; for the lowest level of thinking cf. Hippolytus *RH* 6.11.1, where fr. 77(109) is taken closely with fr. 100(110).10, and for the highest, cf. Aristotle's criticism of the omniscience of Empedocles' god, *Metaph.* 1000b3–6.

62. Frs. 79(106) and 80(108), introduced by Aristotle at *Metaph.* 1009b17 with καὶ γάρ 'E. μεταβάλλοντας τὴν ἕξιν μεταβάλλειν φησὶ τὴν φρόνησιν.

63. Cf. also Heraclitus fr. 119, Diogenes of Apollonia fr. 5, *Regimen* I.25 (on intelligence depending on the right blend of elements), and further, H. Reiche *Empedocles' Mixture* pp. 53–56.

64. The better thought is not conditioned, as it seems to have been for Parmenides (and cf. Heraclitus frs. 30, 118), by a preponderance of one element but by a balance of the ingredients; and here Empedocles fills the gap in Parmenides' theory (of which Theophrastus complains, *Sens.* 4) concerning the state resulting from an exact equality in the mixture.

fragments 19 and 21(27) as a description of the sphere, and identifiable with φρὴν ἱερή, is found several times in Presocratic theory. In the scheme of Anaxagoras, for example, all things were together in the original mixture, and consequently no color or other distinguishing feature could be picked out. Anaximander and Anaximenes earlier had made use of an *archē* with no perceptible character; moreover, the *archē* in a neutral and invariant state, when not subject to rarefaction or condensation, is for Anaximenes the ψυχή for man, and that which surrounds the world, as well as that which existed first of all and from which the world arose.[65]

Empedocles, like Anaximenes and the succeeding tradition through Aristotle and later, also has this link between the soul, or thinking faculty, and that which is around the world. The restored daimons, who include Empedocles, go outward toward the circumference, where there still survives part of the original god under Love. In fragment 47(35) it was shown that Love takes hold of the center and extends her power outward.[66] And in the complementary period Strife consolidates its control from the center while Love in turn is being driven ἐπ' ἔσχατα τέρματα κύκλου. Hippolytus, who gives the only detailed commentary on fragment 107(115),[67] describes there the activity of Strife at this stage as a breaking up of the unity brought about by Love, resulting in the generation of plant, animal, and human life. Conversely, Love is trying to pull back to herself out of pity the parts of the one that Strife is scattering into many (or, in Aristotelian terminology,[68] the parts of the mixture that Strife is destroying). These, from another aspect, are the daimons forcibly severed from their fellows and compelled to take on mortal form in the creation caused by Strife, and Love would therefore be drawing them toward the circumference as she herself retreats toward it. Plutarch too supports this when he speaks of the κατὰ φύσιν χώρα the daimons reach after their exile;[69] the κατὰ φύσιν χώρα for the daimons would be with Love at the ἔσχατα τέρματα κύκλου.

It now becomes easier to see how the question of the continuity of the daimon might be answered. From his own position Empedocles looks back and recognizes that the parts of roots of which he is now constituted

65. Cf. Anaxagoras fr. 1, Anaximenes fr. 2, Aristotle *Phys.* 187a20–23, Simplicius *in Phys.* 24.13f.

66. Cf. the commentary on fr. 47(35).

67. Hippolytus *RH* 7.29.12–24.

68. Cf. Aristotle *Metaph.* 1092b6–7.

69. Plutarch *de Is. et Os.* 361c, cf. Hippolytus *RH* 1.4.3, and also Aetius 1.5.2 on ἀρχὴ ὕλη.

were once integrated into the perfect and unvarying unity of all things under Love, which produced the θεὸς εὐδαιμονέστατος—holy mind.[70] Then came a change. Strife began to take over and to break up the mixture. This is seen as "trusting in Strife"; there is a feeling that something "wrong" was done, and a penalty demanded, but this does not imply that Empedocles remembered what happened or that a choice was open to him. The parts that are now himself have been used for all kinds of *thnēta* and have lived different forms of life in the different elemental masses. None of these inferior forms of life was satisfactory, because their mixtures were out of proportion,[71] or they were unable to become properly constituted, or, in the case of the boy and girl, their time was cut off before they could become settled. In this way the parts of the roots were thought of as driven from one element to another, without a period of rest in which to become developed. Now at length Empedocles sees himself as a recognizable *egō*; he has attained the highest form of life on earth, he has the best mixture of elements, and his *phronēsis* is pure.[72] He, that is his intelligence which now has daimonic status, escapes further disintegration by Strife.

In the *Katharmoi* Empedocles earnestly encourages his fellow citizens to follow his example. They should hinder the work of Strife and promote that of Love by ceasing from quarreling and slaughter, and in their place restoring the universal friendliness characteristic of an earlier age. In so doing they and their kindred may eventually be free of the "joyless land."[73]

The *Physics* gives similar encouragement to Pausanias, but the details are more exact. On one level Empedocles hopes to train Pausanias in healing, so that he will win through to one of the top lives among men. But this is dependent on the fundamental attitude. If Pausanias thinks the right sort of thoughts, "with goodwill and unsullied attention,"[74] then

70. Cf. Aristotle *Metaph.* 1000b3-4, Empedocles fr. 97(134). 4.

71. Fish, for example, have too much fire in their constitution, cf. Theophrastus *CP* 1.21.5.

72. The failure to reach a satisfactory constitution may explain the simultaneous death of body and soul at Aetius 5.25.4. Sextus links fr. 77(109), on the perception of like elements by like, with fr. 105(113), and Empedocles' claim to divinity with both purity of thought and the assimilation of the god within him to the god without (*adv. math.* 1.302); cf. Plato *Phaedo* 79d.

73. Cf. frs. 122(136), 119(130), 113(121).

74. Cf. further the commentary on fr. 100(110). Democritus also seems to have believed that teaching alters the physical pattern of the soul, cf. his fr. 33, G. Vlastos *Phil. Rev.* 1945, pp. 578-92, 1946, pp. 57-62, and C. C. W. Taylor *Phronesis* 1967, p. 9.

his mixture will be improved and perhaps get properly constituted, and so not be dissipated at death; but if, like most men, he thinks about petty things, his mixture will get worse, and at death the thoughts will disintegrate into their different parts of roots, and these will fly off to join their respective families, the separating masses of earth, air, fire, and water.

This section has aimed to show that the theory of the daimon put forward by Empedocles is not "mystic," contradicting his physical theory and outside the tradition of early Greek philosophy. The notion of a characterless *archē* from which the present world arises is developed according to Milesian cosmogony; the connection of thinking with the mixing of the elements is an elaboration of part of Parmenides' *Doxa*, and the theory of a perfect mixture being characterless is accepted by Anaxagoras. The suggestion that the soul is of the same nature as the outer circle of the heavens is present before and after Empedocles. Notably it recurs in Plato, especially in the intelligent and invisible deity of the *Timaeus* at the ἔσχατος οὐρανός, to which the daimon is related, and with a relationship that can be strengthened by thinking the right thoughts.[75] It is found in Aristotle too, in the encircling fifth element, eternal and invariant, which is akin to the *dynamis* of the ψυχή.[76] The poems of Empedocles are an integral part of this same tradition. They put forward a theory which connects an earlier, undifferentiated stage of the universe with a uniting of the elements, recognizing god and mind there, and which further supposes that this divine intelligence still surrounds the cosmos and that the soul in its best state has an affinity with it.

---

75. Cf. Plato *Tim.* 36e, 90a, and also Aristotle *De An.* 404b11–17, where Empedocles' theory is compared with that of the *Timaeus* because both construct the soul out of elements.

76. Cf. Aristotle *Cael.* 269a32, 270b10, *GA* 736b30, 737a1, *EE* 1248a24–27.

4. The Allocation of the Fragments

The method for allocation put forward here is to set out the fragments in groups graded according to the certainty of their place in either poem.[1] The first groups consist of fragments whose contexts are known, and those said by ancient authorities to precede or follow them. In the central groups are fragments less directly related to the first sets, or for which weaker criteria, such as the number of the imperative or similarity of subject matter, are the only clues available. The last groups comprise those lines for which there is no indication to assist the allocation. This scheme of groupings has been presupposed throughout the introduction and commentary, and the unsatisfactory state of the evidence for dividing and allocating the fragments that it reveals has served as a check on any dogmatic conclusions derived from the original lines.

Group I consists of fragments 1, 6, 8, 17, 62, 96, 98, and 103 in Diels-Kranz's ordering, and these are certainly from the *Physics*. From the first book Tzetzes quotes fr. 6, Aetius fr. 8, and Simplicius frs. 17 and 96; fr. 1 is said by Diogenes to be the address of the *Physics* to Pausanias.[2] From the second book Simplicius gives fr. 62 and also sets frs. 98 and 103 in the *Physics*, but without indicating the book.[3]

Simplicius also supplies the evidence for connecting frs. 35, 59, 75, 85, and 104 directly with those of group I. He states that fr. 35 comes before fr. 98 with the words πρὸ τούτων, and that fr. 104 is after fr. 103 with καὶ

---

1. The numbering in this chapter only is that of Diels-Kranz. Elsewhere these numbers are given in parentheses after the corresponding number of the new text and ordering.

2. Tzetzes *ex Il.* 53.23; Aetius 1.30.1; Simplicius *in Phys.* 157.27, 300.20; D.L. 8.60.

3. Simplicius *in Phys.* 381.29, 32.1-2, 331.10.

μετ' ὀλίγον. Immediately before the quotation of fr. 104 here he groups together a phrase from fr. 59, the second line of fr. 75, and fr. 85 with the first line of fr. 98 (the place of which is fixed by the earlier citation) in the summary: καὶ πολλὰ ἄν τις εὕροι ἐκ τῶν Ἐμπεδοκλέους Φυσικῶν τοιαῦτα παραθέσθαι ὥσπερ καὶ τοῦτο.[4]

Because of their relation to group II or on comparably strong grounds frs. 20, 21, 23, 26, 57, 61, 71, 73, and 111 can be set in the *Physics* with reasonable assurance. Simplicius gives fr. 73 as coming after fr. 71 with the words καὶ μετ' ὀλίγα; both precede fr. 75 (from the above group), and all three fragments are said to come closely together. He also quotes fr. 57 with frs. 35 and 59 as referring to the same *katastasis*, and in the summary in Aetius of the generations of living things the stage given in fr. 61 follows that described in fr. 57 and may be assumed to come from the same poem as it.[5] Further, Simplicius has fr. 26 after fr. 21 with the indication ὀλίγον δὲ προελθών, fr. 23 is said to be a *paradeigma* of fr. 21, and fr. 21 to develop further the theory of fr. 17, part of which is repeated in fr. 26. Elsewhere fr. 20 is given as a commentary on fr. 17.29, and so, because of their connection with each other and with the certain fr. 17, frs. 20, 21, 23, and 26 can be added.[6] Fragment 111 is included in group III because the distinctive phrase in the third line, ἐπεὶ μούνῳ σοι ἐγὼ κρανέω τάδε πάντα, shows that this fragment is almost certainly addressed to Pausanias and so belongs in the *Physics* rather than the *Katharmoi*.[7]

The fragments of group IV, which consists of 9, 12, 13, 16, 27–31, 36–38, 53, 54, 86, 87, and 95, with 2–4 and 110, depend for their allocation on a looser connection with those of the first sets, or on the fact that they deal with subjects similar to those treated in them. Plutarch relates fr. 9, and in particular the fourth line, to fr. 8, and frs. 12, 13, and 16 develop the arguments of fr. 17.29–33.[8] In Simplicius, fr. 87 follows fr. 86 with the phrase καὶ μετ' ὀλίγον and is itself followed by fr. 95; the subject of fr. 86 is given as περὶ γενέσεως τῶν ὀφθαλμῶν; fr. 95 is referred to the context of vision, and this apparently is a subject with which fr. 85 (a fragment almost certainly from the second group) deals.[9] Fragment 35

4. Simplicius *in Phys.* 32.11, 331.1–14, and cf. 32.1–6.
5. Simplicius *in Cael.* 530.1–11, 587.1–26, Aetius 5.19.5.
6. Simplicius *in Phys.* 33.8–34.3, 159.6–12, 27; fr. 26.1 and 8–12 repeat fr. 17.29 and 9–13.
7. Karsten, *EAcr*, and Mullach, *FPG*, however, would put this fragment as ἐκ τῶν Ἰατρικῶν; see chap. 1.
8. Plutarch *adv. Col.* 1113a; *MXG* 975b1–8, 976b26–27; Hippolytus *RH* 7.29.10.
9. Simplicius *in Cael.* 529.21–27.

(and fr. 36 has a similar reference) describes the retreat of Strife and advance of Love, and the contrasting stage of the advance of Strife is likely to belong to the same poem. This brings in frs. 30 and 31; frs. 27, 28, and 29, which describe the state of the sphere immediately preceding Strife's rise to power, would also belong in the same work. Fragment 38 introduces a cosmogony, a standard Presocratic theme that would be expected to feature in a physical work, and frs. 37, 53, and 54, which describe this cosmogony's first stages, are all quoted in Aristotle's critical account of Empedocles' physics and are best placed with fr. 38.[10] In this set frs. 2–4 and 110 may also be included, on the grounds of the relative certainty of their allocation. The imperatives in lines 6 and 9–12 of fr. 3, and in frs. 4 and 110, are in the singular and most obviously addressed to Pausanias; according to Sextus, Empedocles' fr. 2 (which also includes a promise given to a second person singular) comes immediately before fr. 3.[11]

Other fragments deal with topics in groups III and IV. Fragments 84, 88, and 94 are concerned with vision, the subject of frs. 86 and 87. Fragments 39–49, 51–52, and 55–56 on the nature of the sun, moon, earth, and sea fulfill the promise of fr. 38 and are the obvious and traditional subjects of physical speculation. Fragment 22 is quoted by Simplicius along with frs. 21, 23, 26, 17, and 8 as furthering the argument he puts forward for their interpretation. Plutarch gives fr. 76 as an example of the relative positions elements may be found in,[12] the subject of the fragment is similar to that of fr. 75, and it is an instance of the general scheme outlined in fr. 71. In addition, fr. 100 on respiration, fr. 89 on ἀπορροαί (with the simile illustrating mixing by means of pores in fr. 91), and fr. 90 on nutrition deal with technical subjects related to what is known elsewhere of the content of the *Physics*.

After group V the allocation becomes more doubtful, but frs. 33, 82, 83, 101, 102, and 105–09 have some points in favor of their assignment to the *Physics*. Of these Plutarch quotes fr. 33 as an illustration of the unifying power of *philia*,[13] and this fragment, along with the biological observations of frs. 82 and 83, perhaps connects with the description of the formation of animals in frs. 71 and 73. Fragments 101 and 102 on breathing and smell fit with fr. 100, and frs. 105–09 on thought and perception add to the account of the functioning of organisms.

10. Aristotle *GC* 333b1–334a5.

11. Sextus *adv. math.* 7.124–25.

12. Plutarch *quaest. conv.* 618b, *fac. lun.* 927f, and cf. Empedocles frs. 53–54.

13. Plutarch *amic. mult.* 95a.

It may be suggested on grounds of subject matter that frs. 63–68, 72, 74, 79–81, and 93 belong to the *Physics*, although there is no indication in the authorities that this is the case. Fragment 72 introduces an account of trees and fishes, fr. 74 touches on the latter (repeating Empedocles' unusual word καμασῆνες), and frs. 79–81 give some description of trees and their characteristics. Group VII, like the other biological observations, would appear more suitable for the *Physics*. Fragment 93 gives an instance of a type of mixture and probably belongs with the other examples of mixing in the *Physics*,[14] but the text of the line is obscure and the exact reference unknown. There are no pointers for the allocation of frs. 63–68, which deal with reproduction and embryology, and according to the notice of Theon there was some account of the embryo in the *Katharmoi*. However, the summary in Aetius of the four stages of the generation of living things, part of which is substantiated by fragments almost certainly belonging to the *Physics*, shows that sexual reproduction was referred to there in connection with the fourth stage.[15] Those fragments, therefore, that are on this subject may be kept in the *Physics*, but with some reservations.

The placing of the last group (VIII) is quite uncertain. Fragments 77 and 78, like frs. 79–81, are concerned with trees, but some editors argue that they belong to the account of the age of Kypris in the *Katharmoi*.[16] Fragments 24 and 25 deal with Empedocles' method of exposition and could belong to either poem, but there are instances of repetition and divergence in the *Physics*. Of the remaining fragments, 27a is referred by Plutarch to the ideal philosopher;[17] this fragment has been allocated to the *Physics* in the present text, although a case could be made for setting it in the *Katharmoi*, either with the fragments relating to the age of Kypris or with those describing the best forms of life. It is possible that fr. 50 was not written by Empedocles.[18]

Apart from fr. 153a and the new fr. 152, the only fragment that is quoted as definitely from the *Katharmoi* is fr. 112, from Diogenes.[19]

---

14. Cf. frs. 33 and 91.

15. Theon Smyrnaeus 104.1: τὸ γοῦν βρέφος δοκεῖ τελειοῦσθαι ἐν ἑπτὰ ἑβδομάσιν, ὡς 'E. αἰνίττεται ἐν τοῖς Καθαρμοῖς; Aetius 5.19.5.

16. Cf., for example, Karsten *EAcr* p. 269, on his lines 366–67; for trees in the *Kath.* cf. fr. 152.

17. Plutarch *princ. phil.* 777c.

18. Cf. Tzetzes *All. Il.* O.85.

19. D.L. 8.54: αὐτὸς ἐναρχόμενος τῶν Καθαρμῶν φησιν . . .

Aristotle says of fr. 135 that it is ὡς Ἐμπεδοκλῆς λέγει περὶ τοῦ μὴ κτείνειν τὸ ἔμψυχον. The universal law, which is the subject of this fragment, is connected by Sextus to the theory of the kinship of living things and the criminal act of killing and eating animals, and according to Hippolytus a prohibition against eating meat was one of the themes of the *Katharmoi*.[20] Those fragments, therefore, that are directly connected with a warning against the slaughter and eating of animals may be allocated to the *Katharmoi*; these are frs. 136, 137, and 139.[21] In fr. 128 the abstention from blood sacrifice and meat eating is set up as an ideal that was realized in the age of Kypris. Fragment 130 is a development of this subject, for it describes the friendship that once existed between men and animals, and a contrast with the present slaughter is implied; it may therefore be put with fr. 128 in group II. Fragment 114 is an almost certain allocation since it includes the address ὦ φίλοι, which appears in fr. 112, the one indisputable fragment from the *Katharmoi*. Fragment 145 is also addressed to a plural audience.

Because of the very title οἱ Καθαρμοί, whether due to Empedocles or not, it would seem that the two phrases which are apparently concerned with purification and ritual, namely frs. 138 and 143, should be allocated to the poem. The specific prohibitions of frs. 140 and 141, and the general one of fr. 144, may be added to group III on a similar basis.

Plutarch states that fr. 115 belongs for Empedocles ἐν ἀρχῇ τῆς φιλοσοφίας, but this gives no clear indication from which poem it comes.[22] Although there is a slight balance in favor of the *Physics* being composed before the *Katharmoi*,[23] Plutarch's notice does not necessarily mean that fr. 115 belongs at the beginning of the *Physics*. Perhaps the *Katharmoi*

20. Hippolytus *RH* 7.30.3–4, Aristotle *Rhet.* 1373b 14–17, Sextus *adv. math.* 9.127.

21. Porphyry, in the context of the quotation of fr. 139, *de abst.* 2.31, speaks of making amends διὰ τῶν καθαρμῶν for former misdeeds, but this is probably a reference to ritual purification rather than to Empedocles' poem.

22. Plutarch *exil.* 607c: ὁ δ' Ἐ. ἐν ἀρχῇ τῆς φιλοσοφίας προαναφωνήσας . . .

23. Anaxagoras seems to have heard of an argument of Zeno (cf. Zeno frs. 1 and 3, Anaxagoras fr. 3), and in frs. 8 and 10 to be replying to Empedocles, whereas there is no trace in Empedocles of his having heard of Zeno's arguments; Zeno and Empedocles were probably working out their reactions to Parmenides at about the same time. Further, the twentieth chapter of *Ancient Medicine* mentions Empedocles as a well-known writer περὶ φύσιος. All this suggests that the *Physics* was composed about 460–455 B.C. If the *Katharmoi* were prior it would be quite a youthful work, and this would make it difficult to account for the fame Empedocles claims for himself in fr. 112; cf. further the commentary on fr. 107(115).

appeared first in Plutarch's text, but ἐν ἀρχῇ τῆς φιλοσοφίας (without the article with ἀρχῇ) is more likely to mean "as a starting point" for Empedocles' philosophy; as such it could give the grounds for the prohibitions that do seem to belong to the *Katharmoi*. If this is so then this fragment brings with it the references to the different lives contained in frs. 117, 127, 146, and 147.

If, from fr. 115, life is now taken to be in some sense an exile from a more fortunate state, then frs. 118, 119, and 124, which refer to present sorrow in contrast with former happiness, could be placed in group V. Also, the fragments that apparently elaborate on the notion of this world as a cave and meadow of Atē, that is, frs. 120–23, should probably be added to them. And Porphyry explains fr. 126 as relating to a theory of incarnation,[24] which would connect the fragment to those in group IV.

Last, there is a group of fragments (VI) for which no clues are provided to guide their placing. Three of these have been left, as Diels prints them, in the *Katharmoi*. Sextus quotes fr. 113 after lines 4–5 of fr. 112, and perhaps it is the beginning of an explanation for the confident tone of these lines. Fragment 116 is obscure, but such a notice of Love's opposition to Ananke could be from either poem; the same is true of fr. 125, except for the slight hint of Clement's quoting it after fr. 118.[25]

Fragments 11 and 15 have been transferred from the *Physics* to the *Katharmoi*. The two fragments belong together, for Plutarch puts fr. 15 after fr. 11 with the words τὸ μετὰ ταῦτα.[26] Plutarch quotes freely from both poems without giving the source, and here the mention of δειλά and ἐσθλά in fr. 15, which men are said to suffer before and after death, fits better with the history of the daimons in the *Katharmoi* than with the more impersonal account in the *Physics* of the arrangements of roots.

Fragment 129 has been moved to the *Physics*. It does not at first sight fit into either poem, and some editors print it separately.[27] If Porphyry is right in referring the fragment to Pythagoras[28] it is unlikely that, although he lived in the generation before Empedocles, Pythagoras should be placed in the golden age of the distant past, as Diels's setting of the fragment suggests. In the present text fr. 129 is placed before fr. 110 on the

---

24. Porphyry ap. Stobaeus *Ecl.* 1.49.60.
25. Sextus *adv. math.* 1.302; Plutarch *quaest. conv.* 745d; Clement *Strom.* 3.2.14.2.
26. Plutarch *adv. Col.* 1113c–d.
27. E.g., Karsten *EAcr* under *Varia*, p. 150.
28. Porphyry *Vit. Pyth.* 30.

assumption that Pythagoras was one of the few wise men whose thought ranged widely and was not blunted by μυρία δειλά. In this way he would be held up as an example of right thinking for Pausanias to imitate.

According to Tzetzes, fr. 134 comes from the *Physics*, from the third book. Since Diels's reasons for supposing that Tzetzes read the *Katharmoi* as the third book of the *Physics* are not altogether convincing, the fragment has been restored to the *Physics*.[29] Fragment 133 seems an obvious predecessor to fr. 134, and since there are no independent indications for its source it has been taken over with fr. 134 to the *Physics*. Similarly, fr. 132 could belong to either poem, but it has been allocated to the *Physics* as an introduction to the account of divinity in frs. 133 and 134. This fragment also serves to link the preceding account of the physical structure of man's thought with the exordium on how that thought should be used. Fragment 131 has been transferred to the beginning of the *Physics*. The Hippolytus context of this fragment, which connects it with the two *kosmoi* established by Love and Strife, suggests that it should be allocated to the *Physics*.[30] The subject of the lines is a prayer to the Muse for help in giving an ἀγαθὸς λόγος about the gods, and this comes most appropriately with the prologue in which the Muse is known to have been addressed, and before the revelation to Pausanias of the new theory of the true nature of the θεοὶ μάκαρες that is set out in the sixth fragment.

Some phrases printed by Diels as full fragments are either so brief or obscure, or the reading so much in doubt, that they cannot intelligibly be accepted as giving Empedocles' original words or as contributing to the evidence for a discussion of his work. These phrases have been printed separately as addenda, with the omission of fr. 18. Fragment 14 has also been omitted, as it seems to be a clumsy combination in *MXG* of frs. 13 and 17.32. The position of fr. 34 has been discussed above, on pp. 18–19; it is kept in the *Physics* in parentheses.

This scheme for the allocation of the fragments is summarized in the following list. Groups I–VIII of the *Physics* fragments and I–VI of the *Katharmoi* are in descending order of certainty of allocation. There is no indication available in the ancient authorities of where fragments in groups VII–VIII of the *Physics* and V–VI of the *Katharmoi* should be placed, and the allocation of the fragments in the preceding group in each poem is not assured.

29. See chap. 1.
30. Hippolytus *RH* 7.31.4.

Summary of the Grouping of the Fragments according to Certainty of Allocation
(Diels-Kranz's numbering)

(a) from the *Physics*

I   1 6 8 17 62 96 98 103
II   35 59 75 85 104
III   20 21 23 26 57 61 71 73; (2s) 111
IV   9 12 13 16 27–31 36–38 53 54 86 87 95; (2s) 2–4 110
V   22 39–49 51 52 55 56 76 84 88–91 94 100
VI   33 82 83 101 102 105–09
VII 63–68 72 74 79–81 93; (T) 131 133 134
VIII 24 25 27a (34) 50 77 78; (T) 129 132

(b) from the *Katharmoi*

I   112 (153a) (fr. 152)
II   128 130 135 136 137 139; (2p) 114 145
III 138 140 141 143 144
IV 115 117 127 146 147
V   118 119 120–24 126
VI 113 116 125; (T) 11 15

(c) Addenda

    5 7 10 19 32 58 60 69 70 92 97 99 142 148–53

Note: (2s) = 2nd person singular, (2p) = 2nd person plural, (T) = transfer

5. The Titles of the Poems

Were the titles Περὶ φύσεως (or φύσιος) and Καθαρμοί given to his poems by Empedocles himself? Probably not, although the question is a vexed one. In the doxography, and in particular in Diogenes Laertius and the *Suda*, most of the Presocratics are credited with a work entitled Περὶ φύσεως, e.g., Anaximander (*Suda*), Xenophanes (*ad* fr. 30), Heraclitus (D.L. 9.5), Zeno (*Suda*). This presupposes that it was customary for authors to give their works titles and that φύσις unsupported was accepted in the fifth century as meaning "(the whole of) nature." Both of these suppositions are disputable. Parmenides' work was known as περὶ τοῦ (ἑνὸς) ὄντος, and that of Melissus as περὶ φύσεως ἢ περὶ τοῦ ὄντος, cf. Simplicius *in Phys.* 70.17, 144.26, *in Cael.* 557.10, and according to Sextus (*adv. math.* 7.65) Gorgias wrote περὶ τοῦ μὴ ὄντος ἢ περὶ φύσεως, deliberately challenging Melissus. In these last two cases περὶ φύσεως looks like a later addition under Peripatetic influence, a suggestion supported by Simplicius, *in Cael.* 556.15–30.

For φύσις to mean "nature as a whole" a limiting genitive, such as τῶν πάντων or τοῦ ὅλου, seems to have been required for the Presocratics, cf. Archytas fr. 1, Philolaus ap. Sextus *adv. math.* 7.92, *Dissoi Logoi* 8.1, D.L. 8.34, and Xenophon *Mem.* 1.1.11 and 14. (The absence of such a genitive in Heraclitus fr. 123 has been shown by Kirk to be a fault in the late tradition of that fragment, see *Heraclitus* pp. 227–31.) Later there could be an explanatory phrase, such as περὶ φύσεώς τε καὶ τοῦ ὅλου, Plato *Lysis* 214b. More important, when Plato uses the phrase περὶ φύσεως ἱστορία at *Phaedo* 96a, he treats it as a new technical term and details its meaning: εἰδέναι τὰς αἰτίας ἑκάστου, διὰ τί γίγνεται ἕκαστον καὶ διὰ τί ἀπόλλυται καὶ διὰ τί ἐστι. There are similar explanations at *Philebus* 59a, *Phaedrus* 270a–d, and *Laws* 891c. The author of *Ancient Medicine* enlarges on Plato's interpretation, . . . οἱ περὶ φύσιος γεγράφασιν ἐξ ἀρχῆς ὅ τι ἐστιν ἄνθρωπος καὶ ὅπως πρῶτον ἐγένετο καὶ ὁπόθεν συνεπάγη, *VM* 20, and cf. also Euripides fr. 910 Nauck. These passages summarize the earlier work of the Presocratics in a concise form; Περὶ φύσεως, far from being a well-established title bestowed by an individual author, is an innovation requiring exposition.

For Aristotle the exposition is no longer necessary. He calls the Presocratics οἱ φυσικοί or οἱ φυσιολογικοί, and their works οἱ περὶ φύσεως λόγοι, τὰ περὶ φύσεως, or τὰ φυσικά. In much the same way as he refers to his own work as περὶ φύσεως or τὰ φυσικά he gives quotations from Empedocles as ἐν τοῖς φυσικοῖς (*Mete.* 382a1), as well as ἐν τῇ κοσμοποιίᾳ (*Phys.* 196a22 and cf. *Metaph.* 1001a12); τὰ φυσικά is also the citation in Simplicius and Aetius for frs. 12(8), 8(17), 53(62), and 48(96). (The whole question is well treated by E. Schmalzriedt in his *Peri Physeos.*) The variety in the reference tells against a fixed, original title. Περὶ φύσεως later became a term used by Peripatetic historians for a work on natural philosophy by those whom Aristotle called οἱ φυσικοί, but this is quite different from its being the title the individual φυσικός gave to his work.

Guthrie gives a comprehensive listing of the meanings and uses of the word *katharmos* (*HGP* vol. 2, pp. 244–45), but this does not justify the title (οἱ) Καθαρμοί as Empedocles'. Aristotle knows his second poem as περὶ τοῦ μὴ κτείνειν τὸ ἔμψυχον, *Rhet.* 1373b14; it is Diogenes who uses οἱ Καθαρμοί (8.63), and Theon who cites 129(143) as a *katharmos* comparable to Plato's educational syllabus, 15.7. *Katharmoi* and books about them are attributed by Plato (*Rep.* 364e) to Orpheus and Musaeus. Probably Empedocles' pleas for the protection of animal and plant life were later associated with Orphic and Pythagorean precepts, and a title appropriate for them used for Empedocles' poem.

6. Concordance of the Ordering of the Fragments

(The figures in parentheses in both tables give the numbering of the fragments according to the arrangement of Diels-Kranz, *Fragmente der Vorsokratiker*. The third column of figures in the second table is that of J. Bollack, *Empédocle* vol. 2.)

I

(1)	4	(27a)	98	(54)	30	(81)	67
(2)	1	(28)	22	(55)	46	(82)	71
(3)	2,5	(29)	22	(56)	45	(83)	72
(4)	6	(30)	23	(57)	50	(84)	88
(5)	134	(31)	24	(58)	139	(85)	84
(6)	7	(32)	138	(59)	51	(86)	85
(7)	135	(33)	61	(60)	140	(87)	86
(8)	12	(34)	49	(61)	52	(88)	89
(9)	13	(35)	47	(62)	53	(89)	73
(10)	136	(36)	20	(63)	56	(90)	75
(11)	104	(37)	31	(64)	54	(91)	74
(12)	9	(38)	27	(65)	57	(92)	143
(13)	10	(39)	33	(66)	55	(93)	76
(14)	—	(40)	34	(67)	58	(94)	90
(15)	106	(41)	35	(68)	59	(95)	87
(16)	11	(42)	41	(69)	141	(96)	48
(17)	8	(43)	38	(70)	142	(97)	144
(18)	—	(44)	36	(71)	60	(98)	83
(19)	137	(45)	39	(72)	63	(99)	145
(20)	26	(46)	40	(73)	62	(100)	91
(21)	14	(47)	37	(74)	68	(101)	92
(22)	25	(48)	42	(75)	70	(102)	93
(23)	15	(49)	43	(76)	69	(103)	81
(24)	18	(50)	44	(77)	64	(104)	82
(25)	17	(51)	28	(78)	64	(105)	94
(26)	16	(52)	32	(79)	65	(106)	79
(27)	21,19	(53)	29	(80)	66	(107)	78

(108)	80	(118)	112	(128)	118	(138)	125
(109)	77	(119)	111	(129)	99	(139)	120
(110)	100	(120)	115	(130)	119	(140)	127
(111)	101	(121)	113	(131)	3	(141)	128
(112)	102	(122)	116	(132)	95	(142)	146
(113)	105	(123)	117	(133)	96	(143)	129
(114)	103	(124)	114	(134)	97	(144)	126
(115)	107	(125)	130	(135)	121	(145)	123
(116)	109	(126)	110	(136)	122	(146)	132
(117)	108	(127)	131	(137)	124	(147)	133
						(148)–(153a)	147–151

II

1	(2)	10	40	(46)	371	79	(106)	536
2	(3)	14	41	(42)	374	80	(108)	537
3	(131)	—	42	(48)	341	81	(103)	529
4	(1)	3	43	(49)	344	82	(104)	531
5	(3)	14	44	(50)	—	83	(98)	461
6	(4)	27	45	(56)	398	84	(85)	463
7	(6)	150	46	(55)	394	85	(86)	410
8	(17)	31, 124	47	(35)	201, 509	86	(87)	411
9	(12)	46	48	(96)	462	87	(95)	439
10	(13)	47, 96	49	(34)	452	88	(84)	415
11	(16)	118	50	(57)	495	89	(88)	417
12	(8)	53	51	(59)	222, 501	90	(94)	435
13	(9)	56	52	(61)	508	91	(100)	551
14	(21)	63	53	(62)	510	92	(101)	562
15	(23)	64	54	(64)	622	93	(102)	556
16	(26)	68	55	(66)	610	94	(105)	520
17	(25)	20	56	(63)	641	95	(132)	—
18	(24)	22	57	(65)	647	96	(133)	—
19	(27)	92,171	58	(67)	616	97	(134)	—
20	(36)	207	59	(68)	608	98	(27a)	99
21	(27)	92, 171	60	(71)	450	99	(129)	—
22	(29/28)	83, 98, 195	61	(33)	409	100	(110)	578, 699
23	(30)	126	62	(73)	454	101	(111)	12
24	(31)	121	63	(72)	479	102	(112)	—
25	(22)	231	64	(77/78)	581, 583–84	103	(114)	—
26	(20)	60	65	(79)	588	104	(11)	57
27	(38)	320	66	(80)	591	105	(113)	—
28	(51)	142	67	(81)	595	106	(15)	58
29	(53)	220	68	(74)	627	107	(115)	110
30	(54)	224	69	(76)	468	108	(117)	—
31	(37)	140	70	(75)	465	109	(116)	—
32	(52)	227	71	(82)	477	110	(126)	—
33	(39)	240	72	(83)	471	111	(119)	—
34	(40)	360	73	(89)	554	112	(118)	—
35	(41)	337	74	(91)	680	113	(121)	—
36	(44)	328	75	(90)	543	114	(124)	—
37	(47)	362	76	(93)	685	115	(120)	—
38	(43)	365	77	(109)	522	116	(122)	—
39	(45)	368	78	(107)	523	117	(123)	—

118	(128)	—		130	(125)	—		142	(70)	512
119	(130)	—		131	(127)	—		143	(92)	682
120	(139)	—		132	(146)	—		144	(97)	625
121	(135)	—		133	(147)	—		145	(99)	420
122	(136)	—		134	(5)	25		146	(142)	—
123	(145)	—		135	(7)	66		147-151	(148)-(153a)	
124	(137)	—		136	(10)	59				cf. 384, 519,
125	(138)	—		137	(19)	402				400, 480, 609
126	(144)	—		138	(32)	406		152	—	—
127	(140)	—		139	(58)	490				
128	(141)	—		140	(60)	503				
129	(143)	—		141	(69)	603				

II. Text

7. ΠΕΡΙ ΦΥΣΕΩΣ

1(2) Sextus *adv. math.* 7.122

ἄλλοι δὲ ἦσαν οἱ λέγοντες κατὰ τὸν 'Ε. κριτήριον εἶναι τῆς ἀληθείας οὐ τὰς αἰσθήσεις, ἀλλὰ τὸν ὀρθὸν λόγον, τοῦ δὲ ὀρθοῦ λόγου τὸν μέν τινα θεῖον ὑπάρχειν τὸν δὲ ἀνθρώπινον. ὧν τὸν μὲν θεῖον ἀνέξοιστον εἶναι, τὸν δὲ ἀνθρώπινον ἐξοιστόν. λέγει δὲ περὶ μὲν τοῦ μὴ ἐν ταῖς αἰσθήσεσι τὴν κρίσιν τὰληθοῦς ὑπάρχειν οὕτως·

> στεινωποὶ μὲν γὰρ παλάμαι κατὰ γυῖα κέχυνται,
> πολλὰ δὲ δείλ' ἔμπαια, τά τ' ἀμβλύνουσι μερίμνας.
> παῦρον †δὲ ζωῆσι βίου† μέρος ἀθρήσαντες
> ὠκύμοροι καπνοῖο δίκην ἀρθέντες ἀπέπταν,
> 5 αὐτὸ μόνον πεισθέντες, ὅτῳ προσέκυρσεν ἕκαστος
> πάντοσ' ἐλαυνόμενοι, τὸ δ' ὅλον ⟨πᾶς⟩ εὔχεται εὑρεῖν·
> οὕτως οὔτ' ἐπιδερκτὰ τάδ' ἀνδράσιν οὔτ' ἐπακουστά
> οὔτε νόῳ περιληπτά.

περὶ δὲ τοῦ μὴ εἰς τὸ παντελὲς ἄληπτον εἶναι τὴν ἀλήθειαν, ἀλλ' ἐφ' ὅσον ἱκνεῖται ὁ ἀνθρώπινος λόγος ληπτὴν ὑπάρχειν, διασαφεῖ τοῖς προκειμένοις ἐπιφέρων

> σὺ ⟨δ'⟩ οὖν, ἐπεὶ ὧδ' ἐλιάσθης,
> πεύσεαι †οὐ πλεῖόν γε† βροτείη μῆτις ὄρωρεν.

2 Procl. *in Tim.* 175c   **4** Plu. *de Is. et Os.* 360c   **5** D.L. 9.73   **7–8**
Plu. *aud. poet.* 17e, D.L. 9.73

93

2 δείλ᾽ ἔμπαια Emperius, Karsten : δειλεμπεα codd. : δείλ᾽ ἔπεα P, δείρ
ἔπεα Q Procl. : δείν᾽ ἔπεα Stephanus   3 δὲ ζωῆς ἰδίου Diels : δὲ ζωῆς
ἀβίου Scaliger : δ᾽ἐν ζωῆσι βίου Wilam., DK   ἀθρήσαντες Scaliger :
ἀθρήσαντος vel ἀθροίσαντος codd.   6 τὸ δ᾽ ὅλον Bergk : τὸ δὲ ὅλον
codd.   πᾶς add. Bergk, Diels : μάψ Stein : τίς ἄρ᾽ H. Fränkel   8 νόῳ
Plu. D.L. : νῶ codd.   δ᾽ add. Bergk   9 παύσεαι N   οὐ πλέον ἠὲ
Karsten, Diels : οὐ πλέον οὔτι H. Fränkel

2(3) Sextus adv. math. 7.124 [post 1(2).8–9]
καὶ διὰ τῶν ἑξῆς ἐπιπλήξας τοῖς πλέον ἐπαγγελλομένοις γιγνώσκειν παρίστησιν
ὅτι τὸ δι᾽ ἑκάστης αἰσθήσεως λαμβανόμενον πιστόν ἐστι, τοῦ λόγου τούτων
ἐπιστατοῦντος, καίπερ πρότερον καταδραμὼν τῆς ἀπ᾽ αὐτῶν πίστεως. φησὶ
γάρ

     ἀλλὰ θεοὶ τῶν μὲν μανίην ἀποτρέψατε γλώσσης,
     ἐκ δ᾽ ὁσίων στομάτων καθαρὴν ὀχετεύσατε πηγήν·
     καὶ σέ, πολυμνήστη λευκώλενε παρθένε Μοῦσα,
     ἄντομαι, ὧν θέμις ἐστὶν ἐφημερίοισιν ἀκούειν,
5   πέμπε παρ᾽ Εὐσεβίης ἐλάουσ᾽ εὐήνιον ἅρμα.

1 ἀποτρέψατε Scaliger : ἀπετρέψατε codd.   2 ὀχετεύσατε Stephanus :
ὠχεύσατε N, ἐχεύσατε E, ὀχεύσατε Lς

3(131) Hippolytus RH 7.31.3
κόσμον γάρ φησιν εἶναι ὁ ᾽Ε. τὸν ὑπὸ τοῦ νείκους διοικούμενον τοῦ πονηροῦ
καὶ ἕτερον νοητὸν τὸν ὑπὸ τῆς φιλίας ... μέσον δὲ εἶναι τῶν διαφόρων ἀρχῶν
δίκαιον λόγον ... τοῦτον δὲ αὐτὸν τὸν δίκαιον λόγον τὸν τῇ φιλίᾳ συναγων-
ιζόμενον Μοῦσαν ὁ ᾽Ε. προσαγορεύων, καὶ αὐτὸς αὐτῷ συναγωνίζεσθαι παρ-
ακαλεῖ, λέγων ὧδέ πως·

     εἰ γὰρ ἐφημερίων ἕνεκέν τινος, ἄμβροτε Μοῦσα,
     ἡμετέρας μελέτας ⟨ἄδε τοι⟩ διὰ φροντίδος ἐλθεῖν,
     εὐχομένῳ νῦν αὖτε παρίστασο, Καλλιόπεια,
     ἀμφὶ θεῶν μακάρων ἀγαθὸν λόγον ἐμφαίνοντι.

1 εἰκάραι φημερίων codd., corr. Miller   2 ἄδε τοι suppl. Wilam. : μέλε
τοι Diels   3 εὐχομένων codd., corr. Schneidewin

4(1) D.L. 8.60
ἦν δ᾽ ὁ Παυσανίας, ὥς φησιν ᾽Αρίστιππος καὶ Σάτυρος, ἐρώμενος αὐτοῦ, ᾧ

δὴ καὶ τὰ Περὶ φύσεως προσπεφώνηκεν οὕτως·

Παυσανίη, σὺ δὲ κλῦθι, δαΐφρονος Ἀγχίτεω υἱέ

Ἀγχίτεω DK (ex *Anth. Gr.* 7.508.1) : Ἀγχίτου codd. (cf. D.L. 8.61.3, Iamb.
Vit. Pyth. 113)

5(3) Sextus *adv. math.* 7.125 [post 2(3).1–5]

μηδέ σέ γ᾽ εὐδόξοιο βιήσεται ἄνθεα τιμῆς
πρὸς θνητῶν ἀνελέσθαι, ἐφ᾽ ᾧ θ᾽ ὁσίης πλέον εἰπεῖν
θάρσει, καὶ τότε δὴ σοφίης ἐπ᾽ ἄκροισι †θοάζει†.
ἀλλ᾽ ἄγ᾽ ἄθρει πάσῃ παλάμῃ πῇ δῆλον ἕκαστον,
5   μήτε τιν᾽ ὄψιν ἔχων †πίστει† πλέον ἢ κατ᾽ ἀκουήν
ἢ ἀκοὴν ἐρίδουπον ὑπὲρ τρανώματα γλώσσης,
μήτε τι τῶν ἄλλων, ὁπόσῃ πόρος ἐστὶ νοῆσαι,
γυίων πίστιν ἔρυκε, νόει δ᾽ ᾗ δῆλον ἕκαστον.

1–2 Clem. *Strom.* 5.59.3   **3** Procl. *in Tim.* 106e, Plu. *mult. am.* 93b

───────────────

2 ἐφ᾽ ᾧ θ᾽ ὁσίης Clem. : ἐφωθοείης codd.   **3** τάδε τοι Procl.   θοάζει
codd., Procl.: θαμίζειν (θαυμάζειν C¹) Plu.: θοάσσεις Karsten: θοάζειν G.
Hermann, Diels   **4** ἀλλὰ γὰρ ἄθρει πᾶς codd., corr. Bergk   **5** πιστὴν
Bergk, H. Fränkel : ὄψει ἔχων πίστιν Ellis   **8** δ᾽ Karsten : θ᾽ codd.

6(4) Clement *Strom.* 5.18.4

ἀλλὰ κακοῖς μὲν κάρτα πέλει κρατέουσιν ἀπιστεῖν.
ὡς δὲ παρ᾽ ἡμετέρης κέλεται πιστώματα Μούσης
γνῶθι, διατμηθέντος ἐνὶ σπλάγχνοισι λόγοιο.

τοῖς μὲν γὰρ κακοῖς τοῦτο σύνηθες, φησὶν ὁ Ἐ., τὸ ἐθέλειν κρατεῖν τῶν ἀλ-
ηθῶν διὰ τοῦ ἀπιστεῖν.

1–2 Theodoret. *Gr. aff.* 1.71

───────────────

1 κάρτα πέλει codd., Theodoret. : χαρτὰ πέλει Diels : κάρτα μέλει Her-

worden, DK   2 ὧδε γὰρ Theodoret.   3 διατμισθέντος Wilam. :
διασσηθέντος Diels

7(6) Aetius 1.3.20

'Ε. τέτταρα μὲν λέγει στοιχεῖα, πῦρ ἀέρα ὕδωρ γῆν, δύο δὲ ἀρχικὰς δυνάμεις,
φιλίαν τε καὶ νεῖκος· ὧν ἡ μέν ἐστιν ἑνωτική, τὸ δὲ διαιρετικόν. φησὶ δὲ
οὕτως·

> τέσσαρα γὰρ πάντων ῥιζώματα πρῶτον ἄκουε·
> Ζεὺς ἀργὴς Ἥρη τε φερέσβιος ἠδ' Ἀϊδωνεύς,
> Νῆστίς θ' ἣ δακρύοις τέγγει κρούνωμα βρότειον.

Δία μὲν γὰρ λέγει τὴν ζέσιν καὶ τὸν αἰθέρα, Ἥρην δὲ φερέσβιον τὸν ἀέρα,
τὴν δὲ γῆν τὸν Ἀϊδωνέα· Νῆστιν δὲ καὶ κρούνωμα βρότειον οἱονεὶ τὸ σπέρμα
καὶ τὸ ὕδωρ.

1–3 S.E., *adv. math.* 9.362, 10.315, Stob. 1.10.11, Hippol. *RH* 7.29.4, 10.7.3,
Probus *Verg. Buc.* 11.4, Tz. *ex. Il.* 53.23, Eus. *PE* 14.14.6   **1** Clem. *Strom.*
6.17.4, Phlp. *in Phys.* 88.6   **2–3** D.L. 8.76, Athenagoras 22, Heraclit. *All.*
24   **3** cf. *Suda* s.v. Nēstis

---

1 γὰρ S.E., Heraclit. : τῶν codd.   ἄκουε] ἔασιν Probus   **2** ἀργὴς S.E.,
Probus, D.L., Athenagoras, Heraclit. : αἰθὴρ codd., Tz. : ἀὴρ Hippol. 10.7
(om. 7.29)   **3** τέγγει κρούνωμα βρότειον codd., S.E., Heraclit. : τέγγει
κρουνῶ μακρόγιον vel μαβρόντιον Hippol. : τ' ἐπικούρου νῶμα βρότειον Athenagoras : ἐπιπικροῖ ὄμμα βροτεῖον D.L. : γε πικροῖς νωμᾶ βρότειον γένος Probus,
Suda

8(17) Simplicius *in Phys.* 157.25

ὁ δὲ 'Ε. τὸ ἓν καὶ τὰ πολλὰ τὰ πεπερασμένα καὶ τὴν κατὰ περίοδον ἀποκ-
ατάστασιν καὶ τὴν κατὰ σύγκρισιν καὶ διάκρισιν γένεσιν καὶ φθορὰν οὕτως
ἐν τῷ πρώτῳ τῶν Φυσικῶν παραδίδωσι·

> δίπλ' ἐρέω· τοτὲ μὲν γὰρ ἓν ηὐξήθη μόνον εἶναι
> ἐκ πλεόνων, τοτὲ δ' αὖ διέφυ πλέον' ἐξ ἑνὸς εἶναι.
> δοιὴ δὲ θνητῶν γένεσις, δοιὴ δ' ἀπόλειψις·
> τὴν μὲν γὰρ πάντων σύνοδος τίκτει τ' ὀλέκει τε,
> 5 ἡ δὲ πάλιν διαφυομένων †θρυφθεῖσα δρεπτή†.
> καὶ ταῦτ' ἀλλάσσοντα διαμπερὲς οὐδαμὰ λήγει,

ἄλλοτε μὲν φιλότητι συνερχόμεν᾽ εἰς ἓν ἅπαντα,
ἄλλοτε δ᾽ αὖ δίχ᾽ ἕκαστα φορεύμενα νείκεος ἔχθει.
⟨οὕτως ᾗ μὲν ἓν ἐκ πλεόνων μεμάθηκε φύεσθαι⟩
10　ἠδὲ πάλιν διαφύντος ἑνὸς πλέον᾽ ἐκτελέθουσι,
τῇ μὲν γίγνονταί τε καὶ οὔ σφισιν ἔμπεδος αἰών·
ᾗ δὲ διαλλάσσοντα διαμπερὲς οὐδαμὰ λήγει,
ταύτῃ δ᾽ αἰὲν ἔασιν ἀκίνητοι κατὰ κύκλον.
ἀλλ᾽ ἄγε μύθων κλῦθι, μάθη γάρ τοι φρένας αὔξει·
15　ὡς γὰρ καὶ πρὶν ἔειπα πιφαύσκων πείρατα μύθων,
δίπλ᾽ ἐρέω· τοτὲ μὲν γὰρ ἓν ηὐξήθη μόνον εἶναι
ἐκ πλεόνων, τοτὲ δ᾽ αὖ διέφυ πλέον᾽ ἐξ ἑνὸς εἶναι,
πῦρ καὶ ὕδωρ καὶ γαῖα καὶ ἠέρος ἄπλετον ὕψος·
νεῖκός τ᾽ οὐλόμενον δίχα τῶν, ἀτάλαντον ἁπάντῃ,
20　καὶ φιλότης ἐν τοῖσιν, ἴση μῆκός τε πλάτος τε·
τὴν σὺ νόῳ δέρκευ, μηδ᾽ ὄμμασιν ἧσο τεθηπώς·
ἥτις καὶ θνητοῖσι νομίζεται ἔμφυτος ἄρθροις,
τῇ τε φίλα φρονέουσι καὶ ἄρθμια ἔργα τελοῦσι,
Γηθοσύνην καλέοντες ἐπώνυμον ἠδ᾽ Ἀφροδίτην·
25　τὴν οὔ τις μετὰ τοῖσιν ἑλισσομένην δεδάηκε
θνητὸς ἀνήρ· σὺ δ᾽ ἄκουε λόγου στόλον οὐκ ἀπατηλόν.
ταῦτα γὰρ ἶσά τε πάντα καὶ ἥλικα γένναν ἔασι,
τιμῆς δ᾽ ἄλλης ἄλλο μέδει, πάρα δ᾽ ἦθος ἑκάστῳ,
ἐν δὲ μέρει κρατέουσι περιπλομένοιο χρόνοιο.
30　καὶ πρὸς τοῖς οὐδ᾽ †ἄρ τι† ἐπιγίγνεται οὐδ᾽ ἀπολήγει·
εἴτε γὰρ ἐφθείροντο διαμπερές, οὐκέτ᾽ ἂν ἦσαν.
τοῦτο δ᾽ ἐπαυξήσειε τὸ πᾶν τί κε, καὶ πόθεν ἐλθόν;
πῇ δέ κε κἠξαπόλοιτο, ἐπεὶ τῶνδ᾽ οὐδὲν ἐρῆμον;
ἀλλ᾽ αὔτ᾽ ἔστιν ταῦτα, δι᾽ ἀλλήλων δὲ θέοντα
35　γίγνεται ἄλλοτε ἄλλα καὶ ἠνεκὲς αἰὲν ὁμοῖα.

1–2 (=16–17) Simp. in Phys. 161.6　　7–13 (om. 9) Simp. in Cael. 141.1,
293.25　　7–8 Simp. in Phys. 25.29, 1318.25, in Cael. 530.14, Stob. 1.10.11,
D.L. 8.76　　9–13 Arist. Phys. 250b30　　11 Simp. in Phys. 1124.23　　12–
13 Simp. in Phys. 160.20, 1125.1　　14 Stob. 2.31.6, Clem. Strom. 5.85.3
17–20 Simp. in Phys. 26.1　　18–20 S.E. adv. math. 9.10　　18 Plu. amic. 63d,
Clem. Strom. 6.17.4　　18, 20 Athenagoras 22　　19–20 S.E. adv. math. 10.317,
Hippol. RH 10.7.3　　20–21 Plu. amat. 756d　　21 Simp. in Phys. 188.26.
Clem. Strom. 5.15.4　　27 Arist. GC 333a19, Phlp. in GC 258.4, 261.22　　29
Simp. in Phys. 1184.7　　32 MXG 975b1, cf. 976b25

5 δρυφθεῖσα E : θρεφθεῖσα Panzerbieter   διέπτη Scaliger   **9** ex Arist.
Phys. 250b30 (cf. 16 (26))   **14** μάθη Bergk : μέθη codd. : μάθησις Stob.,
Clem.   **18** αἰθέρος Plu., Clem.   **20** φιλίη S.E. 10.317, Athenagoras :
φιλία Hippol.   ἐν] μετὰ S.E., Athenagoras, Hippol.   **25** μετὰ τοῖσιν
Brandis : μετ' ὄσσοισιν (ὄσοισιν F) codd.   **30** οὐδ' ἄρ ἐπιγίνεται οὐδ' F :
οὔτ' ἄρ τέ τι γίγνεται οὔτ' Diels   **32** πόθεν οὖν τί κ' ἐπέλθοι *MXG*
976b : παντί τε καὶ ἐλθόν *MXG* 975b   **33** κἠξαπόλοιτο Diels : κε καὶ
κήρυξ ἀπόλοιτο codd. : κῆρ' ἀπόλοιτο Bollack

9(12) *MXG* 975a36
ἔτι εἰ καὶ ὅτι μάλιστα μήτε τὸ μὴ ὂν ἐνδέχεται γενέσθαι μήτε ἀπολέσθαι
τὸ μὴ ὄν, ὅμως τί κωλύει τὰ μὲν γενόμενα αὐτῶν εἶναι, τὰ δὲ ἀίδια, ὡς
καὶ 'Ε. λέγει; ἅπαντα γὰρ κἀκεῖνος ταὐτὰ ὁμολογήσας, ὅτι

> ἐκ γὰρ τοῦ μὴ ἐόντος ἀμήχανόν ἐστι γενέσθαι,
> καί τ' ἐὸν ἐξαπόλεσθαι ἀνήνυστον καὶ ἄπυστον·
> αἰεὶ γὰρ †θήσεσθαι† ὅπῃ κέ τις αἰὲν ἐρείδῃ.

ὅμως τῶν ὄντων τὰ μὲν ἀίδια εἶναί φησι, πῦρ καὶ ὕδωρ καὶ γῆν καὶ ἀέρα,
τὰ δ' ἄλλα γίνεσθαί τε καὶ γεγονέναι ἐκ τούτων. οὐδεμία γὰρ ἑτέρα, ὡς οἴεται, γένεσίς ἐστι τοῖς οὖσιν.

1-2 Philo *aet. mund.* 2

---

1 ἐκ γὰρ τοῦ μὴ ἐόντος scripsi : ἔκ τε μὴ ὄντος codd. : ἐκ τοῦ γὰρ οὐδαμῇ
ὄντος Philo : ἔκ τε γὰρ οὐδάμ' ἐόντος Diels   **2** καί τ' ἐὸν Diels : τό τε
ὄν codd. : τι τό τε ὄν Philo   ἐξαπόλεσθαι Diels : ἐξόλλυσθαι codd. :
ἐξαπολεῖσθαι Philo   ἄπυστον Diels : ἄπρηκτον codd. : ἄπαυστον Philo
3 τῇ γ' ἔσται Panzerbieter, Diels : περιέσται Mullach : τοι θήσετ' Wyttenbach

10(13) *MXG* 976b22
ὁμοίως δὲ καὶ ὁ 'Ε. κινεῖσθαι μὲν ἀεί φησι συγκρινούμενα τὸν ἅπαντα ἐνδελεχῶς χρόνον, οὐδὲν εἶναι λέγων ὡς τοῦ παντός, οὐδὲ κενεόν. πόθεν οὖν τί
κ' ἐπέλθοι; ὅταν δὲ εἰς μίαν μορφὴν συγκριθῇ, ὡς ἓν εἶναι,

> οὐδέ τι τοῦ παντὸς κενεὸν πέλει οὐδὲ περισσόν

1 Aet. 1.18.2 Theodoret. 4.14

οὐδέ τι τοῦ παντὸς κενεὸν Aet. : *οὐδέν (φησι) τό γε κενεὸν* codd.

11(16) Hippolytus *RH* 7.29.10

καὶ ἔστι πάντων τῶν γεγονότων τῆς γενέσεως δημιουργὸς καὶ ποιητὴς τὸ νεῖκος τὸ ὀλέθριον, τῆς δὲ ἐκ τοῦ κόσμου τῶν γεγονότων ἐξαγωγῆς καὶ μεταβολῆς καὶ εἰς τὸ ἓν ἀποκαταστάσεως ἡ φιλία· περὶ ὧν ὁ ᾽Ε. ὅτι ἐστιν ἀθάνατα δύο καὶ ἀγένητα καὶ ἀρχὴν τοῦ γενέσθαι μηδέποτε εἰληφότα, ἄλλα λέγει τοιοῦτόν τινα τρόπον.

> *ἔ⟨στ⟩ι γὰρ ὡς πάρος ἦν τε καὶ ἔσσεται, οὐδέ ποτ᾽ οἴω*
> *τούτων ἀμφοτέρων κενεώσεται ἄσπετος αἰών.*

τίνων τούτων; τοῦ νεῖκος καὶ τῆς φιλίας· οὐ γὰρ ἤρξαντο γενέσθαι, ἀλλὰ προῆσαν καὶ ἔσονται ἀεὶ δια τὴν ἀγεννησίαν φθορὰν ὑπομεῖναι μὴ δυνάμενα· τὸ δὲ πῦρ ⟨καὶ τὸ ὕδωρ⟩ καὶ ἡ γῆ καὶ ὁ ἀὴρ θνήσκοντα καὶ ἀναβιοῦντα.

1–2 Hippol. *RH* 6.25.1

---

1 *ἔστι γὰρ ὡς πάρος ἦν* Lloyd-Jones : *εἰ (ἦν* 6.25) *γὰρ καὶ πάρος ἦν* codd. : *ἢ γὰρ καὶ πάρος ἔσκε* Diels   *ἔσσεται οὐδέ ποτ᾽ οἴω* Miller : *καὶ ἔσται οὐδέπω τοίω* codd.   **2** *κενεώσεται* Diels : *κενώσεται (καινὸς ἔσται* 6.25) codd. : *κεινώσεται* Miller   *ἄσπετος* Miller : *ἄσβετος* codd.

12(8) Aetius 1.30.1

᾽Ε. φύσιν μηδενὸς εἶναι, μίξιν δὲ τῶν στοιχείων καὶ διάστασιν, γράφει γὰρ οὕτως ἐν τῷ πρώτῳ Φυσικῶν·

> *ἄλλο δέ τοι ἐρέω· φύσις οὐδενὸς ἐστιν ἀπάντων*
> *θνητῶν, οὐδέ τις οὐλομένου θανάτοιο τελευτή,*
> *ἀλλὰ μόνον μίξις τε διάλλαξίς τε μιγέντων*
> *ἐστί, φύσις δ᾽ ἐπὶ τοῖς ὀνομάζεται ἀνθρώποισιν.*

1–4 Plu. *adv. Col.* 1111f   1, 3–4 Arist. *Metaph.* 1015a1   1, 3 Arist. *GC* 314b7   3 Arist. *GC* 333b14, Simp. *in Phys.* 161.19, 180.30, 235.23, *in Cael.* 306.5, Phlp. *in Phys.* 840.8, 896.26, *in GC* 14.18, 15.8, 16, 263.21, Alex. Aphr. *in Metaph.* 359.19   3–4 MXG 975b7 (cf. Tz. *ex. Il.* 54.25)   4 cf. Ascl. *in Metaph.* 311.33

1 ἀπάντων] ἐόντων Arist. *Metaph.*, om. *GC* : ἑκάστου Plu.   **2** οὐλομένου
θανάτοιο τελευτή codd. : οὐλομένη θανάτοιο γενέθλη Plu.

13(9) Plutarch. *adv. Col.* 1113a

τοσοῦτον δ' ἐδέησε (ὁ 'Ε.) τοῦ κινεῖν τὰ ὄντα καὶ μάχεσθαι τοῖς φαινομένοις
ὥστε μηδὲ τὴν φωνὴν ἐκβαλεῖν ἐκ τῆς συνηθείας, ἀλλ' ὅσον εἰς τὰ πράγματα
βλάπτουσαν ἀπάτην παρεῖχεν ἀφελὼν αὖθις ἀποδοῦναι τοῖς ὀνόμασι τὸ
νενομισμένον ἐν τούτοις·

> οἱ δ' ὅτε μὲν κατὰ φῶτα μιγέντ' εἰς αἰθέρ' ἵ⟨κωνται⟩
> ἢ κατὰ θηρῶν ἀγροτέρων γένος ἢ κατὰ θάμνων
> ἠὲ κατ' οἰωνῶν, τότε μὲν τό ⟨γέ φασι⟩ γενέσθαι,
> εὖτε δ' ἀποκρινθῶσι, τὸ δ' αὖ δυσδαίμονα πότμον·
> 5 †ἦ θέμις† καλέουσι, νόμῳ δ' ἐπίφημι καὶ αὐτός.

ἃ ὁ Κολώτης παραθέμενος οὐ συνεῖδεν ὅτι φῶτας μὲν καὶ θῆρας καὶ θάμνους
καὶ οἰωνοὺς ὁ 'Ε. οὐκ ἀνήρηκεν, ἅ γέ φησι μιγνυμένων τῶν στοιχείων ἀποτελεῖσθαι, τοὺς δὲ τῇ συγκρίσει ταύτῃ καὶ διακρίσει "φύσιν" τινὰ καὶ "πότμον
δυσδαίμονα" καὶ "θάνατον ἀλοίτην" ἐπικατηγοροῦντας ᾗ σφάλλονται διδάξας
οὐκ ἀφείλετο τὸ χρῆσθαι ταῖς εἰθισμέναις φωναῖς περὶ αὐτῶν.

5 Plu. *praec. reip.* 820f, cf. *adv. Col.* 1112f

---

1 μιγέντ' εἰς αἰθέρ' ἵκωνται Diels : μίγεν φῶς αἰθέρι lac. vi-viii litt. codd. :
μιγὲν φάος αἰθέρος ἵκῃ Mullach   **3** τό γέ φασι scripsi : τον lac. vi litt.
codd. : τὸ λέγουσι Reiske, Diels : τάδε φασι Xylander : τὸ νέμουσι Burnet
5 ἦ θέμις καλέουσι Plu. 820 : εἶναι καλέουσι codd. : ἦ θέμις οὐ καλέουσι
Wyttenbach, Diels : οὐ θέμις ἦ καλέουσι Wilam.   νόμῳ] ὅμως codd. : νόμῳ
Plu. 820

14(21) Simplicius *in Phys.* 159.10 [post 8(17).1-35]
πλείονα δὲ ἄλλα εἰπὼν (ὁ 'Ε.) ἐπάγει ἑκάστου τῶν εἰρημένων τὸν χαρακτῆρα,
τὸ μὲν πῦρ ἥλιον καλῶν, τὸν δὲ ἀέρα αὐγὴν καὶ οὐρανόν, τὸ δὲ ὕδωρ ὄμβρον
καὶ θάλασσαν. λέγει δὲ οὕτως·

> ἀλλ' ἄγε, τῶνδ' ὀάρων προτέρων ἐπιμάρτυρα δέρκευ,
> εἴ τι καὶ ἐν προτέροισι λιπόξυλον ἔπλετο μορφῇ,
> ἠέλιον μὲν λευκὸν ὁρᾶν καὶ θερμὸν ἁπάντη,
> ἄμβροτα δ' ὅσσ' †ἐδεῖτο† καὶ ἀργέτι δεύεται αὐγῇ,

5 ὄμβρον δ' ἐν πᾶσι δνοφόεντά τε ῥιγαλέον τε·
   ἐκ δ' αἴης προρέουσι †θέλημα† τε καὶ στερεωπά.
   ἐν δὲ κότῳ διάμορφα καὶ ἄνδιχα πάντα πέλονται,
   σὺν δ' ἔβη ἐν φιλότητι καὶ ἀλλήλοισι ποθεῖται.
   ἐκ τῶν πάνθ' ὅσα τ' ἦν ὅσα τ' ἔστι καὶ ἔσται ὀπίσσω,
10 δένδρεά τ' ἐβλάστησε καὶ ἀνέρες ἠδὲ γυναῖκες,
   θῆρές τ' οἰωνοί τε καὶ ὑδατοθρέμμονες ἰχθῦς,
   καί τε θεοὶ δολιχαίωνες τιμῇσι φέριστοι.
   αὐτὰ γὰρ ἔστιν ταῦτα, δι' ἀλλήλων δὲ θέοντα
   γίγνεται ἀλλοιωπά· †τόγον διάκρισις† ἀμείβει.

3–12 Simp. *in Phys.* 33.8   **3–4** Plu. *de prim. frig.* 949f   **3, 5** Arist. *GC*
314 b20   **3** Gal. *simpl. med.* 11.461K   **9–12** Arist. *Metaph.* 1000a29   **9–11**
[Arist.] *mund.* 399b26   **9** Clem. *Strom.* 6.17.4   **10–13** Ascl. *in Metaph.*
197.33

---

2 μορφῇ Ald. : μορφή codd.   **3** λευκὸν . . . θερμὸν Arist. : λαμπρὸν . . .
θερμὸν Plu. : θερμὸν . . . λαμπρὸν codd., Gal.   ὅρα EL(Arist.), Plu. : ὁρᾷ F
(Simp. 32)   **4** ὅσσ' ἔδεται DE, ὅσσε δέ τε F (Simp. 33) : ὅσσ' ἴδει τε
Diels : ὅσσ' εἴδει τε Wackernagel   **5** δνοφόεντα (ζοφ-HL) Arist., Plu.
exc. gX : δνοφέοντα codd., gX(Plu.)   **6** θέλημνα ED², θελήματα F (Simp.
33) : θέλυμνα Diels : θελεμνά Wilam.   στερέωμα Simp. 33   **9** scripsi :
ἐκ τούτων γὰρ πάνθ' ὅσα τ' ἦν (παντὸς ἄτην D, πάντ' ἦν F) ὅσα τ' ἔστι
καὶ ἔσται codd., om. γὰρ Diels : ἐκ τούτων γὰρ πάντα ὅσα τε ἦν ὅσα τέ
ἐστι καὶ ἔσται Simp. 33 : ἐξ ὧν πάνθ' ὅσα τ' ἦν ὅσα τ' ἐσθ' ὅσα τ' ἔσται
ὀπίσσω Arist. : ἐκ γὰρ τῶν ὅσα γῆν ὅσα τ' ἔσσεται ὅσα τ' ἔασιν Clem.
14 τόγον διάκρισις D, τόγον διάκρασις E : τόσον διὰ κρῆσις Diels : τὰ γὰρ
δία κρῆσις conieci

15(23) Simplicius *in Phys.* 159.27 [post 14(21).1–14]
καὶ παράδειγμα δὲ ἐναργὲς παρέθετο τοῦ ἐκ τῶν αὐτῶν γίνεσθαι τὰ διάφορα·

   ὡς δ' ὁπόταν γραφέες ἀναθήματα ποικίλλωσιν,
   ἀνέρες ἀμφὶ τέχνης ὑπὸ μήτιος εὖ δεδαῶτε,
   οἵ τ' ἐπεὶ οὖν μάρψωσι πολύχροα φάρμακα χερσίν,
   ἁρμονίῃ μίξαντε τὰ μὲν πλέω, ἄλλα δ' ἐλάσσω,
5 ἐκ τῶν εἴδεα πᾶσιν ἀλίγκια πορσύνουσι,
   δένδρεά τε κτίζοντε καὶ ἀνέρας ἠδὲ γυναῖκας,
   θῆράς τ' οἰωνούς τε καὶ ὑδατοθρέμμονας ἰχθῦς,
   καί τε θεοὺς δολιχαίωνας τιμῇσι φερίστους·

οὕτω μή σ' ἀπάτη φρένα καινύτω ἄλλοθεν εἶναι
10 θνητῶν, ὅσσα γε δῆλα †γεγάασιν† ἄσπετα, πηγήν,
ἀλλὰ τορῶς ταῦτ' ἴσθι, θεοῦ πάρα μῦθον ἀκούσας.

2 ἄμφω codd. : ἄμφι Ald.   δεδαῶτες F   4 ἀρμονίη F, ἀρμενίη DE
μίξαντες D   6 κτίζοντες D   9 μή σ'] μήν F   καινύτω Blass :
καί νυ τῳ D, καί νυ τω F, καί νυ τῷ E   10 γεγάκασιν Diels

16(26) Simplicius in Phys. 33.18 [post 14(21).1-12]
καὶ ὀλίγον δὲ προελθών φησιν

ἐν δὲ μέρει κρατέουσι περιπλομένοιο κύκλοιο,
καὶ φθίνει εἰς ἄλληλα καὶ αὔξεται ἐν μέρει αἴσης.
αὐτὰ γὰρ ἔστιν ταῦτα, δι' ἀλλήλων δὲ θέοντα
γίγνοντ' ἄνθρωποί τε καὶ ἄλλων ἔθνεα θηρῶν,
5 ἄλλοτε μὲν φιλότητι συνερχόμεν' εἰς ἕνα κόσμον,
ἄλλοτε δ' αὖ δίχ' ἕκαστα φορεύμενα νείκεος ἔχθει,
εἰσόκεν †ἓν† συμφύντα τὸ πᾶν ὑπένερθε γένηται.
οὕτως ἧ μὲν ἓν ἐκ πλεόνων μεμάθηκε φύεσθαι,
ἠδὲ πάλιν διαφύντος ἑνὸς πλέον' ἐκτελέθουσι,
10 τῆ μὲν γίγνονταί τε καὶ οὔ σφισιν ἔμπεδος αἰών·
ἧ δὲ τάδ' ἀλλάσσοντα διαμπερὲς οὐδαμὰ λήγει,
ταύτη δ' αἰὲν ἔασιν ἀκίνητοι κατὰ κύκλον.

1-2 Simp. in Phys. 160.16   1 Simp. in Phys. 1185.19   5-6 cf. 8(17).7-8
8-12 Arist. Phys. 250b20, cf. 8(17).9-13

4 θηρῶν Sturz : κηρῶν codd. : θνητῶν Bergk   6 φορεύμενα 8(17).8 :
φορούμενα codd.   7 ἐν E, ὃν F, ὃν D : ἂν Ald. : αὖ Bywater

17(25) Schol. in Plat. Gorg. 498e
παροιμία "δὶς καὶ τρὶς τὸ καλόν", ὅτι χρὴ περὶ τῶν καλῶν πολλάκις λέγειν.
Ἐ. τὸ ἔπος, ἀφ' οὗ καὶ ἡ παροιμία· φησὶ γὰρ

καὶ δὶς γάρ, ὃ δεῖ, καλόν ἐστιν ἐνισπεῖν,

Plu. s.v.s. Ep. 1103f

ἐνισπεῖν] ἀκοῦσαι Plu.

18(24) Plutarch *def. or.* 418c

ἀλλ' ἵνα μὴ τὸ 'Εμπεδόκλειον εἰπεῖν δόξω

κορυφὰς ἑτέρας ἑτέρῃσι προσάπτων
μύθων †μήτε λέγειν† ἀτραπὸν μίαν,

ἐάσατέ με τοῖς πρώτοις τὸ προσῆκον ἐπιθεῖναι τέλος· ἤδη γὰρ ἐπ' αὐτῷ γεγόναμεν.

2 μήτε λέγειν] μὴ τελέειν Knatz, Diels : μήτ' ἐλθεῖν Lloyd-Jones

19(27) Plutarch. *fac. lun.* 926d

ὥσθ' ὅρα καὶ σκόπει, δαιμόνιε, μὴ μεθιστὰς καὶ ἀπάγων ἕκαστον, ὅπου πέ-
φυκεν εἶναι, διάλυσίν τινα κόσμου φιλοσοφῇς καὶ τὸ νεῖκος ἐπάγῃς τὸ 'Ε.
τοῖς πράγμασι· μᾶλλον δὲ τοὺς παλαίους κινῇς Τιτᾶνας ἐπὶ τὴν φύσιν καὶ
Γίγαντας καὶ τὴν μυθικὴν ἐκείνην καὶ φοβερὰν ἀκοσμίαν καὶ πλημμέλειαν
ἐπιδεῖν ποθῇς, χωρὶς τὸ βαρὺ πᾶν καὶ χωρὶς τιθεὶς τὸ κοῦφον

ἔνθ' οὔτ' ἠελίοιο †δεδίττεται† ἀγλαὸν εἶδος,
οὐδὲ μὲν οὐδ' αἴης λάσιον μένος, οὐδὲ θάλασσα

ὥς φησιν 'Ε.· οὐ γῇ θερμότητος μετεῖχεν, οὐχ ὕδωρ πνεύματος, οὐκ ἄνω τι
τῶν βαρέων, οὐ κάτω τι τῶν κούφων, ἀλλ' ἄκρατοι καὶ ἄστοργοι καὶ μονάδες
αἱ τῶν ὅλων ἀρχαί, μὴ προσιέμεναι σύγκρισιν ἑτέρου πρὸς ἕτερον μηδὲ
κοινωνίαν, ἀλλὰ φεύγουσαι καὶ ἀποστρεφόμεναι καὶ φερόμεναι φορὰς ἰδίας
καὶ αὐθάδεις οὕτως εἶχον, ὡς ἔχει πᾶν οὗ θεὸς ἄπεστι κατὰ Πλάτωνα, τουτέστιν
ὡς ἔχει τὰ σώματα, νοῦ καὶ ψυχῆς ἀπολιπούσης.

1 δεδίσκεται Karsten   **2** μένος Bergk : γένος codd. : δέμας Karsten

20(36) Aristotle *Metaph.* 1000b1

εἰ γὰρ μὴ ἦν τὸ νεῖκος ἐν τοῖς πράγμασιν, ἓν ἂν ἦν ἅπαντα, ὥς φησίν ('Ε.).
ὅταν γὰρ συνέλθῃ, τότε δὲ

⟨τῶν δὲ συνερχομένων ἐξ⟩ ἔσχατον ἵστατο νεῖκος.

διὸ καὶ συμβαίνει αὐτῷ τὸν εὐδαιμονέστατον θεὸν ἧττον φρόνιμον εἶναι τῶν

TEXT															104

ἄλλων· οὐ γὰρ γνωρίζει τὰ στοιχεῖα πάντα· τὸ γὰρ νεῖκος οὐκ ἔχει, ἡ δὲ
γνῶσις τοῦ ὁμοίου τῷ ὁμοίῳ.

Ascl. in Metaph. 198.1, Stob. I.10.11

τῶν δὲ συνερχομένων ἐξ suppl. ex Stobaeo

21(27) Simplicius in Phys. 1183.24
τοῦτο δὲ "ἔοικεν 'Ε. ἂν εἰπεῖν, ὅτε λέγει ὅτι το κρατεῖν καὶ κινεῖν ἐν μέρει
τὴν φιλίαν καὶ τὸ νεῖκος ἐξ ἀνάγκης ὑπάρχει τοῖς πράγμασιν," εἰ δὲ καὶ
τοῦτο, καὶ τὸ ἠρεμεῖν ἐν τῷ μεταξὺ χρόνῳ· τῶν γὰρ ἐναντίων κινήσεων ἠρεμία μεταξύ ἐστιν. Εὔδημος δὲ τὴν ἀκινησίαν ἐν τῇ τῆς φιλίας ἐπικρατείᾳ
κατὰ τόν σφαῖρον ἐκδέχεται, ἐπειδὰν ἅπαντα συγκριθῇ,

	ἔνθ' οὔτ' ἠελίοιο διείδεται ὠκέα γυῖα,

ἀλλ', ὥς φησιν,

	οὕτως ἁρμονίης πυκινῷ κρυφῷ ἐστήρικται
	σφαῖρος κυκλοτερὴς μονίῃ περιηγέι γαίων.

3 Simp. in Cael. 591.5, Procl. in Tim. 160d, Ach. Tat Intr. Arat. 6 (37.13),
Anon. in Arat. 1.6 (97.25), M. Ant. 12.3

2 ἁρμονίης Α, ἁρμονίας Μ, ἁρμονίως F   κρυφῷ Α, κρυφῶ Μ, κρύφει F
ἐστήρικται ΑΜ, ἐστήρικτο F   3 σφαίρας κυκλοτερεῖ Anon.   μονιῇ Μ,
μονη lac. iv litt. F : μόνη DE (in Cael.), Procl. : μούνη Ach. : μανία Anon.
περιγηθέι Μ, περιγήθει AF, E (in Cael.) : περὶ γήθει F, περὶ γῆθ ἤ D, πε-
ριήγη Ε² (in Cael.)   γαίων in Cael. : αἰων codd. : χαίρων Ach., Anon., Q
(Procl.): χαῖρον cet. codd. Procl.

22(29/28) Hippolytus RH 7.29.13
καὶ περὶ μὲν τῆς τοῦ κόσμου ἰδέας, ὁποία τίς ἐστιν ὑπὸ τῆς φιλίας κοσμου-
μένη, λέγει ('Ε.) τοιοῦτόν τινα τρόπον·

	οὐ γὰρ ἀπὸ νώτοιο δύο κλάδοι ἀίσσονται,
	οὐ πόδες, οὐ θοὰ γοῦν', οὐ μήδεα γεννήεντα,

ἀλλὰ σφαῖρος ἔην καὶ ἶσος ἔστιν αὐτῷ. τοιοῦτόν τι καὶ κάλλιστον εἶδος τοῦ κόσμου ἡ φιλία ἐκ πολλῶν ἓν ἀπεργάζεται· τὸ δὲ νεῖκος, τὸ τῆς τῶν κατὰ μέρος διακοσμήσεως αἴτιον, ἐξ ἑνὸς ἐκείνου ἀποσπᾷ καὶ ἀπεργάζεται πολλά.

Stobaeus 1.15.2

> ἀλλ' ὅ γε πάντοθεν ἶσος ⟨ἑοῖ⟩ καὶ πάμπαν ἀπείρων,
> σφαῖρος κυκλοτερὴς μονίῃ περιηγέι γαίων.

2 γοῦν' 97(134).3 : γούνατ' codd.   **3** ἑοῖ add. Maas : ἔην Diels   **4** μονίῃ περιηγέι γαίων 21(27).3 : μιμίῃς περιτεθῇ (-τείθη P) χαίρων codd.

23(30) Aristotle *Metaph.* 1000b9
ἀλλ' ὅθεν δὴ ὁ λόγος, τοῦτό γε φανερόν, ὅτι συμβαίνει αὐτῷ τὸ νεῖκος μηθὲν μᾶλλον φθορᾶς ἢ τοῦ εἶναι αἴτιον. ὁμοίως δ' οὐδ' ἡ φιλότης τοῦ εἶναι· συνάγουσα γὰρ εἰς τὸ ἓν φθείρει τἆλλα. καὶ ἅμα δὲ αὐτῆς τῆς μεταβολῆς αἴτιον οὐθὲν λέγει, ἀλλ' ἢ ὅτι οὕτως πέφυκεν·

> αὐτὰρ ἐπεὶ μέγα νεῖκος ἐνὶ μελέεσσιν ἐθρέφθη,
> ἐς τιμάς τ' ἀνόρουσε τελειομένοιο χρόνοιο,
> ὅς σφιν ἀμοιβαῖος πλατέος παρ' ἐλήλαται ὅρκου

ὡς ἀναγκαῖον μὲν ὂν μεταβάλλειν· αἰτίαν δὲ τῆς ἀνάγκης δηλοῖ.

1–3 Simp. *in Phys.* 1184.14   **2–3** Syrian. *in Metaph.* 43.34   **3** Ascl. *in Metaph.* 198.33

---

1 αὐτὰρ ἐπεὶ Simp. : ἀλλ' ὅτε δὴ codd.   ἐν μελέεσσιν F (Simp.) : ἐνιμμελέεσσιν A(Simp.), Diels   ἐρέφθη Simp.   **2** ἐς Simp. : εἰς (ἐπὶ GᵇIᵇ, Syrian.) codd.   **3** ὃ σφιν ἀμοιβᾷς F (Simp.)   παρ' ἐλήλαται Diels : παρελήλατο ETCᵇ, Ascl. : παρήλατο SBᵇ : παρελήλαται Aᵇ, Simp. : παρ' ἐλήλατο Sturz

24(31) Simplicius *in Phys.* 1184.2 [post 21(27).3]
ἀρξαμένου δὲ πάλιν τοῦ νείκους ἐπικρατεῖν τότε πάλιν κίνησις ἐν τῷ σφαίρῳ γίνεται·

> πάντα γὰρ ἐξείης πελεμίζετο γυῖα θεοῖο.

πελεμίζετο A, πολεμίζετο FM   γυῖα] γαῖα F

25(22) Simplicius *in Phys.* 160.26

καὶ ἐκ τούτων δὲ ἄν τις τὸν διττὸν αἰνίττεσθαι διάκοσμον οἴοιτο·

> ἄρθμια μὲν γὰρ ταῦτα ἑαυτῶν πάντα μέρεσσιν,
> ἠλέκτωρ τε χθών τε καὶ οὐρανὸς ἠδὲ θάλασσα,
> ὅσσα φιν ἐν θνητοῖσιν ἀποπλαχθέντα πέφυκεν.
> ὡς δ' αὔτως ὅσα κρῆσιν ἐπαρκέα μᾶλλον ἔασιν
> 5 ἀλλήλοις ἔστερκται ὁμοιωθέντ' Ἀφροδίτῃ·
> ἐχθρὰ μάλιστ' ⟨ὅσα⟩ πλεῖστον ἀπ' ἀλλήλων διέχουσι
> γέννῃ τε κρήσει τε καὶ εἴδεσιν ἐκμακτοῖσι,
> πάντῃ συγγίγνεσθαι ἀήθεα καὶ μάλα λυγρά
> †νεικεογεννέστησιν† ὅτι σφισι †γένναν ὀργᾷ†.

καὶ γὰρ ὅτι καὶ ἐν τοῖς θνητοῖς ἥρμοσται ταῦτα, δεδήλωκεν, ἐν δὲ τοῖς νοητοῖς μᾶλλον ἥνωται καὶ "ἀλλήλοις ἔστερκται ὁμοιωθέντα Ἀφροδίτῃ," καὶ ὅτι κἂν πανταχοῦ, ἀλλὰ τὰ μὲν νοητὰ τῇ φιλίᾳ ὡμοίωται, τὰ δὲ αἰσθητὰ ὑπὸ τοῦ νείκους κρατηθέντα καὶ ἐπὶ πλέον διασπασθέντα ἐν τῇ κατὰ τὴν κρᾶσιν γενέσει ἐν ἐκμακτοῖς καὶ εἰκονικοῖς εἴδεσιν ὑπέστησαν τοῖς νεικεογενέσι καὶ ἀήθως ἔχουσι πρὸς τὴν ἕνωσιν τὴν πρὸς ἄλληλα.

6–7 (πλεῖστον . . . ἐκμακτοῖσιν) Thphr. *Sens.* 16

---

1 ἄρτια F   ταῦτα Diels : αὐτὰ F, ἑαυτὰ DE   **3** ἀποπλαχθέντα D, ἀποπλαγχθέντα EF   **4** κρᾶσιν codd.   **6** ἐχθρὰ Thphr. : ἔχθρα F, ἔργα DE   μάλιστ' ὅσα πλεῖστον ἀπ' ἀλλήλων διέχουσι conieci : πλεῖστον ἀπ' ἀλλήλων διέχουσι μάλιστα codd., om. μάλιστα Thphr. : ⟨δ' ἃ⟩ suppl. Diels   **7** κράσει codd.   **8–9** om. F   **9** νεικεογεννηταῖσι Scaliger, νεικεογεννητῇσι Karsten : νείκεος ἐννεσίῃσιν Panzerbieter, Diels   γένναν ἔοργεν Diels : πᾶν δέμας ὀργᾷ Karsten : γένναι ἐν ὀργῇ conieci

---

26(20) Simplicius *in Phys.* 1124.7

δυνατὸν δὲ καὶ ἐν τῷ ὑπὸ σελήνην ἄμφω θεωρεῖν τήν τε ἕνωσιν καὶ τὴν διάκρισιν ἀεὶ μὲν ἄμφω, ἄλλοτε δὲ ἄλλην ἐν ἄλλοις καὶ ἄλλοις μέρεσιν ἢ ἐν ἄλλοις καὶ ἄλλοις χρόνοις ἐπικρατοῦσαν. καὶ γὰρ καὶ ἐνταῦθα τὸ νεῖκος καὶ τὴν φιλίαν παρὰ μέρος ἐπικρατεῖν ἐπί τε ἀνθρώπων καὶ ἰχθύων καὶ θηρίων καὶ ὀρνέων ὁ Ἐ. φησι τάδε γράφων·

> τοῦτο μὲν ἀμ βροτέων μελέων ἀριδείκετον ὄγκον·

ἄλλοτε μὲν φιλότητι συνερχόμεν' εἰς ἓν ἅπαντα
γυῖα, τὰ σῶμα λέλογχε, βίου θαλέθοντος ἐν ἀκμῇ·
ἄλλοτε δ' αὖτε κακῇσι διατμηθέντ' ἐρίδεσσι
5 πλάζεται ἄνδιχ' ἕκαστα περὶ ῥηγμῖνι βίοιο.
ὡς δ' αὔτως θάμνοισι καὶ ἰχθύσιν ὑδρομελάθροις
θηρσί τ' ὀρειλεχέεσσιν ἰδὲ πτεροβάμοσι κύμβαις.

1 τοῦτον codd.   ἀμβροτέρων Μ, ἂν βροτέων AF : ἀν βροτέων Diels
2 cf. 8(17).7   3 σώματα FM   θαλέοντος F : θαλέθουσιν Karsten
4 ἐρίδεσσι Ald. : ἐρίδεσι Α, ἐρίδεσιν F, ἐργιδέσιος Μ   5 περὶ ῥηγμήνεσι
F, περίρρηγμῖνι Α, Diels   6 ὑδρομελάκροις Μ   7 θηρσί τ' ὀρειλεχέεσσιν Schneider : θηρσί τ' ὀρειμελέεσσιν ΑΜ, θερσί τε ῥημελέεσσιν F   ἠδὲ
πτεροβάσι Μ, ἠδέπερ F

27(38) Clement *Strom.* 5.48.2
σφίγξ δὲ οὐχ ἡ τῶν ὅλων σύνδεσις καὶ ἡ τοῦ κόσμου κατὰ τὸν ποιητὴν
Ἄρατον περιφορά, ἀλλὰ τάχα μὲν ὁ διήκων πνευματικὸς τόνος καὶ συνέχων
τὸν κόσμον εἴη ἄν· ἄμεινον δὲ ἐκδέχεσθαι τὸν αἰθέρα πάντα συνέχοντα καὶ
σφίγγοντα, καθὰ καὶ ὁ Ἐ. φησιν·

el δ' ἄγε τοι λέξω †πρῶθ' ἥλιον ἀρχήν
ἐξ ὧν δὴ† ἐγένοντο τὰ νῦν ἐσορῶμεν ἅπαντα,
γαῖά τε καὶ πόντος πολυκύμων ἠδ' ὑγρὸς ἀήρ
Τιτὰν ἠδ' αἰθὴρ σφίγγων περὶ κύκλον ἅπαντα.

1 πρῶτ' ἐξ ὧν ἥλιος ἀρχήν / τἄλλα τε δῆλ' conieci (δῆλ' H. Weil) : πρῶθ'
ἥλικα τ' ἀρχήν / ἐξ ὧν δῆλ' Diels : ἠλίου ἀρχήν Stein   2 ἐσορώμενα
πάντα codd. corr. Gomperz

28(51) Eustathius *ad Od.* 1.321
οἱ δὲ τὸ ἀνόπαια λέγουσιν ἀντὶ τοῦ ἀφανής, πόρρω τῆς ὄψεως. δοκεῖ δέ
τισι καὶ ἀντὶ τοῦ ἀνωφερὴς εἶναι, ὡρμημένοις ἐκ τῶν Ἐ. εἰπόντος ἐπὶ πυρὸς
τό

καρπαλίμως δ' ἀνόπαιον.

Hdn. *schem. Hom.* (*EM* 311 D)

────────────

δὲ ἀνόπεαν Hdn.

29(53) Aristotle *Phys.* 196a20

. . . ὥσπερ 'E. οὐκ ἀεὶ τὸν ἀέρα ἀνωτάτω ἀποκρίνεσθαί φησιν, ἀλλ' ὅπως ἂν τύχῃ. λέγει γοῦν ἐν τῇ κοσμοποιίᾳ ὡς

οὕτω γὰρ συνέκυρσε θέων τότε, πολλάκι δ' ἄλλως.

καὶ τὰ μόρια τῶν ζῴων ἀπὸ τύχης γενέσθαι τὰ πλεῖστα φησίν.

Arist. *GC* 334a3, Simp. *in Phys.* 327.18, 330.35, 358.11, 1318.28, Phlp. *in Phys.* 261.22, Them. *in Phys.* 49.9

30(54) Aristotle *GC* 334a4 [post 29(53)]

ὅτε δέ φησι πεφυκέναι τὸ πῦρ ἄνω φέρεσθαι, ὁ δ' αἰθήρ, φησί,

μακρῇσι κατὰ χθόνα δύετο ῥίζαις.

31(37) Aristotle *GC* 333a35

ἀλλὰ μὴν οὐδ' αὔξησις ἂν εἴη κατ' 'E., ἀλλ' ἢ κατὰ πρόσθεσιν· πυρὶ γὰρ αὔξει τὸ πῦρ,

αὔξει δὲ χθὼν μὲν σφέτερον δέμας, αἰθέρα δ' αἰθήρ.

δέμας H, γένος cet. codd.

32(52) Proclus *in Tim.* 141e

καὶ γὰρ ὑπὸ γῆς ῥυακές εἰσι πυρός, ὥς πού φησι καὶ 'E.·

πολλὰ δ' ἔνερθ' οὔδεος πυρὰ καίεται.

καὶ οὐ δεῖ θαυμάζειν, πῶς οὖν ἐν ὕδατι ὂν τὸ πῦρ οὐ σβέννυται· χωρεῖ γὰρ πάντα δι' ἀλλήλων, καὶ ἔστι τὸ ἐπικρατοῦν ἄλλο ἐν ἄλλοις, καὶ ἔστι καὶ τὸ φῶς πῦρ διιὸν διὰ πάντων.

ἔνερθεν codd. corr. Sturz

33(39) Aristotle *Cael.* 294a21

οἱ μὲν γὰρ διὰ ταῦτα ἄπειρον τὸ κάτω τῆς γῆς εἶναί φασιν, ἐπ' ἄπειρον αὐτὴν ἐρριζῶσθαι λέγοντες, ὥσπερ Ξενοφάνης ὁ Κολοφώνιος, ἵνα μὴ πράγματ' ἔχωσι ζητοῦντες τὴν αἰτίαν· διὸ καὶ 'E. οὕτως ἐπέπληξεν, εἰπὼν ὡς

εἴπερ ἀπείρονα γῆς τε βάθη καὶ δαψιλὸς αἰθήρ,
ὡς διὰ πολλῶν δὴ γλώσσης ἐλθόντα ματαίως
ἐκκέχυται στομάτων, ὀλίγον τοῦ παντὸς ἰδόντων . . .

1–3 *MXG* 976a35   **1** cf. Simp. *in Cael.* 522.11   **2–3** Clem. *Strom.* 6.149.1

---

2 γλώσσης (γλώσση Ε) codd., Clem. : γλώσσας Wilam., DK : βροτέων
MXG   ἐλθόντα Clem. : ῥηθέντα codd., *MXG*   **3** εἰδότων Η, Clem.

34(40) Plutarch *fac. lun.* 920c

. . . ὥς που καὶ 'Ε. τὴν ἑκατέρων ἀποδίδωσιν οὐκ ἀηδῶς διαφοράν·

        ἥλιος ὀξυβελὴς ἠδ' ἱλάειρα σελήνη,

τὸ ἐπαγωγὸν αὐτῆς καὶ ἱλαρὸν καὶ ἄλυπον οὕτω προσαγορεύσας.

ὀξυμελὴς codd. : ὀξυβελὴς Xylander   ἠδ' ἱλάειρα Diels, cf. s.v. ἱλάειρα
Hsch. : ἡ δὲ λάιρα codd.

35(41) Macrobius 1.17.46

Apollo 'Ελελεύς appellatur ἀπὸ τοῦ ἐλίττεσθαι περὶ τὴν γῆν . . . ἢ ὅτι
συναλισθέντος πολλοῦ πυρὸς περιπολεῖ ut ait E. :

        ἀλλ' ὁ μὲν ἁλισθεὶς μέγαν οὐρανὸν ἀμφιπολεύει.

EM, Suda s.v. hēlios

ἀλλ' ὁ μὲν ἁλισθεὶς *EM* : ἀλλ' ὁ μὲν ἀλεῖσθαι *Suda* : οὕνεκ' ἀναλισθεὶς
(ἀναλλισθεὶς BPR, ἀναλυθεὶς S) codd.   μέγαν] μέσον *EM*

36(44) Plutarch *Pyth. or.* 400b

ὑμεῖς δὲ τοῦ μὲν 'Ε. καταγελᾶτε φάσκοντος τὸν ἥλιον περὶ γῆν ἀνακλάσει
φωτὸς οὐρανίου γενόμενον αὖθις

        ἀνταυγεῖ πρὸς 'Ολυμπον ἀταρβήτοισι προσώποις.

Gal. *us. part.* 3.182K

ἀνταυγεῖ Sturz : ἀνταυγεῖν codd. : ἀνταυγέω Gal.   πρὸς] τὸν Gal.

37(47) *Anecdota Graeca* (Bekker) 1.337.15
ἀγής· τοῦτο ἀπὸ συνθέτου καταλείπεται τοῦ εὐαγής ἢ παναγής. 'Ε.·

   ἄθρει μὲν γὰρ ἄνακτος ἐναντίον ἀγέα κύκλον.

38(43) Plutarch *fac. lun.* 929d
... οἷον αἵ τε φωναὶ κατὰ τὰς ἀνακλάσεις ἀμαυρότερον ἀναφαίνουσι τὴν τοῦ φθέγματος αἵ τε πληγαὶ τῶν ἀφαλλομένων βελῶν μαλακώτεραι προσπίπτουσιν,

   ὡς αὐγὴ τύψασα σεληναίης κύκλον εὐρύν

ἀσθενῆ καὶ ἀμυδρὰν ἀνάρροιαν ἴσχει πρὸς ἡμᾶς, διὰ τὴν κλάσιν ἐκλυομένης τῆς δυνάμεως.

Philo *prov.* 2.70 quemadmodum E.: "lumen accipiens lunaris globus magnus largusque mox illico reversus est ut currens caelum attingeret."

αὐγή Xylander : αὐτή codd.

39(45) Achilles Tatius *Intr. Arat.* 16(43.6)
εἰσὶ δὲ οἳ πρῶτον τὸν ἥλιον λέγουσιν, δευτέραν δὲ τὴν σελήνην, τρίτον δὲ τὸν Κρόνον. ἡ δὲ πλείων δόξα καθ' ἣν πρώτην ἡ σελήνη, ἐπεὶ καὶ ἀπόσπασμα τοῦ ἡλίου λέγουσιν αὐτήν, ὡς καὶ 'Ε.·

   κυκλοτερὲς περὶ γαῖαν ἑλίσσεται ἀλλότριον φῶς.

40(46) Plutarch *fac. lun.* 925b
τῆς δὲ γῆς τρόπον τινὰ ψαύει (ἡ σελήνη) καὶ περιφερομένη πλησίον,

   ἅρματος ὥσπερ ἂν ἴχνος ἑλίσσεται

φησὶν 'E.

ἡ [τε] περὶ ἄκρην

οὐδὲ γὰρ τὴν σκιὰν αὐτῆς ὑπερβάλλει πολλάκις ἐπὶ μικρὸν αἰρομένην τῷ
παμμέγεθες εἶναι τὸ φωτίζον· ἀλλ' οὕτως ἔοικεν ἐν χρῷ καὶ σχεδὸν ἐν
ἀγκάλαις τῆς γῆς περιπολεῖν, ὥστ' ἀντιφράττεσθαι πρὸς τὸν ἥλιον ὑπ' αὐτῆς,
... διὸ λεκτέον οἶμαι θαρροῦντας ἐν τοῖς τῆς γῆς ὅροις εἶναι τὴν σελήνην
ὑπὸ τῶν ἄκρων ἐπιπροσθουμένην.

1 ὡς πέρι χνοίη ἐλίσσεται Panzerbieter, Diels   2 ἄκραν codd., lac. xvii
litt. E, xxv B

41(42) Plutarch *fac. lun.* 929c, cf. 934d
αὐτή (ἡ σελήνη) τε γὰρ ἄδηλός ἐστι τηνικαῦτα κἀκεῖνον (τὸν ἥλιον) ἀπέκρυψε
καὶ ἠφάνισε πολλάκις

                    †ἀπεσκεύασε† δέ οἱ αὐγάς

ὥς φησιν 'E.

      †ἐσ τε αἰαν† καθύπερθεν, ἀπεσκνίφωσε δὲ γαίης
      τόσσον ὅσον τ' εὖρος γλαυκώπιδος ἔπλετο μήνης,

καθάπερ εἰς νύκτα καὶ σκότος οὐκ εἰς ἄστρον ἕτερον τοῦ φωτὸς ἐμπεσόντος.

1 ἀπεσκέδασεν Xylander : ἀπεσκίασεν Bergk : ἀπεστέγασεν Diels   2 ἐς
γαῖαν Xylander : ἔστ' ἂν ἴῃ Diels

42(48) Plutarch *quaest. Plat.* 1006e
καὶ γὰρ οἱ τῶν ὡρολογίων γνώμονες οὐ συμμεθιστάμενοι ταῖς σκιαῖς ἀλλ'
ἑστῶτες ὄργανα καὶ χρόνου μέτρα γεγόνασι, μιμούμενοι τῆς γῆς τὸ ἐπιπροσθοῦν
τῷ ἡλίῳ περὶ αὐτὴν ὑποφερομένῳ, καθάπερ εἶπεν 'E.

      νύκτα δὲ γαῖα τίθησιν ὑφισταμένη φαέεσσι.

ἐφισταμένη Scaliger : ὑφισταμένοιο Diels   φαέεσσι Sturz : φάεσσι codd.

43(49) Plutarch *quaest. conv.* 720
σκοτεινὸς γὰρ ὢν ὁ ἀὴρ κατ' 'E.

νυκτὸς ἐρημαίης ἀλαώπιδος

ἀλαώπιδος Xylander, cf. Hsch. s.v. ἀλαῶπιν· σκοτεινήν : ἀγλαώπιδος codd.

44(50) Tzetzes *All. Il.* 15.86

ἡ Ποσειδῶνος κέλευσις ἐξ Ἴριδος ὑπάρχει
ἢ πρὸς τὴν θάλασσαν αὐτὸν ἢ πρὸς θεοὺς καλοῦσα
ὅπερ φησὶν Ἐμπεδοκλῆς εἴτε τις τῶν ἑτέρων·
Ἶρις δ᾿ ἐκ πελάγους ἄνεμον φέρει ἢ μέγαν ὄμβρον.

45(56) Hephaestio *Enchir.* 1.3.4
θέσει μακραὶ γίνονται . . . καὶ Ἐ.·

ἅλς ἐπάγη ῥιπῇσιν ἐωσμένος ἠελίοιο.

46(55) Aristotle *Mete.* 357a24
ὁμοίως δὲ γελοῖον καὶ εἴ τις εἰπών

γῆς ἱδρῶτα θάλασσαν

οἴεταί τι σαφές εἰρηκέναι, καθάπερ Ἐ.· πρὸς ποίησιν μὲν γὰρ οὕτως εἰπὼν
ἴσως εἴρηκεν ἱκανῶς (ἡ γὰρ μεταφορὰ ποιητικόν), πρὸς δὲ τὸ γνῶναι τὴν
φύσιν οὐχ ἱκανῶς.

Arist. *Mete.* 353b11, Olymp. *in Mete.* 151.4, cf. 155.8, Alex. Aphr. *in Mete.*
67.14, 80.31, 81.16, Aet. 3.16.3

ἱδρῶτα τῆς γῆς εἶναι τὴν θάλατταν codd. : τὴν θάλατταν ἱδρῶτα γῆς
Olymp. : ἱδρῶτα τῆς γῆς Aet.

47(35).1–15 Simplicius *in Cael.* 528.30; 16–17 ex *in Phys.* 32.13
μήποτε δὲ κἂν ἐπικρατῇ ἐν τούτῳ (τῷ κόσμῳ) τὸ νεῖκος ὥσπερ ἐν τῷ σφαίρῳ
ἡ φιλία, ἀλλ᾿ ἄμφω ὑπ᾿ ἀμφοῖν λέγονται γίνεσθαι. καὶ τάχα οὐδὲν κωλύει
παραθέσθαι τινὰ τῶν τοῦ Ἐ. ἐπῶν τοῦτο δηλοῦντα·

αὐτὰρ ἐγὼ παλίνορσος ἐλεύσομαι ἐς πόρον ὕμνων,
τὸν πρότερον κατέλεξα, λόγου λόγον ἐξοχετεύων
κεῖνον· ἐπεὶ νεῖκος μὲν ἐνέρτατον ἵκετο βένθος
δίνης, ἐν δὲ μέσῃ φιλότης στροφάλιγγι γένηται,
5　ἐν τῇ δὴ τάδε πάντα συνέρχεται ἓν μόνον εἶναι,
οὐκ ἄφαρ, ἀλλὰ θελημὰ συνιστάμεν᾽ ἄλλοθεν ἄλλα.
τῶν δέ τε μισγομένων χεῖτ᾽ ἔθνεα μυρία θνητῶν·
πολλὰ δ᾽ ἄμικτ᾽ ἔστηκε κεραιομένοισιν ἐναλλάξ,
ὅσσ᾽ ἔτι νεῖκος ἔρυκε μετάρσιον· οὐ γὰρ ἀμεμφέως
10　πω πᾶν ἐξέστηκεν ἐπ᾽ ἔσχατα τέρματα κύκλου,
ἀλλὰ τὰ μέν τ᾽ ἐνέμιμνε μελέων τὰ δέ τ᾽ ἐξεβεβήκει.
ὅσσον δ᾽ αἰὲν ὑπεκπροθέοι, τόσον αἰὲν ἐπῄει
ἠπιόφρων φιλότητος ἀμεμφέος ἄμβροτος ὁρμή·
αἶψα δὲ θνήτ᾽ ἐφύοντο, τὰ πρὶν μάθον ἀθάνατ᾽ εἶναι,
15　ζωρά τε πρὶν κέκρητο, διαλλάξαντα κελεύθους.
τῶν δέ τε μισγομένων χεῖτ᾽ ἔθνεα μυρία θνητῶν,
παντοίαις ἰδέῃσιν ἀρηρότα, θαῦμα ἰδέσθαι.

ἐν τούτοις δηλοῦται ὅτι ἐν τῇ ἁπλῇ διακοσμήσει ὑποστέλλεται μὲν τὸ νεῖκος,
ἡ δὲ φιλότης ἐπικρατεῖ, ὅταν ἐν μέσῃ τῇ στροφάλιγγι, τουτέστι τῇ δίνῃ,
γένηται, ὥστε καὶ τῆς φιλότητος ἐπικρατούσης ἐστὶν ἡ δίνη, καὶ ὅτι τὰ μὲν
τῶν στοιχείων ἄμικτα μένει ὑπὸ τοῦ νείκους, τὰ δὲ μιγνύμενα ποιεῖ τὰ
θνητὰ καὶ ζῷα καὶ φυτά, διότι πάλιν διαλύεται τὰ μιγνύμενα.

3–17 Simp. *in Phys.* 32.13　　5, 10–13 Simp. *in Cael.* 587.11.14　　7 *EM*
s.v. ethnos　　14–15 Arist. *Poet.* 1461a24, Ath. 10.423f　　15 Plu. *quaest. conv.*
677d

2 λόγου Bergk : λόγῳ codd.　　ἐπιχετεύων A　　5 ἐν τῇ δὴ DE (*in Phys.*) :
ἐν τῇ ἡ δε A : ἐν τῃδι A (*Cael.* 587) : ἔνθ᾽ ἤδη Bergk　　6 ἀλλ᾽ ἐθελημὰ
F　　ἄλλα codd. : ἄλλο *in Phys.*　　8 ἄμικτ᾽ ἐστι κεκερασμένοισιν E,
ἄμικτ᾽ (ἄμμικτα F) ἔστηκε κερασμένοισι DF (*in Phys.*) : ἄμικθ᾽ ἔστηκε κεραιομένοισιν Stein : ἄμεικτ᾽ ἔστηκε κεραιομένοισιν Diels　　ἐλλάξ A　　9
ἀμεμφέος F, ἀμφαφέως A　　10 πω F, τὸ A : οὔπω *Cael.* 587, DE (*in
Phys.*) : πὼ cet. codd. : τῶν Diels　　12 ὑπεκπροθέει F (*in Phys.*)　　13
ἠπιόφρων codd. : πίφρων DE, ἢ περίφρων F (*in Phys.*)　　ἀμφεσσον A
14 θνητὰ φύοντο Ath.　　15 ζωρά τε πρὶν κέκρητο scripsi : ζωρά τε τὰ
πρὶν ἄκριτα codd. : ζωρά τε τὰ πρὶν ἄκρητα Ath., Plu. : ζῷά τε πρὶν
κέκριτο (κέκτητο A^c) Arist. : ζωρά τε πρὶν τὰ κέκρητο Bergk : ζωρά τε τὰ
πρίν, ἔκρητο Diels　　διαλλάσσοντα Ath.　　17 παντοίαισιν ἰδέεσσιν DE

48(96) Simplicius *in Phys.* 300.19

καὶ γὰρ λόγῳ τινι ποιεῖ (ὁ 'Ε.) σάρκας καὶ ὀστοῦν καὶ τῶν ἄλλων ἕκαστον. λέγει γοῦν ἐν τῷ πρώτῳ τῶν Φυσικῶν·

> ἡ δὲ χθὼν ἐπίηρος ἐν εὐστέρνοις χοάνοισι
> τὼ δύο τῶν ὀκτὼ μερέων λάχε Νήστιδος αἴγλης,
> τέσσαρα δ' Ἡφαίστοιο· τὰ δ' ὀστέα λευκὰ γένοντο,
> ἁρμονίης κόλλησιν ἀρηρότα θεσπεσίηθεν.

τούτεστιν ἀπὸ τῶν θείων αἰτίων καὶ μάλιστα τῆς φιλίας ἤτοι ἁρμονίας· ταῖς γὰρ ταύτης κόλλαις ἁρμόζεται.

1–3 Arist. *De An.* 410a4, Alex. Aphr. *in Metaph.* 135.15, Ascl. *in Metaph.* 112.1, Them. *in de An.* 33.12, Sophon. *in de An.* 32.15   2–3 Alex. Aphr. *in Metaph.* 828.8, Syrian. *in Metaph.* 188.17, cf. Simp. *in de An.* 68.5, Phlp. *in de An.* 176.30

---

1 ἐπίειρος LF Alex.   εὐρυστέρνοις B Sophon., CZ Them. : εὐτύκτοις EF, A Alex.   2 τὼ] τῶν ESTUX Arist., (exc. τὰ Z) Ascl., Them., Sophon. : τὰς DE, W Arist., Alex., Syrian. : τὰ F, cet. Arist. : τὼ Steinhart, Diels μοιράων DE, UVW Arist. A Alex., Z Them.   3 λευκὰ γένοντο codd., TVW Arist. : λεύκ' ἐγένοντο cet.

49(34) Aristotle *Mete.* 381b31

τὸ γὰρ ὑγρὸν τῷ ξηρῷ αἴτιον τοῦ ὁρίζεσθαι καὶ ἑκάτερον ἑκατέρῳ οἷον κόλλα γίγνεται, ὥσπερ καὶ 'Ε. ἐποίησεν ἐν τοῖς Φυσικοῖς (Περσικοῖς Ε)·

> ἄλφιτον ὕδατι κολλήσας . . .

καὶ διὰ τοῦτο ἐξ ἀμφοῖν ἐστὶ τὸ ὡρισμένον σῶμα.

[Arist.] *probl.* 929b16, Alex. Aphr. *in Mete.* 199.6, Olymp. *in Mete.* 297.19

50(57) Simplicius *in Cael.* 586.7

ἐρωτᾷ δέ, πότερον οὐχ οἷά τε ἦν τότε οὕτω κινεῖσθαι ἀτάκτως, ὥστε καὶ μίγνυσθαι τοιαύτας μίξεις ἔνια, ἐξ ὧν "συνίσταται τὰ κατὰ φύσιν συνιστάμενα σώματα, οἷον ὀστᾶ καὶ σάρκες" καὶ ὅλως τὰ τῶν ζῴων μέρη καὶ τῶν φυτῶν καὶ αὐτὰ τὰ ζῷα καὶ τὰ φυτά, "καθάπερ 'Ε. γίνεσθαί φησιν ἐπὶ τῆς φιλότητος" λέγων·

ἦ πολλαὶ μὲν κόρσαι ἀναύχενες ἐβλάστησαν.

... ὁ μὲν Ἀλέξανδρος ὡς μίξεως παράδειγμα ἀκούει, ἐξ ἧς συνίσταται τὰ
κατὰ φύσιν σώματα, καὶ συναίρεσθαι δοκεῖ τῷ λόγῳ αὐτοῦ τὸ ἐπὶ τῆς φιλότητος τοῦτο λέγεσθαι μίξεως αἰτίας οὔσης ὥσπερ τοῦ νείκους διακρίσεως. πῶς
δὲ ἂν εἴη μίξεως σημαντικὸν ἡ "ἀναύχενος κόρση" καὶ τἆλλα τὰ ὑπὸ τοῦ
Ἐ. λεγόμενα ἐν τούτοις

> γυμνοὶ δ' ἐπλάζοντο βραχίονες εὔνιδες ὤμων,
> ὄμματα τ' οἶ' ἐπλανᾶτο πενητεύοντα μετώπων,

καὶ πολλὰ ἄλλα, ἅπερ οὐκ ἔστι μίξεως παραδείγματα, ἐξ ἧς τὰ κατὰ φύσιν
συνίσταται;

1 Arist. *Cael.* 300b30, *De An.* 430a29, *GA* 722b20, Simp. *in de An.* 250.23,
in Cat. 337.2, Phlp. *in de An.* 545.19, *in GC* 27.35; Tz. *ad Lyc.* 507, 711, *ad
Alleg. Il.* 4.33

---

1 ἦ codd., Arist. *GA* : om. Arist. *Cael.* : ὡς Tz.   πολλῶν pleri.   ἀν-
αύχενοι βλαστῶσιν Simp. *Cat.*   **2** ἐπλάξοντο E, ἐμπλάζοντο A   **3** οἶα
D, οἷα AE

51(59) Simplicius *in Cael.* 587.18 [post 47(35).10-13]
ἐν ταύτῃ οὖν τῇ καταστάσει "μουνομελῆ" ἔτι τὰ γυῖα ἀπὸ τῆς τοῦ νείκους
διακρίσεως ὄντα ἐπλανᾶτο τῆς πρὸς ἄλληλα μίξεως ἐφιέμενα

> αὐτὰρ ἐπεὶ κατὰ μεῖζον ἐμίσγετο δαίμονι δαίμων,

ὅτε τοῦ νείκους ἐπεκράτει λοιπὸν ἡ φιλότης,

> ταῦτά τε συμπίπτεσκον, ὅπῃ συνέκυρσεν ἕκαστα,
> ἄλλα τε πρὸς τοῖς πολλὰ διηνεκῆ ἐξεγένοντο.

ἐπὶ τῆς φιλότητος οὖν ὁ Ἐ. ἐκεῖνα εἶπεν, οὐχ ὡς ἐπικρατούσης ἤδη τῆς φιλότητος, ἀλλ' ὡς μελλούσης ἐπικρατεῖν, ἔτι δὲ τὰ ἄμικτα καὶ μονόγυια
δηλούσης.

2 Simp. *in Phys.* 327.20, 331.2

---

1 δαίμονι om. A   2 ἕκαστα] ἅπαντα in Phys.

52(61) Aelian *NA* 16.29

'E. ὁ φυσικός φησι περὶ ζῴων ἰδιότητος λέγων καὶ ἐκεῖνος δήπου γίνεσθαί τινα συμφυῆ καὶ κράσει μορφῆς μὲν διάφορα, ἐνώσει δὲ σώματος συμπλακέντα· ἃ δὲ λέγει, ταῦτά ἐστι·

> πολλὰ μὲν ἀμφιπρόσωπα καὶ ἀμφίστερν' ἐφύοντο,
> βουγενῆ ἀνδρόπρῳρα, τὰ δ' ἔμπαλιν ἐξανέτελλον
> ἀνδροφυῆ βούκρανα, μεμιγμένα τῇ μὲν ἀπ' ἀνδρῶν
> τῇ δὲ γυναικοφυῆ, †σκιεροῖς† ἠσκημένα γυίοις.

2 Arist. *Phys.* 198b32, 199b11; Simp. *in Phys.* 372.1, 380.20, 381.3,7,13, 383. 4; Them. *in Phys.* 62.3; Phlp. *in Phys.* 314.13; Plu. *adv. Col.* 1123b

---

1 ἀμφίστερνα φύεσθαι codd., emend. Karsten   2 ἐξανατέλλειν codd., emend. Karsten   3 ἀνδρογενῆ βούπρωρα Simp. *in Phys.* 381.7   ἀπ' Karsten : ὑπ' codd.   4 χλιεροῖς Karsten : στιβαροῖς Bergk : διεροῖς Panzerbieter : στείροις vel σκιροῖς Diels

53(62) Simplicius *in Phys.* 381.29

εἰπόντος δὲ τοῦ 'E. ἐν τῷ δευτέρῳ τῶν Φυσικῶν πρὸ τῆς τῶν ἀνδρείων καὶ γυναικείων σωμάτων διαρθρώσεως ταυτὶ τὰ ἔπη·

> νῦν δ' ἄγ', ὅπως ἀνδρῶν τε πολυκλαύτων τε γυναικῶν
> ἐννυχίους ὄρπηκας ἀνήγαγε κρινόμενον πῦρ,
> τῶνδε κλῦ'· οὐ γὰρ μῦθος ἀπόσκοπος οὐδ' ἀδαήμων.
> οὐλοφυεῖς μὲν πρῶτα τύποι χθονὸς ἐξανέτελλον,
> 5 ἀμφοτέρων ὕδατός τε καὶ εἴδεος αἶσαν ἔχοντες·
> τοὺς μὲν πῦρ ἀνέπεμπε θέλον πρὸς ὁμοῖον ἱκέσθαι,
> οὔτε τί πω μελέων ἐρατὸν δέμας ἐμφαίνοντας,
> οὔτ' ἐνοπὴν †οὔτ'† ἐπιχώριον ἀνδράσι †γύων†.

3 cf. Arist. *Phys.* 199b9

---

1 ἄγε πως F   3 τῶνδ' ἔκλυ' E   5 ἴδεος Diels   8 οὔτ' F, οἶα τ' E, οὔτ' αὖ Ald. : οἶόν τ' Diels   γῆρυν Ald. : γυῖον Stein, Diels : οἴη τ'

ἐπιχώριον ἀνδράσι γυίων Bollack

54(64) Plutarch *quaest. nat.* 917e
ἢ καὶ τὸ συντρέφεσθαι καὶ συναγελάζεσθαι τὰ θήλεα τοῖς ἄρρεσιν ἀνάμνησιν
ποιεῖ τῶν ἀφροδισίων καὶ συνεκκαλεῖται τὴν ὄρεξιν· ὡς ἐπὶ ἀνθρώπων 'Ε.
ἐποίησε

τῷ δ' ἐπὶ καὶ πόθος εἴτε †διὰ πέψεως ἀμμίσγων†

ἀμμίστων uA, ἀμίσθων n : εἰσι δι' ὄψιος ἀμμιμνήσκων (εἰσι Karsten, δι'
ὄψιος Wyttenbach) Diels

55(66) Schol. *in Eurip. Phoen.* 18
'Ε. ὁ φυσικὸς ἀλληγορῶν φησι

σχιστοὺς λειμῶνας . . . 'Αφροδίτης

ἐν οἷς ἡ τῶν παίδων γένεσίς ἐστιν.

λειμῶνας AT, λιμῶνας M, λιμένας B

56(63) Aristotle *GA* 764b15
οὔτε γὰρ διεσπασμένον ἐνδέχεται τὸ σῶμα τοῦ σπέρματος εἶναι, τὸ μὲν ἐν
τῷ θήλει τὸ δ' ἐν τῷ ἄρρενι, καθάπερ 'Ε. φησὶν εἰπών·

ἀλλὰ διέσπασται μελέων φύσις, ἡ μὲν ἐν ἀνδρός

Arist. *GA* 722b12, Phlp. *in GA* 166.25, cf. Gal. *sem.* 4.616K

ἡ δ' ἐν γυναικός add. Phlp.

57(65) Aristotle *GA* 723a23
πρὸς δὲ τούτοις εἰ τὸ θῆλυ καὶ τὸ ἄρρεν ἐν τῇ κυήσει διαφέρει, καθάπερ 'Ε.
λέγει

ἐν δ' ἐχύθη καθαροῖσι· τὰ μὲν τελέθουσι γυναῖκες

ψύχεος ἀντιάσαντα

1 Phlp. *in GA* 30.4, cf. Arist. *GA* 764a1

_____

1 ἐλύθη S   **2** ⟨τὰ δ' ἔμπαλιν ἄρρενα θερμοῦ⟩ add. Diels

58(67) Galen *Hipp. Ep.* 17.1002 K
ὁ μὲν γὰρ Παρμενίδης οὕτως ἔφη "δεξιτεροῖσι μὲν κούρους, λαοῖσι δ' αὖ κούρας." ὁ δὲ 'Ε. οὕτως·

> ἐν γὰρ θερμοτέρῳ τὸ κατ' ἄρρενα ἔπλετο †γαίης†,
> καὶ μέλανες διὰ τοῦτο καὶ ἀδρομελέστεροι ἄνδρες
> καὶ λαχνήεντες μᾶλλον.

1 τοκὰς ἄρρενος ἔπλετο γαστήρ Diels : τὸ κατ' ἄρρενα ἔπλετο γαστρός Sturz
2 ἀδρομελέστεροι Karsten : ἀνδρωδέστεροι codd.

59(68) Aristotle *GA* 777a7, cf. Philoponus *in GA* 208.9
τὸ γὰρ γάλα πεπεμμένον αἷμά ἐστιν, ἀλλ' οὐ διεφθαρμένον. 'Ε. δ' ἢ οὐκ ὀρθῶς ὑπελάμβανεν ἢ οὐκ εὖ μετήνεγκε ποιήσας ὡς τὸ αἷμα (τὸ γάλα codd.)

> μηνὸς ἐν ὀγδοάτου δεκάτῃ πύον ἔπλετο λευκόν.

60(71) Simplicius *in Cael.* 529.28 [post 87(95).1]
ὅτι δὲ περὶ τούτων λέγει τῶν ἐν τούτῳ τῷ κόσμῳ, ἄκουε τούτων τῶν ἐπῶν·

> εἰ δέ τί σοι περὶ τῶνδε λιπόξυλος ἔπλετο πίστις,
> πῶς ὕδατος γαίης τε καὶ αἰθέρος ἠελίου τε
> κιρναμένων εἴδη τε γενοίατο χροῖά τε θνητῶν
> τόσσ' ὅσα νῦν γεγάασι συναρμοσθέντ' 'Αφροδίτῃ

1 δέ τις F, δ' ἔτι c   **4** τόσσ' Karsten : τοία codd. τοῖ' οἷα Wilam.
γεγῶασι A

61(33) Plutarch *amic. mult.* 95a
τοὐναντίον οὖν ἔοικεν ἡ καλουμένη πολυφιλία ⟨τῇ φιλίᾳ⟩ ποιεῖν. ἡ μέν

γὰρ συνάγει καὶ συνίστησι καὶ συνέχει καταπυκνοῦσα ταῖς ὁμιλίαις καὶ φιλοφροσύναις

> ὡς δ' ὅτ' ὀπὸς γάλα λευκὸν ἐγόμφωσεν καὶ ἔδησε

κατ' Ἐ. (τοιαύτην γὰρ ἡ φιλία βούλεται ποιεῖν ἑνότητα καὶ σύμπηξιν), ἡ δὲ πολυφιλία . . .

ἔπηξε LC

62(73) Simplicius *in Cael.* 530.5 [post 60(71).1–4]
καὶ μετ' ὀλίγα·

> ὡς δὲ τότε χθόνα Κύπρις, ἐπεί τ' ἐδίηνεν ἐν ὄμβρῳ,
> εἴδεα ποιπνύουσα θοῷ πυρὶ δῶκε κρατῦναι

1 ἐδείκνεεν A   **2** εἰ δέ ἀποπνοιοῦσα A   θεῶ F

63(72) Athenaeus 8.334b
οὐ λανθάνει δέ με καὶ ὅτι κοινῶς πάντες οἱ ἰχθύες καμασῆνες ὑπὸ Ἐ. ἐλέχθησαν τοῦ φυσικοῦ οὕτως·

> πῶς καὶ δένδρεα μακρὰ καὶ εἰνάλιοι καμασῆνες

64(77–78) Theophrastus *CP* 1.13.2, cf. Plutarch *quaest. conv.* 649c
εἰ δὲ καὶ συνεχῶς ὁ ἀὴρ ἀκολουθοίη τούτοις (τοῖς δένδροις), ἴσως οὐδὲ τὰ παρὰ τῶν ποιητῶν λεγόμενα δόξειεν ἂν ἀλόγως ἔχειν οὐδ' ὡς Ἐ. ἀείφυλλα καὶ ἐμπεδόκαρπά φησι θάλλειν

> καρπῶν ἀφθονίῃσι κατ' ἠέρα πάντ' ἐνιαυτόν,

ὑποτιθέμενός τινα τοῦ ἀέρος κρᾶσιν, τὴν ἐαρινήν, κοινήν.

ἀείφυλλα] ἐμπεδόφυλλον Plu. : δένδρεα δ' ἐμπεδόφυλλα καὶ ἐμπεδόκαρπα τέθηλεν versum Hermann., edd.   κατήρεα Scaliger : κατήορα Stein

65(79) Aristotle *GA* 731a4
καὶ τοῦτο καλῶς λέγει Ἐ. ποιήσας

οὕτω δ' ᾠοτοκεῖ μακρὰ δένδρεα πρῶτον ἐλαίας.

τό τε γὰρ ᾠὸν κύημά ἐστι, καὶ ἔκ τινος αὐτοῦ γίγνεται τὸ ζῷον, τὸ δὲ λοιπὸν τροφή.

Thphr. *CP* 1.7.1, Phlp. *in GA* 63.11

μακρά] μικρά PSY, Phlp.

66(80) Plutarch *quaest. conv.* 683d
τοῦ δ' Ἐ. εἰρηκότος

οὕνεκεν ὀψίγονοί τε σίδαι καὶ ὑπέρφλοα μῆλα

τὸ μὲν τῶν σιδῶν ἐπίθετον νοεῖν, ὅτι τοῦ φθινοπώρου λήγοντος ἤδη καὶ τῶν καυμάτων μαραινομένων ἐκπέττουσι τὸν καρπόν . . . τὰ δὲ μῆλα καθ' ἥντινα διάνοιαν ὁ σοφὸς "ὑπέρφλοια" προσειρήκοι, διαπορεῖν.

ὑπέρφλοα Karsten : ὑπέρφλοια codd.

67(81) Plutarch *quaest. nat.* 912c
ἡ δὲ πέψις ἔοικεν εἶναι σῆψις, ὡς Ἐ. μαρτυρεῖ λέγων

οἶνος ἀπὸ φλοιοῦ πέλεται σαπὲν ἐν ξύλῳ ὕδωρ.

Plu. *quaest. nat.* 919d, Arist. *Top.* 127a19, Alex. Aphr. *in Top.* 357.12, Anon. *in Plat. Theaet.* 24.39

ὑπὸ φλοιῷ Xylander

68(74) Plutarch *quaest. conv.* 685f
αὐτῶν δὲ τῶν ζῴων οὐδὲν ἂν χερσαῖον ἢ πτηνὸν εἰπεῖν ἔχοις οὕτω γόνιμον ὡς πάντα τὰ θαλάττια· πρὸς ὃ καὶ πεποίηκεν ὁ Ἐ.·

φῦλον ἄμουσον ἄγουσα πολυσπερέων καμασήνων.

121   *ΠΕΡΙ ΦΥΣΕΩΣ* 66(80)–71(82)

69(76) Plutarch *quaest. conv.* 618b

καὶ τὸν θεὸν ὁρᾷς, ὃν "ἀριστοτέχναν" ἡμῶν ὁ Πίνδαρος προσεῖπεν, οὐ πανταχοῦ τὸ πῦρ ἄνω τάττοντα καὶ κάτω τὴν γῆν ἀλλ' ὡς ἂν αἱ χρεῖαι τῶν σωμάτων ἀπαιτῶσιν·

> τοῦτο μὲν ἐν κόγχαισι θαλασσονόμοις βαρυνώτοις·
> ναὶ μὴν κηρύκων τε λιθορρίνων χελύων τε,

φησὶν 'Ε.

> ἔνθ' ὄψει χθόνα χρωτὸς ὑπέρτατα ναιετάουσαν.

2–3 Plu. *fac. lun.* 927f

1 θαλασσονόμων Diels

70(75) Simplicius *in Cael.* 530.8 [post 62(73)]
καὶ πάλιν

> τῶν δ' ὅσ' ἔσω μὲν πυκνά, τὰ δ' ἔκτοθι μανὰ πέπηγεν,
> Κύπριδος ἐν παλάμῃσι πλάδης τοιῆσδε τυχόντα

2 Simp. *in Phys.* 331.9

2 παλάμῃσι (-μης F) πλάδης τοιῆσδε codd. : παλάμῃσι πλάδης (πλάσης Ε) τοίης τι *in Phys.*

71(82) Aristotle *Mete.* 387b4
λέγω δὲ καὶ ὀστᾶ καὶ τρίχας καὶ πᾶν τὸ τοιοῦτον ἐν ταὐτῷ· οὐ γὰρ κεῖται ὄνομα κοινόν, ἀλλὰ κατ' ἀναλογίαν ὅμως ἐν ταὐτῷ πάντ' ἐστίν, ὥσπερ καὶ 'Ε. φησι

> ταὐτὰ τρίχες καὶ φύλλα καὶ οἰωνῶν πτερὰ πυκνά
> καὶ λεπίδες γίγνονται ἐπὶ στιβαροῖσι μέλεσσιν.

Olymp. *in Mete.* 335.22

2 λοπίδες E   φολιδονίδες Olymp. : φλονίδες Karsten

72(83) Plutarch *fort.* 98d
τὰ μὲν γὰρ ὥπλισται καὶ ὁδοῦσι καὶ κέντροις,

αὐτὰρ ἐχίνοις
ὀξυβελεῖς χαῖται νώτοις ἐπιπεφρίκασι.

1 ἐχίνοις Vulcob. : ἐχῖνος codd.   **2** ὀξυβελοῖς W, ὀξυβελής O χαῖται
Vulcob. : καί τε N, δέ τε cet. codd.

73(89) Plutarch *quaest. nat.* 916d
σκόπει δή, κατ᾽ Ἐ. γνοὺς ὅτι

πάντων εἰσὶν ἀπορροαὶ ὅσσ᾽ ἐγένοντο·

οὐ γὰρ ζῴων μόνον οὐδὲ φυτῶν οὐδὲ γῆς καὶ θαλάττης, ἀλλὰ καὶ λίθων
ἄπεισιν ἐνδελεχῶς πολλὰ ῥεύματα καὶ χαλκοῦ καὶ σιδήρου.

ἀπορροαί A ante corr. : ἀπορροιαί cet. codd.

74(91) Philoponus *in GA* 123.15
καὶ ὧν μὲν εἰσι τὰ ναστὰ καὶ οἱ πόροι, τουτέστι τὰ κοῖλα καὶ πυκνὰ σύμ-
μετρα, ὥστε δ᾽ ἀλλήλων χωρεῖν, τούτων ἔφασκεν (ὁ Ἐ.) εἶναι μῖξιν καὶ
κρᾶσιν, οἷον ὕδατος καὶ οἴνου, ὧν δὲ ἀσύμμετρα, ἄμικτα ταῦτα ἔφασκεν
εἶναι, ὥσπερ ἔλαιον καὶ ὕδωρ· φησὶ γὰρ

(ὕδωρ) οἴνῳ μᾶλλον †ἐναρίθμιον†, αὐτὰρ ἐλαίῳ
οὐκ ἐθέλει.

ταῦτα λέγων κατὰ παντὸς σώματος τὴν αἰτίαν τῆς τῶν ἡμιόνων ἀτεκνίας
ἀπεδίδου.

Alex. Aphr. *quaest.* 72.26, cf. Arist. *GA* 723a18

_____

1 ἐναρίθμιον codd., Alex. : ἐνάρθμιον Karsten

75(90) Plutarch *quaest. conv.* 663a

εἴτε γὰρ ἐξ ὁμοίων ἀναλαμβάνει τὸ οἰκεῖον ἡ φύσις εἰς τὸν ὄγκον αὐτόθεν ἡ ποικίλη τροφὴ πολλὰς μεθιεῖσα ποιότητας ἐξ ἑαυτῆς ἑκάστῳ μέρει τὸ πρόσφορον ἀναδίδωσιν· ὥστε γίνεσθαι τὸ τοῦ 'Ε.

ὡς γλυκὺ μὲν [ἐπὶ] γλυκὺ μάρπτε, πικρὸν δ' ἐπὶ πικρὸν ὄρουσεν,
ὀξὺ δ' ἐπ' ὀξὺ ⟨ἔβη⟩, †δαλερὸν δαλεροῦ λαβέτως†

Macrobius *Sat.* 7.5.17

_____

1 ἐπὶ om. Macr.   2 ἔβη suppl. Macr.   θερμὸν δ' ἐποχεύετο θερμῷ Macr. : δαερὸν δ' ἐποχεῖτο δαηρῷ Diels : δαερὸν δ' ἐποχεύετο δαερῷ Maas

76(93) Plutarch *def. or.* 433b

ἄλλα γὰρ ἄλλοις οἰκεῖα καὶ πρόσφορα καθάπερ τῆς μὲν πορφύρας ὁ κυαμὸς τῆς δὲ κόκκου τὸ νίτρον δοκεῖ τὴν βαφὴν ἄγειν μεμιγμένον,

βύσσῳ δὲ †γλαυκῆς κρόκου† καταμίσγεται ἀκτίς,

ὡς 'Ε. εἴρηκε.

γλαύκοιο Xylander   καὶ κρόκου J, κρόκον ΠΒ, κρόνου Gu   ἀκτίς] om. ΓΠΒ : αἶθος Xylander : ἀκτῆς Wilam.   γλαυκῇ κόκκου καταμίσγεται ἄνθος Wyttenbach : γλαυκῆς κόκκος καταμίσγεται ἀκτῆς Diels : γλαύκοιο κρόκου καταμίσγεται ἀκτίς Bennet

77(109) Aristotle *De An.* 404b8

ὅσοι δ' ἐπὶ τὸ γινώσκειν καὶ τὸ αἰσθάνεσθαι τῶν ὄντων, οὗτοι δὲ λέγουσι τὴν ψυχὴν τὰς ἀρχάς, οἱ μὲν πλείους ποιοῦντες, ταύτας, οἱ δὲ μίαν, ταύτην, ὥσπερ 'Ε. μὲν ἐκ τῶν στοιχείων πάντων, εἶναι δὲ καὶ ἕκαστον ψυχὴν τούτων, λέγων οὕτως·

γαίῃ μὲν γὰρ γαῖαν ὀπώπαμεν, ὕδατι δ' ὕδωρ,
αἰθέρι δ' αἰθέρα δῖον, ἀτὰρ πυρὶ πῦρ ἀΐδηλον,
στοργὴν δὲ στοργῇ, νεῖκος δέ τε νείκεϊ λυγρῷ.

1–3 Arist. *Metaph.* 1000b6, S.E. *adv. math.* 1.303, 7.92, 121, Hippol. *RH* 6.11.1, Phlp. *in GC* 268.17, Sophon. *in de An.* 12.22   1–2 Ascl. *in Metaph.* 198.11, Gal. *plac. Hipp.* 5.627K, Stob. 1.51.7   1,3 Procl. *in Tim.* 233c;

Phlp. *in de An.* 182.1 **1** Phlp. *in de An.* 150.12, 180.21, 469.20, 489.27, 570.24, Them. *in de An.* 10.20 14.18, 34.8, Sophon. *in de An.* 26.16, Gal. *plac. Hipp.* 5.631K

2 ἠέρι δ᾽ ἠέρα S.E. 1.303 δῖον codd., Gal., Stob. : δῖαν cet., om. Hippol. ἄδηλον E **3** στοργῇ δὲ στοργὴν codd. δέ τε] δέ τι BᵇCᵇ Metaph. : ἐπὶ Hippol. : δέ γε S.E. 7.92, Procl.

78(107) Theophrastus *Sens.* 10

τὸ μὲν γὰρ φρονεῖν εἶναι τοῖς ὁμοίοις, τὸ δ᾽ ἀγνοεῖν τοῖς ἀνομοίοις, ὡς ἢ ταὐτὸν ἢ παραπλήσιον ὂν τῇ αἰσθήσει τὴν φρόνησιν. διαριθμησάμενος γάρ, ὡς ἕκαστον ἑκάστῳ γνωρίζειν, ἐπὶ τέλει προσέθηκεν ὡς

> ἐκ τούτων ⟨ὡς⟩ πάντα πεπήγασιν ἁρμοσθέντα
> καὶ τούτοις φρονέουσι καὶ ἥδοντ᾽ ἠδ᾽ ἀνιῶνται.

διὸ καὶ τῷ αἵματι μάλιστα φρονεῖν· ἐν τούτῳ γὰρ μάλιστα κεκρᾶσθαι τὰ στοιχεῖα τῶν μερῶν.

1 γάρ add. Karsten, lacunam xiv litt. indicat P : ὡς Lloyd-Jones **2** ἥδοντ᾽ ἠδ᾽ Karsten : ἥδονται καί codd.

79(106) Aristotle *Metaph.* 1009b17

καὶ γὰρ ᾽Ε. μεταβάλλοντας τὴν ἕξιν μεταβάλλειν φησὶ τὴν φρόνησιν·

> πρὸς παρεὸν γὰρ μῆτις ἀέξεται ἀνθρώποισιν.

Arist. *De An.* 427a23, Alex. Aphr. *in Metaph.* 306.18, Ascl. *in Metaph.* 277.9, Phlp. *in de An.* 485.23, Them. *in de An.* 87.22, Sophon. *in de An.* 115.26

ἐναύξεται ETAᵇ, Alex.

80(108) Aristotle *Metaph.* 1009b19 [post 79(106).1]

καὶ ἐν ἑτέροις δὲ λέγει ὅτι

> ὅσσον ⟨δ᾽⟩ ἀλλοῖοι μετέφυν, τόσον ἄρ σφισιν αἰεί
> καὶ τὸ φρονεῖν ἀλλοῖα παρίσταται

Arist. *De An.* 427a24, Alex. Aphr. *in Metaph.* 306.24, Ascl. *in Metaph.* 277.17, Phlp. *in de An.* 486.16, cf. Simp. *in de An.* 202.30

---

1 δ' add. Diels : γ' Sturz   μετέφην STAᵇ   τόσον ἄρ] ὅθεν *De An.*, Phlp.
2 καὶ τὸ φαντίζεσθαι καὶ ὀνειρώττειν φρονεῖν Τ (*De An.*)   παρίστατο
codd. : καθίσταται Τ (*De An.*)

81(103) Simplicius *in Phys.* 331.12 [post 70(75).2]
καὶ πολλὰ ἄν τις εὕροι ἐκ τῶν 'Ε. Φυσικῶν τοιαῦτα παραθέσθαι, ὥσπερ καὶ τοῦτο·

τῇδε μὲν οὖν ἰότητι τύχης πεφρόνηκεν ἅπαντα.

82(104) Simplicius *in Phys.* 331.41 [post 81(103)]
καὶ μετ' ὀλίγον·

καὶ καθ' ὅσον μὲν ἀραιότατα ξυνέκυρσε πεσόντα

ἀραιότατα Scaliger : ἀραιότατα codd.

83(98) Simplicius *in Phys.* 31.31
ὅτι γὰρ οὐχ ὡς οἱ πολλοὶ νομίζουσι φιλία μὲν μόνη κατ' 'Ε. τὸν νοητὸν
ἐποίησε κόσμον, νεῖκος δὲ μόνον τὸν αἰσθητόν, ἀλλ' ἄμφω πανταχοῦ οἰκείως
θεωρεῖ, ἄκουσον αὐτοῦ τῶν ἐν τοῖς Φυσικοῖς λεγομένων, ἐν οἷς καὶ τῆς
ἐνταῦθα δημιουργικῆς συγκράσεως τὴν 'Αφροδίτην ἤτοι τὴν φιλίαν αἰτίαν φησί.
καλεῖ δὲ τὸ μὲν πῦρ καὶ "Ηφαιστον καὶ ἥλιον καὶ φλόγα, τὸ δὲ ὕδωρ ὄμβρον,
τὸν δὲ ἀέρα αἰθέρα. λέγει οὖν πολλαχοῦ μὲν ταῦτα καὶ ἐν τούτοις δὲ τοῖς
ἔπεσιν·

ἡ δὲ χθὼν τούτοισιν ἴση συνέκυρσε μάλιστα,
'Ηφαίστῳ τ' ὄμβρῳ τε καὶ αἰθέρι παμφανόωντι,
Κύπριδος ὁρμισθεῖσα τελείοις ἐν λιμένεσσιν,
εἴτ' ὀλίγον μείζων †εἴτε πλέον ἐστὶν† ἐλάσσων.
5 ἐκ τῶν αἷμά τ' ἔγεντο καὶ ἄλλης εἴδεα σαρκός.

1 Simp. *in Phys.* 331.5

3 ὁρμηθεῖσα DE   **4** μεῖζον εἴτε πλέον ἐστὶν ἐλάσσον F   μείζων εἴτε
πλέονεσσιν ἐλάσσων Panzerbieter : εἴτ᾽ ἐν πλεόνεσσιν Dodds   **5** αἷμα
τέγεντο D, αἷματ᾽ ἔγεντο E, αἷματ᾽ ἐγένοντο F : αἷμά τε γέντο Sturz

84(85) Simplicius *in Phys.* 331.3

"καὶ τὰ μόρια τῶν ζῴων ἀπὸ τύχης γενέσθαι τὰ πλεῖστά φησιν," ὡς ὅταν
λέγῃ [83(98).1], καὶ πάλιν

ἡ δὲ φλὸξ ἰλάειρα μινυνθαδίης τύχε γαίης,

καὶ ἐν ἄλλοις [70(75).2]. καὶ πολλὰ ἄν τις εὕροι ἐκ τῶν ᾽Ε. Φυσικῶν τοιαῦτα
παραθέσθαι.

ἡ δή D, ἤδη E   φλόξ om. E   ψύχε DF

85(86) Simplicius *in Cael.* 529.21

ἀλλὰ καὶ περὶ γενέσεως τῶν ὀφθαλμῶν τῶν σωματικῶν τούτων λέγων ἐπήγαγεν

ἐξ ὧν ὄμματ᾽ ἔπηξεν ἀτειρέα δι᾽ ᾽Αφροδίτη.

86(87) Simplicius *in Cael.* 529.24 [post 85(86)]

καὶ μετ᾽ ὀλίγον

γόμφοις ἀσκήσασα καταστόργοις ᾽Αφροδίτη

87(95) Simplicius *in Cael.* 529.26 [post 86(87)]

καὶ τὴν αἰτίαν λέγων τοῦ τοὺς μὲν ἐν ἡμέρᾳ, τοὺς δὲ ἐν νυκτὶ κάλλιον ὁρᾶν

Κύπριδος (φησίν) ἐν παλάμῃσιν ὅτε ξὺμ πρῶτ᾽ ἐφύοντο.

88(84) Aristotle *Sens.* 437b23

᾽Ε. δ᾽ ἔοικε νομίζοντι ὁτὲ μὲν ἐξιόντος τοῦ φωτός, ὥσπερ εἴρηται πρότερον
βλέπειν. λέγει γοῦν οὕτως·

ὡς δ᾽ ὅτε τις πρόοδον νοέων ὡπλίσσατο λύχνον,
χειμερίην διὰ νύκτα πυρὸς σέλας αἰθομένοιο,

ἅψας παντοίων ἀνέμων λαμπτῆρας ἀμοργούς,
οἵ τ' ἀνέμων μὲν πνεῦμα διασκιδνᾶσιν ἀέντων,
5 φῶς δ' ἔξω διαθρῷσκον, ὅσον ταναώτερον ἦεν,
λάμπεσκεν κατὰ βηλὸν ἀτειρέσιν ἀκτίνεσσιν·
ὡς δὲ τότ' ἐν μήνιγξιν ἐεργμένον ὠγύγιον πῦρ
λεπτῇσιν ⟨τ'⟩ ὀθόνῃσι λοχάζετο κύκλοπα κούρην·
αἱ δ' ὕδατος μὲν βένθος ἀπέστεγον ἀμφινάοντος,
10 πῦρ δ' ἔξω δίεσκον ὅσον ταναώτερον ἦεν.

ὁτὲ μὲν οὕτως ὁρᾶν φησιν, ὁτὲ δὲ ταῖς ἀπορροίαις ταῖς ἀπὸ τῶν ὁρωμένων.

1–10 cf. Arist. *Sens.* 437b14. Alex. Aphr. *in Sens.* 23.11　　8 cf. Eust. *ad Od.*
20.21

---

3 ἀμουργούς Alex.　　4 αἵ τ' EMPYGᵃ　　5 φῶς] πῦρ EMPYGᵃ, add.
supra ἤ φῶς il　　ἔξω διάντπται τρείατο θεσπεσίῃσιν ὀθόνῃσιν διαθρῶσκον
P　　7 ἐργμένον L, ἐερμένον W, ἐελμένον EM, ἐεκμένον Y, ἐκμένον Gᵃ
8 add. τ' Diels　　ὀθόνοισιν X, χοανῇσιν P, χθονίῃσι EMYGᵃil　　λοχάζετο
EMYil, λοχάζεται Gᵃ, ἐχείατο L, ἐχεύατο cet. codd.　　αἱ χοάνῃσι δίαντα
τετρήατο θεσπεσίῃσιν coni. Blass ex P v.5, incl. Diels post 8　　9 ἀμφινάοντος Bekker : ἀμφιναέντος (ἀμφὶ καέντος M) codd.　　10 δίεσκον P :
διαθρῷσκον cet. codd.

89(88) Strabo 8.364.3
παρ' 'Ε. δέ

μία γίγνεται ἀμφοτέρων ὄψ,

ἡ ὄψις.

Arist. *Poet.* 1458a5

ὄψ codd. : ὄης (ὁ Bᶜ) Arist.

90(94) Plutarch *quaest. nat.* 39, cf. Aristotle *GA* 779b28
cur aqua in summa parte alba, in fundo vero nigra spectatur? an quod
profunditas nigredinis mater est, ut quae solis radios prius quam ad eam

descendant, obtundant et labefactet? superficies autem quoniam continuo a
sole afficitur, candorem luminis recipiat oportet. quod ipsum et E. approbat :

> et niger in fundo fluvii color exstat ab umbra,
> atque cavernosis itidem spectatur in antris.

91(100) Aristotle *Resp.* 473a15

λέγει δὲ περὶ ἀναπνοῆς καὶ 'Ε. . . . καὶ περὶ τῆς διὰ τῶν μυκτήρων ἀναπνοῆς λέγων οἴεται καὶ περὶ τῆς κυρίας λέγειν ἀναπνοῆς . . . γίνεσθαι δέ φησι
τὴν ἀναπνοὴν καὶ ἐκπνοὴν διὰ τὸ φλέβας εἶναί τινας, ἐν αἷς ἔνεστι μὲν
αἷμα, οὐ μέντοι πλήρεις εἰσὶν αἵματος, ἔχουσι δὲ πόρους εἰς τὸν ἔξω ἀέρα,
τῶν μὲν τοῦ σώματος μορίων ἐλάττους, τῶν δὲ τοῦ ἀέρος μείζους· διὸ τοῦ
αἵματος πεφυκότος κινεῖσθαι ἄνω καὶ κάτω, κάτω μὲν φερομένου εἰσρεῖν τὸν
ἀέρα καὶ γίνεσθαι ἀναπνοήν, ἄνω δ' ἰόντος ἐκπίπτειν θύραζε καὶ γίνεσθαι
τὴν ἐκπνοήν, παρεικάζων τὸ συμβαῖνον ταῖς κλεψύδραις·

> ὧδε δ' ἀναπνεῖ πάντα καὶ ἐκπνεῖ· πᾶσι λίφαιμοι
> σαρκῶν σύριγγες πύματον κατὰ σῶμα τέτανται,
> καί σφιν ἐπὶ στομίοις πυκναῖς τέτρηνται ἄλοξιν
> ῥινῶν ἔσχατα τέρθρα διαμπερές, ὥστε φόνον μέν
> 5 κεύθειν, αἰθέρι δ' εὐπορίην διόδοισι τετμῆσθαι.
> ἔνθεν ἔπειθ' ὁπόταν μὲν ἀπαΐξῃ τέρεν αἷμα,
> αἰθὴρ παφλάζων καταΐσσεται οἴδματι μάργῳ,
> εὖτε δ' ἀναθρῴσκῃ πάλιν ἐκπνέει, ὥσπερ ὅταν παῖς
> κλεψύδρῃ παίζουσα διειπετέος χαλκοῖο·
> 10 εὖτε μὲν αὐλοῦ πορθμὸν ἐπ' εὐειδεῖ χερὶ θεῖσα
> εἰς ὕδατος βάπτῃσι τέρεν δέμας ἀργυφέοιο,
> †οὐδετ' ἐς† ἄγγοσδ' ὄμβρος ἐσέρχεται, ἀλλά μιν εἴργει
> ἀέρος ὄγκος ἔσωθε πεσὼν ἐπὶ τρήματα πυκνά,
> εἰσόκ' ἀποστεγάσῃ πυκινὸν ῥόον· αὐτὰρ ἔπειτα
> 15 πνεύματος ἐλλείποντος ἐσέρχεται αἴσιμον ὕδωρ.
> ὡς δ' αὔτως ὅθ' ὕδωρ μὲν ἔχει κατὰ βένθεα χαλκοῦ,
> πορθμοῦ χωσθέντος βροτέῳ χροῒ ἠδὲ πόροιο,
> αἰθὴρ δ' ἐκτός, ἔσω λελιημένος, ὄμβρον ἐρύκει
> ἀμφὶ πύλας ἠθμοῖο δυσηχέος, ἄκρα κρατύνων,
> 20 εἰσόκε χειρὶ μεθῇ· τότε δ' αὖ πάλιν, ἔμπαλιν ἢ πρίν,
> πνεύματος ἐμπίπτοντος ὑπεκθέει αἴσιμον ὕδωρ.
> ὡς δ' αὔτως τέρεν αἷμα κλαδασσόμενον διὰ γυίων
> ὁππότε μὲν παλίνορσον ἐπαΐξειε μυχόνδε,
> αἰθέρος εὐθὺς ῥεῦμα κατέρχεται οἴδματι θῦον,

25   εὖτε δ' ἀναθρῴσκη, πάλιν ἐκπνέει ἴσον ὀπίσσω.

cf. Michael *in PN* 124.15

---

1 λείφαιμοι NVn, δίαιμοι Mil   **3** πυκναῖς MZil, πυκινοῖς vel πυκνοῖς
cet. codd.   ἄλεξι V, δόναξι Mil   **4** τέρθρα GᵃHᵃLmo, τέθρα cet. codd.,
Mich.   φόνον Mil, φανόν cet. codd.   **5** εὐπορίην LQHᵃf, εὔπνοιαν
pr.z, εὐπορίαν cet. codd.   **6** ἐπαίξοι corr. i, ἐπάξοι pr.i, ἐπάξειε l,
ἐπάξη M pr.z, ἀπαίξη LXGᵃHᵃmo, ἐπαίξη cet. codd.   **8** ἀναθρῴσκη
Karsten : ἀναθρώσκει codd.   ἐκπνέει Diels : ἐκπνεῖ codd.   **9** κλεψύδρη
Diels : κλεψύδραις vel κλεψύδρην codd.   παίζησι il, παίζουσι MZ   διειπετέος Diels, δι' εὐπαγεός P, δι' εὐπετέοις S, διιπετέος ZMil, δι' εὐπετέος
cet. codd.   **12** οὐδέτ' ἐς vel οὐδ' ὅτι ἐς codd. : οὐδ' ἔτ' ἐς Diels, οὐδεὶς
DK : οὐδέ τις Bollack   **13** αἰθέρος Stein, Burnet   **14** ἀποστεγάσει
Pfmo, ἀποστεγάσῃ M pr.z, il   **15** ἐκλείποντος MZil   αἴσιμον Mich. :
αὔξιμον vel αἴσιμον codd.   **17** χωσθέντος GᵃHᵃLQf, χρωσθέντος cet.
codd.   χρωὶ ἠδὲ f, χροιῆδε NPVno, χροιήνδε MZ, χροίνε δέ il, χερὶ ἠδὲ
X   πόρους Mil   **19** ἠθμοῖο PSXZ, ἰσθμοῖο cet. codd.   **21** ἐκπί-
πτοντος MZGᵃiln   ὑπεκθέει MZil, ὑπεκθεῖ cet. codd.   **23** ἐπαίξειε
(ἐπάξειε MZ) codd. : ἀπαίξειε Stein, Diels   **24** αἰθέρος MZil, ἕτερον
cet. codd. : τούτερον Furley   οἶδμα τιταίνον MZil   **25** ἀναθρῴσκη
Karsten : ἀναθρώσκοι il, ἀναθρώσκη MSZ, ἀναθρώσκει cet. codd.   ἐκπνέει
Diels : ἐκπνεῖ codd.

92(101) Plutarch *quaest. nat.* 917e
πότερον αἱ κύνες, ὥς φησιν 'Ε.

κέρματα θηρείων μελέων μυκτῆρσιν ἐρευνῶν,

τὰς ἀπορροὰς ἀναλαμβάνουσιν, ἃς ἐναπολείπει τὰ θηρία τῇ ὕλῃ . . .

Alexander *probl.* 22.7
ζῶντος μὲν οὖν διὰ τὸ συνεχῆ εἶναι τὴν ὀσμὴν ἀπὸ τοῦ θηρίου αἰσθάνονται,
τεθνεῶτος δὲ πέπαυσται ῥέουσα· οὐ γὰρ καταλείπει, ὥσπερ 'Ε., ὡς

. . . ἀπέλειπε ποδῶν ἁπαλῇ περὶ ποίῃ

1 Plu. *curios.* 520f, cf. Anon. *in Plat. Theaet.* 71.3

1 κέρματα Anon. : κέμματα (κόμματα B) codd. : πέλματα J¹, τέρματα cet.
Plu. 520f   ἐρευνῶν Plu. 520f : ἐρευνῶσαι codd.   **2** περιπoία codd. :
πνεύματα θ' ὅσσ' ἀπέλειπε ποδῶν ἁπαλῇ περὶ ποίᾳ Diels : ζώονθ' ὅσσ' DK :
ὀσμᾶθ' ὅσσ' Pearson

93(102) Theophrastus *Sens.* 22
οὐ γὰρ ἴσως καθ' αὑτὸ τὸ ἀναπνεῖν αἴτιον τῆς ὀσφρήσεως, ἀλλὰ κατὰ συμβεβηκός, ὡς ἔκ τε τῶν ἄλλων ζώων μαρτυρεῖται καὶ διὰ τῶν εἰρημένων παθῶν·
ὁ δ' ὡς ταύτης οὔσης τῆς αἰτίας καὶ ἐπὶ τέλει πάλιν εἴρηκεν ὥσπερ ἐπι-
σημαινόμενος

            ὧδε μὲν οὖν πνοιῇς τε λελόγχασι πάντα καὶ ὀσμῶν.

πνοιῇς Stephanus : πνοῆς codd.

94(105) Stobaeus 1.49.53
οἴεται γὰρ καὶ Ὅμηρος ἐν τῷ αἵματι εἶναι τοῖς ἀνθρώποις τὴν περὶ τὰ
θνητὰ φρόνησιν ... Ἐ. δὲ οὕτω φαίνεται ὡς ὀργάνου πρὸς σύνεσιν τοῦ αἵματος ὄντος λέγειν·

            αἵματος ἐν πελάγεσσι †τετραμμένα ἀντιθρῶντος†
            τῇ τε νόημα μάλιστα κικλήσκεται ἀνθρώποισιν·
            αἷμα γὰρ ἀνθρώποις περικάρδιόν ἐστι νόημα.

3 *EM* s.v. αἷμα, cf. Censorinus 6.1, Chalc. *Tim.* 218

────────────

1 τεθραμμένη Grotius   ἀντιθορῶντος P², ἀντιθορόντος Scaliger : ἀμφιθρο-
ῶντος Karsten   **2** κυκλίσκεται Heeren

95(132) Clement *Strom.* 5.140.5

            ὄλβιος

ὡς ἔοικεν, ἄρα ἐστὶν κατὰ τὸν Ἐ.,

            ὃς θείων πραπίδων ἐκτήσατο πλοῦτον,
            δειλὸς δ' ᾧ σκοτόεσσα θεῶν πέρι δόξα μέμηλεν.

γνῶσιν καὶ ἀγνωσίαν ὅρους εὐδαιμονίας κακοδαιμονίας τε θείως ἐδήλωσεν.

96(133) Clement *Strom.* 5.81.2

τὸ γάρ τοι θεῖον, ὁ Ἀκραγαντῖνός φησι ποιητής,

> οὐκ ἔστιν πελάσασθαι ἐν ὀφθαλμοῖσιν ἐφικτόν
> ἡμετέροις ἢ χερσὶ λαβεῖν, ᾗπερ τε μεγίστη
> πειθοῦς ἀνθρώποισιν ἁμαξιτὸς εἰς φρένα πίπτει.

Theodoret. *Gr. aff.* 1.74

---

1 πελάσαι δ' ὀφθαλμοῖς (ὀφθαλμοῖσιν, V) οὐκ ἔστιν ἐφικτόν CV Theodoret.
2 ᾗπερ τε codd. : ᾗπερ γε Karsten

97(134) Ammonius *in Int.* 249.1

διὰ ταῦτα δὲ καὶ ὁ Ἀκραγαντῖνος σοφὸς ἐπιρραπίσας τοὺς περὶ θεῶν ὡς
ἀνθρωποειδῶν ὄντων παρὰ τοῖς ποιηταῖς λεγομένους μύθους, ἐπήγαγε προηγ-
ουμένως μὲν περὶ Ἀπόλλωνος, περὶ οὗ ἦν αὐτῷ προσεχῶς ὁ λόγος, κατὰ δὲ
τὸν αὐτὸν τρόπον καὶ περὶ τοῦ θείου παντὸς ἁπλῶς ἀποφαινόμενος

> οὐδὲ γὰρ ἀνδρομέη κεφαλῇ κατὰ γυῖα κέκασται,
> [οὐ μὲν ἀπὸ νώτοιο δύο κλάδοι ἀΐσσουσι,]
> οὐ πόδες, οὐ θοὰ γοῦν', οὐ μήδεα λαχνήεντα,
> ἀλλὰ φρὴν ἱερὴ καὶ ἀθέσφατος ἔπλετο μοῦνον,
> 5 φροντίσι κόσμον ἅπαντα καταΐσσουσα θοῇσιν.

διὰ τοῦ "ἱερή" καὶ τὴν ὑπὲρ νοῦν αἰνιττόμενος αἰτίαν.

1–5 Tz. *Chil.* 13.80   **1** (1, 3–5 mg.) Olymp. *in Gorg.* 4.3   **4–5** Tz. *Chil.* 7.517

1 οὔτε Ammon., Olymp. mg. : οὐ μὲν Tz.   ἀνδρομέη] βροτέη Tz.   **2** νώτων γε codd., corr. Schneider   ἀΐσσουσιν codd. : ἀΐσσονται Stein, vers. seclusi   **3** πόδες] χέρες Olymp. mg.   γοῦνα καὶ Tz.   μήδεα] στήθεα superscrip. A

98(27a) Plutarch *princ. phil.* 777c

ὁ μὲν γὰρ εἰς ἀρετὴν διὰ φιλοσοφίας τελευτῶν σύμφωνον ἑαυτῷ καὶ ἄμεμπτον
ὑφ' ἑαυτοῦ καὶ μεστὸν εἰρήνης καὶ φιλοφροσύνης τῆς πρὸς ἑαυτὸν ἀεὶ παρ-
έχεται τὸν ἄνθρωπον

οὐ στάσις οὐδέ τε δῆρις ἀναίσιμος ἐν μελέεσσιν.

οὐ δῆρις codd. corr. Xylander   ἀναίσιμος Meziriae : ἀνέσιμος w, ἐναίσιμος
cet. codd.

99(129) Porphyry *Vit. Pyth.* 30
τούτοις καὶ ᾽Ε. μαρτυρεῖ λέγων περὶ αὐτοῦ·

> ἦν δέ τις ἐν κείνοισιν ἀνὴρ περιώσια εἰδώς,
> ὃς δὴ μήκιστον πραπίδων ἐκτήσατο πλοῦτον.
> παντοίων τε μάλιστα σοφῶν ἐπιήρανος ἔργων·
> ὁππότε γὰρ πάσῃσιν ὀρέξαιτο πραπίδεσσιν,
> 5 ῥεῖά γε τῶν ὄντων πάντων λεύσσεσκεν ἕκαστον,
> καί τε δέκ᾽ ἀνθρώπων καί τ᾽ εἴκοσιν αἰώνεσσιν.

τὸ γὰρ "περιώσια" καὶ "τῶν ὄντων λεύσσεσκεν ἕκαστα" καὶ "πραπίδων
πλοῦτον" καὶ τὰ ἐοικότα ἐμφαντικὰ μάλιστα τῆς ἐξαιρέτου καὶ ἀκριβεστέρας
παρὰ τοὺς ἄλλους διοργανώσεως ἔν τε τῷ ὁρᾶν καὶ τῷ ἀκούειν καὶ τῷ νοεῖν
τοῦ Πυθαγόρου.

1–6 Iamb. *Vit. Pyth.* 67   **1–2** D.L. 8.54

---

3 σοφῶν add. τ᾽ Wilam.   **5** ῥεῖ᾽ ὅ γε Cobet   ἕκαστον Iamb. : ἕκαστα
codd.

100(110) Hippolytus *RH* 7.29.25
τοιαύτη τις ἡ κατὰ τὸν ᾽Ε. ἡμῖν ἡ τοῦ κόσμου γένεσις καὶ φθορὰ καὶ
σύστασις ἐξ ἀγαθοῦ καὶ κακοῦ συνεστῶσα φιλοσοφεῖται. εἶναι δέ φησι καὶ
νοητὴν τρίτην τινὰ δύναμιν, ἣν καὶ ἐκ τούτων ἐπινοεῖσθαι δύνασθαι, λέγων
ὧδέ πως·

> εἰ γὰρ καὶ σφ᾽ ἀδινῇσιν ὑπὸ πραπίδεσσιν ἐρείσας
> εὐμενέως καθαρῇσιν ἐποπτεύσεις μελέτῃσιν,
> ταῦτά τέ σοι μάλα πάντα δι᾽ αἰῶνος παρέσονται,
> ἄλλα τε πόλλ᾽ ἀπὸ τῶνδε κτ⟨ήσε⟩αι· αὐτὰ γὰρ αὔξει
> 5 ταῦτ᾽ εἰς ἦθος ἕκαστον, ὅπῃ φύσις ἐστὶν ἑκάστῳ.
> εἰ δὲ σύ γ᾽ ἀλλοίων ἐπορέξεαι οἷα κατ᾽ ἄνδρας
> μυρία δειλὰ πέλονται ἅ τ᾽ ἀμβλύνουσι μερίμνας,

ἢ σ' ἄφαρ ἐκλείψουσι περιπλομένοιο χρόνοιο
σφῶν αὐτῶν ποθέοντα φίλην ἐπὶ γένναν ἱκέσθαι·
10 πάντα γὰρ ἴσθι φρόνησιν ἔχειν καὶ νώματος αἶσαν.

10 Hippol. *RH* 6.12.1, S.E. *adv. math.* 8.286

---

1 καὶ ἐν σφαδίνησιν codd. : κεν σφ' ἀδινῇσιν Schneidewin   **2** ἐποπτεύσεις
scripsi : ἐποπτεύεις codd. : ἐποπτεύσῃς Schneid.   **3** τέ Schneid. : δέ
codd.   **4** τῶνδεκτ(ή.η)ται codd. : τῶνδ' ἐκτήσεαι Diels : τῶνδε κτήσ-
εται Bollack   **5** ἦθος Miller : ἔθος codd.   **6** τἄλλ' οἴων ἐπιρέξεις
codd. corr. Schneid.   **7** δῆλα codd. : δείλα Schneid.   ἅ τ' Diels :
τά τ' codd.   μερίμνας Schneid. : μέριμναι codd.   **8** ἢ σ' Meineke :
σῆς codd.   περιπλομένοιο Miller : περιπλομένοις codd.   **10** νώματος
αἶσαν S.E. : γνωματόσισον codd. : γνώμην ἴσην Hippol. 6.12

101(111) D.L. 8.59
τοῦτόν φησι ὁ Σάτυρος λέγειν ὡς αὐτὸς (ὁ Γοργίας) παρείη τῷ 'Ε. γοητεύοντι.
ἀλλὰ καὶ αὐτὸν διὰ τῶν ποιημάτων ἐπαγγέλλεσθαι τοῦτό τε καὶ ἄλλα πλείω,
δι' ὧν φησι·

    φάρμακα δ' ὅσσα γεγᾶσι κακῶν καὶ γήραος ἄλκαρ
    πεύσῃ, ἐπεὶ μούνῳ σοι ἐγὼ κρανέω τάδε πάντα.
    παύσεις δ' ἀκαμάτων ἀνέμων μένος οἵ τ' ἐπὶ γαῖαν
    ὀρνύμενοι πνοιαῖσι καταφθινύθουσιν ἀρούρας·
5   καὶ πάλιν, ἢν ἐθέλησθα, παλίντιτα πνεύματ' ἐπάξεις·
    θήσεις δ' ἐξ ὄμβροιο κελαινοῦ καίριον αὐχμόν
    ἀνθρώποις, θήσεις δὲ καὶ ἐξ αὐχμοῖο θερείου
    ῥεύματα δενδρεόθρεπτα, †τάτ' αἰθέρι ναιήσονται†,
    ἄξεις δ' ἐξ Ἀίδαο καταφθιμένου μένος ἀνδρός.

1–9 Suda s.v. ἄπνους, Tz. *Chil.* 2.909   **3–5** Clem. 6.30.2

---

4 πνοιαῖσι] θνητοῖσι Clem.   ἀρούρας Clem., Tz. : ἀρούραν codd.   **5**
ἢν κ' P, Suda, ἢν F, ἢν καὶ θέλησθα B : εὖτ' ἐθέλησθα Clem.   παλίντονα
Suda   **6** θήσεις F, (om. ἐπάξεις) Clem. : τήσεις B, στήσεις P, Suda, Tz.
7 θήσεις B²F, θήσει B¹, στήσεις P, Tz.   θερείου P², Tz. : θερείοις BFP¹,
om. Suda   **8** τάτ' αἰθέρι ναιήσονται P¹, ταταιθερυναίης ὄντα B, τάτε
θέρειναήσονται F, τάτ' ἐνθέρει ἀήσονται P² : τά τ' ἐν θέρει ἔσονται Suda :
τά τ' αἰθέρινα θήσονται Tz. : τά τ' αἰθέρι ναιήσονται Diels : τά τ' αἰθέρι
ἀίσσονται Wilam.

8. ΚΑΘΑΡΜΟΙ

102(112) 1,2, 4–11 D.L. 8.61 (3 Diod. Sic. 13.83.2; 10,12 Clem. *Strom.* 6.30.3)

τὴν γοῦν ἄπνουν ὁ Ἡρακλείδης φησὶ τοιοῦτόν τι εἶναι, ὡς τριάκοντα ἡμέρας συντηρεῖν ἄπνουν καὶ ἄσφυκτον τὸ σῶμα· ὅθεν εἶπεν αὐτὸν καὶ ἰητρὸν καὶ μάντιν, λαμβάνων ἅμα καὶ ἀπὸ τούτων τῶν στίχων·

> ὦ φίλοι, οἳ μέγα ἄστυ κάτα ξανθοῦ Ἀκράγαντος
> ναίετ' ἀν' ἄκρα πόλεος, ἀγαθῶν μελεδήμονες ἔργων,
> (ξείνων αἰδοῖοι λιμένες κακότητος ἄπειροι,)
> χαίρετ'· ἐγὼ δ' ὑμῖν θεὸς ἄμβροτος οὐκέτι θνητός
> 5 πωλεῦμαι μετὰ πᾶσι τετιμένος, ὥσπερ ἔοικεν,
> ταινίαις τε περίστεπτος στέφεσίν τε θαλείοις·
> †τοῖσιν ἅμ' ἀν† ἵκωμαι ἐς ἄστεα τηλεθάοντα
> ἀνδράσιν ἠδὲ γυναιξὶ σεβίζομαι· οἱ δ' ἅμ' ἔπονται
> μυρίοι ἐξερέοντες ὅπῃ πρὸς κέρδος ἀταρπός,
> 10 οἱ μὲν μαντοσυνέων κεχρημένοι, οἱ δ' ἐπὶ νούσων
> παντοίων ἐπύθοντο κλύειν εὐηκέα βάξιν,
> δηρὸν δὴ χαλεπῇσι πεπαρμένοι ⟨ἀμφ' ὀδύνῃσιν⟩.

1–2, 4–6 Anth. Gr. 9.569   **1–2** D.L. 8.54   **4–5** D.L. 8.66, S.E. adv.math. 1.302   **4** Plot. 4.7.10.38, Tz. ex.Il. 29.24, Philostr. Vit. Ap. 1.1, Lucian. laps. 2, Suda s.v. Empedokles, Pythagoras

---

2 πόλεος Merzdorf : πόληος F,P (Anth.), πολέως BP¹, Pl (Anth.)   **3** ex D.S. 13.83.2, fortasse falso inser.   **4** ὑμῖν] ὕμμιν Philostr., Suda, Luc. (exc. F): εἰμὶ M (Plot.), F (Luc.)   **5** τετιμημένος B, ABVCR (S.E.)

ἔοικεν *Anth.* : ἔοικα codd.   **6** περίστρεπτος F, P (*Anth.*)   θαλείοις *Anth.*, θαλίος codd.   **7** τοῖσιν ἄμ' ἄν BP¹F, ἄμ' εὖτ' ἄν P² : πᾶσι δὲ τοῖς ἄν Wilam. : πᾶσι δ' ἄμ' εὖτ' ἄν conieci   **10** δ' ἐπὶ Clem. : δέ τι codd.   νοῦσον Clem.   **12** δηρὸν δὴ Sylburg : σιδηρὸν vel σιδηρὰν Clem.   χαλεποῖσι Clem. corr. Bergk   ἀμφ' ὀδύνῃσιν add. Bergk

103(114) Clement *Strom.* 5.9.1

καί μοι σφόδρα ἐπεινεῖν ἔπεισι τὸν 'Ακραγαντῖνον ποιητὴν ἐξυμνοῦντα τὴν πίστιν ὧδέ πως·

> ὦ φίλοι, οἶδα μὲν οὕνεκ' ἀληθείη πάρα μύθοις
> οὓς ἐγὼ ἐξερέω· μάλα δ' ἀργαλέη γε τέτυκται
> ἀνδράσι καὶ δύσζηλος ἐπὶ φρένα πίστιος ὁρμή.

1 οὕνεκ' Meineke : οὖν ἐκ τ' codd.   **2** ἔγωγ codd. corr. Sylburg

104(11) Plutarch *adv. Col.* 1113c

ἐμοὶ μέντοι δοκεῖ μὴ τοῦτο κινεῖν τὸ ἐκφορικὸν ὁ 'Ε., ἀλλ' ὡς πρότερον εἴρηται, πραγματικῶς διαφέρεσθαι περὶ τῆς ἐξ οὐκ ὄντων γενέσεως, ἣν "φύσιν" τινὲς καλοῦσι. δηλοῖ δὲ μάλιστα διὰ τούτων τῶν ἐπῶν·

> νήπιοι· οὐ γάρ σφιν δολιχόφρονές εἰσι μέριμναι,
> οἳ δὴ γίγνεσθαι πάρος οὐκ ἐὸν ἐλπίζουσιν,
> ἤ τι καταθνήσκειν τε καὶ ἐξόλλυσθαι ἁπάντῃ.

ταῦτα γὰρ τὰ ἔπη μέγα βοῶντός ἐστι τοῖς ὦτα ἔχουσιν, ὡς οὐκ ἀναιρεῖ γένεσιν ἀλλὰ τὴν ἐκ μὴ ὄντος, οὐδὲ φθορὰν ἀλλὰ τὴν "ἁπάντῃ," τουτέστι τὴν εἰς τὸ μὴ ὂν ἀπολλύουσαν.

3 τι Ε : τοι Β   ἁπάντῃ Xylander : πάντῃ codd.

105(113) Sextus *adv. math.* 1.302 [post 102(112).4–5]

καὶ πάλιν·

> ἀλλὰ τί τοῖσδ' ἐπίκειμ' ὡσεὶ μέγα χρῆμά τι πράσσων,
> εἰ θνητῶν περίειμι πολυφθερέων ἀνθρώπων;

... συνήσει ὅτι ὁ 'Ε. θεὸν ἑαυτὸν προσηγόρευσεν, ἐπεὶ μόνος καθαρὸν ἀπὸ κακίας τηρήσας τὸν νοῦν καὶ ἀνεπιθόλωτον τῷ ἐν ἑαυτῷ θεῷ τὸν ἐκτὸς κατείληφεν.

2 πολυφθορέων ABCVR

106(15) Plutarch *adv. Col.* 1113d [post 104(11)]
ἐπεὶ τῷ γε βουλομένῳ μὴ ἀγρίως οὕτως μηδὲ ἠλιθίως ἀλλὰ πραότερον συκοφαντεῖν τὸ μετὰ ταῦτα ἐπὶ τοὐναντίον ἂν αἰτιάσασθαι παράσχοι, τοῦ 'Ε.
λέγοντος

οὐκ ἂν ἀνὴρ τοιαῦτα σοφὸς φρεσὶ μαντεύσαιτο,
ὡς ὄφρα μέν τε βιῶσι, τὸ δὴ βίοτον καλέουσι,
τόφρα μὲν οὖν εἰσίν, καί σφιν πάρα δειλὰ καὶ ἐσθλά,
πρὶν δὲ πάγεν τε βροτοὶ καὶ ⟨ἐπεὶ⟩ λύθεν, οὐδὲν ἄρ' εἰσίν.

ταῦτα γὰρ οὐκ ἀρνουμένου μὴ εἶναι τοὺς γεγονότας καὶ ζῶντάς ἐστιν, εἶναι δὲ μᾶλλον οἰομένου καὶ τοὺς μηδέπω γεγονότας καὶ τοὺς ἤδη τεθνηκότας.

1 φρέσι post ἀνήρ codd. corr. Xylander   3 δειλά Bergk : δεινά codd.
4 ἐπεὶ add. Reiske   λύθεν Xylander : λυθέντ' codd.

107(115) 1, 3, 5, 6, 13 Plutarch *exil.* 607c; 1-2, 4-12, 13, 14 Hippolytus *RH* 7.29.14-23

1-2 Simp. *in Phys.* 1184.9, Stob. 2.8.42   6-7 Origen *Cels.* 8.53   9-12 Plu. *de Is. et Os.* 361c, *vit. aer.* 830f; Eus. *PE* 5.5.2   13-14 Ascl. *in Metaph.* 197.20; Phlp. *in GC* 266.4, *in de An.* 73.32, *in Phys.* 24.20; Plot. 4.8.1.19; Hierocl. *in CA* 54

Plutarch *exil.* 607c
ὁ δ' 'Ε. ἐν ἀρχῇ τῆς φιλοσοφίας προαναφωνήσας

1   ἔστιν ἀνάγκης χρῆμα, θεῶν ψήφισμα παλαιόν,
3   εὖτέ τις ἀμπλακίῃσι φόβῳ φίλα γυῖα †μιν†
5   δαίμονες οἵ τε μακραίωνος λελάχασι βίοιο,
6   τρίς μιν μυρίας ὥρας ἀπὸ μακάρων ἀλάλησθαι,
13   τὴν καὶ ἐγὼ νῦν εἶμι, φυγὰς θεόθεν καὶ ἀλήτης,

οὐχ ἑαυτόν, ἀλλ' ἀφ' ἑαυτοῦ πάντας ἀποδείκνυσι μετανάστας ἐνταῦθα καὶ ξένους καὶ φυγάδας ἡμᾶς ὄντας.

Hippolytus *RH* 7.29.14 [post 22(29).1–2, 4]
καὶ τοῦτό ἐστιν ὃ λέγει περὶ τῆς ἑαυτοῦ γεννήσεως ὁ Ἐ.·

13 *τῶν καὶ ἐγὼ ⟨νῦν⟩ εἰμι, φυγὰς θεόθεν καὶ ἀλήτης,*

τουτέστι θεὸν καλῶν τὸ ἓν καὶ τὴν ἐκείνου ἑνότητα, ἐν ᾧ ἦν πρὶν ὑπὸ τοῦ νείκους ἀποσπασθῆναι καὶ γενέσθαι ἐν τοῖς πολλοῖς τούτοις τοῖς κατὰ τὴν τοῦ νείκους διακόσμησιν· 14 *"νείκει" γάρ φησι "μαι⟨νομένῳ πίσυνος," νεῖκος μαι⟩νόμενον καὶ τεταραγμένον καὶ ἄστατον τὸν δημιουργὸν τοῦδε τοῦ κόσμου ὁ Ἐ. ἀποκαλῶν. αὕτη γάρ ἐστιν ἡ καταδίκη καὶ ἀνάγκη τῶν ψυχῶν, ὧν ἀποσπᾷ τὸ νεῖκος ἀπὸ τοῦ ἑνὸς καὶ δημιουργεῖ καὶ ἐργάζεται, λέγων τοιοῦτόν τινα τρόπον·*

4 *ὅς καὶ ἐπίορκον ἁμαρτήσας ἐπομώσει,*
5 *δαίμονες οἵτε μακραίωνος λελάχασι βίοιο,*

"δαίμονας" τὰς ψυχὰς λέγων "μακραίωνας," ὅτι εἰσι ἀθάνατοι καὶ μακροὺς ζῶσιν αἰῶνας·

6 *τρὶς μὲν μυρίας ὥρας ἀπὸ μακάρων ἀλάλησθαι,*

"μάκαρας" καλῶν τοὺς συνηγμένους ὑπὸ τῆς φιλίας ἀπὸ τῶν πολλῶν εἰς τὴν ἑνότητα τοῦ κόσμου τοῦ νοητοῦ. τούτους οὖν φησιν "ἀλάλησθαι" καὶ

7 *φυομένους παντοῖα διὰ χρόνου εἴδεα θνητῶν,*
8 *ἀργαλέας βιότοιο μεταλλάσσοντα κελεύθους.*

"ἀργαλέας κελεύθους" φησὶν εἶναι τῶν ψυχῶν τὰς εἰς τὰ σώματα μεταβολὰς καὶ μετακοσμήσεις. τοῦτ' ἐστὶν ὃ λέγει·

8 *ἀργαλέας βιότοιο μεταλλάσσοντα κελεύθους·*

"μεταλλάσσουσι" γὰρ αἱ ψυχαὶ σῶμα ἐκ σώματος, ὑπὸ τοῦ νείκους μεταβαλλόμεναι καὶ κολαζόμεναι καὶ οὐκ ἐώμεναι μένειν εἰς τὸ ἕν· ἀλλὰ κολάζεσθαι ἐν πάσαις κολάσεσιν ὑπὸ τοῦ νείκους τὰς ψυχὰς μεταβαλλομένας σῶμα ἐκ σώματος.

9   *αἰθέριόν γε (φησί) μένος ψυχὰς πόντονδε διώκει,*
10 *πόντος δ' ἐς χθονὸς οὖδας ἀπέπτυσε, γαῖα δ' ἐς αὐγάς*
11 *ἠελίου φαέθοντος, ὁ δ' αἰθέρος ἔμβαλε δίναις·*
12 *ἄλλος δ' ἐξ ἄλλου δέχεται, στυγέουσι δὲ πάντες.*

αὕτη ἐστὶν ἡ κόλασις ἣν κολάζει ὁ δημιουργός, καθάπερ χαλκεύς τις μετακοσμῶν σίδηρον καὶ ἐκ πυρὸς εἰς ὕδωρ μεταβάπτον· πῦρ γάρ ἐστιν ὁ αἰθήρ, ὅθεν εἰς πόντον μεταβάλλει τὰς ψυχὰς ὁ δημιουργός, χθὼν δὲ ἡ γῆ· ὅθεν φησιν· ἐξ ὕδατος εἰς γῆν, ἐκ γῆς δὲ εἰς τὸν ἀέρα. τούτ' ἐστὶν ὃ λέγει·

10   γαῖα δ' ἐς αὐγὰς
11 ἠελίου φαέθοντος, ὁ δ' αἰθέρος ἔμβαλε δίναις·
12 ἄλλος ⟨δ'⟩ ἐξ ἄλλου δέχεται, στυγέουσι δὲ πάντες.

μισουμένας οὖν τὰς ψυχὰς καὶ βασανιζομένας καὶ κολαζομένας ἐν τῷδε τῷ κόσμῳ κατὰ τὸν Ἐ. συνάγει ἡ φιλία, ἀγαθή τις οὖσα καὶ κατοικτείρουσα τὸν στεναγμὸν αὐτῶν καὶ τὴν ἄτακτον καὶ πονηρὰν "τοῦ νείκους τοῦ μαινομένου" κατασκευὴν καὶ ἐξάγειν κατ' ὀλίγον ἐκ τοῦ κόσμου καὶ προσοικειοῦν τῷ ἑνὶ σπεύδουσα καὶ κοπιῶσα, ὅπως τὰ πάντα εἰς τὴν ἑνότητα καταντήσῃ ὑπ' αὐτῆς ἀγόμενα. . . . τοῦτον εἶναί φησιν ὁ Ἐ. νόμον μέγιστον τῆς τοῦ παντὸς διοικήσεως, λέγων ὧδέ πως·

1 ἔστιν ἀνάγκης χρῆμα, θεῶν ψήφισμα παλαιόν,
2 ἀΐδιον, πλατέεσσι κατεσφρηγισμένον ὅρκοις,

"ἀνάγκην" καλῶν τὴν ἐξ ἑνὸς εἰς πολλὰ κατὰ τὸ νεῖκος καὶ ἐκ πολλῶν εἰς ἓν κατὰ τὴν φιλίαν μεταβολήν.

107(115) fragmentum factum est hoc modo:

  ἔστιν ἀνάγκης χρῆμα, θεῶν ψήφισμα παλαιόν,
  ἀΐδιον, πλατέεσσι κατεσφρηγισμένον ὅρκοις·
  εὖτέ τις ἀμπλακίῃσι φόβῳ φίλα γυῖα †μιν†
  †ὃς καὶ† ἐπίορκον ἁμαρτήσας ἐπομόσσῃ,
5 δαίμονες οἵτε μακραίωνος λελάχασι βίοιο,
  τρίς μιν μυρίας ὥρας ἀπὸ μακάρων ἀλάλησθαι,
  φυόμενον παντοῖα διὰ χρόνου εἴδεα θνητῶν
  ἀργαλέας βιότοιο μεταλλάσσοντα κελεύθους.
  αἰθέριον μὲν γάρ σφε μένος πόντονδε διώκει,
10 πόντος δ' ἐς χθονὸς οὖδας ἀπέπτυσε, γαῖα δ' ἐς αὐγάς
  ἠελίου φαέθοντος, ὁ δ' αἰθέρος ἔμβαλε δίναις·
  ἄλλος δ' ἐξ ἄλλου δέχεται, στυγέουσι δὲ πάντες.
  τῶν καὶ ἐγὼ νῦν εἰμι, φυγὰς θεόθεν καὶ ἀλήτης,
  νείκεϊ μαινομένῳ πίσυνος.

codd. = Hippol. 7.29.14, exc.v. 3 codd. = Plu. 607c

1 ἔστιν Simp. : ἔστι τι codd., Plu.   ἀνάγκης Plu. : ἀνάγκη codd., Simp.
σφρήγισμα Α, σφράγισμα FM (Simp.)   2 κατεσφρηγισμένον Simp. :
κατεσφραγισμένον codd., Stob.   3 φόβῳ φίλα γυῖα μιν codd. : φόνῳ
φίλα γυῖα μιήνῃ Stephanus, edd.   4 ὅς καί] νείκει θ' ὅς κ(ε) Diels : ὅς κεν
τὴν van der Ben : ὅρκον ὅτις κ(ε) temptavi   ἐπομόσσῃ Schneidewin : ἐπομώσει codd.   5 δαίμονες οἵ τε Plu. : δαιμόνιοί τε codd.   μακραίωνες
λελόγχασι βίοιο Plu. : μακραίωνος λελάχασι βίοις codd.   6 μιν Plu. :
μὲν codd. Origen,   ἀλάλησθαι Plu. : ἀλάλασθε codd.   7 φυόμενον
Stein : φυομένους codd. : γινομένην Origen   παντοίαν Origen   χρόνου
Bergk : χρόνον codd., Origen   εἴδεα edd. : ἴδεα codd. : ἰδέαν Origen
9 Plu. (om. μὲν) 361c, 830f, Eus. : αἰθέριόν γε μένος ψυχὰς πόντονδε ἐχθονὸς
διώκει codd.   10 ἀνέπτυσε Plu. 830   αὐγάς] αὖθις Plu. 361 : λυγάς
Χ, λυτάς J Plu. 830   11 φαέθοντος] ἀκάμαντος (ἀκάματος zab 830) Plu.
13 τὴν καὶ ἐγὼ νῦν εἰμι Plu. : νῦν om. codd. : ὡς καὶ ἐγὼ δεῦρ' εἰμί Phlp.,
Ascl.   14 αἰθομένῳ Ascl.

108(117) Hippolytus *RH* 1.3.1

Ε. δὲ μετὰ τούτους γενόμενος καὶ περὶ δαιμόνων φύσεως εἶπε πολλά, ὡς
ἀναστρέφονται διοικοῦντες τὰ κατὰ τὴν γῆν ὄντες πλεῖστοι, οὗτος τὴν τοῦ
παντὸς ἀρχὴν νεῖκος καὶ φιλίαν ἔφη· καὶ τὸ τῆς μονάδος νοερὸν πῦρ τὸν
θεόν, καὶ συνεστάναι ἐκ πυρὸς τὰ πάντα καὶ εἰς πῦρ ἀναλυθήσεσθαι· ᾧ σχεδὸν
καὶ οἱ Στωικοὶ συντίθεται δόγματι, ἐκπύρωσιν προσδοκῶντες. μάλιστα δὲ
πάντων συγκατατίθεται τῇ μετενσωματώσει, οὕτως εἰπών·

ἤδη γάρ ποτ' ἐγὼ γενόμην κοῦρός τε κόρη τε
θάμνος τ' οἰωνός τε καὶ ἔξαλος ἔλλοπος ἰχθύς.

οὗτος πάσας εἰς πάντα τὰ ζῷα μεταλλάττειν εἶπε τὰς ψυχάς.

1–2 Clem. *Strom.* 6.24.3, Ath. 8.365a, D.L. 8.77, Them. *in de An.* 35.13,
Phlp. *in de An.* 140.7, Sophon. *in de An.* 24.39, Eust. *ad Od.* 18.79, Olymp.
in Phd. 58.17, *Anth. Gr.* 9.569, Cyrill. *Jul.* 872c, cf. Chalcid. *Tim.* 197   1
Philostr. *Vit. Ap.* 1.1, Suda s.v. Empedoklēs, Pythagoras   2 Proclus *in R.*
2.333.8

1 ἤτοι μὲν γὰρ codd. : ἤδη ποτ' Ath., Eust.   κοῦρός τε κούρη τε codd. pler.
Phlp. : κούρη (κόρη Philostr.) τε κόρος τε R Phlp., Ath., Them., Philostr.,
Eust., Cyrill., Suda   2 ἐξαλλὸς Β : ἐξ ἀλὸς Eust., Ath., *Anth. Gr.*, Phlp.,

Sophon. : εἰν ἀλλ Clem. : ἐξ ἁλὸς, ἐξαλλὸς var. Olymp. ἔλλοπος Clem. :
ἔμπορος codd., Ath., Phlp., Them., Sophon., Procl. : ἔμπυρος D.L., Anth.
Gr. : ἄμφορος vel νήχυτος Olymp. : φαίδιμος Cyrill.

109(116) Plutarch *quaest. conv.* 745d
ὁ δὲ Πλάτων ἄτοπος ... τὰς δὲ Μούσας ἢ παραλείπων παντάπασιν ἢ τοῖς
τῶν Μοιρῶν ὀνόμασι προσαγορεύων καὶ καλῶν θυγατέρας Ἀνάγκης. ἄμουσον
γὰρ Ἀνάγκη, μουσικὸν δὲ ἡ Πειθώ, καὶ Μούσαις †φιλοδαμοῦσα† πολὺ μᾶλλον
οἶμαι τῆς Ἐ. Χάριτος

στυγέει δύστλητον Ἀνάγκην.

110(126) Stobaeus 1.49.60 (ex Porphyr.)
αὐτῆς γὰρ τῆς μετακοσμήσεως εἱμαρμένη καὶ φύσις ὑπὸ Ἐ. δαίμων ἀνηγό-
ρευται·

σαρκῶν ἀλλογνῶτι περιστέλλουσα χιτῶνι

καὶ μεταμπίσχουσα τὰς ψυχάς.

Plu. *esu. carn.* 998c

ἀλλογνῶτι Plu. : ἀλλοιχῶτι vel ἀλλογνῶτι codd. : ἀλλοιόχρωτι Karsten

111(119) Plutarch *exil.* 607d [post 107(115).1, 3, 5, 6, 13]
"οὐ γὰρ αἷμα" φησίν "ἡμῖν οὐδὲ πνεῦμα συγκραθέν, ὦ ἄνθρωποι, ψυχῆς
οὐσίαν καὶ ἀρχὴν παρέσκεν, ἀλλ' ἐκ τούτων τὸ σῶμα συμπέπλασται γηγενὲς
καὶ θνητόν," τῆς δὲ ψυχῆς ἀλλαχόθεν ἡκούσης δεῦρο, τὴν γένεσιν ἀποδημίαν
ὑποκορίζεται τῷ πραοτάτῳ τῶν ὀνομάτων· τὸ δ' ἀληθέστατον, φεύγει καὶ
πλανᾶται θείοις ἐλαυνομένη δόγμασι καὶ νόμοις· εἶτα ... ἐνδεδεμένη τῷ
σώματι διὰ τὸ μὴ ἀναφέρειν μηδὲ μνημονεύειν

ἐξ οἵης τιμῆς τε καὶ ὅσσου μήκεος ὄλβου

μεθέστηκεν, οὐ Σάρδεων Ἀθήνας ... ἀλλ' οὐρανοῦ καὶ σελήνης γῆν ἀμει-
ψαμένη καὶ τὸν ἐπὶ γῆς βίον.

Clem. *Strom.* 4.13.1, Hippol. *RH* 5.7.30, Stob. 3.40.5

ὅσσου edd. : ὅσου codd., Stob. : οἵου Clem., om. Hippol.

112(118) Clement *Strom*. 3.14.1 (cf. Sextus *adv. math.* 11.96)
Ἡράκλειτος γοῦν κακίζων φαίνεται τὴν γένεσιν, ἐπειδὰν φῇ· (22B20). δῆλος
δὲ αὐτῷ συμφερόμενος καὶ ᾿Ε. λέγων·

κλαῦσά τε καὶ κώκυσα ἰδὼν ἀσυνήθεα χῶρον.

113(121) 1–2, 4 Hierocles *in CA* 54, 2–3 Proclus *in Cra*. 97.23
ἄνεισι δὲ καὶ τὴν ἀρχαίαν ἕξιν ἀπολαμβάνει, εἰ φύγοι τὰ περὶ γῆν καὶ τὸν

ἀτερπέα χῶρον

ὡς ὁ αὐτὸς λέγει,

ἔνθα φόνος τε κότος τε καὶ ἄλλων ἔθνεα κηρῶν,
(αὐχμηραί τε νόσοι καὶ σήψιες ἔργα τε ῥευστά)

εἰς ὃν οἱ ἐμπεσόντες

Ἄτης ἀν λειμῶνα κατὰ σκότος ἡλάσκουσιν.

ἡ δὲ ἔφεσις τοῦ φεύγοντος τὸν τῆς " "Ἄτης λειμῶνα" πρὸς τὸν τῆς ᾿Αληθείας
ἐπείγεται λειμῶνα, ὃν ἀπολιπὼν τῇ ὁρμῇ τῆς πτερορρυήσεως εἰς γήινον ἔρχεται
σῶμα ὀλβίου αἰῶνος ἀμερθείς.

2, 4 Procl. *in R*. 2.157.27   2 Philo *Prov*. (ap. Eus. *PE* 8.14.23), Theo Sm.
149.6   4 Procl. *in Tim*. 339b, Them. *Or*. 178a

───────────

2 φόνοι τελοῦνται Eus. : κοτός τε φόνος τε Theo, Procl.   3 ex Procl. *in*
Cra. 97.23 fortasse falso inser.   4 ἀν λειμῶνα Bentley : ἀνὰ λειμῶνα
codd. : ἐν λειμῶνι Procl.   ἡλάσκουσι] ἰλάσκονται Procl.

114(124) Clement *Strom*. 3.14.2 [post 130(125)]
καὶ πάλιν·

ὢ πόποι, ὢ δειλὸν θνητῶν γένος, ὢ δυσάνολβον,

οἴων ἐξ ἐρίδων ἔκ τε στοναχῶν ἐγένεσθε.

2 Porph. *abst.* 3.27, Eus. *PE* 14.18.28

1 ἡ δειλὸν codd. corr. Scaliger   2 τοίων ἔκ τ' ἐρίδων Porph., Eus. :
οἴων ἐξ ἐρείδων codd.   στοναχῶν] νεικέων Porph.   γενόμεσθα Porph. :
πέπλασθε Eus.

115(120) Porphyry *antr. nymph.* 8 (cf. Plot. 4.8.1.33)
ἀφ' ὧν οἶμαι ὁρμώμενοι καὶ οἱ Πυθαγόρειοι καὶ μετὰ τούτους Πλάτων ἄντρον
καὶ σπήλαιον τὸν κόσμον ἀπεφήνατο. παρά τε γὰρ 'Ε. αἱ ψυχοπομποὶ δυνάμεις λέγουσιν

     ἠλύθομεν τόδ' ὑπ' ἄντρον ὑπόστεγον . . .

116(122) Plutarch *tranq. an.* 474b
οὐ γάρ, ὡς ὁ Μένανδρός φησιν, "ἅπαντι δαίμων ἀνδρὶ συμπαρίσταται / εὐθὺς
γενομένῳ. μυσταγωγὸς τοῦ βίου / ἀγαθός," ἀλλὰ μᾶλλον, ὡς 'Ε., διτταί τινες
ἕκαστον ἡμῶν γινόμενον παραλαμβάνουσι καὶ κατάρχονται μοῖραι καὶ δαί-
μονες·

     ἔνθ' ἦσαν Χθονίη τε καὶ Ἡλιόπη ταναῶπις,
     Δῆρίς θ' αἱματόεσσα καὶ Ἁρμονίη θεμερῶπις,
     Καλλιστώ τ' Αἰσχρή τε, Θόωσά τε Δηναιή τε,
     Νημερτής τ' ἐρόεσσα μελάγκουρός τ' Ἀσάφεια.

2 cf. Plu. *de Is. et Os.* 370d   4 cf. Tz. *Chil.* 12.509

2 θερμερῶπις YhS², γε μερῶπις Δ   3 δηναίη Δ, δαιναίη cet. codd.
4 μελάγκουρος Tz : μελάγκαρπστ' NRS, μελανκαρπώτ' G¹XY¹, μελάγκαρπός
τ' cet. codd.

117(123) Cornutus *Comp.* 17(30.3)
μετὰ δὲ ταῦτα ἡ τῶν λεγομένων Τιτάνων ἐστὶ γένεσις. οὗτοι δ' ἂν εἶεν
διαφοραὶ τῶν ὄντων· ὡς γὰρ 'Ε. φυσικῶς ἐξαριθμεῖται

     Φυσώ τε Φθιμένη τε, καὶ Εὐναίη καὶ Ἔγερσις,

Κινώ τ' 'Αστεμφής τε, πολυστέφανός τε Μεγιστώ,
καὶ †φορίη† Σωπή τε καὶ 'Ομφαίη

καὶ πολλὰς ἄλλας, τὴν εἰρημένην ποικιλίαν τῶν ὄντων αἰνιττόμενος.

3 φορίη NB, φορίην MXPlc, φυρύη cet. codd.   σωπή Bergk : σοφήν MXPlc,
σόφη b, σομφήν V : σομφή Karsten   ὀμφαλήν vel ὀμφαίην codd.

118(128) Porphyry *abst.* 2.20 (1–8), 2.27 (8–10)
τὰ μὲν ἀρχαῖα τῶν ἱερῶν ... τὰ ὑδρόσπονδα, τὰ δὲ μετὰ ταῦτα μελίσπονδα
... εἶτ' ἐλαιόσπονδα· τέλος δ' ἐπὶ πᾶσιν τὰ ὕστερον γεγονότα οἰνόσπονδα.
μαρτυρεῖται δὲ ταῦτα οὐ μόνον ὑπὸ τῶν κύρβεων ... ἀλλὰ καὶ παρ' 'Ε.,
ὃς περὶ τῆς θεογονίας διεξιὼν καὶ περὶ τῶν θυμάτων παρεμφαίνει λέγων·

> οὐδέ τις ἦν κείνοισιν "Αρης θεὸς οὐδὲ Κυδοιμός
> οὐδὲ Ζεὺς βασιλεὺς οὐδὲ Κρόνος οὐδὲ Ποσειδῶν,
> ἀλλὰ Κύπρις βασίλεια,

ἥ ἐστιν ἡ φιλία·

> τὴν οἵ γ' εὐσεβέεσσιν ἀγάλμασιν ἱλάσκοντο
> 5   γραπτοῖς τε ζώοισι μύροισί τε δαιδαλεόδμοις
> σμύρνης τ' ἀκρήτου θυσίαις λιβάνου τε θυώδους,
> ξανθῶν τε σπονδὰς μελίτων ῥίπτοντες ἐς οὖδας,

ἅπερ καὶ νῦν ἔτι σώζεται παρ' ἐνίοις οἷον ἴχνη τινὰ τῆς ἀληθείας ὄντα,

> ταύρων δ' †ἀκρίτοισι† φόνοις οὐ δεύετο βωμός,
> ἀλλὰ μύσος τοῦτ' ἔσκεν ἐν ἀνθρώποισι μέγιστον,
> 10   θυμὸν ἀπορραίσαντας ἐέδμεναι ἠέα γυῖα.

1–7 Ath. 12.510c   **1–3** Eust. *ad Il.* 22.116   **8–10** Eus. *PE* 4.14.7, Cyrill.
Jul. 76.972d

─────────────

2 οὐδ' ὁ Κρ. οὐδ' ὁ Π. codd. : οὐδὲ Κρ. om. Eus.   **4** ἱλάσκονται Ath.
5 δαιδαλεόσμοις codd.   **6** σμύρνοις τε Ath.   ἀκράτου codd.   **7**
ξουθῶν τε σπονδὰς μελίττων ῥιπτοῦντες codd.   **8** ἀκρίτοισι codd., Cyrill. :
ἀκράτοισι Eus. : ἀκρήτοισσι Scaliger : ἀρρήτοισι Fabricius   **9–10** ex *abst.*
2.27, Eus., Cyrill. inser.   **9** ἔσχον Cyrill.   **10** ἀπορρέσαντας codd.

ἐέδμεναι Cyrill. : ἐέλμεναι codd. : ἔδμεναι (ἔσμεναι AH) Eus. : ἐ⟨ν⟩έδμεναι
Diels   ἠέα Vigier : ἦια codd., Eus., Cyrill. : ἤπια Reiske

119(130) Schol. *in Nic. Ther.* 453
τὰ κτίλα ἐπὶ τῶν ἡμέρων καὶ τιθασσῶν τίθεται καὶ ἐπὶ τῶν τῆς ποίμνης
προηγουμένων κριῶν καὶ ἐπὶ τῶν λιπαρῶν. ὁ δὲ 'Ε. ἐπὶ τῶν ἡμέρων καὶ
πραέων·

> ἦσαν δὲ κτίλα πάντα καὶ ἀνθρώποισι προσηνῆ,
> θῆρές τ' οἰωνοί τε, φιλοφροσύνη τε δεδήει.

1 ἦσαν δὲ καὶ P, ἦσαν γὰρ L : ἔνθ' ἦσαν Karsten   **2** φῆρες P   οἰωνοί
τε Sturz : ἄνθρωποί τε codd.

120(139) Porphry *abst.* 2.31
ἐπεὶ δ' ἀναμάρτητος οὐδείς, λοιπὸν ἀκεῖσθαι τοῖς ὕστερον διὰ τῶν καθαρμῶν
τὰς πρόσθε περὶ τὴν τροφὴν ἁμαρτίας. τοῦτο δὲ ὁμοίως γένοιτ' ἄν, εἰ πρὸ
ὀμμάτων ποιησάμενοι τὸ δεινὸν ἀνευφημίσαιμεν κατὰ τὸν 'Ε. λέγοντες·

> οἴμοι ὅτ' οὐ πρόσθεν με διώλεσε νηλεὲς ἦμαρ
> πρὶν σχέτλι' ἔργα βορᾶς περὶ χείλεσι μητίσασθαι.

2 σχέτλια ἔργα βορᾶς πρὶν χείλεσι H. Fränkel

121(135) Aristotle *Rhet.* 1373b16
ἔστι γάρ, ὃ μαντεύονταί τε πάντες, φύσει κοινὸν δίκαιον καὶ ἄδικον ...
καὶ ὡς 'Ε. λέγει περὶ τοῦ μὴ κτείνειν τὸ ἔμψυχον· τοῦτο γὰρ οὐ τισὶ μὲν
δίκαιον τισὶ δ' οὐ δίκαιον,

> ἀλλὰ τὸ μὲν πάντων νόμιμον διά τ' εὐρυμέδοντος
> αἰθέρος ἠνεκέως τέταται διά τ' ἀπλέτου αὐγῆς.

2 τέτακται QYᵇZᵇ   αὐγῆς YᵇZᵇAᶜ, αὖ γῆς cet. codd.

122(136) Sextus *adv. math.* 9.119, cf. Chalcid. *Tim.* 197
οἱ μὲν οὖν περὶ τὸν Πυθαγόραν καὶ τὸν 'Ε. καὶ τὸ λοιπὸν τῶν 'Ιταλῶν πλῆθός
φασι μὴ μόνον ἡμῖν πρὸς ἀλλήλους καὶ πρὸς τοὺς θεοὺς εἶναί τινα κοινωνίαν,
ἀλλὰ καὶ πρὸς τὰ ἄλογα τῶν ζῴων. ἓν γὰρ ὑπάρχειν πνεῦμα τὸ διὰ παντὸς

τοῦ κόσμου διῆκον ψυχῆς τρόπον, τὸ καὶ ἐνοῦν ἡμᾶς πρὸς ἐκεῖνα. διόπερ καὶ κτείνοντες αὐτὰ καὶ ταῖς σαρξὶν αὐτῶν τρεφόμενοι ἀδικήσομέν τε καὶ ἀσεβήσομεν ὡς συγγενεῖς ἀναιροῦντες. ἔνθεν καὶ παρῄνουν οὗτοι οἱ φιλόσοφοι ἀπέχεσθαι τῶν ἐμψύχων . . . καὶ 'Ε. πού φησιν

> οὐ παύσεσθε φόνοιο δυσηχέος; οὐκ ἐσορᾶτε
> ἀλλήλους δάπτοντες ἀκηδείῃσι νόοιο;

123(145) Clement *Protr.* 2.27.3
ταύτῃ τοι ἡμεῖς οἱ τῆς ἀνομίας υἱοί ποτε διὰ τὴν φιλανθρωπίαν τοῦ λόγου νῦν υἱοὶ γεγόναμεν τοῦ θεοῦ· ὑμῖν δὲ καὶ ὁ ὑμέτερος ὑποδύεται ποιητὴς ὁ Ἀκραγαντῖνος 'Ε.·

> τοιγάρτοι χαλεπῇσιν ἀλύοντες κακότησιν
> οὔποτε δειλαίων ἀχέων λωφήσετε θυμόν.

124(137) Sextus *adv. math.* 9.129 [post 122(136)]
καὶ

> μορφὴν δ' ἀλλάξαντα πατὴρ φίλον υἱὸν ἀείρας
> σφάξει ἐπευχόμενος μέγα νήπιος †οἱ δὲ πορεῦνται†
> λισσόμενον θύοντες· †ὁ δ' ἀνήκουστος† ὁμοκλέων
> σφάξας ἐν μεγάροισι κακὴν ἀλεγύνατο δαῖτα.
> 5 ὡς δ' αὔτως πατέρ' υἱὸς ἑλὼν καὶ μητέρα παῖδες
> θυμὸν ἀπορραίσαντε φίλας κατὰ σάρκας ἔδουσιν.

ταῦτα δὴ παρῄνουν οἱ περὶ τὸν Πυθαγόραν, πταίοντες· οὐ γὰρ εἰ ἔστι τι διῆκον δι' ἡμῶν τε καὶ ἐκείνων πνεῦμα, εὐθὺς ἔστι τις ἡμῖν δικαιοσύνη πρὸς τὰ ἄλογα τῶν ζῴων.

1–2 Plu. *superst.* 171c, Origen *Cels.* 5.49, cf. Chalcidius *Tim.* 197

---

1 διαλλάξαντα Γ, διαλλάξαντι W   εἴρας XN, εἰρὰς Y, εἰρά W, ἱερᾶ J² ἐν ἱεροῖς Dn (Plu.)   **2** σφάξει Origen, σφάζει codd.   οἱ δὲ πορεῦνται LE, οἶδα πορεῦντα N : οἱ δ' ἐπορεῦνται Bergk : οἱ δ' ἀπορεῦνται DK : οἰκτρὰ τορεῦντα Zuntz   **3** λισσόμενον (λισσόμενοι ς) θύοντες codd. : λισσόμενον θύοντος Hermann : λισσόμενοι θύοντες Wilam.   δὲ νήκουστος Bergk : δ' αὖ νήκουστος Diels   **6** ἀπορραίσαντε Karsten : ἀπορραίσαντα codd.

125(138) Aristotle *Poet.* 1457b13
ἀπ᾽ εἴδους δὲ ἐπὶ εἶδος οἷον

χαλκῷ ἀπὸ ψυχὴν ἀρύσας

καὶ "τάμων ἀτειρέι χαλκῷ" [129(143)]· ἐνταῦθα γὰρ τὸ μὲν ἀρύσαι ταμεῖν, τὸ δὲ ταμεῖν ἀρύσαι εἴρηκεν· ἄμφω γὰρ ἀφελεῖν τί ἐστιν.

χαλκὸν ἀπὸ ψυχῆς ἀερείσας Nᵃ

126(144) Plutarch *coh. ir.* 464b
ἐπὶ πᾶσι τοίνυν τὸ μὲν τοῦ ᾽Ε. μέγα καὶ θεῖον ἡγούμην, τὸ

νηστεῦσαι κακότητος.

127(140) Plutarch *quaest. conv.* 646d
καὶ οὐ μόνης ὡς ἔοικε κατ᾽ ᾽Ε, τῆς

δάφνης [τῶν] φύλλων ἄπο πάμπαν ἔχεσθαι

χρή, ἀλλὰ καὶ τῶν ἄλλων φείδεσθαι δένδρων ἁπάντων καὶ μὴ κοσμεῖν ἑαυτοὺς ταῖς ἐκείνων ἀκοσμίαις, βίᾳ καὶ παρὰ φύσιν τὰ φύλλα συλῶντας αὐτῶν.

128(141) Gellius 4.11.9, cf. 4.11.2, Geoponica 2.35.8
videtur autem de κυάμῳ non esitato causam erroris fuisse, quia in E. carmine qui disciplinas Pythagorae secutus est, versus hic invenitur:

δειλοί, πάνδειλοι, κυάμων ἄπο χεῖρας ἔχεσθαι.

πάνδειλοι om. Gp.   ἐλέσθαι vel ἐλέσθαις ς: ἔχεσθε (-σθαι CH) Gp.

129(143) Theon 15.7, Aristotle *Poet.* 1457b14
κατὰ ταῦτα δὴ καὶ ἡ τῶν πολιτικῶν λόγων παράδοσις τὸ μὲν πρῶτον ἔχει καθαρμόν τινα οἷον ἡ ἐν τοῖς προσήκουσι μαθήμασιν ἐκ παίδων συγγυμνασία. ὁ μὲν γὰρ ᾽Ε.

κρηνάων ἄπο πέντε ταμὼν ταναήκεϊ χαλκῷ

δεῖν ἀπορρύπτεσθαι.

Arist. *Poet.* 1457b14

πέντ' ἀνιμῶντά φησιν ἀτειρεί (ταμόντα ταναήκει man. pr.) codd. τεμὼν
(ταμὼν Bekker) ἀτειρέι Ar. exc. ταναήκει R : τάμοντ' ἐν ἀτειρέι Diels

130(125) Clement *Strom.* 3.14.2 [post 112(118)]
καὶ ἔτι

  ἐκ μὲν γὰρ ζωῶν ἐτίθει νεκρὰ εἶδε' ἀμείβων.

εἶδε Sylburg : ἠδὲ codd.

131(127) Aelian *NA* 12.7, cf. Schol. Aphth. ap. Hermanni *Orphica* 511
λέγει δὲ καὶ 'Ε. τὴν ἀρίστην εἶναι μετοίκησιν τὴν τοῦ ἀνθρώπου, εἰ μὲν ἐς
ζῷον ἡ λῆξις αὐτὸν μεταγάγοι, λέοντα γίνεσθαι· εἰ δὲ ἐς φυτόν, δάφνην. ἃ
δὲ 'Ε. λέγει ταῦτά ἐστιν

  ἐν θήρεσσι λέοντες ὀρειλεχέες χαμαιεῦναι
  γίγνονται, δάφναι δ' ἐνὶ δένδρεσιν ἠυκόμοισιν.

1 θήρεσσι Schol. : θηρσὶ δὲ codd. 2 ἐν Schol.

132(146) Clement *Strom.* 4.150.1 cf. Theodoret. 8.36
φησὶ δὲ καὶ ὁ 'Ε. τῶν σοφῶν τὰς ψυχὰς θεοὺς γίνεσθαι ὧδέ πως γράφων·

  εἰς δὲ τέλος μάντεις τε καὶ ὑμνόπολοι καὶ ἰητροί
  καὶ πρόμοι ἀνθρώποισιν ἐπιχθονίοισι πέλονται·
  ἔνθεν ἀναβλαστοῦσι θεοὶ τιμῇσι φέριστοι.

133(147) Clement *Strom.* 5.122.3, cf. Eusebius *PE* 13.31.49
ἦν δὲ ὁσίως καὶ δικαίως διαβιώσωμεν, μακάριοι μὲν ἐνταῦθα, μακαριώτεροι
δὲ μετὰ τὴν ἐνθένδε ἀπαλλαγήν, οὐ χρόνῳ τινὶ τὴν εὐδαιμονίαν ἔχοντες, ἀλλ'
ἐν αἰῶνι ἀναπαύεσθαι δυνάμενοι

  ἀθανάτοις ἄλλοισιν ὁμέστιοι αὐτοτράπεζοι
  †ἐόντες† ἀνδρείων ἀχέων ἀπόκληροι, ἀτειρεῖς,

ἡ φιλόσοφος 'Ε. λέγει ποιητική.

1 αὐτοτράπεζοι Eus. : ἔν τε τραπέζαις codd.   **2** ἐόντες] εὔνιες Scaliger : εὔφρονες? Zuntz : τέρπουτ' van der Ben : ἐόντες post ἀπόκληροι transposui ἀχαιῶν codd., corr. Stephanus   ἀτειρεῖς Eus., ἀτηρεῖς codd.

9. Addenda

134(5) Plutarch *quaest. conv.* 728e

ἔλεγε δὲ τῆς ἐχεμυθίας τοῦτο γέρας εἶναι τοὺς ἰχθῦς καλεῖν ⟨ἔλλοπας⟩ οἷον ἐλλομένην τὴν ὅπα καὶ καθειργομένην ἔχοντας. καὶ τὸν ὁμώνυμον ἐμοὶ τῷ Παυσανίᾳ Πυθαγορικῶς παραινεῖν τὰ δόγματα †στέγουσαι φρενὸς ἀλλ' ὅπερ ἐλάσσω†, καὶ ὅλως θεῖον ἡγεῖσθαι τὴν σιωπὴν τοὺς ἄνδρας.

στεγάσαι φρενὸς ἔλλοπος εἴσω Wyttenbach

135(7) Hesychius s.v. ἀγέννητα

ἀγέννητα· στοιχεῖα παρ' 'Ε.

136(10) Plutarch *adv. Col.* 1113b

ἃ ὁ Κολώτης παραθέμενος οὐ συνεῖδεν, ὅτι φῶτας μὲν καὶ θῆρας καὶ θάμνους καὶ οἰωνοὺς ὁ 'Ε. οὐκ ἀνήρηκεν, ἅ γέ φησι μιγνυμένων τῶν στοιχείων ἀποτελεῖσθαι, τοὺς δὲ τῇ συγκρίσει ταύτῃ καὶ διακρίσει φύσιν τινὰ καὶ πότμον δυσδαίμονα καὶ θάνατον ἀλοίτην ἐπικατηγοροῦντας ἢ σφάλλονται διδάξας, οὐκ ἀφείλετο τὸ χρῆσθαι ταῖς εἰθισμέναις φωναῖς περὶ αὐτῶν.

137(19) Plutarch *prim. frig.* 952b

καὶ ὅλως τὸ μὲν πῦρ διαστατικόν ἐστι καὶ διαιρετικόν, τὸ δ' ὕδωρ κολλητικὸν καὶ σχετικόν, τῇ ὑγρότητι συνέχον καὶ πῆττον· ἢ καὶ παρέσχεν Ε. ὑπόνοιαν ὡς τὸ μὲν πῦρ νεῖκος οὐλόμενον, σχεδύνην δὲ φιλότητα τὸ ὑγρὸν ἑκάστοτε προσαγορεύων.

138(32) [Arist.] *lin. insec.* 972b30

τὸ ἄρθρον διαφορά πώς ἐστιν· διὸ καὶ 'Ε. ἐποίησε †διὸ δεῖ ὀρθῶς†.

δύω δέει ἄρθρον Diels

139(58) Simplicius *in Cael.* 587.18
ἐν ταύτῃ οὖν καταστάσει μουνομελῆ ἔτι τὰ γυῖα ἀπὸ τῆς τοῦ νείκους διακρίσεως ὄντα ἐπλανᾶτο τῆς πρὸς ἄλληλα μίξεως ἐφιέμενα.

140(60) Plutarch *adv. Col.* 1123b
ταῦτα μέντοι καὶ πολλὰ τούτων ἕτερα τραγικώτερα τοῖς 'Ε. ἐοικότα τεράσμασιν ὧν καταγελῶσιν, εἰλίποδ' ἀκριτόχειρα καὶ βουγενῆ ἀνδρόπρῳρα.

141(69) Proclus *in R.* 2.34.26
ὅτι καὶ ὁ 'Ε. οἶδεν τὸν διπλοῦν τῶν γεννήσεων χρόνον. διὸ καὶ τὰς γυναῖκας καλεῖ διγόνους καὶ τὴν ὑπεροχὴν τοῦ πλήθους τῶν ἡμερῶν αὐτὸς εἶπεν καὶ ὅτι τὰ ὀκτάμηνα ἄγονα.

142(70) Rufus *Ephes.* 229, p.166.11
τὸ δὲ βρέφος περιέχεται χιτῶσι, τῷ μὲν λεπτῷ καὶ μαλακῷ· ἀμνίον αὐτὸν 'Ε. καλεῖ.

143(92) Aristotle *GA* 747a34
'Ε. δ' αἰτιᾶται τὸ μῖγμα τὸ τῶν σπερμάτων γίνεσθαι πυκνὸν ἐκ μαλακῆς τῆς γονῆς οὔσης ἑκατέρας· συναρμόττειν γὰρ τὰ κοῖλα τοῖς πυκνοῖς ἀλλήλων, ἐκ δὲ τῶν τοιούτων γίνεσθαι ἐκ μαλακῶν σκληρὸν ὥσπερ τῷ καττιτέρῳ μειχθέντα τὸν χαλκόν.

144(97) Aristotle *Part. An.* 640a19
'Ε. οὐκ ὀρθῶς εἴρηκε λέγων ὑπάρχειν πολλὰ τοῖς ζῴοις διὰ τὸ συμβῆναι οὕτως ἐν τῇ γενέσει οἷον καὶ τὴν ῥάχιν τοιαύτην ἔχειν ὅτι στραφέντος καταχθῆναι συνέβη.

145(99) Theophrastus *Sens.*9
τὴν δ' ἀκοὴν ἀπὸ τῶν ἔξωθεν γίνεσθαι ψόφων, ὅταν ὁ ἀὴρ ὑπὸ τῆς φωνῆς κινηθεὶς ἠχῇ ἐντός. ὥσπερ γὰρ εἶναι κώδωνα τῶν †ἴσων† ἤχων τὴν ἀκοήν, ἣν προσαγορεύει σάρκινον ὄζον· κινουμένην δὲ παίειν τὸν ἀέρα πρὸς τὰ στερεὰ καὶ ποιεῖν ἦχον.

146(142) Voll. Herc. N. 1012 col.18

δῆλον γὰρ ὡς οἱ μὲν κήρυκες φθένξονται, ἡ δ᾽ Ἑλλὰς φθένξεται. μία δὴ
δύναμις τοῦ σημαινομένου. τὰτὸ δὲ καὶ παρ᾽ Ε. γέγονεν ὅτε λέγεται·

> τὸν δ᾽ οὔτ᾽ ἄρ τε Διὸς τέγεοι δόμοι αἰγ[ιόχοιο
> οὔ]τ[ε ποτ᾽] Ἀΐδεω δέ [··········]κ[···] στέγος

147(148–150) Plutarch *quaest. conv.* 683e

καὶ μάλιστα τοῦ ἀνδρὸς οὐ καλλιγραφίας ἕνεκα τοῖς εὐπροσωποτάτοις τῶν
ἐπιθέτων ὥσπερ ἀνθηροῖς χρώμασι τὰ πράγματα γανοῦν εἰωθότος, ἀλλ᾽
ἕκαστον οὐσίας τινὸς ἢ δυνάμεως δήλωμα ποιοῦντος οἷον ἀμφιβρότην χθόνα
τὸ τῇ ψυχῇ περικείμενον σῶμα, καὶ νεφεληγερέτην τὸν ἀέρα καὶ πολυαίματον
τὸ ἧπαρ.

148(151) Plutarch *amat.* 756e

"ζείδωρον" γὰρ αὐτὴν (Ἀφροδίτην) Ε., "εὔκαρπον" δὲ Σοφοκλῆς ἐμμελῶς
πάνυ καὶ πρεπόντως ὠνόμασαν.

149(152) Aristotle *Poet.* 1457b22

... ἢ ὃ γῆρας πρὸς βίον, καὶ ἑσπέρα πρὸς ἡμέραν· ἐρεῖ τοίνυν τὴν ἑσπέραν
γῆρας ἡμέρας καὶ τὸ γῆρας ἑσπέραν βίου ἢ ὥσπερ Ε. δυσμὰς βίου.

150(153) Hesychius s.v. βαυβώ

βαυβώ· τιθήνη Δήμητρος. σημαίνει δὲ καὶ κοιλίαν ὡς παρ᾽ Ε.

151(153a) Theon 104.1

τὸ γοῦν βρέφος δοκεῖ τελειοῦσθαι ἐν ἑπτὰ ἑβδομάσιν, ὡς Ε. αἰνίττεται ἐν
τοῖς Καθαρμοῖς.

152 Herodian Καθολικὴ Προσῳδία,

παρὰ μέντοι Ε. ἐν β᾽ Καθαρμῶν ἐστιν εὑρέσθαι ἐκτεταμένον τὸ α, ὡς δῆλον
κἀκ τῆς συγκριτικῆς παραγωγῆς· μανότερος γὰρ ἔφη ὡς τρανότερος·

> τῶν γὰρ ὅσα ῥίζαις μὲν ἐπασσυτέραι[σιν] ἔγερθε
> μᾶνοτέροις [δ᾽ ὄ]ρπ[ηξ]ιν ὑπέστη τηλεθ[άοντα].

III. Translation and Commentary

10. *Physics*

FRAGMENTS 1-6   THE RIGHT APPROACH

1(2)

The powers spread over the body are constricted, and many afflictions burst in and dull their meditations. After observing a small part of life in their lifetime, subject to a swift death they are borne up and waft away like smoke; they are convinced only of that which each has experienced as they are driven in all directions, yet all boast of finding the whole. These things are not so to be seen or heard by men or grasped with mind. But you now, since you have come aside to this place, will learn within the reach of human understanding.

Sextus quotes this fragment soon after 77 (109) to show that, although E. supposed that the external world can be known by means of the like elements of which we are constituted, there is evidence for the alternative view, that the criterion of truth resides not in the senses but in reason. Proclus, on *Tim.* 34c, quotes line 2 in support of Plato's statement that we are subject to chance and speak in a random way; according to E. we are exiles from god and open to the constant attacks of afflictions that blunt our vision of reality. Plutarch uses line 4 on the brevity of life to corroborate Plato's remark that human conceit is futile (cf. *Laws* 716a–b), and lines 7–8 (οὕτως . . . περιληπτά) in conjunction with Xenophanes' words (DK 21 B34.1–2) to show that truth is hard to come by. Diogenes Laertius, in his life of Pyrrho, puts the same quotation, together with line 5, with evidence from Archilochus, Euripides, Xenophanes, Heraclitus, Zeno of Elea, and even Homer as backing for skepticism. (For E.'s assimilation later to the ranks of the Skeptics cf. Cicero *Acad.* 1.12.44, 2.5.14, 23.74).

1 στεινωποὶ παλάμαι: the "devices" for understanding (cf. ἄθρει πάσῃ παλάμῃ and πόρος νοῆσαι, 5(3).4, 7) are the sense organs, with that of touch being spread over the whole body. The metaphor of the road to understanding is common in Parmenides (e.g., frs. 2.4, 7.2, 8.18) and is taken up again by E. in frs. 5(3). 4–7 and 96(133); cf. Lactantius 3.28.12 "E. angustas esse sensuum semitas queritur." κέχυνται: the line is quoted in the Epicurean *Corpus* (Vol. Herc. VII² f. 22, c. 29) with τέτανται, the verb of 91(100).2.

2 ἔμπαια: justified by Karsten from Aeschylus *Ag.* 187 and Proclus' explanation, πολλὰ γὰρ ἐμπίπτοντα τοῖς ὄντως ἡμῖν δειλοῖς . . . ἀμβλύνει τὴν τῶν ὄντων θεωρίαν. The line is echoed in 100(110).7.

3 δὲ ζωῆσι βίου: corrected plausibly to δ' ἐν ζωῆσι βίου by Wilamowitz. Burnet (*EGP* p. 204, n. 3) adopts Scaliger's δὲ ζωῆς ἀβίου and compares τὸ δὴ βίοτον καλέουσι, 106(15).2.

4 ὠκύμοροι καπνοῖο δίκην: Homeric phrasing, cf. *Il.* 18.95, 458, 23.100, *Od.* 1.266, and also Lucretius 3.455–56. The line obviously precludes individual survival after death.

6: cf. Heraclitus fr. 2 ζώουσιν οἱ πολλοὶ ὡς ἰδίαν ἔχοντες φρόνησιν, and E. 33(39).3.

7–8 οὕτως . . . περιληπτά: ἐπιδερκτά and ἐπακουστά are forms found only here in classical Greek; with νόῳ περιληπτά cf. νοήσει περιληπτόν, Plato *Tim.* 28a. Diels translates, "So wenig lässt sich dies für die Menschen sehen oder hören . . .," and similarly Guthrie, "So little are these things to be seen or heard by men" (*HGP* vol. 2, p. 138). The sense seems to be that τάδε, the general subject, almost equivalent to τὸ ὅλον, is not perceptible or understandable to the average man. Men usually are mistaken in method, attitude, and aim, and easily distracted (cf. 100(110). 6–7); they are also unable to go beyond their immediate experience, which they misinterpret and overrate. The contrast is one familiar from Heraclitus and Parmenides, between the man who knows and the run of mortals who learn nothing, a contrast E. makes again in 95(132), where he calls the man who has understanding ὄλβιος, as against the δειλός who has only an unclear *doxa*. (Cf. especially Heraclitus frs. 1 and 2 and Parmenides fr. 6.4–7.)

8 ἐπεὶ ὧδ' ἐλιάσθης: this Homeric phrase has been interpreted as addressed to E. with the sense "since you have strayed (or come down) to this earth," or to Pausanias similarly; it has also been construed as

"since you have shared my exile" (cf. Guthrie *HGP* vol. 2, p. 138, n. 4).
A less strained sense, "since you have come to me (to learn)," seems preferable and in accord with 100(110) and 101(111). LSJ, s.v. λιάζομαι,
gives "stray from the straight path," but the opposite is implied, viz.
"recoil (from error) to learn the truth."

9 οὐ πλεῖόν γε: Karsten's emendation οὐ πλέον ἠέ has been followed
by Stein and Diels. H. Fränkel's οὐ πλέον οὔτι is plausible on the interpretation that E. claims to be a θεὸς ἄμβροτος and to have superhuman
wisdom, but as Diels-Kranz points out, this does not accord with Sextus'
introductory remark that truth can be reached ἐφ' ὅσον ἱκνεῖται ὁ
ἀνθρώπινος λόγος. E.'s attitude is more modest here, and the fragment
should be taken in conjunction with 5(3) and 100(110). Men generally
do not grasp the truth of things, but this does not mean that it is unattainable. If Pausanias, under E.'s guidance, makes careful use of the
evidence provided by his senses and brings in *nous* to supplement their
deficiencies, then, within the given limitations, it is possible to achieve
genuine understanding.

2(3)

But turn from my tongue, o gods, the madness of these men, and from hallowed lips
let a pure stream flow. And I entreat you, virgin Muse, white-armed, of long
memory, send of that which it is right and fitting for mortals to hear, driving the
well-reined chariot from the place of reverence.

Sextus gives these lines in conjunction with 5(3) as coming ἑξῆς on the
preceding fragment, and he uses them to show that, having previously
inveighed against the senses, E. still wishes to claim that their evidence
can be reliable. The fragment has been divided after the fifth line, for the
person addressed changes from the Muse to Pausanias, and a transitional
passage is needed. That Sextus does omit a considerable number of lines
from his quotations without indicating that he does so is supported by
his citation of Parmenides earlier at 7.111. There frs. 7.2–6 and 8.1–2
of Parmenides run straight on from fr. 1.1–30, although it is known
from Plato (*Soph.* 237a, 258d) and Simplicius (*in Cael.* 557.25 to 558.1–2)
that the lines were not consecutive.

1 τῶν μὲν μανίην: the *mania* has two aspects—the futility of what is
put forward and the impiety of transgressing the boundaries of *themis*
in professions of knowledge. Referring to Sextus' phrase οἱ πλέον ἐπαγγελ-

λόμενοι γιγνώσκειν, Diels gives Parmenides as an example of those whom E. is criticizing, but from the careful consideration E. gives to Parmenides' work and the use he makes of some Eleatic arguments, this seems unlikely. As in the previous fragment, and in keeping with the Presocratic tradition, E.'s attack is a general one on all who put forward rash and ill-considered opinions. The ritualistic language of this fragment makes it more than the stock poetic request for divine assistance; its general tone seems more suited to the *Katharmoi* and shows how the edges of a division between the two poems as religious versus scientific are blurred.

2 ὀχετεύσατε: Stephanus' emendation. The metaphor from irrigation is used again in fr. 47(35).2.

3 πολυμνήστη Μοῦσα: Burnet and Guthrie translate the epithet as "much-wooed," Diels "vielgefeierte," and Bignone "molto contesa." Karsten, however, has "memor" and LSJ "much-remembering," "mindful," a sense, appropriate here, that is argued for by E. Fraenkel in his note on Aeschylus *Ag.* 821 (but Denniston and Page claim the passive "much-remembered," as at *Ag.* 1459). A play on the Homeric word is probably intended; cf. the different meaning E. gives to the Homeric μινυνθάδιος, μυχός, ὄρπηξ, ἀλλότριος φώς, etc. ἄντομαι in the next line is an example; in Homer it means "meet," usually with hostile intent, and it is first found with the sense "meet with prayers," "entreat," here in E.

4–5: Sturz, Karsten, and Burnet put a stop after ἀκούειν and take the chariot as object of πέμπε, but ἄντομαι does not seem to have been used with an infinitive (cf. Euripides *Andr.* 921–22 ἄντομαί σε Δία καλοῦσα . . . πέμψον με). Guthrie (*HGP* vol. 2, p. 127) omits ἄντομαι and supplies an object for the verb, translating, "in so far as it is lawful for us creatures of a day to hear, escort me, driving the chariot . . .," but this reads strangely. To whom does the chariot belong? Karsten suggests that Εὐσεβίης be taken with ἄρμα, comparing Χαρίτων ἄρματα, Simonides 148.10 (Bergk), and ἄρμα Πιερίδων, Pindar *Pyth.* 10.65. Burnet supposes that the Muse will drive E.'s chariot, but this would make the fragment contradictory—if E. was already at the shrine of Piety he would not be asking to keep within the bounds of *themis*. Parmenides (fr. 1) represented himself as driven in his chariot by the daughters of the Sun *to* the abode of the goddess, but E.'s prayer is rather for the Muse to come in her chariot, παρ' Εὐσεβίης, to his assistance; so Aphrodite in a golden chariot from her father's house to Sappho, fr. 1.6–8. For the literary convention of a goddess coming in a chariot cf. the examples cited by Page, *Sappho and Alcaeus* p. 7.

3(131)

If for the sake of any one of mortal men, immortal Muse, (it pleased you) that our cares came to your attention, now once more, Kalliopeia, answer a prayer, and stand by as a worthy account of the blessed gods is being unfolded.

Hippolytus understands the Muse addressed in this fragment to be an allegory for the δίκαιος λόγος, a principle described as an intermediary between Love and Strife but working with Love for unity. The interpretation is unwarranted, for the epithets given to the Muse in fr. 2(3).3 and the mention of her in fr. 6(4).2 show that E. is working within the framework of Pierian inspiration.

1–3 εἰ γὰρ . . . Καλλιόπεια: on the ὕμνος κλητικός cf. E. Fraenkel *Philologus* 1931, pp. 3–9, and further references given by Lloyd-Jones, *JHS* 1963, p. 83, n. 7. The structure of the appeal "If ever in the past . . . come now" is a common one, cf. Sappho fr. 1.5–7 with Page *Sappho and Alcaeus* p. 17, n. 3, and Lloyd-Jones *JHS* 1963, pp. 83–84. ἐφημερίων has been taken as masculine, as in 2(3).4. Schneidewin (*Philologus* 1851, p. 167), followed by Stein, supposes ἐφημερίων to be neuter, writes τί σοι for τινος, ἡμετερής for ἡμετέρας, and supplies ἔμελε. It has then been argued that since E. is referring to an earlier work of his own, namely the *Physics*, the fragment belongs to the *Katharmoi* (cf. Diels *SPAW* 1898, p. 399). However, with a supplement on the lines suggested by Wilamowitz, the reference to a previous poem by E. fails. The sense is quite general: "If in the past a poet's work has pleased you, come now and bring inspiration in answer to an appeal." (For αὖτε as the repetition not of an action but of a type of action cf. Page *Sappho and Alcaeus* p. 13, n. 3, and for E.'s use of ἡμέτερος for "of men in general" cf. 96(133). 2.) Hippolytus' mention, in the context of the fragment, of the κόσμοι brought about by Love and Strife makes the lines more suited to the *Physics* than to the *Katharmoi*, and it is in the *Physics* that the Muse is addressed (cf. 2(3).3–5) and that an ἀγαθὸς λόγος about the gods is revealed in detail (cf. 8(17).26, where, after an account of the four roots and Love and Strife, E. adds, σὺ δ' ἄκουε λόγου στόλον οὐκ ἀπατηλόν).

4 ἀμφὶ θεῶν . . . ἀγαθὸν λόγον: cf. Xenophanes fr. 34.1–2 and Parmenides 8.50–51 for their announcement of a new and personal *logos*; E. too has a new conception of θεός.

4(1)

And you, Pausanias, son of wise Anchitos, hear me.

The line is one of the eight fragments quoted specifically from the *Physics*; the phrasing is Homeric, cf. *Il.* 8.152, 11.197, 450. Nothing definite is known about Pausanias. Since the *Physics* was addressed to him he was assumed to have been Empedocles' devoted and favored disciple, and so he figures in the biographers (cf. the supposed intimacy between Parmenides and Zeno, D.L. 9.25). According to Heraclides Ponticus, Pausanias was present at the feast following the cure of the ἄπνους, and he organized a search for Empedocles on his subsequent disappearance; however, he later told the people that E. would not return and that they must sacrifice to him as if he had become a god (cf. D.L. 8.67–69). The whole account is denied by Timaeus, who claims that if it were true, Pausanias, being a wealthy man, would have set up a statue or shrine to E. (D.L. 8.71). Galen cites Pausanias, Philistion, and E. together as Italian doctors (*meth. med.* 1.1, 10.6K, and cf. Heraclides Ponticus on E. explaining the problem of the ἄπνους to Pausanias, D.L. 8.60). Pausanias is also called a doctor and a native of Gela in the epigram quoted by Diogenes immediately after this fragment:

> Παυσανίην ἰητρὸν ἐπώνυμον Ἀγχιτέω υἱόν
> φῶτ' Ἀσκληπιάδην πατρὶς ἔθρεψε Γέλα,
> ὃς πολλοὺς μογεροῖσι μαραινομένους καμάτοισι
> φῶτας ἀπέστρεψεν Φερσεφόνης ἀδύτων.

The epigram, however, as chapter 1 has shown, is almost certainly spurious. Anchitos, the father of Pausanias, is known elsewhere only in an anecdote told by Iamblichus (*Vit. Pyth.* 113), in which a young guest of Anchitos is about to avenge his father with an attack on his host but is calmed by E.'s music.

5(3)

And do not let (it) compel you to take up garlands of glory and honor from men, on condition that you speak recklessly, overstepping propriety, and so then sit on the high throne of wisdom. But come, observe with every power in what way each thing is clear, without holding any seeing as more reliable compared with hearing, nor echoing ear above piercings of the tongue; and do not keep back trust at all from the other parts of the body by which there is a channel for understanding, but understand each thing in the way in which it is clear.

Sextus gives the lines immediately after 2(3) as a continuous quotation.

Clement mentions the (later) distinction that was made in the Pythagorean school between the ἀκουσματικοί and the genuine philosophers, and he claims that the Peripatetics similarly separated *doxa* from εὐκλεία and truth; the first two lines of this fragment are then quoted anonymously, followed by evidence for the same distinction from Heraclitus, frs. 104 and 29, Demosthenes, *de cor.* 296, and Parmenides, fr. 1.29–30. Proclus, praising the caution Plato shows in the *Timaeus* (29d) regarding the ability of mortal men to give an exact account of the gods and of the universe, complains that a similar hesitation was not found in Heraclitus, who contrasted his own knowledge with the ignorance of others, or in Empedocles, who guaranteed to reveal the truth, or in the Stoics. Plutarch quotes the second half of the third line, as a well-known phrase, to describe Meno's high opinion of his own training in argument.

1–3 μηδέ σέ . . . θοάζει: because lines 4–8 are clearly addressed to Pausanias, and fr. 2(3) is addressed to the Muse, there would have been a break in Sextus' quotation, cf. the commentary on 2(3); it is hard to see how lines 1–3 could be interpreted as spoken to the Muse, and Clement, Proclus, and Plutarch all put the lines in a context of human wisdom. If some verses have been omitted by Sextus, then they would give the transitional passage and also perhaps provide a subject for βιήσεται; this is preferable to supposing that the flowers themselves exercise compulsion, as is assumed by Diels-Kranz (cf. ἄεθλια κάλ' ἀνελέσθαι *Od.* 21.117). μή with the future indicative seems here to be used with a prohibitive force (cf. W. W. Goodwin *Syntax of the Moods and Tenses of the Greek Verb* p. 19, par. 70, but also B. L. Gildersleeve *Syntax of Classical Greek from Homer to Demosthenes* p. 270), and the subject may well have been a general one, even τάδε, i.e., "what I am about to tell you." Karsten marks a lacuna after εἰπεῖν, takes θάρσει as imperative, ends the line with θοάσσεις, and translates, "aude, et sic in sapientiae culmen evolabis." This suits the contexts given in Clement and Proclus of the wisdom of the one who knows the truth as contrasted with general ignorance, but it goes against the more modest approach of the previous fragments. Perhaps the infinitive θοάζειν is a correct conjecture, with the general sense, "Do not be seduced by the glamor of a reputation for wisdom into putting my words to an improper use" (cf. Xenophanes' claim to honor because of his *sophia*, fr. 2.11–12).

5 ὄψιν ἔχων πίστει: the dative πίστει is a syntactical oddity here, and the translation given by Diels-Kranz is unsatisfactory. Ellis's suggestion of ὄψει ἔχων πίστιν meets with difficulty in the accusatives of the following

line; ὄψιν ἔχων πιστήν is better, and for the construction with the comparative cf. *Od.* 18.162.

6 τρανώματα γλώσσης: probably not "the clear instructions of the tongue" (Burnet), or "what the tongue makes plain" (Guthrie), but "the piercings of the tongue" by pores that account for the sense of taste, connecting with τετραίνω (rather than τρανόω, a late verb), cf. 91(100).3 πυκναῖς τέτρηνται ἄλοξιν.

7–8 μήτε . . . ἕκαστον: the early editors, Sturz, Karsten, and Mullach, put a stop after νοῆσαι and take the passage as a contrast between the deceptive evidence given by the senses and the true understanding reached by νοῦς independently of them. But this is forcing the construction to give a skeptical slant which is at variance with E.'s position elsewhere, as for example 14(21).1, 26(20), and 77(109). E. rather is picking up the Eleatic distinction between perception and reason (cf. Parmenides frs. 7.4–5 and 6.6–7) and contradicting it; to a considerable extent the senses can help us to understand the structure and functioning of the universe. Perception of the familiar earth, air, sea, and fire, for example, reveals the qualities of the roots of which all things are composed; a sharp biological eye sees essential similarities in organic formations. But there is a limit to the senses, and νοῦς then works independently, as in grasping the nature of Philotēs (8(17).21) or of the god (96(133).1–3). It is less certain whether E. has Heraclitus in mind (cf. fr. 101a ὀφθαλμοὶ τῶν ὤτων ἀκριβέστεροι μάρτυρες), but the combination of perceiving with learning is in the Presocratic tradition, cf. Heraclitus fr. 55, Xenophanes fr. 24 (the god's seeing and hearing being without specific organs), and the Hippocratic *Regimen* 1.23, where seven senses are listed as the means to γνῶσις, a list that could serve as a commentary on τὰ ἄλλα γυῖα of lines 7–8: ἀκοὴ ψόφου, ὄψις φανερῶν, ῥῖνες ὀδμῆς, γλῶσσα ἡδονῆς καὶ ἀηδίης, στόμα διαλέκτου, σῶμα ψαύσιος, θερμοῦ ἢ ψυχροῦ πνεύματος διέξοδοι ἔξω καὶ ἔσω. Alcmaeon thought of πόροι as channels stretching from the organ to the brain, Theophrastus *Sens.* 26, Chalcidius *Tim.* 279 (DK 24 A10), but when E. calls each sense a πόρος νοῆσαι, and eyes and hands the "highway of persuasion that leads to the φρήν for men" (96(133).2–3), is he being as literal as Alcmaeon? It may be true that νοῦς "coordinates and interprets the testimony of the senses into an understanding of the whole" (von Fritz *CPh* 1946, p. 20), but there are reasonable grounds for supposing that this works on a physical basis. Blood, the heart-blood in particular, is the organ of thought (94(105), Theophrastus *Sens.* 10), the channels of blood are stretched throughout the body, noticeably in the eye, ear, nose, tongue, and hand, and the blood moves to

and from the surface of the skin; it is likely that the blood channels convey
sensations from the organs to the thorax, cf. further the commentaries on
91(100) and 94(105).

6(4)
*It is indeed the habit of mean men to disbelieve what is authoritative, but do you
learn as the assurances of my Muse urge, after the argument has been divided within
your breast.*

Clement interprets these lines as the general inclination of the κακοί,
through distrust, to overcome the truth; E.'s own doctrine, however, car-
ries conviction. The point of view is supported with reference to the
Greek principle of learning like by like, and with quotations from Prov-
erbs 26:5, 1 Corinthians 1:22, Matthew 5:45, and Romans 3:29. Theodoretus gives the first two lines as agreeing with Heraclitus fr. 34. According to E., disbelievers are κακοί, according to Heraclitus those without understanding are like the deaf. The theme is developed and brings
in Parmenides fr. 4.1, Solon fr. 16, and E. again with 96(133).

1 κάρτα πέλει: a weak phrase. Diels suggested χάρτα πέλει, translating, "mali homines gaudent diffidere eis qui optinent" (*PPF* p. 107), but
later adopted κάρτα μέλει: "doch Niedrigen liegt es nur zu sehr am
Herzen, den Starken zu misstrauen" (*Vors.*[3] p. 225). The datives are
ambiguous. Both contexts understand κακοῖς as masculine and take it
with the finite verb, κακός here implying "slow-learning" (cf. Sophocles
Ajax 964, *OT* 545, *Phil.* 910), combined with a moral slur. κρατέουσιν
may also be masculine, and opposed to κακοῖς, as "those who are superior
in knowledge," including E., but it is more likely to be neuter, equivalent
to τὰ ἀληθῆ, which have the backing of the Muse. (On neuter references
for κρατεῖν cf. Mullach *FPG* p. 33.) The μέν and δέ contrast (which is
avoided in Theodoretus' adaptation of the second line) seems to be
between what the κακοί do—distrust the truth—and what the πιστώματα
of the Muse urge—attention to the *logos* (cf. 103(114).1–3).

2 πιστώματα: not "effata" (Karsten) or "arcana" (Bergk), but rather
"the objective reliable signs that justify confidence" (cf. Verdenius
Mnemosyne 1948, p. 13); similarly Διὸς πιστώματα, Aeschylus *Eum.* 214,
and cf. Aristotle *Rhet.* 1376a17.

3 γνῶθι: on γιγνώσκειν in E., where the meaning is shifting from
"recognize an object directly by the senses" to "understand a thought"

(although to understand a thought is still to recognize and understand its object), cf. von Fritz *CPh* 1946, p. 17, n. 1. διατμηθέντος . . . λόγοιο: σπλάγχνα, like φρήν, 96(133).3, and περικάρδιον αἷμα, 94(105).3, refers to the part of the thorax that is the physical basis of thinking, where the *logos* is in some sense incorporated. The process of incorporation is not made clear in this fragment (and there is little help to be gained from passages like Plato *Phdr.* 265e and Vergil *Aen.* 8.20). It seems that, provided the recipient is in the right condition for assimilating the *logos*, there is a dividing and separating (cf. Parmenides fr. 7.5–6) or (if Diels's διασσηθέντος is accepted) a sifting of the *logos* in and around the heart; the thoughts thus received then increase and strengthen εἰς ἦθος ἕκαστον; cf. further the commentary on 100(110).

FRAGMENTS 7–11   BASIC PRINCIPLES: FOUR ROOTS, LOVE, AND STRIFE

7(6)

Hear first the four roots of all things: bright Zeus and life-bringing Hera and Aidoneus and Nestis, whose tears are the source of mortal streams.

These lines on the πολυθρύλητα στοιχεῖα of E. are given generally in listings of Presocratic ἀρχαί, and the authorities quoting them are concerned mainly with the allocation of the divine names to the different roots. But Sextus also allies the Stoics to E. as positing similar elements, Heraclitus claims that the lines are in imitation of *Iliad* 3.276–79, and Clement gives them a Pythagorean context. Hippolytus at *RH* 7.29 divides the roots into δύο ὑλικά—earth and water, and δύο ὄργανα—air and fire, but at 10.7 he takes all four as ὑλικά in contrast to the active principles of Love and Strife. Clement adds 8(17).18 and 14(21).9 to the first line as a continuous quotation; in Stobaeus, 20(36) is appended to the fragment. Tzetzes refers it to the first book of the Περὶ Φύσεως.

1 ῥιζώματα: "root clumps," literally of trees (cf. Theophrastus *CP* 3.3.4), but used also of ancestry (Theodectes 3), and in Aeschylus of the offspring (*Sept.* 413). Nearer to E.'s meaning is the use of ῥίζα by Hesiod, *Erga* 19 (and cf. Homer *Od.* 9.390), and by Aristotle of the inquiry of the philosophers of old into ἀρχαὶ καὶ ῥίζαι γῆς καὶ θαλάττης, *Mete.* 353b1. The notable parallel is the Pythagorean oath

οὐ μὰ τὸν ἀμετέρᾳ ψυχᾷ παραδόντα τετρακτόν,
παγὰν ἀενάου φύσεως ῥίζωμά τ᾽ ἔχουσαν (or ῥίζωματ᾽ ἔχουσαν)

quoted at Aetius 1.3.8, Sextus *adv. math.* 7.94, Porphyry *Vit. Pyth.* 20, and Iamblichus *Vit. Pyth.* 150. It is impossible to date the oath, but it does not appear in the earlier tradition, and the introduction of φύσις in this sense is suspiciously late. If there is a connection, the Pythagoreans are more likely to have borrowed the unusual term ῥίζωμα from E. than vice versa (cf. also θνητῶν πηγή, 15(23).10). The poetic word implies for E. "foundation," "living source of increase and growth," and perhaps also "basic nature"; cf. the comprehensive use of ῥίζα and ῥιζοτόμος, Theophrastus *HP* 9.8 and also Lucretius 2.103 and Proclus *in Tim.* 130c.

2 Ζεὺς . . . ᾽Αἰδωνεύς: the allocation of the divine names to the different roots was disputed even in antiquity. One tradition, which identified Aidoneus with air and Hera with earth, was put forward by the Homeric allegorists and applied to E. by Diogenes and Hippolytus (cf. Heraclitus *All.* 24, 41, Stobaeus 1.10.11, Hippolytus *RH* 7.29.4, D.L. 8.76, and for the connection, Diels *Doxographi Graeci* pp. 88–99). In Hippolytus, Aidoneus as air is argued from the etymology, ὅτι πάντα δι᾽ αὐτοῦ βλέποντες μόνον αὐτὸν οὐ καθορῶμεν, and the epithet φερέσβιος, applied by E. to Hera, is taken to refer to earth. But Aidoneus (i.e., Hades) is most easily understood as earth (cf. the arguments put forward by Millerd *Empedocles* p. 31), and φερέσβιος, an epithet of earth in Hesiod and the Homeric Hymns, may well have been deliberately transferred by E. to the root of air, which in one form is the breath essential to life (cf. Aristophanes *Nubes* 570: Αἰθέρα σεμνότατον, βιοθρέμμονα πάντων); this would be in accordance with his custom of putting established phrasing in a new setting. The "Homeric" line of interpretation should therefore almost certainly be rejected as a late rereading of E. Similarly the interpretation put forward by Knatz ("Empedoclea" pp. 1–9) and Thiele (*Hermes* 1897, pp. 68–78), and approved by Burnet (*EGP* p. 229, n. 3), which refers Zeus to *aithēr*, Hera to earth, and Aidoneus to fire, may be disregarded. This view has no support from the many ancient commentators on the lines, and the identification of Zeus with E.'s *aithēr* requires the rejection of all E.'s uses of ἀήρ for the element of air. The best tradition is the Theophrastean one, which gives Zeus as fire, Hera as air, and Aidoneus as earth, cf. Aetius 1.3.20, Philodemus *piet.* 2 (DK 31 A33), and also Plutarch *de Is. et Os.* 363d. Hera as air appears in the *Cratylus* (404c), this view has support from Menander 1.5.2 (DK 31 A23), and it was this interpretation of the names of the elements that was taken over by the

Stoics, cf. Cicero *ND* 2.66 and the long list of parallel references cited by
Pease *ND* vol. 2, p. 716. For discussions of the question cf. Millerd *Empedocles* pp. 30–32, Bignone *Empedocle* pp. 542–44, Guthrie *HGP* vol. 2, pp.
144–46.

3 *Νῆστις . . . βρότειον*: there are variant readings of this line, but
the contexts in Aetius and Heraclitus confirm the phrase *τέγγει κρούνωμα
βρότειον*. In Eustathius, Nestis is given as a Sicilian goddess (*Il.* 1180.14),
but apart from the mention of her here and at 48(96).2 she does not
appear in classical literature. Two attempts to explain the name were
given. One, originating from Simplicius (*in de An.* 68.13–14), gives the
derivation *ἀπὸ τοῦ νάειν καὶ ῥεῖν*; the other, from Hippolytus (*RH*
7.29.4), connects her with *νῆστις* = "fasting" (cf. 126(144) *νηστεῦσαι
κακότητος*) and interprets, *ὅτι τροφῆς αἴτιον γινόμενον τρέφειν οὐκ εὐτονεῖ
τὰ τρεφόμενα*. All agree that she represents the root of water, and
Sturz suggested that as Aidoneus is earth, Nestis may be Persephone, the
name referring to underground streams. If Nestis was a Sicilian name for
Persephone rather than an obscure water nymph, this would give a
pointed contrast with the Olympian couple and balance the four (which
are *ἰσά τε πάντα*, 8(17).27) more exactly. This, however, is only conjecture, and E. did not have a strict terminology for the roots; see the
table of terms in chap. 2.

8(17)

*A twofold tale I shall tell: at one time it grew to be one only from many, and at
another again it divided to be many from one. There is a double birth of what is
mortal, and a double passing away; for the uniting of all things brings one generation into being and destroys it, and the other is reared and scattered as they are
again being divided. And these things never cease their continual exchange of position, at one time all coming together into one through love, at another again being
borne away from each other by strife's repulsion. (So, insofar as one is accustomed
to arise from many) and many are produced from one as it is again being divided,
to this extent they are born and have no abiding life; but insofar as they never cease
their continual exchange, so far they are forever unaltered in the cycle.*

*But come, hear my words, for learning brings an increase of wisdom. Even as I said
before, when I was stating the range of my discourse, a twofold tale I shall tell:
at one time it grew to be one only from many, and at another again it divided to be
many from one—fire and water and earth and measureless height of air, with
pernicious strife apart from these, matched (to them) in every direction, and love*

among them, their equal in length and breadth. Contemplate her with the mind, and do not sit staring dazed; she is acknowledged to be inborn also in the bodies of men, and because of her their thoughts are friendly and they work together, giving her the name Joy, as well as Aphrodite. No mortal has perceived her as she whirls among them; do you though attend to the progress of my argument, which does not mislead.

All these are equal and of like age, but each has a different prerogative, and its particular character, and they prevail in turn as the time comes round. Moreover, nothing comes to birth later in addition to these, and there is no passing away, for if they were continuously perishing they would no longer exist. And what would increase this whole, and from where would it come? How would it be completely destroyed, since nothing is without them? No, these are the only real things, but as they run through each other they become different objects at different times, yet they are throughout forever the same.

This is the longest and most important of the extant fragments. It is quoted in full by Simplicius from the first book of E.'s *Physics (in Phys.* 157.27), and since Simplicius also describes the opening verses as τὰ εὐθὺς ἐν ἀρχῇ παρατεθέντα (*in Phys.* 161.14–15), the fragment has been put earlier than it had been in Diels's arrangement. The contexts of the various lines quoted in a considerable range of sources give the substance of the fragment as follows: as Love and Strife alternately gain the ascendancy over all things the cosmos is brought into existence and destroyed in unceasing succession (Simp. *in Phys.* 157.25, *in Cael.* 140.30, 293.19–23, 530.11–12, D.L. 8.76; on Arist. *Phys.* 250b27–251a5 and Simp. *in Phys.* 1124.19–1125.24, cf. below on 16(26).8–12); Love and Strife are motive principles working on the four elements of earth, air, fire, and water, and they are not perceptible to the senses but intelligible by νοῦς (Simp. *in Phys.* 25.24, 188.23, D.L. 8.76, S.E. *adv. math.* 9.10, 10.317, Plu. *amat.* 756d, Hippol. *RH* 10.7.3, Clem. *Strom.* 5.15.4, 6.17.4); E. thought of the four elements as equal in some way, prevailing inevitably in turn; birth is explained by their uniting and death by their separation, for nothing can be added to or subtracted from their sum (Arist. *GC* 333a16, Phlp. *in GC* 257.32, 261.21, Simp. *in Phys.* 157.25, 161.13, 1184.5, *MXG* 975b10, 976b22).

1–2 (= 16–17) ηὐξήθη . . . εἶναι, διέφυ . . . εἶναι : the infinitives are consecutive, cf. Goodwin *MT* par. 775. What is the subject of the finite verbs? Guthrie translates, "at a certain time one alone grew out of many," but gives an alternative on the lines suggested above in a foot-note (*HGP* vol. 2, p. 153). The unexpressed subject is probably πάντα (cf. below on line 4 and 14(21).7) or τὸ ὅλον (cf. 1(2).6), the "twofold tale" being the two cosmic changes (1) from many to one, and (2) from one to many. When the lines are repeated at 16–17 the uniting and sepa-rating totality is spelled out as fire, water, earth, and air, to which Love and Strife are added.

3–5 ἀπόλειψις: the abstract noun is unusual in epic and in its opposi-tion to γένεσις (Parmenides' word is ὄλεθρος, fr. 8.21); normally the meaning is "desertion" (Thucydides, Demosthenes, Xenophon) or "failing" (of rivers or of the moon in Aristotle). θρεφθεῖσα, Panzerbieter's emendation of Simplicius' θρυφθεῖσα, with Scaliger's διέπτη for δρεπτή, balances τίκτει τ' ὀλέκει τε. Karsten keeps θρυφθεῖσα, changes ὀλέκει to αὔξει, and δοιή (admittedly an unusually early use of the singular) to τοίη; but this is unnecessary surgery to remove the idea of a second or double generation. Bollack tries δρυφθεῖσ' ἀποδρύπτει, translating "dispersant, se disperse." Other recent views on the lines are summarized by A. A. Long in *The Pre-Socratics*, ed. A. P. D. Mourelatos, pp. 404–12. τὴν μέν . . . ἡ δέ: Diels refers the two pronouns to γένεσις, "at valent etiam mutatis mutandis de ἀπολείψει" (*PPF* p. 112). Sturz had under-stood the first pronoun as γένεσις and the second as ἀπόλειψις, but it seems rather that both pronouns should refer to both nouns, the compact expression being elucidated by the verbs. There is a first generation and a "failing" of mortal things when θνητά are brought to birth and then destroyed by the many coming into one, and a second when θνητά are again reared and scattered as many "divide" (a distinctive Empedoclean sense; διαφύομαι = "germinate" Thphr. *CP* 2.17.7, "intervene" or "grow between" Hdt. 1.61, Thphr. *CP* 3.7.9, and later "be inseparably connected with").

6–8 ταῦτα: like πάντα in line 3, which unite and separate, identified in line 18 as earth, air, fire, and water. φορεύμενα: Ionic form; Stobaeus has φρουρούμενα. Lines 6–8 add the information that the move from many to one is the work of Love, and that from one to many is due to Strife; the alternation between the two is unceasing. The last two lines are repeated at 16(26).5–6, line 7 at 26(20).2, and line 8, with some variation, at 26(20).4. The connection of likeness and unity with Love, and of enmity and separation with Strife, is found again at 25(22).4–8. Lines 6–8 are part of the outline of E.'s cosmic scheme, as the first two lines of the fragment and the phrase πάντων σύνοδος show. He is con-cerned here with the eternal succession of the two phases of all things coming into one through Love and separating into many through Strife. This is universal activity which later is to be found at work in individual organisms, in the same way as the materials that make up the individual are identified with the world masses. (For the attempts to deny any cosmic reference at all cf. note 110 in chapter 2.)

9 οὕτως . . . φύεσθαι: the line has been supplied here from Aristotle *Phys.* 250b30 and Simplicius *in Phys.* 33.26; for this and the following four lines cf. the commentary on 16(26).8–12 with the Aristotelian context.

14 ἀλλ' ἄγε μύθων κλῦθι: one of several formulaic monitions to Pausanias found throughout the poem, especially when a new and important point is to be made, cf. 4(1), 5(3).4, 6(4).3, 15(23).11, 17(38).1, 53(62).1, 100(110).10. Here the explanation of the nature and function of the four roots and Love and Strife gives body to the schematic outline of the first verses of the fragment. μάθη: Stobaeus has μάθησις and omits τοι, which has the support of Clement's paraphrase; Simplicius gives μέθη (which Sturz tried to justify by referring to Plato *Lysis* 222c), changed by Bergk to μάθη. This would be the only occurrence of the noun, except for the Doric genitive in Hesychius: μάθας, μαθήσεως. For the literal increase that learning brings cf. 100(110).4–5.

15 πείρατα μύθων: cf. Homer *Il.* 23.350 of Nestor ἑκάστου πείρατ' ἔειπε.

16–17: cf. lines 1–2.

18: previously the roots had been given under somewhat enigmatic divine names (cf. 7(6).1–2), but they are now listed in familiar terms. The first three—fire, water, and earth—are straightforward. For the fourth Simplicius has ἠέρος, and Plutarch and Clement αἰθέρος; the epithet is ἄπλετον in Simplicius and Clement and ἤπιον in Plutarch, Sextus, and Athenagoras, ἤπιον perhaps coming into the text from Parmenides B 8.56–57; for ἄπλετον cf. 121(135).2. Burnet (*EGP* p. 219, n. 3; p. 228, n. 2) accepts αἰθέρος here, denying that the element was ever called ἀήρ by E. αἰθήρ admittedly is the most common word for this root in E., but his terminology is not fixed (cf. 91(100).13, 25(22).2, 91(100).15, and the table in chap. 2). Elsewhere ὑγρὸς ἀήρ and Τίταν αἰθήρ refer to the same root, the former in its occupation of the lower atmosphere and the latter in that of the higher, cf. the commentary on 27(38).3–4.

19–20: the formal introduction of the uniting and separating agents, already mentioned briefly in lines 7–8. νεῖκος οὐλόμενον: cf. νείκεος ἔχθει line 8. The baneful nature of Strife, and the innate hatred that brings about separation, is emphasized from the start, giving Aristotle grounds for regarding it as a principle of evil, cf. *Metaph.* 985a4–10, Plutarch *de Is. et Os.* 370e. ἀτάλαντον ἀπάντῃ: "equal in every way," "uniform," as in Hesiod *Theog.* 524 and Parmenides fr. 8.44. It is not that Strife is materially equal in weight to each or all of the roots but that its power can stretch evenly and comprehensively over them all.

20 ἐν τοῖσιν: alternatively μετὰ τοῖσιν, cf. line 25. No significant contrast need be made with δίχα τῶν in the previous line, except perhaps that Strife as a separating agency works apart, and Love from within, cf. Guthrie *HGP* vol. 2, p. 154. ἴση μῆκός τε πλάτος τε: like ἀτάλαντον ἀπάντῃ above, for Love's uniform extension over the roots.

21: the contrast between visual perception and intellectual recognition is clearly made, with a corresponding distinction in objects. Earth, air, fire, and water are visible, and their nature can be understood from observation (cf. 14(21).1–6), but Love is not a material entity like them and can be grasped only by νοῦς, so Parmenides fr. 4.1. There is also an underlying separation of subjects, familiar from Heraclitus and Parmenides, of the one who has reached true understanding from the ordinary masses, who in comparison are like people sleeping or stunned; cf. Heraclitus fr. 1, Parmenides fr. 6.7, and E. earlier at 1(2).1–6. Like the nature of Love, that of the supreme god is not to be reached or understood by the senses, cf. 96(133).1–3.

22 νομίζεται: changed by Karsten to ἐνίζεται on the grounds of the verse contradicting lines 25–26, but the second reference is to the elements. Men recognize the presence of Philotēs, or Aphrodite, well enough within their bodies and observe the effects on human thinking and action, but its universal working on the roots is not perceptible and has not been understood as the functioning of the same principle as that which powerfully influences themselves.

24 Γηθοσύνην: Homeric, cf. *Il.* 21.390 and also 13.29 (where "the ascription to nature of a distinctly human emotion is unique in Homer," Leaf ad loc.). ἐπώνυμον: cf. *Il.* 9.562.

25 μετὰ τοῖσιν: Brandis's correction for the unmetrical μετ' ὅσσοισιν, giving a reference to the roots, as in line 20. Other suggestions are μεθ' ἅπασιν (Sturz), μεθ' ὅλοισιν (Panzerbieter), γ' ὅσσοισιν (Preller), and τ' ὅσσοισιν (Ellis).

26 ἄκουε . . . ἀπατηλόν: a direct challenge to Parmenides' deprecation of his *Doxa*, fr. 8.52.

27 ταῦτα . . . ἔασι: whether or not there is a lacuna after line 26, the subject of line 27 is the roots. This is clear (1) in the continuation in lines 34–35 (for it is the roots which in running through each other become the

various phenomena), (2) in the near repetition of lines 29 and 34 in 16(26), where the reference is to the elements, and (3) in the ancient commentaries on line 27. It is the four roots that are equal and of like age, and that make up the totality of the world mass, allowing for no addition or subtraction. Love and Strife are not "things" like the roots and cannot be compared with them; their control can extend over them, however, as was explained in lines 19–20, and the question of their eternity is taken up separately in 11(16). The roots are ἴσα πάντα (cf. Parmenides fr. 9.4 of fire and night—ἴσοι ἀμφότεροι), but Aristotle queries what is meant by this. Granted that for E. the elements are absolutely basic and incapable of being transformed into each other (cf. GC 315a15–16), then if they are quantitatively comparable there must be a common unit of measurement, which would deny their ultimate nature. This would also be the case if they were dynamically comparable, cf. Mete. 340a14, and chap. 2, n. 79. But if the comparison is analogical, e.g., one is as hot as another is white, it is qualitative, and the elements should be called "similar," not "equal," cf. Aristotle GC 333a20–34, Philoponus in GC 257.32–258.4, 261.21–25, Joachim on Aristotle GC, pp. 231–33. E. was probably being straightforward and assuming that the roots were equal in age, honor, and power, and in their total sums (cf. lines 27–29 here, and also, e.g., the equal amounts and pressures involved in 91(100).6–21). The basic argument against any one element predominating had probably been put forward already by Anaximander, cf. Aristotle Phys. 204b28, Simplicius in Phys. 479.32, and Kahn Anaximander p. 186, n. 1.

28 τιμῆς . . . ἑκάστῳ: cf. Parmenides on fire and night, fr. 8.57–58. Each root has its own individual and inalienable nature, which is preserved throughout, as explained by Simplicius, in Phys. 159.13, introducing 14(21) after this fragment. This assumption of permanent, inherent characteristics is essential to the idea of an element, and the emphasis E. placed on it is one of his important contributions to Greek science. Difficulties, however, arise with the positing of a stage of such mingling of the roots that these characteristics are not discernible; see chap. 2.

29 ἐν . . . χρόνοιο: the reference is still to the roots, cf. below on 16(26).1, where the line is repeated with κύκλοιο for χρόνοιο.

30 οὐδ †ἄρ τι† ἐπιγίγνεται: P. Maas accepts the elision of the iota of τι here (Greek Metre, trans. H. Lloyd-Jones, pp. 73, 74), giving as parallels ἔστι τι Ἀνάγκης χρῆμα—a doubtful variant for 107(115).1—and Theocritus 30.12, against which cf. A. S. F. Gow Theocritus, ad loc.

Karsten emended to ἄρ οὔτ' ἐπιγίγνεται, and Diels in some despair to ἄρ τέ τι γίγνεται, cf. *SPAW* 1897, p. 1069. Professor H. Lloyd-Jones has suggested in a personal communication οὐδ' ἄρτι(= now, lately) τι γίνεται. For the sense cf. Parmenides fr. 8.36–37 and also Lucretius 2.296.

31 εἴτε . . . ἦσαν: cf. the emphatic statement of this Eleatic argument by Melissus, fr. 7(2) εἰ τοίνυν τριχὶ μὴ μυρίοις ἔτεσιν ἑτεροῖον γίνοιτο, ὀλεῖται πᾶν ἐν τῷ παντὶ χρόνῳ. Karsten suspects a missing line after line 31, but εἴτε "non respondet alterum, quia alterum lemma variata forma l. 32 continuatur," Diels *PPF* p. 114.

32–33 τοῦτο . . . ἐρῆμον: here E. takes over Parmenides' arguments for the denial of birth and death to what is (cf. fr. 8.6–7, 19–20) and applies them to the four roots, which have no temporal starting or stopping points. Further, Parmenides had claimed that μὴ ὄν could not intervene to prevent what is from reaching its like, nor could there be any variation in density or rarity, cf. fr. 8.23–25, 44–48. E. reinterprets these points, first by asserting that the roots occupy all the available place (τῶνδ' οὐδὲν ἐρῆμον), and then by equating μὴ ὄν with κενόν, resulting in a denial of empty place to interrupt or alter the consistency of the roots, cf. 10(13).

33 ἀλλ' αὔτ' ἔστιν ταῦτα: picking up the τῶνδε of the previous line, the reference continues to be to the roots, cf. 14 (21).13.

34 ἠνεκὲς αἰὲν ὁμοῖα: the Eleatic argument for self-consistency (cf. Parmenides fr. 8.46–48) is applied to the individual roots, completing the point made in line 28—each root has its own τιμή and ἦθος, which are preserved inviolate through the various arrangements and rearrangements of parts in the formation of θνητά. Parmenides was led from the premise ἐπεὶ πᾶν ἔστιν ὁμοῖον to conclude that his subject was unique (cf. G. E. L. Owen *CQ* 10 (1960) pp. 92–93), but E., in positing a mosaic shifting of four eternal roots in a *plenum*, retained their temporal and spatial continuity while allowing plurality and divisibility.

9(12)

It is impossible for there to be a coming into existence from that which is not, and for what exists to be completely destroyed cannot be fulfilled, nor is to be heard of; for when and where it is thrust, then and there it will be.

Philo quotes the first two lines of the fragment anonymously, to show that nothing can come from or pass away into nothing. The three lines and the author are given in *MXG*, where the fragment is connected with 12(8).3–4 as supporting the assertion that since the roots are eternal, there is no absolute genesis or destruction, but an apparent genesis arises from their arrangements and rearrangements.

1 ἐκ γὰρ τοῦ μὴ ἐόντος: a suggested amalgam of ἔκ τε μὴ ὄντος (*MXG*) and ἐκ τοῦ γὰρ οὐδαμῇ ὄντος (Philo), so Bollack: ἔκ τοῦ γὰρ μὴ ἐόντος. Diels has ἐκ τε τοῦ γὰρ οὐδάμ᾽ ἐόντος, but Parmenides usually negates ὄν with μή, cf. frs. 2.7, 7.1, 8.7, and 12, and he frequently has the article, e.g., frs. 2.7, 4.2, 8.32, 35, and 37. ἀμήχανόν ἐστι: almost equivalent to "is logically impossible," cf. G. E. R. Lloyd *Polarity and Analogy* pp. 423–24.

2 ἀνήνυστον καὶ ἄπυστον: cf. Parmenides frs. 2.7–8, 8.8–9, 8.17, and Melissus fr. 2. ἄπυστον is Mangey's suggestion, adopted by Diels, for Philo's ἄπαυστον, which makes no sense here; there is a similar corruption at Parmenides fr. 8.21, where the MSS D and E of Simplicius *in Cael.* read ἄπαυστος for ἄπυστος. The ἄπρηκτον of *MXG* may be an attempt to make sense of ἄπαυστον. For a defense of ἄπαυστον as the *lectio difficilior* cf. Bignone *Empedocle* pp. 398–400.

3 †θήσεσθαι†: Panzerbieter, followed by Diels, emends to τῇ γ᾽ ἔσται, which gives the line a rhetorical flourish. The subject is obviously ἐόν, and the verse so read would make it clear that the preceding two lines had a double reference. There can be no genesis from what is not, nor destruction of what is, in any temporal or spatial sense; ἐόν always exists, and as a *plenum* it occupies all available space, so that there is no time when nor place where it is not. ἐρείδω has a slightly different meaning at 100(110).1.

10(13)
There is no part of the whole that is empty or overfull.

The line is quoted by Aetius under the heading Περὶ κενοῦ and is listed by Theodoretus among several theories on the theme. *MXG* gives it as the condition prevailing after the coming together into unity.

E. is picking up Parmenides' argument on the spatial continuity and consistency of his subject (cf. fr. 8.22–25): there cannot be different degrees of existence at different parts. For Parmenides there is no μὴ ὄν to interrupt the consistency, but E. moves one stage further and identifies μὴ ὄν in its spatial sense with κενόν—an identification adopted by Melissus and similarly used in his denial of variance, cf. Melissus fr. 7.(7)–(8), and also Anaxagoras, fr. 5. The invariance is most marked in the homogeneity of the sphere under Love (which may have induced the context in *MXG*) but always holds true; the roots are incapable of expanding or contracting, and they keep their character inviolate through the mosaic-like arrangements and rearrangements in the *plenum*.

Diels prints as a separate fragment (B 14) the phrase just before this verse in *MXG*: τοῦ παντὸς ⟨δ᾽⟩ οὐδὲ⟨ν⟩ κενεόν. πόθεν οὖν τί κ᾽ ἐπέλθοι; but this makes for needless repetition and may well be an imperfectly remembered conflation of 8(17).32 and 10(13).

11(16)

They are as they were before and shall be, and never, I think, will endless time be emptied of these two.

Hippolytus gives as the subject of the fragment Love and Strife, at *RH* 7.29 attributing the lines to E. but at 6.25 to "the Pythagoreans." He comments that the character of Love is peaceful and unifying whereas Strife is destructive and separates, and that the action of the two continues without beginning or end.

1 ἔ⟨στ⟩ι γὰρ ὡς πάρος ἦν τε καὶ ἔσσεται: a suggestion made in a personal communication by Professor H. Lloyd-Jones for the MSS εἰ γὰρ καὶ πάρος ἦν καὶ ἔσται.

The Homeric formula (e.g., *Il.* 1.70) has the three tenses. After dealing in 8(17).27–35, 9(12), and 10(13) with the four roots, denying them beginning or end in time, spatial variation, and the possibility of addition to or subtraction from their totality, E. then moves on to his motive principles and postulates for them an eternal existence. (Since they were probably not thought of as material bodies in the same way as the roots were, the question of spatial stopping and starting points for them does not arise; see chap. 2.)

FRAGMENTS 12–15 MIXING AND SEPARATING

12(8)

Here is another point: of all mortal things no one has birth, or any end in pernicious death, but there is only mixing, and separating of what has been mixed, and to these men give the name "birth."

The fragment is quoted by Aetius from the first book of the *Physics*. An appropriate place for it is after the general exposition of 8(17) and the related Eleatic arguments. For his next point, E. in this and the following four fragments turns to the world we know and the language we use, showing first that there is no real genesis or destruction of mortal things but only arrangements and rearrangements of their component elements.

1 φύσις: the word is here taken by Plutarch to mean γένεσις in contrast to θάνατος: ὅτι γὰρ ἀντὶ τῆς γενέσεως εἴρηκε τὴν φύσιν, ἀντιθεὶς τὸν θάνατον αὐτῇ δεδήλωκεν ὁ ʼE. (*adv. Col.* 1112a and cf. 1112f). This is the sense also given to φύσις in this context in Aristotle *GC* 314b7 (cf. *Phys.* 193b12), *MXG* 975b6; Philoponus *in GC* 14.14, 15.6–8, 15–17, 263.20–24; Simplicius *in Cael.* 306.3, *in Phys.* 161.18, 180.25–30, 235.20–23; in Alexander it is taken as equivalent to ἕνωσις, *in Metaph.* 359.17–21. At *Metaph.* 1014b35 Aristotle quotes the fragment, without the second line giving the required balance of θάνατος to φύσις, to illustrate the meaning of φύσις as οὐσία (and cf. *GC* 333b11–14, though Joachim argues for φύσις as γένεσις here, *ad GC* 314b7–8). Although such a meaning, or something akin to it, must be implied in E.'s other uses of the word at 56(63) and 100(110).5, this fragment, quoted in its entirety by Plutarch, should probably be given his interpretation. The controversy has continued into modern times, cf. A. O. Lovejoy *PhR* 1909, p. 371; Burnet *EGP* pp. 10–11, 363–64, 205 n. 4; Ross *Ar. Metaph.* vol. 1, pp. 297–98. Opposed to these are W. A. Heidel *Proceedings of the American Academy* 1910, p. 98; Kirk *Heraclitus* pp. 228–30; Kahn *Anaximander* p. 23; Guthrie *HGP* vol. 2, p. 140; and cf. G. A. Seeck *Hermes* 1967, pp. 36–41; J. Owens *Canadian Journal of Philosophy* 1976, pp. 87–100; N. van der Ben *Phronesis* 1978, pp. 204–06. ἀπάντων: the variant ἑκάστου reflects a frequent confusion, cf. 8(17).8, 19 and 51(59).2.

2 θανάτοιο τελευτή: Lovejoy, loc. cit., understands the phrase as (no) "end of death," i.e., θνητά never stop dying, but it is more likely to mean "end that is death," like the standard θανάτοιο τέλος, e.g., Homer *Il.* 3.309, 5.553, 16.502,855, 22.361, and Aeschylus *Sept.* 906. E. seems simply to be saying that despite our normal way of speaking, θνητά are not really born, nor (paradoxically) do they die, because strictly speaking they are temporary arrangements of parts of immortal "roots." The

coming into such an arrangement is φύσις, and the dissolution of the arrangement marks the end of that individual as such. This is spelled out in the next fragment.

3 μίξις: for the assumption that the *mixis* of parts of roots to make an organism is a mosaiclike arrangement in which the pieces retain their character, and not a kind of "chemical" mixture, see chap. 2.

4 ἐπὶ τοῖς . . . ἀνθρώποισιν: cf. line 5 of fr. 13(9). It would not seem that φύσις was a common word for E.'s contemporaries to adopt, but he may have had in mind the verbal usage, as in the next fragment. When a *mixis* is formed, there occurs what is termed γενέσθαι (or φύεσθαι).

13(9)

When they have been mixed in the form of a man and come to the air, or in the form of the race of wild animals, or of plants, or of birds, then people say that this is to be born, and when they separate they call this again ill-fated death; these terms are not right, but I follow the custom and use them myself.

The fragment comes, with 12(8), 104(11), and 106(15), in Plutarch's defense of E. against the charge put forward by Colotes, that E., in abolishing generation, abolished life itself. As Plutarch points out, E. is not doing away with living creatures but showing that terms like birth and death, when applied to them, are misleading; organisms are formed by a mingling in a certain arrangement of parts of eternal roots, and they cease to exist as such when the arrangement breaks up. Provided it is recognized that the terms are not strictly accurate, that birth is really mingling and death separating, the conventional expressions may still be used.

1 μιγέντ' εἰς αἰθέρ' ἵ⟨κωνται⟩: Diels's suggestion for the MSS μίγεν φῶς αἰθέρι and a lacuna of 6–8 letters; he adds, "fortasse φὼς Byzantinorum more vocis φῶτα explicandae causa superscriptum" (*PPF* p. 109). On this reading the subject would be the roots, and the sense would be, "when parts of the roots have formed into an arrangement or mixture with human shape and come to the air." "Coming to the air" may be a poetic paraphrase for "being born" (cf. Lucretius 1.170) but could be more exact, for E.'s theory is that the fetus is ἄπνους and takes its first breath at birth, the intake of air compensating for a loss of moisture, cf. Aetius 4.22.1, 5.15.3.

3 τό ⟨γέ φασι⟩ γενέσθαι: Panzerbieter's filling of the second lacuna

in the fragment. The subject, from the first line, consists of people in general, who speak inaccurately of birth when there is only *mixis*.

5 †ᾗ θέμις† καλέουσι: the reading at 820f, but εἶναι καλέουσι at 1112f. Attempts to make a satisfactory rendering include ἔν γε νόμῳ κ. Reiske, εἰκαίως κ. Karsten, and ἀλοίτην κ. Wyttenbach (cf. DK 31 B10). Stein suggested the conflation ἢ θέμις ἐστί, καλοῦσι, taking θέμις in a weaker sense and close to νόμος. But if θέμις is stressed as "right" (cf. 2(3).4 and Hesiod *Theog.* 396), a negative is obviously required. Wyttenbach had ἢ θέμις ⟨οὐ⟩ for 820f, and Wilamowitz ⟨οὐ⟩ θέμις ᾗ (cf. *Hermes* 1930, p. 246). Diels adopts Wyttenbach's reading as the most reasonable suggestion, on the Homeric pattern with the dative. On the inaccuracy of conventional naming cf. Parmenides fr. 8.38, Anaxagoras fr. 17.

14(21)

But come, if the form of my preceding argument was in any way incomplete, take note of the witnesses of these to what I have said before: sun with its radiant appearance and pervading warmth, heavenly bodies bathed in heat and shining light, rain everywhere dark and chill, and from earth issue firmly rooted solids. Under strife they have different forms and are all separate, but they come together in love and are desired by one another. From them comes all that was and is and will be hereafter—trees have sprung from them, and men and women, and animals and birds and water-nourished fish, and long-lived gods too, highest in honor. For these are the only real things, and as they run through each other they assume different shapes, for the mixing interchanges them.

Simplicius quotes the fragment in full at *in Phys.* 159.13, after the whole of 8(17), as a continuation of the account of the roots, showing that each has its own character and is recognizable in a familiar form—"sun," for example, is fire, "sky" is air, and "rain" and "sea" are water (cf. the table in chap. 2). At *in Phys.* 33.8 Simplicius follows lines 3–12 of this fragment on 47(35), there to point out that mixing results when both Love and Strife are at work.

1 τῶνδ' . . . ἐπιμάρτυρα: the genitives are clumsy. Stein suggested τῶν for τῶνδ', and Diels followed Wilamowitz with τόνδ', taking ἐπιμάρτυρα as masculine singular rather than neuter plural; but a number of phenomena will be pointed out by E. in support of the theory put forward, and the line should probably be left as in Simplicius.

2 λιπόξυλον: "lacking wood," and so "feeble," "defective"; found also at 60(71).1 applied to πίστις but apparently not elsewhere, cf. λίφαιμος, 91(100).1. μορφή: used by Parmenides of fire and night (fr. 8.53), but here the sense is "form of argument." To express his meaning more clearly E. will offer as evidence of the existence and character of the four roots the familiar elemental masses around us.

4 ὅσσ' †ἐδεῖτο†: emended by Diels to ὅσσ' ἴδει τε and further corrected by Wackernagel to ὅσσ' εἴδει τε (cf. SPAW 1884, p. 366; Philologus 1931, pp. 134–35). The word εἶδεος is related to ἱδρώς, and the definition in Hesychius is εἶδεος· θάλπους, καύματος. The ἄμβροτα are the moon and stars, the moon being composed of air shut in by fire, and the stars of fire squeezed out from the air (cf. [Plut.] Strom. ap. Eus. PE 1.8.10, Aet. 2.13.2). If the reading εἶδει is right, and the sense of heat uppermost, then in this line E. would be pointing to the ἄμβροτα as instances of a combination of fire and air; cf. 53(62).5, where heat rather than moisture (which is given in ὕδατος) is indicated.

6 †θέλημα†: the vocabulary of lines 5–6 is uncommon (δνοφόεντα, ῥιγαλέον, and στερεωπά are ἅπ. λεγ.), and the form and sense of this word cannot be decided. θελημά (cf. 47(35).6) is inappropriate, and ἐθελυμνά (advocated by Karsten and Stein from the Suda and Favorinus) unsatisfactory. Diels followed Sturz with θέλυμνα, as a simple form of the Homeric προθέλυμνα (Il. 9.541, 10.15, 13.130, and cf. O'Brien ECC pp. 266–67), but now θελεμνά is generally accepted from the definition in Hesychius: ὅλον ἐκ ῥιζῶν. At GC 315a10, in an obvious reference to this fragment, Aristotle says of E., λέγει τὸν μὲν ἥλιον λευκὸν καὶ θερμόν, τὴν δὲ γῆν βαρὺ καὶ σκληρόν, but "close-packed" or "firmly rooted" is not exactly βαρύ. Also, the verb προρέουσι, associated in epic with the free flowing of rivers and streams (cf. Il. 21.260, Od. 5.444, and especially Hes. Theog. 792), is difficult to understand with a subject of this kind. Perhaps E. wrote no more than θάλασσα (cf. the reference in Simplicius' introduction of the fragment), the weight and hardness mentioned by Aristotle both being implied in στερεωπά—rocks and stones brought along by the water. In any case the theory of an exclusive tetrad of opposites cannot be fastened on E. from this fragment.

7–8: the subject is the four roots, mentioned under familiar names and forms in the preceding lines, and the statement is a general one about their activity when influenced by the motive principles—under Strife (only here in the Physics called κότος) they keep their individual forms in separated masses, in Love they come together into a unity. When both

Love and Strife are active, as Simplicius explains (*in Phys.* 33.4), *thnēta* result.

9: I have accepted Aristotle's version of the line, but with ἐκ τῶν for ἐξ ὧν, as at 15(23).5 and 83(98).5. E. has adopted the common formula for past, present, and future, probably as a deliberate challenge to Parmenides' denial of tenses (fr. 8.5). The list that follows, comprising plant, animal, bird, fish, human, and divine life, is repeated at 15(23).6, the θεοὶ τιμῇσι φέριστοι significantly also appearing in the *Katharmoi* as the highest in the series of lives, cf. 132(146).3.

13–14: line 13 repeats 8(17).34, but there is a change in the second line of the couplet. The emphasis in 8(17) is on the permanence and changelessness of the roots, here it is on their ability to produce all kinds of *thnēta* as they mingle with each other (cf. 47(35).16–17). As against Diels's suggestion for the completion of line 14 a connection is required, and E. does not elsewhere use τόσος without a corresponding relative. Stein and Mullach independently argued for διάπτυξις γὰρ ἀμείβει, a rearrangement of Karsten's suggestion from Simplicius' commentary on 12(8).3: ἀλλὰ μόνον μίξιν τε καὶ διάλλαξιν μιγέντων, καὶ σύνοδον διάπτυξίν τε γενέσθαι ἐν μέρει αἴσης (*in Phys.* 161.20). I conjecture τὰ γὰρ διὰ κρῆσις ἀμείβει, for the tmesis comparing Parmenides fr. 8.41.

15(23)

As painters, men well taught by wisdom in the practice of their art, decorate temple offerings when they take in their hands pigments of various colors, and after fitting them in close combination—more of some and less of others—they produce from them shapes resembling all things, creating trees and men and women, animals and birds and water-nourished fish, and long-lived gods too, highest in honor; so let not error convince you in your mind that there is any other source for the countless perishables that are seen, but know this clearly, since the account you have heard is divinely revealed.

Simplicius quotes the lines as an illustration given by E. of the theory set out in 14(21), refers them to this present world in which plant, animal, and human life results from the activity of both Love and Strife, and connects them with 16(26).1–2 and 11–12. For a discussion of the simile see chap. 2, pp. 38–39.

2 ἀμφὶ . . . δεδαῶτε: the duals δεδαῶτε (line 2), μίξαντε (line 4),

and κτίζοντε (line 6) are puzzling; the earlier editors attempted to avoid them by reading δεδαῶτες (which is given in the Simp. MS F), μάξαν τε, and κτίζουσι respectively. Duals for plurals in Homer, e.g., at *Il.* 3.279, 8.186, 16.371, and 17.387, have been discussed by P. Chantraine (*Grammaire Homérique* vol. 2, p. 28), J. Wackernagel (*Vorlesungen über Syntax* pp. 77–80), and E. Schwyzer and A. Debrunner (*Griechische Grammatik* vol. 2, p. 46); more recently C. Segal has suggested a formal reason for the duals in *Iliad* book 9 ("The Embassy and the Duals of *Iliad* 9.182–98," *GRBS* 1968, pp. 109–14). The duals here may have resulted from the Simplicius MSS reading of ἄμφω for ἀμφί, or perhaps E. is allowing himself a striking flexibility in the forms, cf. 124(137).6.

4 ἁρμονίῃ μίξαντε: "mixed" colors are referred to in Theophrastus *Sens.* 77–78 (on Democritus), Plato *Tim.* 68d, and [Aristotle] *Col.* 792a–b and *Mete.* 372a5. In the introduction it was argued that the mixing of colors in "harmony" described in this fragment is not a blending to produce further shades but the setting of pigments of different colors side by side; the φάρμακα are the appropriate colors ready before the painters start on their pictures. Cf. also 48(96).4, and J. B. Skemp's translation of Plato *Pol.* 277c: "because [the outline] has still to be painted in colours properly balanced with one another." It is uncertain whether a correlation is to be made between the four roots and the four simple colors of black, white, red, and "ochre" (cf. W. Kranz, "Die ältesten Farbenlehren der Griechen," *Hermes* 1912, pp. 126–28). The correspondence is made for E. at Stobaeus *Ecl.* 1.5.3; four colors as canonic are attributed to the Pythagoreans (Aet. 1.15.7, and cf. [Arist.] *De Mundo* 396b13); and they seem to be the ones generally used by fifth-century painters. The number of colors, however, is not as important as the fact that only a few are required in order to produce (in two dimensions) all kinds of θνητά.

6–8: this list was also given in 14(21).11–13. The same wide variety of θνητά comes from the four roots as the painter can reproduce in his art with a few colors.

9 καινύτω: established by Blass from Hesychius καινύτω· νικάτω, the only known appearance of the active form of καίνυμαι.

10 γεγάασιν: Diels's emendation to γεγάκασιν *metris causa* is generally accepted; he compares γεγάκειν in Pindar (*Ol.* 6.49), and Hesychius has the participle γεγακώς. E.'s forms elsewhere are γεγᾶᾱσι 60(71).4, and γεγᾶσι 101(111).1. The line is uncharacteristically stilted and perhaps should be rearranged, e.g.,

πηγὴν ὅσσα γε θνητῶν ἄσπετα δῆλα γεγᾶσιν.

The metaphor of $\pi\eta\gamma\dot{\eta}$, with $\dot{\rho}\dot{\iota}\zeta\omega\mu\alpha$, for the source $\dot{\alpha}\varepsilon\nu\dot{\alpha}ov$ $\varphi\dot{\upsilon}\sigma\varepsilon\omega\varsigma$ appears in the Pythagorean oath by the tetractys, Aetius 1.3.8, and cf. 7(6).1.

11 $\theta\varepsilon o\tilde{v}$ $\pi\dot{\alpha}\rho\alpha$: $\theta\varepsilon\dot{o}\varsigma$ is taken to refer (1) to E. himself as a god, e.g., by Bidez, *Biographie* p. 102, and by W. Nestlé, "Der Dualismus des Emped-okles," *Philologus* 1906, pp. 545–57, comparing 102(112).4; (2) to Aphrodite/Philotēs by Bollack, *Empédocle* vol. 1, p. 265, n. 2, and p. 310; and (3) to the Muse, by Karsten, Diels, Bignone, and others. (3) is surely correct. The $\mu\tilde{v}\theta o\varsigma$ of the physical poem comes from the Muse, addressed in 2(3).4, and specifically as Calliope in 3(131).1–4; her $\pi\iota\sigma\tau\dot{\omega}\mu\alpha\tau\alpha$ guarantee the truth of E.'s *logos*, as at 3(131).4 and 6(4).2–3, and cf. Parmenides fr. 1.22–23. Self-reference here would be an example of the *mania* condemned in 2(3).1 and 5(3).1–3; cf. the commentary on 1(2).9.

FRAGMENTS 16–22 MANY TO ONE IN THE COSMOS: THE SPHERE

16(26)

They prevail in turn as the cycle moves round, and decrease into each other and increase in appointed succession. For these are the only real things, and as they run through one another they become men and the kinds of other animals, at one time coming into one order through love, at another again being borne away from each other by strife's hate, until they come together into the whole and are subdued. So, insofar as one is accustomed to arise from many, and many are produced from one as it is again being divided, to this extent they are born and have no abiding life; but insofar as they never cease their continual exchange, so far they are forever unaltered in the cycle.

The fragment is quoted in full by Simplicius as coming soon after 14(21); he refers it to the genesis of one from many under Love, of many from one under Strife, and of $\theta\nu\eta\tau\dot{\alpha}$ in this world $\kappa\alpha\tau\dot{\alpha}$ $\pi\varepsilon\rho\iota\dot{o}\delta ov\varsigma$. It is a re-wording of the fundamental principle of the uniting and separating of the four roots by reason of the agency of Love and Strife. Lines 1, 3–4, 5–6, and 8–12 repeat 8(17).29, 34–35, 7–8, and 9–13 respectively. Lines 2 and 7 are new, filling in, in a striking manner, the processes involved; $\kappa\dot{\upsilon}\kappa\lambda o\varsigma$ (line 1) and $\kappa\dot{o}\sigma\mu o\varsigma$ (line 5) are important variants on the endings of 8(17).29 and 7.

Commentators tend to complicate the simple explanatory structure of the fragment. The subject is the four roots, the "many." As usual, E. starts his account with the roots in separation. At the appropriate time in the cycle they are in control. In appointed succession they then move from many to one (their masses getting smaller as they mingle) and from one to many (their masses increasing). As they run through each other in both processes they become men and animals. They move from many to one through Love, and from one to many because of Strife, until, coming (again) into one they are subdued. The unity of the four roots described in line 7, which entails the loss of their visible individual characteristics, is the opposite state of affairs to that of line 1. In going from many to one and from one to many they have temporary existences as men and other animals, but in persisting through the recurring exchange of position they are unaltered.

1 ἐν δὲ μέρει . . . κύκλοιο: repeated from 8(17).29 with κύκλοιο for χρόνοιο, itself a refinement on the Homeric περιπλομένων ἐνιαυτῶν (Od. 1.16, and in the singular 11.248). The substitution is a deliberate (and perhaps a pioneer) assertion that time is cyclical, as Aristotle observes later, "to say that things that come into being form a circle is to say that there is a cycle of time" (Phys. 223b30–34, Oxford trans.). κύκλοιο in the first line, picked up by κατὰ κύκλον in the last, sets the fragment in the large-scale context of recurring time.

The subject of κρατέουσι here and in 8(17).29 is the four roots. E. uses singular and plural verbs with this subject, and also masculine and neuter adjectives. In 8(17) the line is obscure and could perhaps refer to a Milesian world picture of warring opposites with regional and seasonal aggressions and compensations, but the context of 16(26) contrasts the time of domination with a time of getting smaller and bigger (i.e., of becoming one from many and many from one), and of complete subjection. The roots are subdued when they are together, and conversely, when they prevail they are separate.

2 φθίνει . . . αἴσης: the roots have a turn at being dominant and separate, and also a turn at getting smaller and at getting bigger; this is explained in lines 5–6 as moving from many to one under Love and moving from one to many under Strife. Exchanging position either way involves "running through each other," and in running through each other the roots become men and other animals. They get smaller as their individual masses dwindle while mingling, and they get bigger as the bits return to their own kind.

3 αὐτὰ γὰρ ἐστιν ταῦτα: "for there are these very things," "these are

the real things" (cf. αὐτὸς οὗτος, LSJ s.v. αὐτός 1.7), rather than "they are themselves" (O'Brien) or "Ils sont, toujours même" (Bollack). "There are just these" (Guthrie) shifts the emphasis slightly. The roots running through each other become different things at different times (8(17).35), things with different faces (14(21).14), and here, more explicitly, men and other animals.

5 εἰς ἕνα κόσμον: the roots run through each other producing men and animals, at one time when going from many to one, and at another when going from one to many, but they stop doing so when dominant and many or subdued and one. Coming into one *kosmos* in line 5 is the same process as coming into one whole in line 7, a more precise version here of εἰς ἓν ἅπαντα at 8(17).7. *Kosmos* is used in the sense of "total world order" as it was by Heraclitus, fr. 30, and probably the Pythagoreans (Aet. 2.1.1) and Parmenides (D.L. 8.48). For this sense of *kosmos* in the Presocratics cf. Kirk *Heraclitus* pp. 307–24, Guthrie *HGP* vol. 1, pp. 454–59, and G. Vlastos *Plato's Universe* chap. 1.

7 τὸ πᾶν: when used elsewhere by E. means "the whole," "the sum total," 8(17).32, 10(13).1, 33(39).3, and so here, rather than an adverb, "completely." Nor should it be taken as the subject of γένηται, involving an unwarranted change of subject from, and then back to, the four roots, and leaving συμφύντα unaccounted for. (O'Brien's elaborate metrical argument for τὸ πᾶν as subject, *ECC* pp. 322–23, is incorrect, for it is not the case that all the following lines except 8 "have a third foot trochaic caesura dividing the line according to sense," and his translation, "until (the time comes when) they grow together as one and the whole is defeated," does not fit the text he prints.) τὸ πᾶν therefore belongs with συμφύντα in the sense of the roots "coming together into the whole." The word before the participle is in doubt and is given variously as ἕν, ὅν, or ὄν; Diels suggested ἐς ἕν (*PPF* p. 118). εἰσόκεν εἰς συμφύντα τὸ πᾶν would be more appropriate, and for the order cf. LSJ s.v. εἰς, B. ὑπένερθε γένηται: the roots are "underneath" in the opposite sense to their prevailing (cf. line 1), because they are not separate and dominant masses but are in such a mixing of discrete particles that none of their characteristics is visibly distinct. Line 7 is a rewording of line 5 as line 1 is of line 6.

8–12: quoted separately by Aristotle (*Phys.* 250b20) and repeated from 8(17).9–13. The lines are given to illustrate movement and rest in E., movement when Love makes one from many or Strife many from one, and "rest" in the times—or time—between. For the many to become one implies a time (of "rest") when they were many, and for the one to

divide into many implies a time (of "rest") when there was the one. That
Aristotle did not spell out the implications may be a fault, but he is free
of the grosser error of deliberate concealment and misinterpretation, see
chap. 2 and the discussions cited there.

10: the line sums up 12(8) and 13(9), as well as lines 2–6. The roots
appear to undergo both genesis and an early death in their compound
forms of men and other animals; this happens as they run through each
other, getting "smaller" (going from many to one) and "bigger" (moving
from one to many). Lines 11–12 give the contrast to line 10. The "exchange of position" results in temporary compounds, but the permanence
of the exchange from many to one and from one to many in a circle (or
cycle) of time ensures the permanence of the roots. (Long argues that the
activity described in line 8 takes an extended period of time but that the
one in line 9 is immediate; the activities also of lines 5 and 7 take an
extended time whereas that of line 6 is immediate, *Pre-Socratics* p. 412.
But the participles in lines 5, 6, 7, and 9 are all present, and it is perverse
to read such an extreme time difference into the similar constructions.)
ἀκίνητοι is "unaltered" in a mainly temporal sense, cf. Parmenides
fr. 8.26, 38, and Owen *CQ* 1960, p. 97.

17(25)

For what is right is worth repeating.

The line is given by the scholiast as the source of the proverb δὶς καὶ τρὶς
τὸ καλόν, and by Plutarch to justify a second refutation of Epicurus.
Except at *Laws* 754c, (with δίς only), Plato uses the δὶς καὶ τρίς version,
Gorg. 498e, *Phlb.* 60a, *Laws* 956e. Repetition of lines in whole or in part
in the extant fragments of E. are as follows: 8(17).1–2 at 16–17, 6 at 12
and at 16(26).11, 7–8 at 16(26).5–6, 9–13 at 16(26).8–12, 29 at 16(26).1,
34 at 14(21).13 and 16(26).3; 14(21).10–12 at 15(23).6–8; 16(26).4 at
113(121).2; 19(27).1 at 21(27).1; 22(29).1–2 at 97(134).2–3; 47(35).7
at 16; 88(84).5 at 10; 91(100).7–8 at 24–25. Repetition is so obviously
a feature of E.'s method that attempts to alter the arrangement of the
fragments solely to avoid it are unjustified. Repetitions, formally in the
epic tradition, are used as summaries, reminders, and reinforcements,
and minor differences are often significant, e.g., περιπλομένοιο χρόνοιο/
κύκλοιο at 8(17).29 and 16(26).1. Most often the repetition is a development or a particular application of what has been said previously in a

general context. Here the reference is likely to be to the considerable repetition of 8(17) in 16(26), but the fragment may also imply advance notice of a more comprehensive reiteration—an outline of the whole cosmology followed by detailed consideration of particular sections (cf. the commentary on 18(24) and Parmenides' program, fr. 8.2–4).

18(24)

Joining one chief point to another, so as not to pursue only one path of discourse.

μὴ τελέειν is generally accepted by all but Bollack, who retains Plutarch's reading, finding a parallel in 47(35).1–2. The construction in both versions is strained and perhaps should be emended (in a personal communication Professor H. Lloyd-Jones suggested μήτ' ἐλθεῖν), but the sense is clear, and the context in Plutarch refers to E. avoiding the exclusive pursuit of one argument. The fragment corroborates the suggestion that E.'s method is to give the main points of his argument—the κορυφαί (cf. 8(17).15 πιφαύσκων πείρατα μύθων)—and then to develop in further (but not exhaustive) detail the sections of especial relevance or interest. It expressly contradicts the claim advanced by Bollack, Hölscher, and Solmsen that the *Physics* is an account of "a single linear development" (A. A. Long's phrase, *The Pre-Socratics* p. 398).

The program that follows summarizes the cosmic stages, starting from the roots in separation, from which the strifeless sphere is derived. There is then the particular account of the entry of Strife, the articulation of the cosmic masses and the related meteorology, followed by a return, in the nature of a digression, to the complementary stage of the retreat of Strife and the resulting monstrous forms. Fragment 53(62) resumes the account with the full-scale zoogony and biology that logically follow the cosmogony given prior to the digression.

19(27)

There the shining form of the sun is not shown, nor the shaggy might of earth, nor sea.

The meaning of δε(ί)δίσσομαι is "frighten" or "fear," and Karsten's δεδίσκεται is therefore generally accepted. Bollack, however, argues for the retention of δεδίσσεται with a sense related to δείκνυμι. He also retains γένος, comparing 25(22).7 and 100(110).9, but the reference here is to the earth as we know it, cf. $\alpha i\theta\acute{\epsilon}\rho\iota o\nu$ $\mu\acute{\epsilon}\nu o\varsigma$ 107(115).9. $\lambda\acute{\alpha}\sigma\iota o\nu$ implies strength and roughness, and cf. the analogues of hair, 71(82).

The roots in separation provide a logical starting point for E.'s account of the cosmic stages. Plutarch's context sets the lines firmly in a description of the four elements completely unmixed under Strife, prior to their being brought into a *harmonia* by the power of Love. The $\varphi o\beta\epsilon\rho\grave{\alpha}$ $\grave{\alpha}\kappa o\sigma\mu\acute{\iota}\alpha$ is comparable to that described by Plato at *Tim.* 53a–b. Even if Plutarch's quotations are not always accurate, it would be perverse to reject him as a key authority on E. and to refer these lines to an opposite state of affairs than that described by him. (Plutarch is said to have written a ten-book commentary on E., cf. Hippolytus *RH* 5.20.6 and the discussion by O'Brien, *ECC* p. 33, n. 2. For the lines as a supposed reference to elements under Love, cf. the commentary on 21(27) below.)

Sun, earth, and sea as we know them are not recognizable when the elemental masses are completely distinct ($\grave{\alpha}\kappa\rho\alpha\tau o\iota$ $\kappa\alpha\grave{\iota}$ $\grave{\alpha}\sigma\tau o\rho\gamma o\iota$ in Plutarch's paraphrase) and in their "natural," i.e., logically prior, state. Earth is at the center (cf. Aristotle *Cael.* 295a30), surrounded by water, air, and fire in concentric layers, each clinging to its own kind and shunning association with any other. Aristotle implies at *Metaph.* 1050b23, 985a25, and *Phys.* 250b26 that the separate elements are at rest, but at *Cael.* 301a15 that they are moving, and this is supported by the participles in the Plutarch context. Perhaps neither rest nor motion in an absolute sense is appropriate, for, according to Plutarch, both start with the increasing influence of Love, cf. 927a.

I suggest there is a vibration (comparable to the uninterrupted shaking of the winnower) as the roots continue to try to shun each other but, in the absence of void, cannot do so completely —a natural (and mindless) $\grave{\alpha}\kappa o\sigma\mu\acute{\iota}\alpha$, subsequently resolved into the preferable $\grave{\alpha}\rho\mu o\nu\acute{\iota}\alpha$ and $\kappa o\iota\nu\omega\nu\acute{\iota}\alpha$ imposed by Philotēs. (Cf. Simplicius *in Cael.* 530.17–20: when the elements are separated by Strife and unmixed there is no *syntaxis* in the relation of sky to earth.)

20(36)
Strife was retreating from them to the extremity as they were coming together.

Since the complete line is given in Stobaeus immediately after 7(6), $\tau\tilde{\omega}\nu$ refers to the four roots. Schneidewin was the first to suggest inserting the line in 47(35) in place of line 7 (which is repeated at line 16), and he was followed by Diels, Kirk-Raven, and Guthrie (*HGP* vol. 2, p. 178, n. 4), but this attributes carelessness to Simplicius' quotation unnecessarily. The line helps to bridge the κορυφαί of 19(27) and 21(27) with the transition from unmixed roots under Strife to mixed under Love. The verb takes the genitive in the sense of "retire from," "give up possession of" (cf. LSJ s.v. ἐξίστημι II), and ἔσχατον is accusative of end of motion (cf. 47(35).10 ἐπ' ἔσχατα τέρματα κύκλου). In Aristotle's truncated version the sense is closer to "whenever everything came together, then Strife's position was at the extremity," and the immediate context is a carping criticism of the god for the comparative poverty of his knowledge resulting from his lack of acquaintance with Strife; fr. 77(109) is quoted to support the criticism. More important, Aristotle points out that Strife is a cause of genesis no less than Love, and Love a cause of destruction— συνάγουσα γὰρ εἰς τὸ ἕν φθείρει τὰ ἄλλα.

21(27)

There the swift limbs of the sun are not distinguished . . . in this way it is held fast in the close covering of harmony, a rounded sphere, rejoicing in encircling stillness.

Simplicius quotes from Eudemus in support of a time of rest between the initiation of movement and control by Love, and that by Strife; in the complete ἐπικράτεια of Love all things come together. For E. this means that the minute particles of roots are so mingled that it is impossible to pick out any one and distinguish it from another. (On the mixing of the elements in the sphere, and Aristotle's commentary, see chap. 2. J. Longrigg's article, *CR* 1967, pp. 1–4, is a reworking of the Arundel thesis, pp. 146–49.) In 19(27).1 the *eidos* of the sun is not apparent because all the particles of fire have come together, and here the particles cannot be discerned (except perhaps by Lynceus, cf. Aristotle *GC* 328a16) because they are closely mingled with other minute parts of earth, air, and water; cf. also the commentary on φθίνει εἰς ἄλληλα 16(26).2. (ἔνθα is probably spatial as in 69(76).3 and almost certainly 113(121).2 and 116(122).1.) Partial repetition in the two lines does not mean that they are to be conflated (cf. on 17(25) above), especially when they are referred to opposite states of affairs.

2 κρυφῷ: surely not "Verliess" (DK), "ténèbres" (Bollack), or

"obscurity" (Guthrie) for the rejoicing, intelligent god. The parallel is Parmenides B 8.29–31. E., like Parmenides, has a metaphor of constraint for the uniform stability and changelessness which in this case are imposed by *harmonia* (another name for Philia/Aphrodite, and less personalized as a cohesive principle, 48(96).4).

3 σφαῖρος: according to the scholiast on Aratus a masculine form of σφαῖρα coined by E. on the analogy of Ἕσπερος for Ἑσπέρα. For the seemingly redundant κυκλοτερής cf. Parmenides 8.43—εὐκύκλου σφαίρης —but E. may be deliberately emphasizing the shape, which was not the main feature of Parmenides' simile. περιηγέι: Simplicius has περιγηθέι, defended by O'Brien *ECC* 284, with inadequate parallels. Bollack reads περιγηθέι γαίων here and περιηγέι χαίρων at 22(29/28).4, but the change in the line is weak and περιγηθής unsuitable for the abstract noun μονίη. For the joy of the god cf. Gēthosunē as another name for Philia, 8(17).24.

μονίη: whether μονίη means "rest" (from μένω) or "solitude" (from μόνος) has been extensively discussed; cf. Jaeger *TEGP* p. 141, Burnet *EGP* p. 210, Guthrie *HGP* vol. 2, p. 169, n. 3, O'Brien *ECC* pp. 22–24, Bollack *Empédocle* vol. 3, p. 137, Kahn *Gnomon* 1969, p. 441. The available evidence, however, strongly supports the sense "stillness" (Guthrie's translation), "absence of change or movement"—cf. the Homeric καμμονίη, Xenophanes fr. 26 and Parmenides fr. 8.29–31; Eudemus, the main authority for the line, understood the word as ἀκινησία. (Tyrtaeus 1.54, with Diehl's references, is arguable support.) "Rejoicing in solitude" is not a Greek characteristic, and Plato has to defend the god's solitude as being no impediment to his happiness, *Tim.* 34b, but repose and freedom from disturbances feature as a desirable state of affairs in the mainstream of Greek thought from Homer (*Od.* 6.42–46) onward. μονίη would still have an aural association with μόνος, however, and the unusual word was probably deliberately chosen for its ambiguity. The combination, attributed to Heraclitus and Parmenides, of "a philosopher's interest in literal, original and paradigmatic meaning, with something of the poet's sensitivity to the psychological suggestiveness and acoustic associations of words" could be claimed for E., cf. Mourelatos *The Pre-Socratics* p. 347.

22(29/28)

For two branches do not spring from his back, he has no feet, no swift knees, no organs of reproduction, but he is equal to himself in every direction, without any beginning or end, a rounded sphere, rejoicing in encircling stillness.

The fragment is here given as a conflation of Diels's 29 and 28. Hippolytus quotes the first two lines, and his version of what follows—ἀλλὰ σφαῖρος ἔην καὶ ἴσος ἐστὶν αὐτῷ—is an unmetrical summary, after a previous warning that the quotation was not exact. (σφαῖραν ἔην at Simplicius *in Phys.* 1124.1 is unhelpful. ἔην is not given in F; without it there are not the additional complications of a tense change and a neuter form. Moreover, οὐδετέρως preceding ποτὲ καλεῖ σφαῖρον looks contradictory; the clause in Simplicius should perhaps be transposed to the end of the sentence at *in Phys.* 1124.4.)

Line 4 repeats 21(27).3, and line 2, with one small change, is applied to the denial of human form to the φρὴν ἱερή of 97(134). The absence of Strife, which features here as a state of the cosmos under Love, is also applicable to the individual wise man, as at 98(27a), and M. Antoninus uses line 4 as a paradigm for the philosophic state. Furthermore, Hippolytus quotes 107(115) after this fragment, relating the entry of Strife into the sphere, and the consequent disruption, to the embodiment of the daimons in a variety of mortal forms. Intelligence and the absence of *stasis* result from the physical structure of component parts achieving homogeneous mingling through the activity of Love. Such is the character of the sphere here described; and the description connects with that of the wise man and shows how the daimon of the *Katharmoi* is to be understood.

1 κλάδοι: for the similarity of parts in animals and plants, cf. hair and leaves at 71(82). ἀίσσονται: "shoot up," cf. Pindar *Nem.* 8.40 of a tree, but also "move about rapidly," and the ambiguity is probably deliberate (Hesiod *Theog.* 150). The absence of arms, legs, and generative organs also characterizes the οὐλοφυεῖς τύποι of 53(62), the prehuman forms that arise at the beginning of the transition from Love's control to Strife's control. The denial of human form in this fragment may well be a development of Xenophanes fr. 23.2 (as Plato later—the god has no need of hands for grasping or for self-defense, nor of feet for the movement appropriate to him, *Tim.* 33d), but E. is involved in a more general and radical rethinking of what it means to be a god, elaborating a theory of cosmic divinity that was already adumbrated in Presocratic thinking (see chap. 3).

3 ὅ γε πάντοθεν ἶσος ⟨ἐοῖ⟩: ⟨ἐοῖ⟩ is supplied by P. Maas, and the phrase is an obvious echo of οἱ γὰρ πάντοθεν ἶσον and ἑωυτῷ πάντοσε τωυτόν at Parmenides fr. 8.49 and 57. E. has copied Parmenides in the concepts of uniqueness, uniformity, balance, and stability but has used

them for a stage in a cosmic alternation, derived from and giving way to plurality and change. There is also a material content, and so Parmenides' simile of a sphere is now applied literally. πάμπαν ἀπείρων fills out the physical description, for the sphere, even more than the circle, has no spatial starting or stopping point. There is also the implication that there are no internal frontiers dividing one element off from another, as is the case in the cosmos under Strife.

FRAGMENTS 23–46 ONE TO MANY IN THE COSMOS: THE PRESENT WORLD

23(30)

But when great strife had grown in the frame and leapt upward to its honors as the time was being completed, a time of exchange for them, which has been defined by a broad oath

This important fragment refers in strong poetical terms to the inevitable end of the dominion of Love and, with the increase of Strife, the beginning of movement as the one breaks into many. In Aristotle's commentary on the lines (*Metaph.* 1000b9–20) Love and Strife are both viewed as generative and destructive—Strife destroys the one but brings many into existence, and Love generates the one but destroys everything else. (But E. is praised for his consistency in keeping the elements permanent.) E., however, gives no reason for the change apart from *anankē*, which itself requires explanation. Simplicius (*in Phys.* 1184) reiterates Aristotle's complaint, and in this context gives interesting parallels. That "this is the way things are and must be" is E.'s explanation for the cyclic time of 8(17).29, the beginning of movement in the sphere at 24(31), and the oracle of *anankē*, strengthened by broad oaths, which gives the time for the separation of the daimon from the gods. Asclepius summarizes the first line as ἡνίκα τὸ νεῖκος ἐπεκράτησε (cf. Simplicius' setting of the lines ἐπὶ τῆς τοῦ νείκους ἐπικρατείας), paraphrases the second, and after quoting the third explains that the oath is called broad ὡς πάλιν χορηγοῦντα τὰ πάντα. It is quite clear that we have a reference to the assumption of power by Strife as a recurring event.

1 αὐτὰρ ἐπεί: cf. 51(59).1, rather than Aristotle's pedestrian version, but Aristotle's ἐθρέφθη "had grown," "had increased in size" (cf. *Il.* 2.661), and not ἐρέφθη (accepted by Bollack and translated "l'emporta"). μέγα is most obviously attributive. ἐνὶ μελέεσσιν: the long iota of the

preposition is acceptable, as at 26(20).5, cf. P. Maas, *Greek Metre* p. 79. μελέεσσιν, like γυῖα in the following fragment, refers to the frame or structure of the sphere, consisting, before the breakup, of the four roots perfectly harmonized. Strife is now "in" the frame in the sense that it is and will be active there. The reverse procedure, of retreat from the μέλη, is given in 47(35).11.

2 ἀνόρουσε: the language is violent, and the image is perhaps that of a military attack. Strife, from the circumference of the sphere (cf. 20(36).1), makes for the center, consolidates its position, and then makes forays outward over more and more territory; τιμαί sums up the victorious outcome.

3 ἀμοιβαῖος: the time given to Love to dominate comes to an end and is replaced by a time given to Strife. Bollack takes ὅρκου with it and translates "en lieu d'une large enceinte." A period of time cannot, however, be recompensed by a ὅρκος but only by a similar period, as letters (Hdt. 6.4) or invitations to dinner (Pindar *Ol.* 1.39) are exchanged, or soldiers replaced (*Il.* 13.793), or keys fitted to doors (Parmenides fr. 1.14). That the predominance of Love must be recompensed by the predominance of its opposite is an application of the idea of cosmic justice and retribution worked out in time found in Anaximander's fragment, and of *metra* governed by *logos* in Heraclitus. The time has been "marked out," ἐλήλαται, by an oath, as a wall or trench is defined (cf. LSJ s.v. ἐλαύνω III.2 and esp. Hesiod *Theog.* 726 and Herodotus 1.146, 6.62). There is no need to wonder who swears the broad oath. Its function is to add solemnity and certainty to the necessary exchange of times of power for the cosmic forces, in somewhat the same way as Parmenides speaks of the necessity of invariance in terms of the bonds of Anankē, and as Plato brings in εἱμαρμένη for the reversal of the cycle in the myth (*Pol.* 272d6–e7).

24(31)
For one by one all the parts of god began to tremble.

Strife's attack on the sphere destroys both its unity and its rest. Simplicius quotes the line after 21(27) with a repeated πάλιν: at the commencement again of Strife's dominion, then again there is movement in the sphere and the parts become articulated.

ἐξείης: "in turn," "one after the other," as at *Il.* 15.137 and 22.240; for πελεμίζετο cf. *Il.* 8.443 of Olympus shaking under the feet of Zeus.

πάντα . . . γυῖα θεοῖο: the "limbs" are not personal, for this is denied at 22(29) and 97(134), nor are they bits of elements that can be distinguished, for no section of the mixture can be picked out as having discernible characteristics (cf. 21 and 19[27]); they are the totality of spatial parts, like μέλη at 23(30).1 and 47(35).11. θεοῖο is important as the only identification in the fragments of the sphere with god, though Ammonius gives the reference of φρὴν ἱερή at 97(134).3 as περὶ τοῦ θείου παντός. That E. ascribes divinity to the sum total of the four roots in a state of perfect mixture under Love is obviously relevant to an understanding of the nature of the daimon, cf. the commentary on 107(115).

25(22)

For all these—sun and earth and sky and sea—are one with the parts of themselves that have been separated from them and born in mortal things. In the same way, those that are more ready to combine are made similar by Aphrodite and feel mutual affection. But such as are most different from each other in birth and mixture and in the molding of their forms are most hostile, quite inexperienced in union, and grieving deeply at their generation in strife, in that they were born in wrath.

There is little help for the interpretation of this fragment from the two sources, for although Simplicius connects the lines with the general behavior of the roots in the cosmic changes of 16(26).1–2, 11–12, his Neoplatonism contrasts intelligible and perceptible worlds, and Theophrastus takes lines 6–7 out of context as an illustration of pain resulting from the interaction of opposites. O'Brien discusses the fragment at confusing and confused length (*ECC* pp. 305–12), Bollack tries diagrams (vol. 1, pp. 181–83), and M. C. Stokes concludes that an analysis of fr. 22 supports his supposition that "in talking about unity and plurality E. did not know what he was talking about" (*One and Many in Presocratic Philosophy* p. 172). But the basic argument in this and the following fragment is clear. E. is anxious to show (1) that earth, air, fire, and water have the same character in the parts of themselves that make up mortal things as in their discernible world masses, and (2) that the activity of Love and Strife, as we know them, is similar to, and a prime illustration of, their cosmic functions. Lines 1–3 make the first point: as Strife's control increases, the four roots come together as the sun, earth, sea, and sky we perceive, but the process is not complete; parts of the four roots are still mixed with each other as *thnēta*, and over these Love and Strife are both active. Lines 4–5 give the working of Love, and 6–9 of Strife. Some individual mixtures can still be combined, and Love makes them similar to each other so that they want to come together; others, however, are incapable of such unions, and since they cannot come together as wholes, nor can their separate parts join with "their own dear kind" (cf. fr. 100(110).9), they have a wretched existence as a result of Strife's activity. The reference here is to *thnēta* in general, with the particular application to the different forms of life in the following fragment.

2 ἠλέκτωρ . . . θάλασσα: in apposition to the subject ταῦτα πάντα. The discernible masses of the four roots are friendly with the parts of themselves (μέρεσσιν as the antecedent to ὅσσα) that make up the constituent portions of mortal things, for they have the same characteristics and are of the same family. With ἄρθμια here cf. ποθέοντα and φίλην γένναν in 100(110). 9, and of fire θέλον πρὸς ὁμοῖον ἱκέσθαι, 53(62).6.

3 φιν: the pronoun, despite the Doric form, is probably not to be emended (e.g., to νῦν as by Stein) but to be taken generally—"(the parts) which have strayed, as far as they (the subjects in line 2) are concerned, and have been cut off and born in mortal things . . ."

4 ὡς δ' αὔτως: one or more lines which would make the comparison more specific may have been lost between 3 and 4, but the point is that, as with the four roots, the cosmic behavior of Love and Strife is the same as that experienced now. ὅσα refers back to ὅσσα and μέρεσσιν—"as many (separated parts) as are better adapted for mixing (κρήσει would be preferable to κρῆσιν) are made like by Aphrodite (cf. 60(71).4) and are desired by one another." There are two processes in this outline: (1) Aphrodite brings separate parts of roots into mixtures where suitable proportions are available (cf. 48(96).4), and (2) the mixtures combine as the result of the same form of attraction that brings about sexual union. The details of "molding," "gluing," and "nailing" of the parts into wholes are given later, cf. frs. 60–87, especially 60(71), 62(73), and 86(87).

6 ἐχθρὰ μάλιστ' ὅσα πλεῖστον ἀπ' ἀλλήλων διέχουσι: my conjecture for the Simplicius line ἐχθρα πλεῖστον ἀπ' ἀλλήλων διέχουσι μάλιστα. μάλιστα is not given by Theophrastus, who starts his direct quotation with πλεῖστον. Diels's addition (from Panzerbieter) of ⟨δ' ἄ⟩ is harsh and leaves πλεῖστον unconnected with ἐχθρα. ἐχθρα πλεῖστον is metrically unpleasing, despite O'Brien's defense of it, *ECC* p. 310. A contrast is obviously needed between what can be mixed and is brought together by Love, and what cannot and is kept apart in enmity by Strife.

7 γέννη . . . ἐκμακτοῖσι: Theophrastus refers the line to an explanation of pain by the interaction of opposites (whereas pleasure is explained

by an interaction of likes); this would seem to involve the theory of pores, since there can be no mixing where the pores do not fit (cf. the commentary on 77[109]). But even if he has taken lines 6–7 out of context there is still support for their reference, namely collections of parts of different roots that cannot come easily, if at all, into further combinations. They are incompatible because of the way they are (γέννη), the lack of proportion in their composition (κρήσει), and their shape. Like mixtures are brought together by Love, unlike ones stay separate; detailed references to what can and cannot mix come later. As well as the implications for sensation and knowledge, lines 6–8 provide a framework of medical relevance for the structure of living things, cf. *Reg.* 1.6.29 προσίζει τὸ σύμφορον τῷ συμφόρῳ, τὸ δὲ ἀσύμφερον πολεμεῖ καὶ μάχεται καὶ διαλλάσσει ἀπ' ἀλλήλων.

9: νεικεογεννέστῃσιν is impossible as it stands. Karsten, after Scaliger, suggests νεικεογεννητῇσι from νεικεογενέσι in the Simplicius context. The sense would be passive—"strife-generated"—and preferable to the Panzerbieter-Diels νείκεος ἐννεσίῃσιν, which brings in a new notion, unknown to Simplicius' paraphrase. My suggestion ὅτι σφισι γένναι ἐν ὀργῇ to resolve the corruption at the end of the line would give E.'s own explanation for the unusual νεικεογεννητῇσιν. The grief and anger at being generated in a world of increasing strife are personalized in the *Katharmoi*, cf. 112(118), 114(124), and 123(145).

26(20)

This is well known in the mass of mortal limbs: at one time, in the maturity of a vigorous life, all the limbs that are the body's portion come into one under love; at another time again, torn asunder by evil strifes, they wander, each apart, on the shore of life. So it is too for plants, and for fish that live in the water, and for wild animals who have their lairs in the hills, and for the wing-sped gulls.

The fragment is given only by Simplicius to show how Love and Strife prevail in turn among men and other living organisms. The lines have been variously interpreted as referring, for example, to sexual intercourse (Kranz), health and sickness (Bignone), life in the womb (Panzerbieter), the "fantastic situation" of 50 (57).1–3 (Guthrie), and a hypothetical "third stage of increasing Strife" (O'Brien). But, as Stokes observes (*One and Many* p. 165), E. is using something *conspicuous* among men as an illustration of what is less obvious. So far in the poem E. has given an outline of the nature of the roots, the way in which they all unite under

Love and move apart under Strife, and their mixing and separating in
the seeming birth and death of *thnēta*. We then have a more detailed account of the many in separation, their coming into one in the sphere,
and the breakup of the sphere into many, with the subsequent emergence
of the visible masses of sun, earth, sky, and sea. This large-scale uniting
and separating can be illustrated by what is familiar among men, plants,
fish, animals, and birds. E. continues with some meteorological details
and then in 47(35) picks up the question of living things in general; in
the many-to-one stage limbs and monsters arise initially, and in 53(62)
we have the origins of man in the present movement of one to many.
In this context what is familiar and conspicuous among living organisms,
and an illustration of uniting and separating on a larger scale, is of
course birth and growth, and death, or as E. prefers to put it, parts coming
together into a σῶμα and subsequently disintegrating. Fragment 26(20)
is a fuller explanation (as Love and Strife are now seen to be involved),
in more poetical terms, of 12(8), where it was said that there is no birth
or death for *thnēta*, ἀλλὰ μόνον μίξις τε διάλλαξίς τε μιγέντων.

1 τοῦτο: so Diels for τοῦτον. The reference would be to a more general
statement of the activity of Love and Strife—possibly that given in the
previous fragment—which is illustrated by something "outstanding" or
"well known" in the body.

3 τὰ σῶμα λέλογχε: what is well known is that the limbs which the
body had and now holds as its portion (for the perfect cf. 93(102).1,
107(115).5) are at one time coordinated and vigorous in the prime of life
(which E. explains as due to Love) but at another lose their strength,
wither, and decay.

4 κακῇσι . . . ἐρίδεσσι: a variant of νεῖκος οὐλόμενον, for the specific manifestations of strife among men in war and disease.

5 περὶ ῥηγμῖνι βίοιο: cf. *Il.* 1.437, 8.501. The seashore is the border
line between land and sea, and the shore of life would be a border line
too, that between life and death, where one hovers when sick, or old, or
wounded. The violence implicit in ῥηγμῖνι (cf. ῥήγνυμι) repeats that of
the previous line, and there may be a link with ῥέω. E. perhaps wishes
to cover both the loss of limbs in battle and the wasting of the body in
illness as physical consequences of Strife's disruption, cf. σήψιες ἔργα τε
ῥευστά related to Strife and the joyless land in 113(121), and also Plato
Tim. 84c τῆς τοῦ σώματος φύσεως ἐξ ἀνάγκης ῥυείσης (quoted by Bignone, p. 410). The separate limbs of 50(57) are not relevant here in the
illustration of the less by the more obvious. Too much stress need not be

laid on πλάζεται in line 5 in a passage already rich in metaphor (cf. Stokes *One and Many* p. 166 and also Parmenides fr. 16.1); the word implies isolation and insecurity as well as physical movement.

6–7: plants (more literally "bushes"), fish, animals, and birds complete the list of the forms of life affected, like men, by Love and Strife, and like them, strong and flourishing at one time, withering, disintegrating, and dying at another. The lines connect with the *Katharmoi* (1) when E. gives a sense in which he has experienced life as a *thamnos*, bird, and fish in 108(117), and (2) in the exhortation to refrain from violating plant and animal life (frs. 124–29), which would promote Strife's disintegration of wholes. The recall of this list at 13(9) is support for line 5 here referring to the διάλλαξις of the roots (εὖτε δ' ἀποκρινθῶσι, 13(19).4) at the time of so-called death.

7 κύμβαις: the species of bird is probably not significant (e.g., as moving between sky and sea, so Bollack *Empédocle* vol. 3, p. 107); the gull, a "headfirst diver" (if that is the sense from κύβη) is the most obvious form of bird life in a harbor town.

27(38)

Come now, I shall tell you from what sources, in the beginning, the sun and all those others which we now see became distinct—earth and swelling sea, moist air, and Titan sky, whose circle binds all things fast.

Clement quotes the lines with approval for showing *aithēr* as a containing and binding principle. In the context of E.'s poem the fragment obviously marks a transition to a new section. After the identification of the visible elemental masses with the four roots in the previous two fragments, frs. 27–46 give details of how these masses came to have their present form and position in the cosmogony brought about by Strife's activity. Then, with 47(35), E. breaks off and returns to the many-to-one stage for the beginning of his account of *thnēta*.

1: Clement's text is defective, and ἥλιον is probably out of position, for the sun cannot be the source of the other elements that are equal to it. Sturz and Karsten suggest a lacuna after the first line where the other three roots would have been listed, but this is unduly repetitive; and Diels's ἥλικα as a substantive is an unsatisfactory guess. Hence my conjecture, with the addition of something like ⟨τἆλλα τε⟩.

4 Τιτὰν αἰθήρ: αἰθήρ and ἀήρ are both used for air, cf. the commen-

tary on 31(37), 83(98), and the list of terms for the roots in chap. 2. The terms are used here in a cosmogonical context for the two obvious divisions of air—the mist close to the earth's surface, and the bright sky above, seen as the encircling οὐρανός, containing and confining the world within itself (cf. 25(22).2 for οὐρανός as air; also ὁ κύκλος τοῦ οὐρανοῦ Hdt. 1.131). The air has been hardened or "frozen" by the fire that is now running beneath it, an idea probably going back to Anaximenes, cf. Aetius 2.11.12, 14.3, and the doxography at DK 31 A51. There is no reason to suppose, as does O'Brien, *ECC* pp. 291–92, that E. is so confused as to use *aithēr* for a mixture of two elements. Although Titan may later have been related to the sun (but I argued that "Titania astra," Vergil *Aen.* 6.725, is probably the sun and stars, *PVS* 1964, pp. 27–28), here the connotations for air are the vast size and strength of an Atlas, needed to hold fast the cosmos.

28(51)
swiftly upward

Eustathius says that the words in E. refer to fire. There is also the reference to fire in *Et. M.* 311d wtih the spelling ἀνόπεαν, and the definition is οἱ μὲν ἀφανῆ, τινὲς δὲ τὸ ἄνω φέρεσθαι. In Homer, *Od.* 1.320, ἀνόπαια in ὄρνις δ' ὣς ἀνόπαια διέπτατο is the hole in the roof to which the smoke from the fire ascends, cf. F. H. Witton *AJP* 1958, pp. 414–15. If the reference is to fire in E., it would apply to the first movements of fire under Strife, when the parts of the roots begin to separate out and to move away from the center. Some air and fire were separated first, then the sea was sweated out from the earth, and the misty layer of air settled around the earth, cf. Aetius 2.6.3, Simplicius *in Cael.* 528.21–24, [Plut.] *Strom.* 10, Philo *prov.* 2.60.

29(53)
for it chanced to be running in this way then, but often in other ways

The line is quoted twice by Aristotle and is also in the commentators. The subject is air, called by Aristotle with reference to E. both αἰθήρ and ἀήρ, and the context is the κοσμοποιία, when Strife begins to separate the roots, διέκρινε μὲν γὰρ τὸ νεῖκος, ἠνέχθη δ' ἄνω ὁ αἰθήρ, *GC* 334a1. Aristotle's complaint is that air does not act systematically. Strife is directly responsible for the initial separating, but then τύχη seems to take over.

At one time air goes upward, at another fire, and air moves downward (as in the next fragment) and, presumably from ἄλλως, in other directions too. Despite his criticism, Aristotle provides support for the present continuation of the separation, indicated in 31(37) and 32(52). On the disorder following the initial separating, cf. Tzetzes *ex. Il.* 42.17 (DK 31 A66): ποτὲ μὲν τοῦ πυρὸς ὑπερνικῶντος καὶ καταφλέγοντος, ὁτὲ δὲ τῆς ὑδατώδους ὑπερβλυζούσης καὶ κατακλυζούσης ἐπιρροῆς.

30(54)

(Air) with deep roots sank down over the earth.

Aristotle gives the fragment in the same context as the previous one. Sometimes air moves up, but at times fire does, cf. 53(62).6, and air moves down and covers the surface of the earth as mist. (κατά with the accusative is "on," "over," "throughout," rather than "down into," cf. LSJ s.v. κατά B.I.2.) According to Aristotle, E. says that the cosmos is ἐπὶ τοῦ νείκους νῦν as πρότερον ἐπὶ τῆς φιλίας, but Aristotle finds no precise explanation for the cause of motion. It would seem that E. (1) gave a general account of the beginning of movement brought about by Strife, as at 23(30) and 24(31), and then, (2) in explaining the formation of the visible masses, showed that the general tendency of the roots was to move to their own kind, cf. the next fragment; Aristotle's complaint is that a logical connection between (1) and (2) is required. The present state of affairs, until the movement of the roots is completed, Aristotle can ascribe only to chance. The vocabulary of the fragment recalls Hesiod *Erga* 19; cf. the commentary on 33(39).

31(37)

Earth increases its own bulk, and air increases air.

The continuing collection of parts of fire, earth, air (and presumably water) into distinctive masses as described by E. is, for Aristotle, not a true αὔξησις (which involves a complete merging) but a *prosthesis* of the parts. The increase of the bulk of earth is due to the natural tendency of the roots, i.e., the way they act of their own accord, when not kept together by Aphrodite riveting, gluing, or nailing them. An ordered arrangement of parts is the result, in nature, of constraint applied to the material by

Aphrodite, and in the case of man a disciplined mental effort is needed, cf. 100(110).1–9. Lucretius takes up the wording of the fragment in 2.1114–15. The line and its context is one of many counterexamples to O'Brien's explanation that *aithēr* for E. is always a mixture of fire and air, *ECC* pp. 291–92.

32(52)

And many fires burn beneath the surface of the earth.

Like 29(53), the fragment shows that the separation of the elements into four masses is not yet complete. All the fire has not yet gone "upward," but some still remains within the earth. Earlier, after the separation of the sea, fire in the earth warmed some of the remaining water to produce hot springs; it hardened parts of earth into rock and, as some of it moved up, produced trees, and then men and women, cf. [Arist.] *probl.* 937a11, Plutarch *de prim. frig.* 953e, Seneca *QNat* 3.24.1, Aetius 5.26.4, and the commentary on 53(62).1–2. The evidence for fire in the earth was at hand in the volcanic areas of Sicily and southern Italy, with Etna as a prime example.

33(39)

If the depths of earth, and extensive air, are without limit, as has come foolishly from the tongue of the mouths of many who have seen but a little of the whole

The fragment contains a criticism of the simplistic but understandable view that the sky stretches upward and the earth downward indefinitely, cf. ἐπ' ἀπείρονα γαῖαν *Il.* 7.446, *Od.* 1.98, Hesiod *Theog.* 187, and, on the depths of Tartarus *Theog.* 807; as in 1(2).1–6, however, E. has little sympathy with the limited scope of popular beliefs. Clement quotes the last two lines in a criticism of general ignorance about the nature of divinity, but Aristotle and *MXG* refer the three lines specifically to Xenophanes, and Aristotle complains of Xenophanes' laziness in positing a bottomless earth to save himself from having to think of a reason for its staying still. Simplicius did not know of a relevant passage from Xenophanes, but from Achilles *Isag.* 4.34.11 we have fr. 28, where it is said that the earth has an upper limit at our feet—τὸ κάτω δ' ἐς ἄπειρον ἱκνεῖται. For E. the amount of earth, as of fire, air, and water, is limited;

from his explanation of eclipses, and of the earth being held still by the rotation of the sky, it is clear that he envisaged it as spherical, cf. 41(42), 42(48), Aristotle *Cael.* 295a17, 300b3, κυκλοτερής at Aetius 2.20.13, and the explanation of tropic circles, 2.23.3.

1 : δαψιλός is a form of δαψιλής unique to E.

2 : γλώσσης ἐλθόντα is more likely to have been displaced by βροτέων ῥηθέντα than the other way around.

34(40)
sharp-arrowed sun and kindly moon

The line is quoted by Plutarch as a pleasing distinction made by E. between the sun and the moon. After the separating of the roots into distinguishable masses, E., in the Presocratic tradition, gives an account of the sun and the moon. ἠελίοιο ὠκέα γυῖα in 21(27) is some support for ὀξυμελής, but the contrast with the moon is not so obvious. ὀξυβελής is more appropriate and means "sharp-arrowed" rather than "sharp-shooting," cf. "sharp-pointed" for the hedgehog, 72(83).2. The form ἰλάειρος, if the emendation is correct, is found only in E.; it occurs again in 84(85) of φλόξ for, probably, the fire in the eye. There the first two syllables are short, as one would expect from ἰλαρός (but ἵλαος at *Il.* 1.583). Rather than a change of quantity here I suspect a half-foot lacuna before ἠδ', or the two phrases may come from different lines. The meaning of ἰλάειρα would seem to be both "kindly" and "pleasant" (cf. Plutarch's ἄλυπον), in contrast, in a Mediterranean climate, to the sun's harshness.

35(41)
but (the sun), after being collected together, moves round the great sky

For Macrobius ἀμφιπολεύει is, exceptionally, equivalent to περιπολεῖ, and the subject is the sun, explained as a collection of parts of fire. The uncompounded ἀλίζειν is used for people, especially soldiers, assembling, and here metaphorically for the parts of fire coming together to form the sun. One would expect a complementary description of the moon to follow with ἡ δέ. For E.'s sun as fire, cf. πυρὸς ἄθροισμα μέγα D.L. 8.77, and Aetius 2.6.3. On the *Stromateis* notice that the *physis* of the sun is not fire, cf. the next fragment.

36(44)

he shines back to Olympus with fearless face

Ὄλυμπος is used in the sense of the extreme limit of the sky (as in Parmenides fr. 11), which E. sees in the *Katharmoi* as the home of the gods. Beneath it are air and fire. Plutarch quotes this line in the context of a seemingly absurd explanation of the sun as an *anaklasis* of the light of the sky.

The surface of the sun facing the sky draws to itself parts of the fire in it, on the principle (1) of parts of the same element being primitively aware of each other and coming together (cf. on 100(110).9), and (2) of a convex surface attracting light. Now the shape of the moon for E., according to Plutarch, is φακοειδές, "lentiform" (*Qu. Rom.* 288b, DK 31 A60), and the comparison with a common object is typical of E. Aristotle, *Cael.* 287a20, uses φακοειδές, along with σφαιροειδές and ᾠοειδές, as a standard shape, and the Latin word directly relates the lentil seed to the form of a lens, i.e., disc-shaped from the front view but an elongated double convex from the side (cf. *Enc. Brit.* 13th ed., *Gray's Manual of Botany* 1970, and *OED* s.v. lentil). No notice is extant on the shape of the sun for E., but I suspect it was lentiform too, larger than the moon (cf. 37[47]), with a diameter equal to that of the earth (Aet. 2.21.2). From E.'s known interest in reflections and the movement of light (cf. Arist. *De An.* 418b20, *Sens.* 446a26) and the knowledge of convex refraction at the time (cf. Theophrastus *Ign.* 73), this fragment, taken with 35(41) and 43(49), can perhaps be interpreted on the following lines. The lentiform sun moves round the spherical earth, and as it does so it attracts the fire from the *ouranos* into its upper convex surface, and then, through the lower surface, it transmits heat and light to the earth below. At night, when the sun travels under the earth, the bulk of the earth itself blocks off the light from our part of the earth's surface.

There is, however, a different account, found only in Aetius and the *Stromateis* (Aet. 2.20.13, Eus. *PE* 1.8.10 [DK 31 A56 and 30]), but adopted and elaborated in modern commentators (cf., for example, the extraordinary diagrams in Bollack, vol. 1, pp. 188–89, vol. 3, pp. 259, 270, 291, 299). It is a strange theory of two rotating suns, the one being the apparent sun, the other a semicosmos filled with fire, corresponding to a semicosmos of air mixed with a little fire (which was supposed to explain night). Thankfully this absurdity can be discarded: (1) it conflicts with the fragments, for (a) fr. 36(44) does not fit it on any acceptable sense of Olympus, (b) fr. 42(48) offers a reasonable and quite different explanation of night, and (c) all the sun fragments refer quite clearly to the sun we know; (2) there is no trace of such a theory elsewhere—if it were genuine one would have expected some comment from Aristotle, the commentators, or Plutarch; (3) it is at variance with the main lines of Presocratic cosmology and the Greek tradition generally (and indeed what could E. have said that could be summarized in such anachronistic language as Aet. 2.20.13?); (4) it is inherently absurd and contradicted by the simplest observation; and (5) confusions have often crept into the doxography by the time of Aetius and the *Stromateis*. E. may have spoken of something like "half of the sun, which is like a lentil in shape, collecting fire," which was incorrectly summarized as a hemisphere of fire and then taken as a hemisphere of the cosmos filled with fire.

37(47)

she contemplates the bright circle of her lord facing her.

The line is quoted for the form ἀγής, compounded in εὐαγής. This means "bright," "brilliant," for the sun at Parmenides fr. 10, and so it does here, rather than "pure," "holy," although the aural ambiguity is probably deliberate, cf. μονίη 21(27). No subject is given for this line, but the moon is obviously appropriate, cf. Parmenides again, fr. 15.

38(43)

as the ray, after striking the broad circle of the moon

The moon shines because it reflects the sun's light. The discovery is attributed to Thales at Aetius 2.28.5 and is said to have been adopted by Pythagoras, Parmenides, E., and Anaxagoras. Plato names Anaxagoras in this context (*Cra.* 409b), and Plutarch both Anaxagoras and E., *fac. lun.* 929b and d, and cf. the next fragment. When the moon is struck on its convex surface by the sun's rays it collects the light, but since it is νεφοειδής and made of compressed air it does not refract it; thus we see only a pale reflection of the sun, without its heat and brightness, cf. Plutarch's context here, and also Aetius 2.25.15.

39(45)

a circle of borrowed light moves swiftly round the earth

ἀλλότριον φῶς is Parmenides' adaptation of the Homeric phrase, cf. *Il.* 5.214, *Od.* 18.219, Parmenides fr. 14. The Homeric sense is "a man from somewhere else," and Parmenides, "a light from somewhere else." There can be no doubt that Parmenides, and E. after him, assumed that the moon took its light from the sun. The recognition of this, and that the moon moves round the earth, are two basic advances in selenology.

40(46)
as the course of the chariot turns round and back, round the summit she

The text of this fragment is corrupt, but from Plutarch's context E. is comparing the moon to a chariot in the closeness of its rotation round the earth. With the reading ὡς πέρι χνοίη (which scans oddly), the simile refers to the nave of the chariot wheel scraping the post on the turn, but perhaps Plutarch's text can be kept. The sense then is that the course of the moon round the earth is as close as that of the chariot round the post. The chariot traces a semicircle as it turns, whereas the moon traces a full circle round the earth. The point is the closeness to the "top" of the earth's surface (ἡ ἄκρη) on the turn, not an elliptical-shaped course. From the context it looks as if E. related the phases of the moon, as well as lunar eclipses, to the extent to which the moon is overshadowed by the earth, but no further details are available. The distance of the moon from the earth is given as half that of the moon from the sun, Aetius 2.31.1.

41(42)
She dispersed his rays to earth from the upper side, and cast on the earth a shadow equal to the breadth of the silvery moon.

Again the text is corrupt. ἀπεσκεύασε does not scan in the line, and the sense is strange. Diels's ἀπεστέγασεν keeps the meter, but "uncover" (cf. 91(100).14) is the opposite to what is required; ἀπεσκέδασε is preferable. καθύπερθεν: "from the upper side," cf. *Od.* 10.353; and †ἔσ τε αἶαν† probably contains a reference not to the earth, which comes in the second part of the line, but to the moon or sky—the substitution of something like ἐς αὐτήν would give the required sense. In an eclipse of the sun the moon is directly between the sun and the earth. This would mean, according to E., that the upper convexity of the moon dispersed the sun's rays in the sky, and the dark undersurface cast a shadow on the earth equal to the moon's own breadth. The sun and the earth have the same diameter (Aet. 2.21.2), but the moon is smaller than both, and so it darkens only part of the earth. There is no need to suppose that E. influenced, or was influenced by, Anaxagoras in the explanation of eclipses. Their accounts are not the same (for Anaxagoras still seems to find a use for Anaximenes' "dark objects") and were probably reached independently. γλαυκώπιδος: Athena's epithet for the brightness of her eyes, and so here of the bright-faced or silvery moon (cf. LSJ s.v. γλαυκός); at 934d, when discussing the changing colors of the moon, Plutarch quotes E.'s γλαυκῶπις for bluish gray.

42(48)
and earth causes night by coming under the rays.

E.'s understanding of the cause of night is authenticated by this line and is therefore preferable to the "hemisphere of air" theory in the doxographical transmission from Aetius, cf. the commentary on 36(44). As the sun goes under the earth, the imposition of the earth's bulk prevents its light from reaching our surface. It is tempting to assume that E. realized that this meant it was daytime then for the antipodes. In his astronomical observations E. may have used a measuring device such as the one described by Plutarch here.

43(49)
of desolate, blind-eyed night

When the sun is beneath the earth the air on our surface is dark. The night is ἀλαῶπις because it is without the eye of the sun (cf. the Cyclops, *Od.* 9.516), and ἐρῆμος because of the sense of vastness and solitude.

44(50)
and Iris brings wind or heavy rain from the sea.

Tzetzes is not certain about the attribution of the verse to E., because, as he goes on to say, he has only a summary and not the text. The line does not appear in the early editors, nor now in Bollack. The succession of dactyls is unpleasing and the meaning is not immediately clear. Wind is not usually associated with Iris, and as Zeus' messenger, and the bridge between Olympus and earth, she comes with rain not from the sea but from a bright sky. Here there may be a conflation with the more sophisticated view of moisture being drawn up from the sea, blown onto land, and then descending as rain, with the rainbow then linking the three areas of sea, air, and earth.

45(56)
salt was crystallized under pressure from the rays of the sun.

The line is quoted as an example of lengthening in *thesis* (i.e., ἅλς for ἅλς). With the aorist ἐπάγη it may come in the context of the early formation of the world, when salt was crystallized by the sun in much the same way as parts of earth were hardened into rock by the fire in it, cf. the commentary on 32(52) and 46(55). Kypris makes use of the hardening properties of fire, 62(73).

46(55)
sea, sweat of earth

The kind of analogy in 71(82) is here used on a larger scale. Men perspire as the result of intense activity in the sun; in the same way, the salt water commenced to exude from the earth as it was put under pressure by the initial cosmic rotation and also heated by the sun, cf. Aetius 2.6.3, 3.16.3, and Lucretius 5.488. Aristotle dismisses this as poetic metaphor and an inadequate explanation for the saltness of the sea. Fresh water in the sea that provides nourishment for fish (cf. Aelian *NA* 9.64) may be explained by 45(56): continued action by the sun crystallizes out some of the salt, leaving that part of the water salt free.

FRAGMENTS 47–52 MANY TO ONE AND INDIVIDUAL LIFE: LIMBS AND MONSTERS

47(35)
But I shall turn back to the path of song I traced before, leading off from one argument this argument: when strife had reached the lowest depth of the whirl and

love comes into the center of the eddy, in her then all these things unite to be one only; not immediately, but coming together from different directions at will. And, as they were being mixed, countless types of mortal things poured forth, but many, which strife still restrained from above, stayed unmixed, alternating with those which were combining, for it had not yet perfectly and completely stood out as far as the furthest limits of the circle, but part remained within and part had gone out of the frame. And, in proportion as it continually ran on ahead, a mild, immortal onrush of perfect love was continually pursuing it. Immediately what were formerly accustomed to be immortal became mortal, and formerly unmixed things were in a mixed state, owing to the exchanging of their ways. And, as they were being mixed, countless types of mortal things poured forth, fitted with all kinds of forms, a wonder to see.

This is one of the most important fragments for an understanding of E., and it is to be taken closely with 8(17) and 16(26). Fragment 16(26) contains the *logos* from which E. is going to draw off this new one (cf. his method at 18(24).1); there E. picked up from 8(17) the main cosmic movements of many to one under Love, and one to many under Strife. This was followed through from 19(27) to 24(31). Then, in 25(22) and 26(20), the characteristics of the four roots and of Love and Strife as experienced by men were shown to be consistent with them in their cosmic role. The main points of the cosmogony of our world followed, as the four roots, the many, separate out from their unity.

The first stages of ἄλλοτε δ' αὖ διχ' ἕκαστα φορεύμενα νείκεος ἔχθει have been explained, and in this fragment we go back to ἄλλοτε μὲν φιλότητι συνερχόμεν' εἰς ἕνα κόσμον for further details, cf. 16(26).5–6, 8(17).7–8, and Simplicius *in Cael.* 587 (which gives lines 10–13 here as an explanation of line 5, itself a rewording of 16(26).5). The details, however, are few, as Aristotle complained, *Cael.* 301a14. There was perhaps little more than the general description of the rise of *thnēta* given in this fragment, and of the formation of single limbs and monsters. Mythical creatures are firmly put in an era other than our own, and this is confirmed by Simplicius, *in Cael.* 587, who relates 50(57) and 51(59) to the same *katastasis* as 35(47).5 and 10–13.

2 ἐξοχετεύων: "drawing off" of water into channels, and here of a minor theme from the main topic of the explanation of our present world. There are a number of unusual words in this fragment as a whole, which have caused confusion in the MSS tradition.

3–4: the δίνη and the στροφάλιγξ must both refer to the cosmic rotation started at the separation of the four masses, cf. Aristotle *Cael.* 295a17, Simplicius *in Cael.* 528.20, Aetius 2.6.3. Strife has reached the "undermost depth" of the whirl in the sense that it has control of the whole rotation to the center. Earth, air, fire, and water at this stage are immortal (i.e., not made up into mortal things) and unmixed, cf. lines 14–15; and the cosmos as we know it has passed away, cf. Aetius 2.4.8, ᾽E. τὸν κόσμον φθείρεσθαι κατὰ τὴν ἀντεπικράτειαν τοῦ νείκους καὶ τῆς φιλίας, and Simplicius *in Cael.* 293.18. Then, and the metaphor is probably military, Love strikes at the center from her position at the ἔσχατα τέρματα κύκλου and gradually consolidates her hold on the field from there, compelling Strife in turn to make a gradual retreat. With γένηται Love could not already be at the center (pushed there by Strife, as is assumed by Guthrie *HGP* vol. 2, p. 179, O'Brien *ECC* p. 117, and others) if she comes to be there. The subjunctive is probably acceptable for the recurring event, as Simplicius gives in his paraphrase—ὅταν γένηται. I would maintain that Love stays at the ἔσχατα τέρματα κύκλου during the increase of Strife, i.e., that at the extreme circumference there is a band of elements in the state of perfect mixture that was enjoyed in the sphere, that this is regarded also as the abode of the gods, and that to it human thought in its best condition is related. In Aetius this area—the subtraction of ὁ κόσμος from τὸ πᾶν— is called ἀρχὴ ὕλη (1.5.2; cf. Aristotle on the existence of the divine, outside space and time, at the circumference of the world, *Cael.* 1.9; and also chap. 3).

5–6: a more elaborate version of what it means for the many to come into one, outlined at 8(17).7, 16(26).5, 26(20).2, and cf. the commentary on 20(36).1. There is a contrast here between ἄφαρ and θελημά (or ἐθελημά); Love does not gain the whole territory in one swoop, but "volunteers" come to join from different parts.

7: cf. the commentary on 20(36); there is no need to substitute that line for line 7 here, despite the repetition at line 16; such a repetition, of the details after the outline, is in E.'s style.

8–9: with ἔστηκε, ἄμ(ε)ιχθ' would be needed, and the tense sequence is awkward but not impossible, cf. ἐξέστηκεν in line 10; perhaps the MSS ἔστηκε as an imperfect of στήκειν can be accepted, as it is by Diels-Kranz, Bollack, and Solmsen. μετάρσιον: a description of Strife as acting "from above" rather than "in suspense" (Guthrie's translation). Strife puts up a dogged resistance and, while Love is bringing the roots together, is able to keep parts of them separate even as it retreats.

10 ἐπ' ἔσχατα τέρματα κύκλου: cf. 20(36) ἐξ ἔσχατον ἵστατο νεῖκος, referring to the outer edge of the circumference, to which Strife retreats

when the many come into one, and which is now Love's last area during the separation into many; cf. the commentary on lines 3–4. Aristotle is continuing the Presocratic tradition, of which E. is firmly a part, by describing the region in both physical and theological terms, *Cael.* 1.9.

11: μελέων with ἐξεβεβήκει for the parts, or frame, of the universe, as in 23(30).1, and cf. 24(31). Strife has control over some parts of the elemental masses, and elsewhere it has given up territory before the advance of Love.

13 ὁρμή: the word does not give increased material status to Love and should not be translated "stream" (cf. LSJ s.v.). The language is metaphorical, of the pursuer and the pursued, and the emphasis is on the effect for the four roots of the tussle between being held separate and being brought together. ἠπιόφρων, "gentle-thinking," "mild" (perhaps a coinage by E.), and ἄμβροτος are transferred from Philotēs, who is also ἀμεμφής, "perfect," "without reproach." ἀμεμφέως in line 9, however, of Strife's movement, is closer to "perfectly," in the nonmoral sense of "completely."

15 ζωρά τε πρὶν κέκρητο: for the reading, and for the sense of ζωρός as "unmixed," cf. my note in *CR* 1962, pp. 109–11; the objections raised by O'Brien, *CR* 1965, pp. 1–4, West, *CR* 1966, p. 136, and Solmsen, *CR* 1967, pp. 245–46, I find unconvincing.

16–17: the immortal and unmixed roots take on a variety of forms as they mix with each other under the increasing power of Love. Although the language of these lines could well refer to the many wondrous kinds of life around us, and 16(26).4–5 seems to imply a race of men arising as the many come into one, I do not think that E. described a world under increasing Love that is identical to the present one. He found in this part of his scheme a means of relegating to another era the hybrid creatures of myth and alien religion. At 53(62) he returns from his digression to the exposition of our world, which was left at 46(55), and describes the rise of human life after the cosmogony. Fragment 51(59) shows that the strange creatures arose as the roots were coming closer and closer together, whereas πῦρ κρινόμενον at 53(62).2 gives the generation of men and women when fire is separating out of the mixture.

48(96)

And the kindly earth received into its broad hollows of the eight parts two of the brightness of Nestis and four of Hephaistos; and these came to be white bones, marvelously held together by the gluing of Harmony.

The first three lines are quoted approvingly by Aristotle for showing that it is not the elements of which something is made that give it its character, but the *logos* of their combination. This understanding of explanation by form is elaborated by the commentators, and in a similar context in the *De Anima* Philoponus and Simplicius see Pythagorean influence. In his commentary in *in Phys.* Simplicius quotes the four lines and says that they come from the first book of E.'s *Physika*. The fragment therefore belongs before 53(62), which is from the second book. In the first book this would seem to be the most suitable place for the fragment—after 47(35) as giving a detail of the formation of ἔθνεα μυρία θνητῶν (and ἀρηρότα is repeated from line 17), and before the description of the individual limbs. The fragment is similar to 83(98), but because E. connects blood with human thought, 83(98) would seem to go better with the physiological fragments relating to life as we know it.

1 ἐπίηρος: the masculine is not found elsewhere. It is glossed by Simplicius as ἐναρμόνιος, with χόανα as ἐν οἷς ἡ τῶν μιγνυμένων γίνεται κρᾶσις (cf. *in de An.* 68.2–10 with *Il.* 18.470 quoted). The earth is the receptacle and also provides one quarter of the material. εὐστέρνος (ἅπ. λεγ.), like εὐρύστερνος, is appropriate for mother earth, but the epithet is somewhat infelicitously transferred. There is an alternative, easier, reading, εὐτύκτοις "well-made," but it is unsuitable for holes in the earth.

2 τώ: Steinhart's suggestion for τῶν (the majority), τάς, and τά of the MSS. The neuter in line 3 makes the reading τὰς δύο τῶν μοίραων difficult, and E. does not use μοῖρα elsewhere. λάχε: similar to συνέκυρσε at 83(98).1, and probably the basis for Aristotle's question whether Love is the cause of any chance mixture or only of mixture κατὰ λόγον (*De An.* 408a21). Both seem to be involved—sections of the elements come together in the general many-to-one movement, and where the proportions are appropriate, Love makes an organic part. Νήστιδος αἴγλης: the commentators take the phrase as referring to both water and air, and give the *logos* of bone as 4 parts fire : 2 earth : 1 water : 1 air; the radiance or bright transparency in the meaning of αἴγλη can refer to water or air. Air is included in 83(98) as αἰθὴρ παμφανόων, but the four elements, in almost equal proportion in the heart-blood, are needed there to explain the physical constitution of thought. There is no reason to suppose that all four are constituents of everything. Four parts fire : 2 earth : 2 water is a very simple *logos*, and it is unlikely that E. gave more intricate details of proportions than those for bone and blood, relying on the painting

simile, 15(23), as a general guide. (The structure of sinews and nails is given in Aetius 5.22.1, and hands and tongue are mentioned by Theophrastus, *Sens.* 11.) E.'s achievement is in the understanding of the principle of proportions of elements in the formation of organisms, rather than in any sophistication in the principle's development.

3 ὀστέα λευκὰ γένοντο: the excess of fire in the proportion accounts for the dryness and whiteness of bones (cf. Simplicius, Philoponus, and Sophonias on *De An.* 409b21); the hard and brittle quality would also be accounted for, cf. the commentary on 62(73). Sinews, according to Aetius (5.22.1), have twice as much water as they do fire and earth, and when they are hardened by air in this proportion they become claws and nails. The phrasing here is an adaptation of Homer's ὀστέα λευκὰ λέγοντο, *Il.* 24.793; the separateness of the bones picked up is recalled in this fashioning of individual bones that are not yet part of an organic whole, cf. 50(57).

4 ἁρμονίης: a name for Philia, as Simplicius explains (and the reference is reinforced by the rare word θεσπεσίηθεν), the artisan of living forms and their parts, cf. 85(86), 86(87), 60(71), 62(73), 70(75). The "gluing" does not imply an additional ingredient, but water is worked into the earth and the compound hardened by the fire (cf. the next fragment). The technique is like that of Hephaistos or Prometheus, cf. Hesiod *Theog.* 571, *Erga* 60–61, Ovid *Met.* 1.80–83.

49(34)
when he had glued barley meal with water

Aristotle quotes the fragment as an example of the mutual relationship between wet and dry ingredients, which bind each other, so that a compound body is formed from both. The words obviously belong in the context of the craftsmanship of Love in making living kinds, but the participle is masculine. I suggest that the fragment is part of a simile in which Love is compared to a baker, who kneads together wet and dry ingredients into a malleable dough, pats it into shape, and "gives it to fire to harden," cf. 62(73). It could well be an illustration of 48(96), with κολλήσας picking up the unusual κόλλησιν. On the other hand there is the faint possibility that the reading ἐν τοῖς Περσικοῖς in *probl.* 929b16 and *Mete.* MS E is correct, and that the fragment refers to the preparation of food on campaign.

50(57)

Here many heads sprang up without necks, bare arms were wandering without shoulders, and eyes needing foreheads strayed singly.

The heads, arms, and eyes in this extraordinary fragment seem to have been thought of as shooting up from the earth (as the result of the first mingling of the roots as they move from many to one) and then moving or floating aimlessly. Aristotle was interested enough to quote the first line three times: (1) as a mild joke with reference to the synthesis of truth and error, *De An.* 430a27; (2) as an additional problem in the discussion of combinations resulting from disordered movement, *Cael.* 300b25; and (3) in dismissing the notion of separate parts coming together, *GA* 722b17. Simplicius, on the *Cael.* passage, disagrees with Alexander's interpretation of the line as a μίξεως παράδειγμα on the grounds that the disordered movements belong with the many-to-one phase of 47(35).5. Philoponus (*in GA* 28 and *in de An.* 545) explains that at first Strife, not Love, was dominant, which is why the limbs were in isolated and disordered movement, and they would have continued so had Love not been able eventually to bring them together. Aristotle firmly puts line 1 ἐπὶ τῆς φιλότητος in the passages cited in *Cael.* and *GA*; in the same section in *Cael.* he states that E. did not give a cosmogony ἐπὶ τῆς φιλότητος (*Cael.* 301a16 and the context given at a10), and further, at *GA* 722b25, he contrasts the world then, ἐπὶ τῆς φιλότητος, with what is now the case. The evidence from Aristotle confirms the suggestion that E. used the many-to-one phase briefly, as a way of both accounting for, and dismissing from the present time, the hybrid creatures of myth.

1 ᾗ μέν: "here," "on the earth," as at *GA* 722b25. ἐβλάστησαν: "sprang up," like shoots from the earth; the verb is used for the different forms of life at 14(21).10. This is the only known occurrence of ἀναύχενες in Greek.

2: arms are "bare" because they are not attached to shoulders (or to hands, for Philoponus adds αἱ μεγάλαι χεῖρες to the list of separate parts, and the phrase may conceal a direct quotation, *in GA* 28.3); cf. also μουνομελῆ, Simplicius *in Cael.* 587.18, discussed at 139(58), and the heads, hands, and feet at *in Phys.* 372.4.

3: the eyes are not in pairs or fixed in sockets; and there were further weird examples of single limbs—Simplicius adds καὶ πολλὰ ἄλλα after this line. E. indulges himself in the exotic vocabulary but firmly removes creatures like the Cyclops from the consideration of life as we know it by putting them, and the parts of which they are made, in a different era. For separate limbs and parts as Peak Cult offerings, cf. B. C. Dietrich *Hist.* 1969, pp. 259–60.

51(59)

But as god mingled further with god they fell together as they chanced to meet each other, and many others in addition to these were continually arising.

Simplicius sets the line in the same *katastasis* as 47(35).10–13; ἐπὶ τῆς φιλότητος is the time when Love is not yet dominant but is in the process of becoming so, and there are still τὰ ἄμικτα καὶ μονόγυια. Love and Strife are related as potential victor and vanquished. Although ἐμίσγετο is used in Homer for hostile engagement (but, except for *Il.* 4.456, with further qualification to give to the verb a definitely hostile sense), in E. the verb is constantly used of the roots combining, and so producing a mortal compound, cf. 12(8).3, 13(9).1, 47(35).7 and 16, and also δι᾽ ἀλλήλων θέοντα at 8(17).34, 14(21).13, 16(26).3. δαίμονι δαίμων therefore refers to the roots which are gods, cf. the commentary on 7(6). There is no conflict with the one other use of δαίμων, in the *Katharmoi* at 107(115).5, for there the δαίμονες in their physical aspect are to be seen as (perfect) combinations of their constituent earth, air, fire, and water, which are singly, and in perfect combination, "gods." (The conclusion of O'Brien's long discussion [*ECC* pp. 325–36] is that δαίμονι δαίμων here means "the pieces of Love in separate limbs [which] mix with one another.")

2 ταῦτα: the subject is still the roots. They first cause the genesis of single limbs as their parts come together, and then, as they mingle further, combinations of limbs. ὅπῃ συνέκυρσεν ἕκαστα: the clause is quoted on its own by Simplicius, at *in Phys.* 327.19 with 29(53), and at *in Phys.* 331.2, to illustrate τύχη in E. The disorder of the roots here, when the many begin to come into one, is like that of their initial separation when the one is becoming many, cf. the commentary on 29(53). In both cases the disorder is temporarily controlled by Love in the production of *thnēta*.

3: ἐξεγένοντο with χθονός understood, cf. ἐξανέτελλον at 52(61).2 and 53(62).4, as well as ἐβλάστησαν in 50(57).

52(61)

Many creatures with a face and breasts on both sides were produced, man-faced bulls arose and again bull-headed men, (others) with male and female nature combined, and the bodies they had were dark.

The four lines are given by Aelian in a brief context of E. speaking of composite creatures, with two forms in one body. βουγενῆ ἀνδρόπρῳρα in line 2 became a well-known phrase for biform creatures, quoted twice by Aristotle, and then by Plutarch and the Aristotelian commentators.

1 ἐφύοντο: Karsten, followed by most editors, changed the infinitives here and in the next line to imperfects. A large number of strange creatures were continually being born and coming up from the earth (cf. the commentary on line 3 of the previous fragment), but from the contexts of 50(57) it seems they are also formed by combinations of the wandering single limbs; e.g., Aristotle, after quoting 50(57).1, adds ἔπειτα συντίθεσθαι τῇ φιλίῃ (’Ε. ἔφη), De An. 430a30. κόρσαι in 50(57).1 is more precisely the front half of the head or the temples (cf. Il. 4.502); if two of these meet, a Janus-like, double-faced head results, and this would be the sense of ἀμφιπρόσωπα. There are precedents for such creatures in myth. Otus and Ephialtes were punished in Tartarus by being tied back to back on either side of a column, and this composite figure, like Janus, seems to be connected with a calendar symbol. (Cf. Hyginus *fab.* 28, and Toepffer s.v. Aloadai *PW*; *Culex* 234 has the giants face to face, however. Plutarch uses ἀμφιπρόσωπος of Janus, *Num.* 19.6) Similarly the two-headed dog, Orthros-Sirius, regarded the old and the new year, and the three faces of Hecate at the crossroads looked in different directions. Multiple-headed creatures were familiar in the representations of Cerberus, Scylla, and Hydra, and cf. the three-headed serpent ἀμφιστρεφέες, *Il.* 11.40. ἀμφίστερνα: the double Ephialtes-Otus figure has two sets of breasts as well as two faces, but E. may have in mind a creature similar to the triform Geryon, with two upper parts from one waist. For Aristophanes' myth, cf. the commentary on line 3.

3 ἀνδροφυῆ βούκρανα: the Minotaur was the most famous example of the bull-headed man. Dionysus had the epithet βουγενής (Plut. *de Is. et Os.* 364f) and had representations with a bull's head or horns, as did the river gods, in particular Achelous, who took on this form in his fight with Heracles (cf. ἀνδρείῳ κύτει βούπρῳρος, Soph. *Trach.* 12–13); and there was ῞Ηρα βοῶπις and also Io. The bull-man biforms are exemplars of all the composite creatures from Greek mythology, such as Centaurs, Harpies, Erynnes, and in particular from Hesiod's *Theogony*, Echidne and her children, the Chimaera and Sphinx; there are similar hybrids in the religions of Egypt and Carthage. E. dismissed these creatures of myth

from the world as we know it and, while offering an explanation of their genesis, relegated them to a different era (as Plato later placed the non-reproducing earth-born men and animals in a different time cycle, in the *Politicus* myth, 271a–c).

It is an exaggeration to read Darwinism back into E. from the ancient comments on this line. Aristotle gives a counterargument to his own teleological principles when he says that some creatures have been preserved because they were put together ἀπὸ τοῦ αὐτομάτου in an appropriate way—ὅσα δὲ μὴ οὕτως, ἀπώλετο καὶ ἀπόλλυται, καθάπερ ’Ε. λέγει τὰ βουγενῆ ἀνδρόπρῳρα (*Phys.* 198b29–32. ἀπόλλυται need not refer the quotation to the present; E.'s phrase is an example—from the past —of the general principle). To be consistent, E. should have extended his notion to plants and spoken of ἀμπελογενῆ ἐλαιόπρῳρα, which is absurd. For Aristotle the mortality of the βουγενῆ ἀνδρόπρῳρα would be explained by a corruption of the seed (*Phys.* 199b5–10). In E. we do not find an understanding of selection and mutation with divergence of parts of the species from the original stock, or new functions and organs developing out of old ones, with the passing on of heritable variations (except in the interesting case of the backbone being vertebrated because it had broken in the womb, cf. Aristotle *Part. An.* 640a19). Instead, there are the simpler recognitions that (1) for survival a species or "animal-kind" must be able to reproduce itself, and (2) it must have appropriate organic parts fulfilling mutual needs, cf. ἐγένετο ζῷα καὶ ἔμενεν διὰ τὸ ἀλλήλοις ἐκπληροῦν τὴν χρείαν and ὅσα μὴ κατὰ τὸν οἰκεῖον συνῆλθε λόγον, ἐφθάρη, Simplicius *in Phys.* 372.3–11. The Epicureans later countered this by denying the genesis of composite creatures in the first place, cf. Lucretius 5.878–924.

μεμιγμένα: the participle brings in an additional set of creatures (listed, like βουγενῆ ἀνδρόπρῳρα, without a connecting particle), rather than adding a further complication to the preceding ones. Androgynous forms belong with other hybrids in a different era from the present. The best known was Hermaphroditos, a private and public cult figure in the 4th century and probably earlier, cf. Theophrastus *Char.* 16.10, *Anth.* 2.102, 9.783; others include Agdistis and Phanes, and with a change of sex, Attis, Caeneus, and Teiresias. There are also the spherical creatures of Aristophanes' myth (Plato *Symp.* 189d–190a). One of their kinds was ἀνδρόγυνον; the name survives but the type has disappeared, explains Aristophanes. His creatures double up human forms and are then halved. There is no way of knowing whether the notion was first suggested by these lines of E., and then exaggerated and caricatured.

4 σκιεροῖς γυίοις: γυῖα is used in Homer and E., and generally, of the body as a whole. If the reading is correct, σκιεροῖς must refer to the color (cf. τὸ σκιερὸν μέλαν φαίνεται, of the sea's surface, [Arist.] *Col.* 791a23). The creatures here are dark colored or swarthy, in the same way as men are described as μέλανες at 58(67).2. The various emendations (cf. the *ap. crit.*) to give meanings like "warm," "sturdy," "lively," "sterile," or "hard" are unnecessary. All the creatures mentioned in this fragment pass away as the many come more and more into one, so Aristotle *Metaph.* 1000b12: in bringing the elements into one, Love destroys everything else.

FRAGMENTS 53–72 ONE TO MANY AND INDIVIDUAL LIFE: HUMANS, ANIMALS, AND PLANTS

53(62)
And now hear this—how fire, as it was being separated, brought up by night the shoots of men and pitiable women, for the account is to the point and well informed. First, whole-nature forms, having a share of both water and heat, sprang up from the earth; fire, as it tended to reach its like, kept sending them up, when they did not as yet show the lovely shape of limbs, or voice or language native to man.

Simplicius quotes the fragment from the second book of the *Physics*, which, *contra* the DK ordering, obviously puts it after 48(96) of the first book. It has the appearance of a fresh start, emphasized by the request for particular attention, and after the digression on the many-to-one stage (with which frs. 47(35)–52(61) are concerned), it goes back to the present one-to-many separation to give the account of the rise of human life following the cosmogony. κρινόμενον πῦρ, which initiates this stage, is the antithesis of ἐπεὶ κατὰ μεῖζον ἐμίσγετο δαίμονι δαίμων of 51(59).1, which produced the mythical creatures of the other era. That the present time is fundamentally an unhappy one is indicated here by πολυκλαύτων, as it is by other expressions in the *Katharmoi* fragments 112(118), 114(124), and 123(145). Hesiodic pessimism is given a philosophical basis in the view of life increasingly dominated by a separative principle.

1 πολυκλαύτων: the passive sense "much-lamented," and so "pitiable," is earlier and more appropriate here than the active "tearful," cf. Aeschylus *Pers.* 674, Euripides *Ion* 869, and the passive πολύκλητος, *Il.* 4.438, 10.420.

2 ἐννυχίους: "by night," but also of the dead (cf. Soph. *OC* 1558), as ἀνήγαγε of bringing up from the dead (and cf. Hes. *Theog.* 626). The origin of human life, like the abode of the dead, is shrouded in darkness. The darkness may be literal in that the early forms of men and women come up before day and night are distinguished. From line 6 it is clear that some fire has already been separated out, but the sun may not yet have been articulated and its light shed around—πρὶν τὸν ἥλιον περι-απλωθῆναι, as in the notice on the origin of trees, Aetius 5.26.4. ὅρπηκας (or probably ὀρπηκας): used especially of saplings (cf. fr. 152). With this word E. relates human to plant life (cf. line 4, and also 65(79), 71(82), and Aet. 5.26.4) and provides a nonmythical explanation for the au-tochthonous traditions as well as giving a new context to Homeric vocabulary (cf. *Il.* 21.37–38 on Lycaon, with ἐννύχιος and ὅρπηκας). κρινόμενον πῦρ: in the further movement of one to many, fire was sep-arating from the earth and moving toward the fire already under the circumference of the cosmos, i.e., parts of fire were being picked out and becoming distinguishable because of the tendency of parts of the same root to converge when not brought into a compound by Love, cf. line 6 here and 100 (110).9. As fire is being separated it brings up the first forms of human life from the earth.

3: an affirmation, in the introduction to this key topic, of the veracity and authority of E.'s account, cf. 3(131).3, 6(4), 15(23).11, 103(114).1–2. The first adjective is ἅπ. λεγ. and the second rare without a genitive.

4 οὐλοφυεῖς τύποι: "whole-nature" or perhaps "whole-growing" forms; the adjective, like ἀνδροφυής and γυναικοφυής in 52(61), is a unique compound. These τύποι (1) originate human life, (2) come up from the earth, (3) have a due amount of water and heat, and (4) have not (yet) any defined limbs or voice. Despite the hint in ὅρπηκας (line 2), their growth from earth, and their early genesis (Aet. 5.26.4), they are unlikely to be trees, which are self-reproductive and have articulate limbs. There is no suggestion of an evolution from trees to men (cf. Simp. *in Cael.* 586.23, Phlp. *in Phys.* 318.27); and, if they were trees, why should they be described in such an obscure way? Nor can they be compared with the first race of men in Aristophanes' myth (Plato *Symp.* 189d), who have their limbs and sex clearly differentiated; only in ἀνδρόγυνον is there an echo of E., not of his "whole-nature" forms but of one of the "wrong" combinations of unattached limbs (cf. the commentary on 52(61).3).

In this context Simplicius criticizes Aristotle's suggestion that σπέρμα, as the true οὐλοφυές, is relevant here, and he adds a definition of the adjective: ὃ καθ' ὅλον ἑαυτὸ πᾶν ἐστιν (Arist. *Phys.* 199b9, Simp. *in Phys.* 382.15, and cf. Aristotle's use of ὁλοφυής for birds, where there is no distinction of thorax and abdomen, *Part. An.* 693a25). The τύποι seem rather to be primitive shapes of warm, moist earth (cf. on line 5). As such they recall the modeling of Pandora by Hephaistos (Hes. *Erga* 61, *Theog.* 571) and the spontaneous generation in the autochthonous myths, but the concept is firmly in the Presocratic tradition. It relates to the theory of the earliest forms of life in Anaximander (cf. Aet. 5.19.4), Xenophanes (frs. 27 and 29), Anaxagoras, and Archelaus (cf. D.L. 2.9 and 17), and to the "embryos" in the (probably) Presocratic account in Diodorus (1.7, and cf. A. Burton *Diodorus Siculus I* pp. 44–47, for a survey of the evidence on the sources here), as well as providing a precedent for the Epicurean theory of "wombs" (Lucretius 5.805–20).

5: the τύποι have a due part (αἶσα, cf. φλόγος αἶσα, Parm. fr. 12.2) of water and heat (for the sense of εἴδεος cf. the commentary on 14(21).4); they are sent up from the earth (sense and scansion connect χθονός with the verb, cf. "E. natos homines ex terra ait ut blitum," Varro fr. 27, DK 31 A72), which implies an accretion of earth to the other ingredients. Earth, moisture, and warmth provide the material for primitive life (cf. the commentary on line 4; the parallel with *Genesis* 2:7 is obvious). From the last sentence of Aetius 5.19.5 it would seem that the *aisa* determined the kind of living creature that would develop—some tending to water, some, with an excess of fire, flying into the air, and the heavier ones earthbound (cf. again the different kinds of life arising when the "membranes" break, Diod. Sic. 1.7.4–5).

6 θέλον πρὸς ὁμοῖον ἱκέσθαι: cf. σφῶν αὐτῶν ποθέοντα φιλὴν ἐπὶ γένναν ἱκέσθαι, 100(110)9. Parts of the same root are primitively aware of and tend toward their like when not restrained into compounds by Love, cf. the commentary on 81(103).

7: the τύποι as yet have no articulate limbs, nor flesh and blood (which require air, cf. 83(98).2 and 5). The further articulation is due to the separative power of Strife, but the μελέων ἐρατὸν δέμας and the detailed structure of the organism are due to Love, in much the same way as Aphrodite adds *charis* to the shape made by Hephaistos, Hesiod *Erga* 65

8: I prefer the Aldine reading of this line: οὔτ' ἐνοπὴν οὔτ' αὖ ἐπιχώριον ἀνδράσι γῆρυν. Diels and most editors change γύων to γυῖον (with οἷον τ' after ἐνοπήν), but the singular is rare and un-Homeric, and reads oddly as referring to the "Schamglied." Bollack has οἴη τ' and γυίων, which makes the vocal organ a γυῖον. The point is surely that the τύποι are as yet mute (the μέλη have been dealt with in the previous line) and cannot speak a particular language (cf. οὐδ' ἴα γῆρυς, *Il.* 4.437) or make even an inarticulate cry (cf. ἐνοπήν τε γόον τε, *Il.* 24.160).

54(64)
And on him desire too

Plutarch quotes the fragment in a context of the farrowing habits of sows. He wonders if the greater fertility of domestic sows can be due to the herding of the two sexes together, so that proximity "reminds" the male of copulation and provokes mutual desire, which according to E. is the case among human beings. The causal chain of proximity–memory–desire is partially confirmed by the Aetius notice (5.19.5) that the generation following the οὐλοφυεῖς τύποι was self-reproducing, the stimulus for the male coming from female beauty. One would expect this line to refer to the three links in some way, and the commonly accepted version is τῷ δ' ἐπὶ καὶ πόθος εἶσι, δι' ὄψιος ἀμμιμνῄσκων, cf. *ap. crit.* But this is illogical; it is not that desire reminds him through sight but that desire is reminded through sight, i.e., that sight reminds him and stimulates desire. Other suggestions are δι' ἄψιος αἷμ' ἀναμίσγων (Ellis *CR* 1902, p. 270) and Bollack's διαμπερέως ἀμμίσγων. The fragment is hopelessly corrupt, and as with other lines having Plutarch as the only source (e.g., 40[46], 41[42], 76[93], and cf. 75[90]), it may be that his memory failed him. Perhaps the original was something like τῷ δ' ἐπὶ καὶ πόθος ἱκνεῖται μεμνημένος ὄψει, with ἀμμίσγων in the next line for the copulation following the desire.

55(66)
the divided meadows of Aphrodite

From the context and the plowing metaphor in *Phoen.* 18, λειμῶνας and not λιμένας is the correct reading, E.'s reference to the female genitals being the more obscene, according to the scholiast. The οὐλοφυεῖς τύποι precede the generation of men and women; the fragments, therefore, dealing with human reproduction and embryology would appropriately come soon after 53(62).

56(63)
But the substance of the limbs is separated, part in (the body of) the man

Aristotle quotes the fragment to criticize E. (with Democritus) for having the *sōma* of the seed "torn apart," some in the male and some in the female (*GA* 764b17), and elsewhere he explains that for E. the two parts are like a σύμβολον (722b11). Galen elaborates on this, adding that the separated parts are brought together in the union stimulated by desire (*sem.* 4.616K). σῶμα in the Aristotelian context shows that φύσις here must mean the actual substance or structure of the embryo, which is pulled apart and then put together again (cf. φύσις at 100(110).5 and μελέων φύσις, Parm. fr. 16.3; however, φύσις is "birth" in 12(8), cf. the commentary there). The line obviously continued with a reference to the female, and this is indicated in Aristotle and Philoponus. The Philoponus context (*in GA* 166.25) also shows that E. is thinking of each organic part being divided (rather than different "limbs" from each, although this is also suggested, *in GA* 27.4). This makes E. more modern than Aristotle here, and in line with recent findings on the nature of genetic material. "Each human cell has two sets of chromosomes. One group is provided by the male parent of an individual, and the other group by the female parent" (*Enc. Brit. Macr.* 1974, 6.742).

57(65)

They were poured in pure places; some met with cold and became women

The subject must be some neuter plural expression for semen. The "pure places" refer to the female receptacle, purified by the evacuation of the menses (cf. LSJ s.v. κάθαρσις II). In the context at *GA* 723a24 Aristotle quotes the fragment as evidence that sex is determined at conception. Aristotle refers to it again at *GA* 764a1–6, where E. is said to explain sex differentiation not by right and left, but by the temperature of the womb. This means, according to Aristotle (and cf. Philoponus *in GA* 166.8), that if conception takes place soon after menstruation the womb is warmer and the resulting embryo male; if later in the month, a "cold" womb causes the offspring to be female. This is in fact wrong (for the high temperature comes with ovulation at the middle and not the beginning of the menstrual cycle), but it need not be foisted on E.; his words simply relate the temperature of the womb to the sex of the offspring, cf. the commentary on the next fragment.

58(67)

For the male was in the warmer . . . this is the reason why men are dark, more powerfully built, and hairier.

The whole context of this fragment is disputed. If γαίης is accepted, the reference is to the early genesis of human life from the earth, when, according to Aetius 5.7.1–2, the first men appeared in the south and east, and the first women in the north, which aligns them with hot and cold respectively. γαστρός, however, was suspected by Sturz but accepted by Karsten; Diels's suggestion is τοκὰς ἄρρενος ἔπλετο γαστήρ. Galen quotes the fragment with Parmenides fr. 17 as linking the right side of the womb with the male, but the notice is abbreviated. He wants support for a Hippocratic connection of right, black, and hot; the first is related to male in the embryology of Parmenides, and the last two in that of E. Galen is surely not so confused here (as Longrigg argues, *Philologus* 1964, pp. 297–99) as to refer a fragment supposedly dealing with north and south parts of the earth to right and left in the womb. As Galen is the only authority for the line, it is sensible to accept his embryological context for it. I suspect that only the first line gives E.'s exact words, with the quotation possibly ending at ἔπλετο; γαίης was then an attempt to finish the line from the following καί (and any genitive is suspect there because of the distance from ἐν θερμοτέρῳ). The last two lines look like a summary, for καί μέλανες διὰ τοῦτο is prosaic and an exact repetition from the Hippocratic quotation Galen is defending; also, the succession of spondees in καὶ λαχνήεντες μᾶλλον is untypical and unpleasing. (Censorinus, 6.8.10, DK 31 A81, links male and female with right and left in E. and Anaxagoras, "but his interpretation should probably be ruled out" states G. E. R. Lloyd, *JHS* 1962, p. 60, n. 19; yet in Aristotle *GA* 764a36 there is an imprecise reference on the sexes of twins which might support this link for E. The link could be accommodated by supposing that on E.'s theory males are conceived when the womb is warmer, and the resulting embryo later attaches itself to the right side of the uterine lining; the converse would be true for females. The interval before any attachment is in fact five days.)

2 μέλανες: not necessarily a reference to Ethiopians, but a conventional contrast between swarthy men and pale women. ἁδρομελέστεροι is Karsten's suggestion from the ἁδροτής–ἀδροτής confusion in Homer; ἀνδρωδέστεροι is tautologous.

3 λαχνήεντες: hair is the human analogue of leaves (71(82).1), and growth in abundance is due to heat. Hairiness connects also with specific maleness in the denial of anthropomorphic attributes to divinity, 97(134).3.

59(68)

On the tenth day of the eighth month it became a white pus.

Aristotle is in agreement with E. that milk is a form of blood (cf. *GA* 739b25; Kranz changed τὸ γάλα to τὸ αἷμα in the present context, and Diels deleted it, but the sense is clear). But he criticizes him for supposing that it is decomposed or putrefied rather than concocted blood—either E. has misunderstood or he is using an inappropriate metaphor. There is a metaphor like this in 67(81), for wine as "rotten" water. The general theory of an agent (here probably heat) acting on a liquid and causing a basic change is implied, and this was important in the medical theories of κρᾶσις and πέψις. In this fragment the language is influenced by the similarity of πύον to πυός, and colostrum *is* an unpleasant-looking, puslike substance in the two or three days before the appearance of the milk.

The tenth day of the eighth month is a precise date, and it is hard to see the reason why it is given. Mammary growth in pregnancy is an obvious indication of organic change, but there is no noticeable sudden alteration on or around the date given here. And by some process which is still obscure, it is the delivery that actually initiates lactation, so that milk is available even for the seven-month child. It can only be assumed that there is some other, irretrievable, significance in the numbers involved.

60(71)

But if your belief about these things in any way lacked assurance, how, from the combining of water, earth, air, and sun came the forms and color of mortal things which have now arisen, fitted together by Aphrodite

Simplicius quotes 85(86), 86(87), 87(95), and then here gives the general principle of the work of Aphrodite in this present world in producing the variety of life as we know it from the combinations of four elements. Two other fragments that show Kypris at work follow, 62(73) and 70(75). This fragment has therefore been put as an introduction to the biological and physiological section. In the present world there is an increasing separation of elements, but Aphrodite is able to counteract this for a time by bringing together parts of the separating elements into temporary compounds, with the resulting variety of *thnēta*.

1 λιπόξυλος: the adjective is unique to E., cf. 14(21).2. E.'s appeal is

to reason. Any doubts Pausanias may still have about the reliability of the account of the different forms of life being produced from a mingling of four elements will be allayed by the evidence from phenomena observable now.

2–4: the language recalls 15(23); the artist working with his colors in two dimensions is now seen to be an exemplar of Aphrodite creating a three-dimensional world from the four elements. συναρμοσθέντα in line 4 recalls ἁρμονίῃ μίξαντε at 15(23).4 and reinforces the notion that it is not a chemical mixture which is involved, but a fitting together to make a whole, cf. συνάρμοσας of a boat, Euripides *Hel.* 233, and of the wooden horse, *Tro.* 11; cf. also Galen's notice that for E. all σώματα on earth are produced from four elements οὐ μὴν κεκραμένων γε δι' ἀλλήλων, ἀλλὰ κατὰ μικρὰ μόρια παρακειμένων τε καὶ ψαυόντων, *Hipp. nat. hom.* 15.49K. χροία: cf. Parmenides fr. 8.41, Anaxagoras fr. 4.4; the form is possibly neuter plural, cf. DK *ad* 31 B 71.

61(33)
As when the sap (of the fig tree) has riveted and set white milk

The fragment is an example of an agent working on a liquid and solidifying it. Plutarch quotes the simile to illustrate the close bond of *philia* contrasted with divisive *polyphilia*. In Homer the like-worded simile relates to speed, *Il.* 5.902; Aristotle makes the comparison for the action of semen, *GA* 771b23 and cf. 737a14. ὀπός is the sap of the fig tree used for curdling, but, in curdling, the juice also putrefies the milk, which makes the change like that in 59(68) and 67(81). ἔδησε: ἔπηξε LC (Plut.), and this is the verb used with ὀπός in Homer loc. cit., and in Aristotle *HA* 522b2; for δεῖν as "harden," "set," cf. [Hippocrates] *Off.* 17. The exact application of the simile is not known, but the use of γόμφος in 86(87), and Plutarch's connection with *philia*, suggest that it belongs in the general context of Aphrodite's work on the elements to produce specific compounds.

62(73)
And as, at that time, when Kypris was busily producing forms, she moistened earth in water and gave it to swift fire to harden

The fragment is quoted without comment by Simplicius, along with

85(86), 86(87), 87(95), 60(71), and 70(75), all of which mention Aphrodite/Kypris as a craftsman responsible for forms of life and their organic parts; and, adds Simplicius, E. is speaking about this *kosmos*. The language here is of the potter and his clay shapes, moistened and then fired. εἶδος is used by E. for the kinds of animate life, in the *Physics* 60(71).3 and cf. 15(23).5, 83(98).5, 25(22).7, and in the *Katharmoi* 107(115).7 and 130(125).

2 εἴδεα ποιπνύουσα: Stein suggested αἰθέρ᾽ ἐπιπνείουσα to bring in all four elements, but air is not an ingredient in the hard substance of bone, 48(96), or in the τύποι, 53(62), and emendation is unnecessary. For ποιπνύω with an accusative, cf. Pindar *Pyth.* 10.64, and the analogous σπεύδω, LSJ s.v., I. κρατῦναι: "strengthen," "harden," but in 91(100).19 "get possession of," "control"; for the sense here cf. Xenophon *Lac.* 2.3 and [Hippocrates] *Fract.* 7.

63(72)
How tall trees and fishes in the sea

The line is quoted by Athenaeus to show E.'s use of the rare word καμασῆνες for fish in general (cf. also 68(74).1). This section gives scope to E.'s wide-ranging biological interests and observations within the framework of the explanation of *thnēta* as combinations of earth, air, fire, and water.

64(77–78)
(Trees ever-bearing leaves and ever-bearing fruit flourish) with fruit in abundance all the year due to the air.

A first line was made from ἐμπεδόκαρπα and θάλλειν in Theophrastus, and Plutarch's identification of ἐμπεδόφυλλον in E. with ἀειθαλές, *quaest. conv.* 649c. ἠέρα in line 2 fits the Theophrastean context, referring in particular to the climate, in this case temperate and springlike. There is no indication of the poem to which the fragment belongs, and Stein, following Karsten, assigned it to the age of Kypris in the *Katharmoi*, cf. 118(128). But there is no hint in Theophrastus or Plutarch that the reference is to a condition that no longer exists, and it is more appropriate to assign it to the group of fragments dealing with the nature of trees, but cf. the commentary on fr. 152.

From Theophrastus and Plutarch here, and Aetius 5.26.4, E.'s explanation of nondeciduous trees, with the laurel, olive, and date palm singled out, can be pieced together. All trees, as the first ζῷα, and therefore closer to the greater influence of Love, have a symmetry in the combination of their constituent elements (and so they combine the *logos* of male and female). The moisture in them, however, is evaporated by summer heat, which causes the leaves to shrivel and fall, and the nourishment taken in is not retained because of the funnel-like arrangement of their pores. But evergreens have an excess of moisture, which survives the summer evaporation, and a symmetrical arrangement of pores that admit regular nourishment. Generally, the temperate zone in which these trees grow balances internal with external symmetry, and so they remain constant.

It is botanically impossible for trees to have fruit all year round in the same way as they do leaves (for the flower precedes the fruit), and the reference must be to a tree regularly bearing a heavy crop. The lines recall the orchard of Alcinous (*Od.* 7.114–18), where the fruit does not fail summer or winter, and this is because the temperate zephyr allows the trees to bear their fruit at different times. In the orchard are pears, apples, pomegranates, figs, and olives, and E.'s interest in date palms was noted above (Aet. 5.26.4, where it is also said that fruits are the excess of water and fire in the plant). Of these the olive and palm are nondeciduous, extremely long-lived, and consistently have abundant fruit. The explanation of such fruitfulness is in the harmony between the *krasis* of the tree's constitution and that of the surrounding air or climate, which nicely blends heat and cold. In the unique compound adjectives with ἐμπεδο- I suspect E. is making use of a mild pun on his own name.

65(79)

In this way tall trees produce olive eggs first

Aristotle praises E. for his vocabulary here, for a fruit is analogous to an egg in that each is a κύημα, with the seed surrounded by the nourishment necessary for its growth; in plants this is a consequence of their bisexual nature. Theophrastus elaborates on this comparison along similar lines. Philoponus, less plausibly, reads μικρὰ δένδρεα, taken as accusative with ἐλαίας in apposition, and no subject specified; he says that the olive stones can be called eggs and olives and also small trees, because of their potential for growth.

μακρὰ δένδρεα: cf. *Od.* 7.114 again of Alcinous' orchard. ᾠοτοκεῖ:

with ἐλαίας as an extended accusative (rather than a genitive singular, which would make a strange circumlocution, and the form would probably be ἐλαίης). The verb later became a technical biological term contrasted with ζῳοτοκεῖν. As Aristotle recognized, E. had the insight to see not merely a resemblance in their oval shape between an olive and an egg but a true analogy based on the functioning of the parts, and this in turn confirms the basic kinship between plant and animal life, which is a key point of the *Katharmoi*.

66(80)

This is why pomegranates come late in the season, and apples are exceptionally succulent.

The discussion in Plutarch starts with Homer's μηλέαι ἀγλαόκαρποι (*Od.* 7.115) and then introduces this line. The explanation for the late ripening of pomegranates is clear. It is a question of the internal structure of the plant and the outside temperature (cf. the commentary on 64(77–78), and ἀήρ is again used in this connection). The pomegranate has relatively little moisture, and so it cannot reach the right consistency in the summer heat but waits until the air is cooler. Plutarch, however, does not understand what E. means by ὑπέρφλοια μῆλα. He says that E.'s epithets are not ornamental but always explain some essential fact or function. Two suggestions are made. Either the prepositional prefix means "excessive," and -φλοια "freshness," "bloom," as in Aratus (*Phaen.* 335), or it means "outside"; the husk of an apple is the shiny covering of the seeds, and the edible part is therefore "outside the husk." Yet if the adjectives are not attributive, the same explanation has to cover both pomegranates and apples. Perhaps it is that outside cool air is in sympathy with and encourages the moisture within. For the pomegranate the late season gives its meager moisture a chance to develop, for the apple a temperate climate results in an excess of moisture and so a succulent fruit.

ὀψίγονοι: again a Homeric word is given a new context, and the tie between the plant and human world is strengthened in the application of the word for the men born later to the late fruit of the season. ὑπέρφλοα: Karsten's emendation, *metris causa*.

67(81)

Water from the skin, fermented in wood, becomes wine.

Like 59(68) and 61(33), this is an example of a change in a liquid brought about by putrefaction. Aristotle dismisses the suggestion that wine is (of the genus) water; Plutarch concentrates on σῆψις, identifying it with πέψις for E. in his first quotation of the line, and seeing it as a characteristic of wine in the second. In the previous fragment φλοιός seemed to refer to the (edible) part of the apple surrounding the seeds, and I suggest it has a similar meaning here, as the part of the grape surrounding the seeds. In wine making, after the pressing, the juice and skins of the grapes are put into wooden casks or vats (which is surely the meaning of ἐν ξύλῳ, for ξύλον is wood cut and put to some use); fermentation is induced spontaneously by the (yeast) particles present in the grape itself, and especially on the skin. During the transformation of the grape juice into wine there is a "vigorous evolution of carbon dioxide giving the impression of boiling" (*Chambers Enc.* 1968, s.v. fermentation). The processes of concoction and putrefaction are closely related or even indistinguishable, and to their more obvious medical and physiological associations is here added a phenomenon from plant life.

68(74)

leading the songless tribe of prolific fish

The point of Plutarch's quotation is that E. recognized that fish are prolific, more so than creatures of land or air. πολυσπερής, Homer's adjective for "widespread men," was understood by Plutarch as "much-sowing," "fertile," and, characteristically, E. makes use of the ambiguity latent in the adjective. The general context in *quaest. conv.* is a discussion of salt as an erotic stimulant, and this is suggested as a reason for Aphrodite's birth from the sea and the numerous offspring of Poseidon and the sea gods. If the feminine participle referred to Aphrodite one would expect Plutarch to mention this as corroborative evidence, but Nestis would be more appropriate for the subject as having command of the creatures in her element. The particular force of ἄμουσον surely is that fish are bloodless and so are denied a sophisticated form of *phronēsis*, one consequence of which is that they have no articulate voice. (The assertion that the line refers to Aphrodite leading fish from land to sea in another era, cf. O'Brien *ECC* pp. 190–94, nullifies the point of Plutarch's citation, for if the fish are coming from land they would not be prolific because they live in the salt sea; and it would be extraordinary for E. to be talking about fish in another era, and not those we know. In the commentary on 47(35) it was argued that E. treated the many-to-one era in a digression to accommodate some creatures of myth; his main task is to account for the present world, when the many are being separated out. The τύποι sent up by fire from the earth go to the element to which they are akin, according to the character of their mixture, so Aetius 5.19.5; any excess of the opposite element is overcome by the surrounding "home" element, cf. Aristotle *Resp.* 477b1–478a11 and Theophrastus *caus. plant.* 1.21.5.)

69(76)

For those with heavy backs who live in the sea, this (is found) in mussels, and indeed you will notice that earth is on the top surface of the flesh of tritons and stony skinned turtles.

The three lines are quoted by Plutarch in *quaest. conv.* in a context of the right criterion for seating guests, where it is suggested that affinity rather than rank should be considered. In nature, fire is not always above earth, but the god—Pindar's ἀριστοτέχνης who is Zeus, but for E. Aphrodite—makes an arrangement in accordance with the function of the organism. Similarly, with the quotation of the last two lines in *fac. lun.*, Plutarch argues against a "natural" position for earth and fire but says that their places are assigned as is appropriate or useful.

1 θαλασσονόμοις: Diels changed the compound to θαλασσονόμων and put a colon at the end of the second line, but E. surely is speaking of three different kinds of "hard-backed sea dwellers"—mussels, which are completely enclosed in a hard covering, tritons (possibly including sea snails), and the reptilian turtles. The collection and hardening of earth on the back is an arrangement of elements achieved by Love for the protection of the organism, in defiance of the movement of the elements to their own kind under Strife. From a comparison with the following fragment it is fair to deduce that E. understood that the carapace is the turtle's bone structure "on top," in fact, the backbone and ribs joined by bony plates.

70(75)

But of those which are compact within and loosely formed without, having chanced on this kind of flaccidity at the hands of Kypris

Simplicius quotes these lines without comment as the last of six fragments, said to come fairly close together, which show Aphrodite/Kypris as a craftsman, fashioning the elements into organisms and organic parts, in *Cael.* 529–30, and cf. the commentary on 60(71). The second line is quoted at *in Phys.* 331.9 as the fourth of seven examples (from many more, adds Simplicius) in E.'s *Physics* on the use of chance. This is given in the verbs συγκυρεῖν, 29(53), 51(59).2, 83(98).1, 82(104), and τυγχάνειν, here and at 84(85), and in the noun τύχη, 81(103). In this fragment the combination of τυγχάνειν and the work of Kypris is like that of συγκυρεῖν and Kypris for the production of blood and flesh, 83(98) and cf. 82(104), and τυγχάνειν and Aphrodite for that of eyes, 84(85) and 85(86). Aristotle complains that E. uses τύχη without identifying it with Philia or Neikos and without giving any explanation of it (*Phys.* 196a12–24 quoting 29[53]). It would seem that, as the four roots are moving haphazardly but in the general direction of separated masses, some of the parts are united into organic compounds by Kypris, as a potter, carpenter, smith, or sculptor works the material he "chances on" to a shape of his own design.

1 μανά: the lengthened first alpha of this adjective is the point of the quotation of fr. 152. The reference to the "rare" or "loosely formed" covering would be to any flesh-covered creature, in contrast to those mentioned in 69(76).

71(82)

As the same things, hair, leaves, the close-packed feathers of birds, and scales on strong limbs grow.

The fragment supports Aristotle's brief comment on bones, hair, and the like being analogous; it is recalled in *HA* 487b20 and imitated in Lucretius 5.788. In a similar way E. related eggs and olives, 65(79); called the ear a "shoot," Theophrastus *Sens.* 9; spoke of the ὄρπηκες of men and women; and conversely called trees the first ζῷα, 53(62) and Aetius 5.26.4. In more general terms all things "think" and feel pleasure and pain, cf. 78(107) and 81(103). This serves to break down the barriers between plant, bird, animal, and human life, and so makes it easier to understand the transition between them made by the daimon of the *Katharmoi*. The acute observation here of the connection between leaves, scales, feathers, and hair relates the forms of life in different elements and the structure of

less and more advanced and articulate types, as well, perhaps, as showing
the first awareness of biological analogy and homology.

72(83)

but for hedgehogs sharp-pointed hairs bristle on their backs.

The fragment is used by Plutarch to illustrate the well-worn theme that
animals are better endowed than men for their own defense, whereas the
compensation for man is his power of reasoning. This is unlikely to be the
context in E.'s poem, which asserts that all things have *phronēsis*, 78(107)
and 81(103). The fragment seems rather to belong to the previous one,
adding another humble example to the list there. χαίτη: the word for
human hair, the mane of a horse or lion, and leaves (cf. LSJ s.v.) is well
chosen, in this setting, for the hedgehog's spines. (J. Longrigg's attempt
to find a further analogue for E. in gills and lungs is unwarranted guesswork and fails to take into account Aet. 5.24.2, cf. "Empedocles' Fiery
Fish," *JWI* 1965, pp. 314–15.)

FRAGMENTS   73–83   PERCEPTION AND THOUGHT

73(89)

There are effluences from all things in existence.

This line is quoted in the course of a complex answer to the question,
"Why does the octopus change color?" In addition to Theophrastus'
explanation that it does so out of cowardice (and for self-defense, *soll. an.*
978e), Plutarch suggests that minute particles detached from rocks and
sprayed by the sea pass into the porous skin of the octopus; when the
creature is frightened, it contracts its body so that the effluences are held
on the surface of the skin and do not penetrate (cf. a similar explanation
in *amic. mult.* 96f). This is considered as a particular application of E.'s
theory, according to which all bodies have pores closely packed on their
surfaces, and effluences are given off not only by the roots but also by
compounds; these effluences are capable of entering the pores that are
symmetrical, cf. Plato *Meno* 76c and Theophrastus *Sens.* 7. The theory is a
general one of mixture (as in 14(21).13–14 of the roots, δι' ἀλλήλων δὲ

θέοντα γίγνεται ἀλλοιωπά· τὰ γὰρ διὰ κρῆσις ἀμείβει, and Theophrastus *Sens.* 12, ὅλως γὰρ ποιεῖ τὴν μίξιν τῇ συμμετρίᾳ τῶν πόρων), but
in practice it seems to have been restricted to explaining perception and
growth, and various phenomena such as reflections (Aetius 4.14.1, *Pap.
Ox.* 1609.13.94, DK 31 B109a) and the attraction of the magnet (Alex.
Aphr. *quaest.* 72.26 on 74(91), and Plutarch *quaest. nat.* 916d). Aristotle
unfavorably contrasts E.'s explanation of ποιεῖν–πάσχειν and μίξις by
means of pores and effluences with that of the atomists, whose postulation
of indivisible solids interspersed by void allowed a more systematic and
comprehensive account of all forms of change, *GC* 324b25–35. Further
criticisms are that any explanation using pores and effluences is superfluous (since bodies adapted by nature for reciprocal contact will interact
even without pores) and is also inconsistent with E.'s denial of void, *GC*
325b5–11, 326b7–28, and cf. Theophrastus *Sens.* 13. It has been suggested
that some light may be thrown on the question whether the pores are
empty or full by referring to the original meaning of *poros*, a "ford,"
which can yield and allow entry to a body but which shows no gap before
the body enters, cf. Guthrie *HGP* vol. 2, p. 234, n. 3; but this is to rein-
state Aristotle's "divisible body," *GC* 326b26–28. From the account of
the magnet it seems that E. supposed the pores to be filled with air that is
displaced by a concentration of effluences (cf. the commentary on the
next fragment, and also Philoponus *in GC* 178.2).

Alcmaeon was probably the first to have spoken of pores in an anatomical sense, but in his case they were channels leading from the sense
organ to the brain, Theophrastus *Sens.* 25–26; E. perhaps had this in mind
in the phrase πόρος νοῆσαι, 5(3).7. E. speaks of πόρος ὕμνων, 47(35).1,
but in the extant fragments does not use the word πόρος for his description
of pores in the body; instead he uses ἄλοκες, 91(100).3. His theory of pores
and effluences was discussed and elaborated in the medical writers (e.g.,
Reg. I.23, *Anon. Lond.* 26, 31–34, and cf. 36), and was taken up especially
by Democritus and Epicurus for their account of "idols" (cf. Theophr.
Sens. 50, Lucretius 1.309–28, 2.69, 4.46–109). The theory seems to have
originated with E., for although Parmenides is cited with E., Anaxagoras,
Democritus, and Epicurus as explaining perception by symmetry of pores
(Aet. 4.9.6), he is not mentioned elsewhere in this connection, and his
name may well have been included from a misunderstanding of Aristotle's *Metaph.* 1009b12–25.

74(91)
(Water) combines more with wine, but refuses with oil.

ἐνάρθμιον is ἄπ. λεγ. but an obvious correction for the unmetrical ἐναρ-ίθμιον, cf. ἄρθμιος, 8(17).23 and 25(22).1. For the use of ἐθέλειν here cf. Plato *Soph.* 252e. Philoponus, like Plutarch in the context of the previous fragment, mentions the universal application of E.'s theory of pores and implies that he used the terms κοῖλα and πυκνά, although they are not found in this sense in the extant fragments. There is evidence of three examples used in connection with the theory. (1) Here, as Philoponus explains, symmetry of κοῖλα and πυκνά in water and wine accounts for their combining, and lack of symmetry for the inability of water to mix with oil. (2) Alexander applies the theory here to the working of the magnet. The effluences from the stone disperse the air obstructing the pores of the iron, then the effluences from the iron move toward the pores of the stone and, being commensurate, fit into them; the iron follows of itself. (3) Philoponus, paraphrasing Aristotle, also gives E.'s use of the theory to explain the sterility of mules. According to E. the semen of the horse and ass have commensurate κοῖλα and πυκνά, and from the mingling of the two soft substances a hard (and sterile) compound results; Aristotle finds this explanation, like (1) above, unsatisfactory, cf. *GA* 747a35–b26 and the commentary on 143(92).

75(90)
So sweet seized on sweet, bitter rushed to bitter, sharp came to sharp, and hot coupled with hot.

In this fragment it seems likely that θερμόν in Macrobius is a simplification of a more unusual word in the original. Hesychius gives μέλαν, καὶ τὸ καιόμενον for δαερόν, and θερμόν, καυματηρόν, λαμπρόν for δαηρόν. Diels therefore suggests δαερὸν δ' ἐποχεῖτο δαηρῷ, and Maas δαερὸν δ' ἐποχεύετο δαερῷ (cf. DK vol. 1, p. 344, n. 5), for the synizesis comparing *Il.* 24.769. This keeps the balance of the repetition of the quality (cf. 77[109]) and retains ἐποχεύετο from Macrobius. Bollack writes ἀλερὸς δ' ἐποτεύεθ' ἀληρῷ, and Maas has three lines from a combination of the two sources. The verbs with their forceful metaphors should probably be taken as past, rather than "gnomic," as Burnet and Kranz suggest, though the activity described still continues. According to Theophrastus, E. explained growth as well as mixture and perception by pores and effluences, and both Plutarch and Macrobius refer the fragment to nutrition, cf. Theophrastus *Sens.* 12 and Aristotle *De An.* 416a30. It would seem that the food is broken up by a σῆψις in the stomach (cf. Galen *def. med.* 99, 19.372K, Plato *Phaedo* 96a–b); it then passes to the liver, where it is transformed into blood (cf. τὴν δὲ γαστέρα πέττουσαν, τὸ δὲ ἧπαρ ἐξαιματοῦν, Simp. *in Phys.* 372.5, πολυαίματον τὸ ἧπαρ, Plutarch *quaest. conv.* 683e). The blood moves through the body and gives to each part what is necessary for its nutrition and growth, cf. Aetius 5.27.1.

In Alcmaeon an indefinite number of opposite *dynameis* are cited as acting in the body, Aetius 5.30.1, and in *Ancient Medicine* the number is also indefinite, the example quoted including salt, bitter, sweet, and acid; special significance is denied to hot and cold. E. here gives the action of obvious *dynameis* in different kinds of food, but without connecting them specifically to the roots. After E., when his doctrine of four roots prevailed in medical theory, the number of powers in the body was restricted to four, and the opposites were conflated with the humors, cf. *VM* 14, 16, and chap. 1.

76(93)
And the gleam of bright saffron mixes in with the linen.

Many suggestions have been put forward for the interpretation of this line. Diels translates his text "Mit der Byssosfarbe aber wird des blauen Holunders Beere gemischt" and cites Hesychius to justify his interpretation of βύσσος as the color. Yet the context in Plutarch refers the line to dyeing rather than to a mixing of colors, no parallel is offered for a mixing of this particular kind, and three initial spondees are heavy (77(109).3 is exceptionally solemn). On the same line is Wyttenbach's version followed by Karsten and Stein, and also by Millerd, but with ἀκτίς for ἄνθος, and the translation "the brilliance of the scarlet dye mixed thoroughly with the grey cloth." This is unsatisfactory for there is still the metrical difficulty, and γλαυκός, which implies some brightness of color, should probably not be taken with βύσσος, since it is important for the material which is to be dyed to be as neutral as possible, cf. Plato *Rep.* 429d. With Bennet's reading, the only change required is in the gender of the adjective, ἀκτίς can be used metaphorically to indicate brightness or penetration (cf. LSJ s.v.), and saffron was well known as a dye, cf. Aeschylus *Pers.* 660, *Ag.* 239. The simile from an everyday craft is typical of E., and an apt illustration of the affinity of certain substances and of the fast union resulting. The fragment's place in the poem is not known, but it may belong with the description of the forms produced by Kypris. It has been grouped with the fragments dealing with effluences and with the attraction of elements in nutrition and perception, because Plutarch quotes the line as an example of a combination of ingredients that are οἰκεῖα and πρόσφορα. His purpose is to give support to the theory that μαντικὴ ἀναθυμίασις, having some affinity to the soul, fits into, fills, and holds fast its rarefied structure.

77(109)

With earth we perceive earth, with water water, with air divine air, with fire destructive fire, with love love, and strife with baneful strife.

These lines on ἡ γνῶσις τοῦ ὁμοίου τῷ ὁμοίῳ are the most widely quoted from E.'s work. Aristotle, in *De An.* 404b16, connects the lines with Plato's *Timaeus*, cf. *Tim.* 35a, 45b, and Sextus with Plato and Pythagoreanism, although he gives the theory as being of some antiquity (cf. *Od.* 17.218). There is a hint of the theory in Alcmaeon, cf. Aristotle *De An.* 405a30, and after E. the attraction of like to like was important in the cosmogonies of Anaxagoras and Democritus, cf. Simp. *in Phys.* 27.11 and Democritus fr. 164. Galen explains the fragment by connecting a root with each sense, saying that sight involves fire, hearing air, touch earth, taste moisture, and smell "vapor," but this is a neat simplification; it is known from 88(84) that both fire and water are involved in vision, and Theophrastus remarks in *Sens.* 9 that E. did not deal with touch or taste, except under a general heading of perception by means of pores.

E. explained perception in general terms by symmetry of pores and the attraction of similars. (Cf. Theophrastus *Sens.* 10 and 7, where asymmetry of pores in the sense organ and object explains why organs cannot distinguish each other's objects—the pores are too wide or too narrow for contact.) Theophrastus also adds that for E. *phronēsis* is the same or much the same as *aisthēsis*. This is from Aristotle, who puts E. with Democritus and "almost everyone else" as identifying *phronēsis* and *aisthēsis*, and supposing this to be an ἀλλοίωσις (*Metaph.* 1009b12; cf. Galen's description of E.'s theory of perception as ἀλλοίωσις ἐκ τῶν ὁμοίων, *Plac. Hipp. Plat.* 5.627K). It is clear that E. supposed that the attraction of like for like covered a whole range, from the basic form of a part of one root being aware of another part like itself and moving toward it (cf. 53(62).6 and 100(110).9), through compounds that can sense and combine with similar compounds, to perfect mixtures that are assimilated to their like, the process of highest (i.e., purest) thought. It would not be possible to make a distinction, in Peripatetic terminology, between *aisthēsis* and *phronēsis*

at any particular point along the scale, and as Theophrastus asks, *Sens.*
12, τί διοίσει τὰ ἔμψυχα πρὸς τὸ αἰσθάνεσθαι τῶν ἄλλων; for on this
theory nothing is inanimate or without sensation at however simple a
level. Now if, with the fire within, we perceive the fire without, we increase the fire in our constitution (this notion is already in Parmenides,
and probably Heraclitus; see chap. 3), and so with earth, air, and water.
Further, we have control to some extent over our perceptions and
thoughts, and over the increase, for better or worse, of what is perceived
and thought. But this control also applies to that which unites and that
which separates the constituents, which on a moral plane means that we
can increase the strength of Love or Strife in us by concentrating on its
like in the outside world, cf. further the commentary on 100(110).10.

2 δῖον: cf. *Il.* 16.365, with αἰθήρ as feminine in Homer. ἀίδηλον: the
adjective, as probably in Parmenides fr. 10.3, is ambiguous here between
"destructive" and "unseen." The two epithets in this line are reminders
of the divine status of the roots.

78(107)
*All things are fitted together and constructed out of these, and by means of them they
think and feel pleasure and pain.*

From the Theophrastean context Stein was probably correct in attaching
these two lines to 77(109), cf. Simplicius *in de An.* 27.34–37. The principle
that all things have *phronēsis*, in varying degrees according to their
elemental structure, connects with 77(109) and also with 81(103) and
100(110).10; here it is also combined with an explanation of pleasure
and pain.

E.'s theory of pleasure is difficult to reconstruct, as there are only two
brief notices in Theophrastus (*Sens.* 9, 16) and two in Aetius (4.9.15 and
5.28.1), the second of which is corrupt. Desire is said to arise from a deficiency in the constituent elements; and this deficiency, which needs to
be remedied, is of something bearing a resemblance to the subject. Pleasure occurs with the action of like on like and the replenishment of the
deficiency by a similar mixture; pain is caused by contraries, for dissimilar
compounds are hostile to each other, Aetius 5.28.1, Theophrastus *Sens.*
9 and 16 quoting 25(22).6–7.

From this scanty evidence (and adding *Sens.* 23) it seems that, as with
aisthēsis and *phronēsis*, all things, on however simple a level, are capable of

feeling pleasure and pain. Satisfactory perception and cognition, i.e., arising from a symmetry of subject and object, is pleasant, and the same holds true for nutrition, cf. Aetius 4.9.14. The animal is aware of its need for nourishment, and this, like perception, is based on the attraction of like to like, cf. the commentary on 75(70); deficiency causes *orexis*, and pleasure arises from the replenishment. The other desire E. interprets is that of sex, again an *orexis* for a unity of likes, that brought about by Aphrodite, and for a return to a former harmony, cf. Aetius 5.19.5, E. 8(17).22 and 54(64).

Theophrastus says that E. explained pain by contraries, but pain relates to perception, which is by likes, *Sens.* 16. E.'s meaning, however, is likely to be less sophisticated than Theophrastus expects. The simple and general statement here covers a great number of instances and involves the six fundamentals. It could be illustrated by pain encountered in nutrition when the food absorbed cannot be assimilated to the body, in perception when there is a lack of symmetry as with the bright light or loud noise (cf. *Sens.* 8), and in human relations when attempts at friendship turn to hostility because of incompatibility. A further implication made explicit by Theophrastus is that ignorance is painful, *Sens.* 23.

1 ⟨ὡς⟩: an informal suggestion made by Professor H. Lloyd-Jones in place of Karsten's commonly accepted ⟨γάρ⟩. πεπήγασιν ἁρμοσθέντα: almost a technical phrase of E.'s for the formation of organic compounds, cf. 70(75), 85(86), 60(71).4.

79(106)

For man's wisdom grows according to what is present.

This line is taken with the following fragment by Aristotle and the commentators; it is also related in *Metaph.* to Parmenides fr. 16, Anaxagoras, and an unknown Homeric phrase, and in *De An.* to *Od.* 18.136. The point made is that according to earlier thinkers *aisthēsis* and *phronēsis* are not distinguished (cf. the commentary on 77[109]); both are *sōmatikon* and of like by like. Alexander gives the sense in which πρὸς παρεόν is to be taken: πρὸς τὸ παρὸν γὰρ καὶ τὸ φαινόμενον ἡ φρόνησις γίνεται, *in Metaph.* 306.17. According to E., then, the external condition affects the internal structure, and so the quality and quantity of the individual's wisdom; in Aristotle's summary, when men change their *hexis* they change their thinking, *Metaph.* 1009b19. It is worth noticing the connection

Asclepius makes with medical theory. Following Aristotle he says that for E. a change of *hexis* is a change of *phronēsis* ὡς ἂν ταῖς κράσεσι τοῦ σώματος ἑπομένων τῶν ψυχικῶν δυνάμεων, καθάπερ καί τινες τῶν ἰατρῶν εἰρήκασι, in *Metaph.* 277.6. A satisfactory mixture of bodily elements is a healthy state (and pleasant, cf. the previous fragment) and conducive to thought, which thrives in the appropriate environment. Specifically human understanding differs from animal perception in its complexity and in the extent to which it is in the individual's control, cf. the commentaries on 80(108) and 100(110).

80(108)
Insofar as they have changed in their nature, so far changed thoughts are always present to them.

This fragment comes with the previous one in the two quotations by Aristotle and the commentators, and it emphasizes it. There it was said that the external condition affects the growth of the thinking, and here that an internal change of structure results in a change of thought. Simplicius and Philoponus relate the lines specifically to dreaming, to the effect that dreams at night are conditioned by a man's physical changes during the day, Simplicius *in de An.* 202.25, Philoponus *in de An.* 486.13, and cf. the reading of T at Aristotle *De An.* 427a25. Explanations of dreams are rare among the Presocratics, and E.'s is well accommodated to his general theory. In the discussion Aristotle does not mention dreams but loss of consciousness (*Metaph.* 1009b25; the phrase on Hector is not in the extant text of Homer). If the "Homeric" reference is relevant to E., as κεῖσθαι ἀλλοφρονέοντα suggests, there is here the extreme case of a blow to the physical system resulting in incoherent and uncharacteristic thoughts, comparable perhaps to the fantasies resulting from a modern anesthetic.

81(103)
There by the will of chance all things have thought

The line is quoted with the following fragment without comment by Simplicius as an illustration of the use of τύχη in E., cf. the commentary on 70(75).

ἰότητι: cf. the Homeric θεῶν ἰότητι, *Il.* 19.9, *Od.* 7.214, in pessimistic contexts. τῇδε must be local, meaning "there" in the mixture of earth, air, fire, and water as it happens to be, for it is out of these that all things are constructed and by means of them that thought is to be explained, cf. the commentary on 78(107).

82(104)
And insofar as the finest happened to have fallen together

This is the last of the lines quoted by Simplicius on τύχη, coming, he says, shortly after the previous fragment. συνέκυρσε is used of random movement in 29(53) and 51(59).2, and again, with reference to the elements, in the first line of the following fragment. The "finest" of the four roots are air and fire, and if the connection with the following fragment is correct, it is the amount of these, balancing to a more or less precise degree the amount of earth and water, that together with them are made by Aphrodite into blood, the organ of thought for men. It is not a defect in Love's workmanship but the quantity of the constituent ingredients—and this is a matter of "chance"—which accounts for the thoughts of some men being inferior to those of others (but the individual can improve his own thought structure, cf. the commentary on 100[110]). There is a similar explanation for other compounds; the coming together of the ingredients is fortuitous (cf. Aristotle *GC* 333b10–11), but where the proportions in which they come together are appropriate, Aphrodite produces an organism or organic part, cf. the commentaries on 60(71) and 70(75).

83(98)
And earth, anchored in the perfect harbors of Aphrodite, chanced to come together with them in almost equal quantities, with Hephaistos and rain and all-shining air, either a little more, or less where there was more. From these came blood and the forms of different flesh.

The first line is quoted by Simplicius in the list of fragments on τύχη (cf. the commentary on 70[75]), and the five lines in a general discussion of Love and Strife both being active in the present world, of Philia/Aphrodite as the craftsman, and here specifically of E.'s terminology for the roots; fire is called Hephaistos, *hēlios*, and *phlox*, water *ombros*, and air *aithēr*. The fragment explains the formation of blood, and it is the blood around the heart that is the organ of human thought, cf. 94(105).3. Theophrastus gives the reason for this: διὸ καὶ τῷ αἵματι μάλιστα φρονεῖν· ἐν τούτῳ γὰρ μάλιστα κεκρᾶσθαι τὰ στοιχεῖα τῶν μερῶν (*Sens.* 10). Blood is composed of fire, air, earth, and water combined in a ratio approximating to 1 : 1 : 1 : 1. The exact proportion was present throughout the sphere under Love's complete control, and the combination which now comes nearest to that is found in blood. The importance of blood as the instrument of thought and the best work of Aphrodite, which is explained in the *Physics*, immediately illuminates the prohibition against bloodshed, set out forcefully in the *Katharmoi*. How well the organ functions depends on the proportion of the constituent ingredients in its physical structure. Two further examples are given by Theophrastus in his notice that a particular skill is due to the μέση κρᾶσις in an organ—the orator, who has a good mixture in his tongue, and the craftsman, who has one in his hands, *Sens.* 10–11.

1 ἡ δὲ χθών: as in 48(96), earth gives a secure hold to the other elements, as well as being an integral part of their composition.

2: for the variety of terms for the four roots cf. the table in chap. 2.

3: the metaphor of "perfect harbors" is unexpected. In other comparable fragments Aphrodite/Kypris is active, fitting together, 60(71); nailing, 86(87); gluing, 48(96); molding, 85(86); working with her hands, 70(75) and 87(95); and generally being busy, 62(73). I suspect that the reference here is to the womb, where the tissues are first formed, cf. Sophocles *OT* 1208, and E.'s metaphor at 55(66). The harbor is "perfect," but the somewhat random coming together of the roots into it results in the imperfection; Kypris produces the best possible result from the given material, cf. the activity of the Demiurge, Plato *Tim.* 41d.

4 †εἶτε πλέον ἐστίν†: Professor Dodds suggested εἶτ' ἐν πλεόνεσσιν to me for this crux. The proportion is not perfect, cf. ἴση μάλιστα in line 1, and so the amount of earth does not exactly match the separate amounts of fire, air, and water, but may be a little more (with less of the other three) or less (where they are more).

5 ἄλλης εἴδεα σαρκός: cf. Aetius 5.22.1 'Ε. τὰς μὲν σάρκας γεννᾶσθαι ἐκ τῶν ἴσων τῇ κράσει τεττάρων στοιχείων. The *eidos* is given by the proportion of the constituent ingredients—with less earth there is blood, and with more, flesh, cf. Hipp. *Nat. Puer.* 15 of the fetus: τοῦ αἵματος . . . πηγνυμένου σὰρξ γίνεται.

FRAGMENTS 84–93 SIGHT, RESPIRATION, AND SMELL

84(85)
The gentle flame met with a slight portion of earth.

The verse comes after the first line of the previous fragment in the list of quotations by Simplicius illustrating E.'s use of τύχη, *in Phys.* 331.7. In the introduction to the previous fragment at *in Phys.* 32, *phlox* was listed with Hephaistos as one of E.'s terms for fire. It is not known to which of the μόρια τῶν ζῴων the verse refers, but from the description of the constituent fire and the amount of earth it is reasonable to suggest the eye. μινυνθαδίης: literally "short-lived" in Homer, cf. of Hector, *Il.* 15.612, and men in general, *Od.* 19.328. The adjective is a reminder that the combination of ingredients that constitute the bodily parts is temporary, cf. 12(8).

85(86)
Out of these the goddess Aphrodite fashioned untiring eyes.

If the previous fragment refers to eyes a lacuna follows, as water and air are also in the eye, cf. Theophrastus *Sens.* 7. This line occurs with the two following fragments in Simplicius' list of examples of the work of Kypris/ Aphrodite on the roots to produce organic parts.

For ἔπηξε cf. the similar use of the verb at 70(75), 78(107), and also 106(15).4.

86(87)
Aphrodite, having fitted (them) with rivets of affection

The line is given by Simplicius as coming soon after the previous one, and presumably in the same context of the formation of eyes. ἀσκεῖν, like πηγνύναι, is for the work of a craftsman. The γόμφοι (cf. 61[33]), rather than nailing the eyes to the skull or connecting them with each other (cf. 89[88]), bind the constituent elements to each other (cf. *Tim.* 43a of the gods working on fire and water). They are bonds of affection in that Love brings the elements together and also makes them want to stay together, contrary to their tendency to stay with their own kind, cf. 14(21).8 and 25(22).5.

87(95)

When they first grew together in the hands of Kypris

The line comes after the two previous fragments in the same context of Kypris/Aphrodite as the craftsman, but it is concerned with the specific reason why some see better at night and others by day. The subject of the verb would then be an expression for parts of fire and water, for eyes with less fire in their constitution see better by day, and those with less water, by night, cf. Theophrastus *Sens.* 8 and the commentary on the next fragment.

88(84)

As when a man who intends to make a journey prepares a light for himself, a flame of fire burning through a wintry night; he fits linen screens against all the winds which break the blast of the winds as they blow, but the light that is more diffuse leaps through, and shines across the threshold with unfailing beams. In the same way the elemental fire, wrapped in membranes and delicate tissues, was then concealed in the round pupil—these kept back the surrounding deep water, but let through the more diffuse light.

The fragment is given by Aristotle with a brief comment that E. at one time, apparently, explains vision by an issue of light from the eye and at another by effluences from the objects seen. Alexander paraphrases the fragment in his commentary on Aristotle here and refers it to Plato's exposition of E.'s theory in the *Meno* (76c–d). Eusebius mentions the adjective in κύκλοπα κούρην as a poetic application of Κύκλωψ (*Od.* 20.19). The whole passage is Homeric in vocabulary and rhythm, as well as in the simile form, cf. especially lines 1 and *Od.* 2.20, 2 and *Il.* 12.279 and 8.563, 3 and *Il.* 2.397, 4 and *Il.* 5.525, and 8 and *Il.* 18.595.

2 διὰ νύκτα: "through the night," cf. *Il.* 2.57 and commonly in Homer; here, for the time the flame burns rather than the extent of the journey.

3 ἀμοργούς: the meaning is unclear, even to Alexander, but an appropriate sense is "linen" (cf. ὀθόνῃσι in line 8) from the famous Amorgian flax, cf. Bollack *Empédocle* vol. 3, p. 322. The traveler prepared the

lantern by lighting the wick, and then, since he was going out in bad weather, shielded the flame with screens of fine material attached to the frame (horn plates were also used for this purpose). παντοίων ἀνέμων is probably an independent genitive, the point being that, whatever the winds, the flame is safe because it is protected on four sides.

5 ταναώτερον: translated "more diffuse," but literally "longer" or "more stretched out"; Alexander's paraphrase gives τοῦ δὲ πυρὸς τὸ λεπτότατον.

6 κατὰ βηλόν: not the sky, as Alexander paraphrases from the Homeric threshold of Olympus, or a part of the lantern, but most obviously the threshold of the traveler's house, where he pauses a moment to find his way by the lantern's unfailing light (cf. ὄμματα ἀτείρεα, 85[86]).

7 ὠγύγιον: an obscure word which seems to mean "ancient," "born long ago"; here, perhaps, from the contrast with ἄφθιτον for the water of Styx (Hesiod *Theog.* 805), "without a known beginning," and appropriate therefore for the element of fire.

8 λοχάζετο: Guthrie accepts the reading λοχεύσατο from Förster and Ross, with the gynecologically peculiar sense "fire gave birth to," *HGP* vol. 2, p. 235. Burnet had kept λοχάζετο with Aphrodite as subject and translated, "even so did she entrap the elemental fire, the round pupil," but Bollack understands "ainsi alors Aphrodite couchait . . ." (vol. 3, p. 325). But the verb is more likely to be middle, with the general sense that the fire "kept itself concealed" in the dark aperture of the pupil—there is still the poetic ambiguity of the little girl with her soft wrappings and the center of the eye with its protective covering, cf. the note below on the whole fragment. The line ⟨αἳ⟩ χοάνῃσι δίαντα τετρήατο θεσπεσίῃσιν, which was made up by Blass from a reading in P of line 5 (cf. *ap. crit.*) and inserted here, should be discarded, cf. also Bollack *Empédocle* vol. 3, p. 327. The syntax of the relative pronoun is strange, the composition from the version of a line four verses earlier in P is unwarranted, and it would be a physiological oddity to have χοάναι, "funnel-shaped holes," in the protective membranes. (O'Brien seems unaware that the line on which he bases much of the argument of his article, *JHS* 1970, pp. 140–79, is an intrusion into the text.) If anything is to be salvaged from the confused line in P, it is that there are pores in the fire.

The structure of the eye as presented here is remarkably accurate. Seven extant fragments deal with the eyes; it is clear that E. was interested in and may well have examined in detail their composition and functioning (Alcmaeon is said to have dissected the eye, cf. DK 24 A10). The conclusions appear to be as follows: the fiery part of the eye (i.e., the lens, cf. Theophrastus *Sens.* 37 and J. I. Beare *Greek Theories of Elementary Cognition* p. 10) is concealed behind the dark opening of the pupil and protected by membranes and tissues (in fact, by the colored membrane of the iris and by the ciliary processes and fibers). These are composed of earth and air (cf. Theophrastus *Sens.* 7, where Diels's addition of ⟨ὕδωρ καὶ⟩ is unnecessary and confusing). Surrounding the membranes, and prevented by them from quenching the fire, is water (in effect in the anterior and posterior chambers, and there is also the vitreous body behind; the general correctness of E.'s account can be seen from a comparison with figs. 13.13 and 13.18 in *Gray's Anatomy* 1973, pp. 1045 and 1048). There are pores in the fire and in the water, and these "alternate" in that the water is on either side of the fire (τοὺς δὲ πόρους ἐναλλὰξ κεῖσθαι τοῦ τε πυρὸς καὶ τοῦ ὕδατος, Thphr. loc. cit.; for a restricted sense of ἐναλλάξ cf. ἴσχειν τὼ ποδ' ἐναλλάξ, Aristoph. *Nub.* 983). Vision occurs when effluences from objects fit into these pores, dark colors being seen when their effluences fit into the pores of water, and light colors when their effluences fit into the pores of fire (cf. Plato *Meno* 76c, Thphr. *Sens.* 7, Aristotle *Sens.* 438a4; 77(109) is a general statement of awareness and recognition, and not relevant for the detailed functioning of the eyes, cf. the commentary on that fragment). Eyes that have less fire, i.e., a smaller pupil and lens, see better by day, and those with more fire, by night (Thphr. *Sens.* 8; this is an obvious conclusion from the dilation of pupils in poor light). The former type of eyes are black or dark, the latter *glaukos* (a conjecture criticized by Aristotle, *GA* 779b15). And, according to Theophrastus *Sens.* 8, the best eyes have equal proportions of fire and water (i.e., the amount of fire in the lens and the amount of water in the surrounding chambers are equivalent; the vitreous body would not come into the calculations).

But in quoting the fragment in the *De Sensu* Aristotle says that at one time E. apparently explains vision by fire coming from the eye, as here, and at another by effluences from what is seen. (For a discussion of the two versions, cf. A. A. Long, *CQ* 1966, pp. 262–64; W. J. Verdenius, *Studia Vollgraff* 1948, pp. 155–64; D. O'Brien, *JHS* 1970, pp. 140–46 and the bibliography given, pp. 157–58.) There is no incompatibility here. From Plato and Theophrastus it is clear that for E. vision occurs when the effluences fit into the pores of the eye (cf. *Meno* 76c, *Sens.* 7), and there is no question of a coalescence of fire from the eye and light from the object, as in Plato *Tim.* 45b, *Theaet.* 156d. But light from fire within the eye is as necessary for vision as external light, and the two are complementary (for eyes with less fire see better by day, and those with more, by night,

Sens. 8). The main point of the lantern simile, moreover, is to show the function of the membranes, which keep the water in the eye from the fire but allow the fire to penetrate.

(There is a faint possibility that E. understood the working of the lens to be comparable to that of the sun, cf. the commentary on 36(44): effluences are collected on the outer convex surface and then refracted from the inner convex surface to the back of the eye, in fact, to the retina. The fire in the eye would then be like a lantern, but with only two opposite sides emitting light. The light penetrates outside the organ to contribute to the light necessary for sight (and also probably to account for "flashing" eyes), but it also refracts the image of light-colored objects through the vitreous body to the back of the organ, in order to give the actual perception of the object. As well as receiving effluences into its pores, the eye, like any other object, gives off its own, cf. the commentary on 73[89].)

89(88)
from both (eyes) comes one seeing

The point of the fragment is not known, as it is quoted by Aristotle and Strabo only for the form ὄψ instead of ὄψις. And since the word is ambiguous, the sense may be either that the two eyes focus on a single subject or that one vision results from the impression on two eyes. The former is the version attributed to Pythagoras and Parmenides (for the rays from each eye embrace the object like outstretched hands, Aet. 4.13.9–10), but the latter is more appropriate for E.'s theory. Perhaps he adapted Alcmaeon's view, or saw independently, that a "path" from each eye joins at the point where the two impressions are combined (and this also explains why the two eyes move together, cf. Chalcidius, DK 24 A10). The next stage for E. would be for the composite impression to be accepted by the blood and taken to the heart, rather than received in the brain.

90(94)
And black color in the depths of a river comes from the shadow, and is seen in the same way in hollowed caverns.

The fragment occurs in one of the eight "questions" from Plutarch's *quaest. nat.*, preserved only in the Latin translation of Gilbert Longeuil.

The "question" is, "Cur aqua in summa parte alba, in fundo vero nigra spectatur?" The first suggestion, for which E.'s lines are quoted in support, is that the surface is illuminated by the sun, but the force of the rays is diminished when they penetrate deep water. Now, E. held water to be black and fire white, and black to be perceived by the water in the eye, and white by the fire (Thphr. *Sens.* 17, and cf. the commentary on the previous fragment). Water, therefore, when it is out of reach of the sun's illumination, as in the depths of a river or in underground caves, appears black, cf. 14(21).5. The fragment and its context imply an interest on E.'s part in the nature and extent of the penetration of water by light. Gilbert Longeuil's translations from the Greek, where they can be checked, are not accurate, cf. F. H. Sandbach's introduction to the Loeb translation, *Plutarch's Moralia* XI, p. 142. I tentatively suggest the following as an attempt at restoring the original Greek:

$$\kappa\alpha\grave{\iota}\ \mu\acute{\epsilon}\lambda\alpha\nu\ \grave{\epsilon}\nu\ \beta\acute{\epsilon}\nu\theta\epsilon\iota\ \pi o\tau\alpha\mu o\widetilde{\upsilon}\ \chi\rho\widetilde{\omega}\mu'\ \grave{\epsilon}\kappa\ \sigma\kappa o\tau\acute{o}\epsilon\nu\tau o\varsigma,$$
$$\mathring{\eta}\delta'\ \grave{\epsilon}\nu o\rho\widetilde{\alpha}\tau\alpha\iota\ \acute{o}\mu\widetilde{\omega}\varsigma\ \tau\alpha\widetilde{\upsilon}\tau'\ \grave{\epsilon}\gamma\kappa o\acute{\iota}\lambda o\iota\sigma\iota\nu\ \grave{\epsilon}\nu\ \mathring{\alpha}\nu\tau\rho o\iota\varsigma.$$

91(100)

This is the way in which all things breathe in and out: they all have channels of flesh, which the blood leaves, stretched over the surface of the body, and at the mouth of these the outside of the skin is pierced right through with close-set holes, so that blood is contained, but a passage is cut for air to pass through freely. Then, when the smooth blood rushes away from the surface, a wild surge of blustering air rushes through, and when the blood leaps up, the air breathes out again. It is like a girl playing with a clepsydra of shining bronze—when she puts the mouth of the pipe against her pretty hand and dips it into the smooth body of shining water, no liquid yet enters the vessel, but the mass of air pressing from within against the close-set perforations holds it back until she releases the compressed current, and then, as the air escapes, a due amount of water enters. Similarly, when she has water in the hollow of the bronze vessel, and the neck and passage are closed by human hand, the air outside, pressing inward, keeps the water in at the gates of the harsh-sounding strainer, controlling the defenses, until the girl releases her hand; then, the reverse of the former process—as the air rushes in, a due amount of water runs out before it. In the same way, when the smooth blood surging through the body rushes back and inward, a flooding stream of air at once comes pouring in, and when the blood leaps up, an equal amount (of air) in turn breathes back out again.

Despite Aristotle's interest in E.'s theory of respiration, as shown by the length of the quotation, he criticizes E. on three counts: (1) for not explaining the purpose of respiration, (2) for not making clear the kinds of ζῷα included in his theory, and (3) for supposing that nose-breathing is primary breathing. The lines are paraphrased somewhat ineptly by Michael of Ephesus, and briefly summarized at Aetius 4.22.1. An intimidating amount has been written on these twenty-five lines. Ancient commentaries are well summarized in Karsten *EAcr* pp. 245–51, and in recent times the most interesting discussions are by J. U. Powell, *CQ* 1923, pp. 172–74; H. Last, *CQ* 1924, pp. 169–73; M. Timparano Cardini, *PP* 1957, pp. 250–70; D. J. Furley, *JHS* 1957, pp. 31–34; N. B. Booth, *JHS* 1960, pp. 10–15; G. E. R. Lloyd, *Polarity and Analogy* 1966, pp. 328–33; G. A. Seeck, *Hermes* 1967, pp. 36–41; T. D. Worthen, *Isis* 1970, pp. 520–30; D. O'Brien, *JHS* 1970, pp. 140–83; and cf. further his bibliographies on pp. 170 and 176, n. 177. The fragment as a whole is here discussed after the notes.

1 πάντα: cf. 93(102); a general theory of respiration is to be given, and, as Aristotle complains, we do not know exactly what types of life are included in it. λίφαιμοι: translated "bloodless" by Burnet, Kirk-Raven, and others, but it is said in lines 4–5 that there is blood in the tubes. Booth, Guthrie, and Bollack have "partly filled with blood," "containing little blood," and "pauvre en sang" respectively from Aristotle *Resp.* 473b2, but these do not explain the adjective and go ill with the language of "rushing" and "leaping" that characterizes the movement of this blood. The prefix is generally passive, "left by" and so "without," but it can be active, cf. Euripides *Or.* 1305, and the description of Heracles in Theocritus 13.73 as λιπαναύτης, i.e., "a sailor who leaves," "a deserter." From this it is possible that σύριγγες λίφαιμοι are "channels that the blood leaves," as they are filled alternately with blood and air; cf. also Sophocles *Ajax* 1412.

2 πύματον κατὰ σῶμα: "over the surface of the body," πύματος being used not in the occasional late sense of "nethermost" but as in Homer for "outermost," cf. *Il.* 6.118, 18.608, and also ῥινὸς ὕπερ πυμάτης, *Il.* 13.616, of Menelaus' strike above "the outside top end—i.e., the bridge—of the nose" between the eyes, which are dislodged by the blow.

4 ῥινῶν ἔσχατα τέρθρα: "the outer extremities of the skin," i.e., the epidermis above the cutis; the meaning of ἔσχατα is clinched by comparing ἔσχατα τέρματα κύκλου, 47(35).10, the outside limit or circumference of the cosmos. The great controversy over whether ῥινῶν is genitive plural of ῥινός ("skin") or of ῥίς ("nose") is like that on μονίη, 21(27).3,

22(28).4, as "rest" or "solitude." In both cases the first is the meaning appropriate to the context, but the ambiguity in the word chosen allows E. also to suggest the second, cf. Kahn's reference to "studied ambiguity in E.," *Gnomon* 1969, p. 439. Other examples of such "studied ambiguity" are ἄδηλον, 77(109).2, πολυκλαύτων, 53(62).1, πολυμνήστη, 2(3).3, and πύον, 59(68).1. In the general theory, it would seem, E. supposed that primitive animal types breathe in and out through pores in the skin (and perhaps there is an implication that plants "breathe" through their leaf surfaces), but in the higher animal types there are two particularly large "holes" in the surface—the nostrils—which are primary examples of pore-breathing. And this would account for Aristotle's second and third criticisms. For Aristotle primary breathing is not nose-breathing but involves the special apparatus of the *artēria*.

If this interpretation of the lines is right, then the link between E.'s simple theory of nose-breathing as a form of skin-breathing with an oscillatory movement of blood and air, and the complexities of Plato's "circulation" of air involving skin, lungs, nose, and mouth (*Tim.* 79), may well be the medical emphasis on unimpeded cutaneous and nasal respiration in the healthy body, cf. Philistion *Anon. Lond.* 20.43–50. The account in Aetius 4.22.1 and 5.15.3 seems to mean that at birth the mucus in the body is ejected through the nose and mouth—the process is hastened by holding the baby up by its feet—as a preliminary to cutaneous and nasal inhalation of air. The instances of ῥίς and ῥινός in Homer are listed by O'Brien, *JHS* 1970, pp. 173–74.

6 ἔνθεν: "from there," i.e., from the holes at the surface. For the movements of fire and air in lines 6–8 Bollack aptly compares the vocabulary in the to-and-fro fighting between Achilles and the river, *Empédocle* vol. 3, pp. 483–84, and *Il.* 21.233–71, especially 233–34.

8–25: the simile is in the standard Homeric form: (1) *x* is the case, (2) it is as when *y*, (3) even so is *x* the case. (3) repeats the original state of affairs given in (1), often in similar wording, cf. *Il.* 13.587, 21.361, 22.138, 188, 306 of Achilles and Hector, and many others. So here lines 22–24 repeat the general sense of 6–8; there is no reason to suppose that E. would deliberately avoid the repetition of (1) in (3). The child "playing" is introduced because it allows a possible move with the clepsydra (immersing it full of air in the water) that would not be shown in its orthodox use. (A child today will play in a similar manner with a drinking straw and a glass of liquid; the straw has only one perforation at the bottom end whereas the clepsydra has many, but it works on the same principle.)

9 κλεψύδρῃ: Diels's emendation; the accusative would refer to a well-known game. The clepsydra was a common household contrivance used for transferring small amounts of liquid from one container to another, and perhaps for measuring. It had a narrow opening at the top, which could be plugged by hand, and a perforated base, cf. the illustrations in Last, *CQ* 1924, p. 170, and Bollack *Empédocle* vol. 3, p. 484. The clepsydra is used here in a simile in which the movement of air into and out of the openings of the body in respiration is compared to that of water into and out of the perforated base of the clepsydra; the fragment does not describe a controlled experiment of any kind. Worthen, *Isis* 1970, p. 527, aptly compares William Harvey saying that the heart is like a force pump; the clepsydra, like the force pump, is a basic model rather than an experimental device. διειπετέος: Bollack rejects the emendation and writes δι' εὐπετέος χαλκοῖο on the grounds that the extant examples of a clepsydra are pottery.

13 ἀέρος (perhaps ἠέρος) ὄγκος: the emphatic assertion of the corporeality of air matching the pressure of ὕδατος δέμας.

15 πνεύματος ἐλλείποντος (ἐμπίπτοντος, line 21): the genitive absolutes on the movement of air correspond to the temporal clauses, lines 6 and 23, and 8 and 25, on the movement of blood, giving syntactical confirmation of the correspondence of air in the clepsydra to blood in the body. αἴσιμον ὕδωρ: cf. the same phrase in line 21. The "due amount" of water that enters and leaves the clepsydra is equivalent to the quantity of air it previously contained.

16 ὅτε . . . ἔχει: corresponds to εὖτε . . . βάπτῃσι, lines 10–11, the girl being the subject of both verbs; in her game she first has air in the clepsydra, and then water.

19: air outside keeps the water in the clepsydra in a state of siege; the gates are the exit for the water, i.e., the perforations, through which it rushes at the first opportunity. The irregular gurgling made by the water entering and filling the strainer accounts for its being called δυσηχής. ἰσθμοῖο, interpreted as "of the neck end," is irrelevant in the context, and the reading ἠθμοῖο preferable.

22 κλαδασσόμενον: glossed by Michael, in *PN* 124.15, as μετὰ ῥύμης καὶ ταραχῆς.

23: Homeric phrasing, cf. *Od.* 22.270 of the suitors retreating before Odysseus.

This fragment gives the first extant Greek physiological theory to connect respiration with the movement of the blood. E. recognizes that the blood is in continuous motion as air is inspired and exhaled; the movement, however, is not circular but oscillatory, being to and from the body's surface in the same "channels." The details of the comparison with the clepsydra are set out below, and some explanatory notes added.

Respiration and the Simile of the Clepsydra

Breathing in:				
A(i)	*static:*	blood inside	(restraint of pores)	air outside, lines 4–5
A(ii)	*inhale:*	blood to center away from holes	*followed by*	air in through holes, lines 6, 23–24
a(i)	*static:*	air inside	(air pressure)	water outside, lines 10–14
a(ii)	*unplug:*	air out up away from holes	*followed by*	water in through holes, line 15
Breathing out:				
B(i)	*static:*	blood withdrawn at center		air inside
B(ii)	*exhale:*	blood to surface toward holes	*follows*	air out through holes, lines 8, 25
b(i)	*static:*	air outside		water inside, lines 16–19
b(ii)	*unplug:*	air in down toward holes	*follows*	water out through holes, lines 20–21

Notes

Air in (a) and (b) is the analogue of blood in (A) and (B), and water in (a) and (b) is the analogue of air in (A) and (B); the correspondence is reinforced by the syntax of subordination, cf. the commentary on line 15.

The detailed explanation of a(i) and b(i) establishes that a stream of air and a stream of liquid can occupy the same amount of space and exert equivalent pressures.

Holes at the base of the clepsydra are analogous to pores in the skin (including, I suggest, the two big "pores" of the nostrils). There is some correspondence between the restraint of the pores at the surface of the body and the pressure of air at the perforated surface of the clepsydra in keeping the two elements separate at the "static" stage of A(i) and a(i).

The deliberate unplugging by the child in a(ii) and b(ii) is analogous to the mechanical initiation of movement in the blood.

The failure of the comparison, that air goes right outside the clepsydra through the top vent in a(ii) but blood does not leave the body, is diminished by concentrating on the movements in relation to the perforated surface in each case.

There is no implication of void in E.'s theory of respiration. Line 23 refers to the area of the heart and lungs that expands with blood and air during inhalation and returns to normal during exhalation. It is not that a previous "void" is filled but that additional material is taken in, and the chest expands to accommodate it.

92(101)

Tracking with nostrils fragments of animal bodies (which they) left from their paws on the soft grass

It is not certain that the two lines are consecutive, but the immediate context in the sources suggests a close relationship. Plutarch quotes the first in a simile about hounds trained to concentrate on a single scent (*curios.* 520e–f) and, under the heading of why spoors are difficult to track in spring (*quaest. nat.* 917e), as part of an explanation of how dogs keep to a trail by picking up the ἀπορροαί left by animals. The second line is quoted by Alexander in a question about the extinction of the body's distinctive odor at death.

1 κέρματα: the first word was obviously puzzling, as the variants show. There are only late parallels for κέρματα as "fragments," but κείρω is well established (and cf. κερματίζω, Plato *Rep.* 525e, *Tim.* 62a). μυκτῆρες, specifically for "nostrils," was not used in the previous fragment, but it was obviously available if an unambiguous reference to nasal breathing only were needed.

2: for various suggestions for filling the lacuna, cf. the *ap. crit.* If this line follows the preceding one, a neuter plural subject for the verb would be needed, relating to the previous genitives. Perhaps the original was something like ⟨ὅσσ'⟩ ἀπέλειπε ποδῶν ⟨τοιαῦτ'⟩ ἀπαλῇ περὶ ποίῃ, cf. τὰς ἀπορροίας . . . ἃς ἐναπολείπει τὰ θηρία τῇ ὕλῃ in Plutarch's paraphrase, *quaest. nat.* 917e. Whatever the reading, it is clear that a physical explanation of smell is put forward. The odor is a series of effluent particles that meet the nostrils of the trained hound, and so indicate the trail, cf. the next fragment.

93(102)

In this way all things are apportioned breathing and smelling.

Theophrastus briefly summarizes E.'s theory of smell at *Sens.* 9 and criticizes it in some detail in 21–22, where the quotation is given as the climax of E.'s account. The context shows that ὀσμή (or ὀδμή) is to be understood as the sense rather than the object of smell, but the ambiguity, strengthened by the plural, persists; the emission of odors, as well as the ability, however primitive, to perceive them, is general. The point that leads to the climax of this line in Theophrastus is that smelling relates to breathing and is explicable by it: ὄσφρησιν δὲ γίνεσθαι τῇ ἀναπνοῇ, *Sens.* 9. Theophrastus counters this with examples of animals that do not breathe but have a sense of smell, and also by saying that if the keenest sense of smell accompanies the most vigorous breathing, then those with short or labored breath should be most sensitive to smells, which is not the case (*Sens.* 21–22). For Theophrastus, breathing is not the αἴτιον of smell but is connected with it κατὰ συμβεβηκός; however, his excessive zeal in criticizing E. leads to inconsistencies in his own theory (cf. G. M. Stratton *Theophrastus and the Greek Physiological Psychology before Aristotle* pp. 39–40). Odor, for E., is the actual emanation from the object that stimulates the sense when it is symmetrical with the pores of the organ. In man and developed forms of animal life the organ is most obviously the nostrils, and despite Theophrastus, it seems E. was aware that respiratory difficulties affect the sense of smell, cf. Aetius 4.17.2. It was argued in the commentary on 91(100) that pores over the skin, including the nostrils, are involved in respiration, so it is likely that E. recognized the sensitivity to smell that extends over the body in lower forms of life— and the wide application of both kinds of smelling is indicated by πάντα here, corresponding to that in 91(100).1. On the modernity of E. here cf. *Chambers Enc.* s.v. "Taste and Smell," where it is said that the entry of odorous molecules into ultramicroscopic holes pierced in the outer cover- ing of the body's structure is still the accepted explanation of the working of this sense, and *Enc. Brit. Macr.* IV, p. 188a, where the entry of odorant particles into special receptive "sockets" on the cell surface is put for- ward as one of the latest theories in the still unresolved debate over how smell works.

FRAGMENTS 94–101 MIND, HOLY MIND, AND THE ADVANTAGE OF RIGHT THINKING

94(105)
(the heart) nourished in seas of blood coursing to and fro, and there above all is what men call thought, because, for men, blood around the heart is thought.

The lines are quoted in Stobaeus from Porphyry's *De Styge*. The cognitive function of the concentration of blood around the heart is connected to Homeric evidence that the heating of the heart-blood in anger results in temporary loss of reason.

1 : Grotius's τεθραμμένη is generally accepted for τετραμμένα, except by Bollack, who keeps the MSS reading, *Empédocle* vol. 3, p. 445. He suggests an adaptation of Homer's description of the four springs by Circe's cave (*Od.* 5.70–71) for the four elements centered around the heart. (Variations, however, on τετραμμένος occur in the same fourth foot position six times in Homer, which may account for the reading here.) A subject is required, possibly κραδίη (the heart being the first organ to be articulated in the embryo, Censorinus 6.1, DK 31 A84), rather than φρήν or φρόνησις, which would preempt νόημα in the following lines. ἀντιθορόντος (Scaliger's emendation of ἀντιθ(ο)ρῶντος) could not be "leap to meet" (LSJ) but "leap up in turn," cf. κραδίη ἐκθρῴσκει, *Il.* 10.94, and ἀναθρῴσκειν of the blood in 91(100).8, 25. Blood moves to and from the heart as it balances the intake and exhalation of air in respiration.

2 μάλιστα: for thought by other means in the body cf. 1(2).1 and 5(3).4–8. κικλήσκεται: the suggestion κυκλίσκεται is unsuitable, as the movement of the blood for E. is oscillatory and not circulatory, and the verb is unknown.

3 ἀνθρώποις: all things think (cf. 100(110).10), and the quality of the thought depends on the constituent elements. For men these are best blended in the blood, but there is thinking inferior and superior to that of man, cf. chap. 3. περικάρδιον: first attested here but taken up in medical writings and in the Aristotelian commentators, cf. Rufus *Onom.* 163, Galen *us. part.* 6.16, Simplicius *in Phys.* 392.24. The third line is quoted separately in the Etymologies and frequently paraphrased, e.g., Cicero *Tusc.* 1.19 "E. animam esse censet cordi suffusum sanguinem," Macrobius *Somn. Scip.* 1.14 and Tertullian *De Anim.* 5 "E. a sanguine animam," Galen *Plac. Hipp.* 2.8.

In the fifth century Greek medicine was divided on the question of the heart or brain being the center of intelligence. The context of this fragment shows the survival of the adducement of Homeric evidence for the connection of the heart with thinking. It is hard to assess the influence E. might have had in the debate, but his stand is echoed in some of the Hippocratic writings, in Aristotle, and in the Epicureans and Stoics. (In *De Corde* 10, for example, man's intelligence is situated specifically in the left chamber of the heart; this was thought to be filled with an airlike substance having some affinities to Stoic *pneuma*, cf. C. R. S. Harris *The Heart and the Vascular System in Ancient Greek Medicine* pp. 94, 238–41, and passim.) E.'s particular innovation, however, is to relate thought not to the heart but to the blood coursing around it, cf. Aetius

4.5.8, Theodoretus 5.22. A detailed commentary giving evidence from observation on the connection of the constitution of the blood with intelligence is found in the Hippocratic *Flat.* 14, ending ἔχοιμι δ' ἂν πολλὰ τοιαῦτα εἰπεῖν, ἐν οἷσιν αἱ τοῦ αἵματος ἐξαλλαγαὶ τὴν φρόνησιν ἐξαλλάσσουσιν, and cf. *Reg.* 1.25 and *Anon. Lond.* 1 on Hippias of Croton. For E. it is the exact mixture of the four roots in the blood that accounts for thought, and also probably for the prohibition against bloodshed given in the *Katharmoi* (cf. Theophrastus *Sens.* 10 and frs. 122–25). It also seems likely that blood played a physical part in bringing to the cardial nexus the understanding achieved by the πόροι νοῆσαι spread over the body, 5(3).4, 7, and cf. 1(2).1. There is a concentration of blood in the individual organs, which accounts for their relative efficiency (cf. Theophrastus *Sens.* 24), and in respiration the blood in the vessels oscillates between the pores at the surface of the body and the area of the heart.

95(132)

Happy the man who has gained the wealth of divine understanding, wretched he who cherishes an unenlightened opinion about the gods.

The fragment is given by Clement in a series of "thefts" from Greek texts to parallel Christian writings, and he emphasizes the connection of knowledge with happiness, and ignorance with unhappiness. But there is also in the fragment the Parmenidean contrast between knowledge and light and *doxa* and darkness (and cf. σκοτίη γνώμη, Democritus fr. 11).

The fragment connects closely with the next two, which give part of the content of the required understanding, with 99(129) in the example of the man who did achieve understanding, and with 100(110), which shows how the individual will be ὄλβιος or δειλός. The physiological term πραπίδες in line 1 here, 99(129).2, 4, and 100(110).1 strengthens the connection, and the phrase πραπίδων ἐκτήσατο πλοῦτον is actually repeated at 99(129).2. The remaining fragments from here to the end of the *Physics* cohere and plausibly belong together in this position, cf. chap. 4. On πραπίδες and thought cf. Hesiod *Theog.* 656 and the commentary on 100(110).

96(133)

It is not possible to bring (the divine) close within reach of our eyes or to grasp him with the hands, by which the broadest path of persuasion for men leads to the mind.

Clement quotes the fragment with Solon fr. 16 and John 1.18 on the
divine as invisible. Theodoretus, no doubt copying him, connects it with
6(4).1–2 (which supports the assignation to the *Physics*), Solon fr. 16, and
Antisthenes fr. 24 in the context of relying on πίστις when the senses
prove inadequate. (Solon's fr. 17 is even more relevant: πάντῃ δ' ἀθαν-
άτων ἀφανὴς νόος ἀνθρώποισιν.) The fragment contrasts knowledge
within the range of the senses (the senses, for example, perceive the
characteristics and activity of earth, air, fire, and water) and knowledge
outside the range of the senses, such as that of the nature of the divine,
cf. the commentary on Philia, 8(17).21, 25–26.

1 πελάσασθαι: the transitive use of the middle is paralleled in *Il.*
17.341; for the meaning of the line cf. Diels *Hermes* 1880, pp. 171–72,
with reference to *Il.* 1.587, 3.306.

2 ᾗπερ: Karsten's emendation has been retained, the relative referring
to both sight and touch, which are the most convincing of the senses. The
"wagon road" exaggerates the πόρος νοῆσαι of 5(3).7, cf. ἐπὶ φρένα
πίστιος ὁρμή, 103(114).3 and Parmenides fr. 4.4. The road to understanding via the senses is direct and unimpeded, but it is not the way by
which the divine is grasped.

97(134)
*For he is not equipped with a human head on a body, [two branches do not spring
from his back,] he has no feet, no swift knees, no shaggy genitals, but he is mind
alone, holy and inexpressible, darting through the whole cosmos with swift thoughts.*

The five lines are quoted by Ammonius in a context of E.'s censure of
anthropomorphic gods, where, in particular, Apollo is referred to, and in
these lines, τὸ θεῖον πᾶν. Tzetzes, *Chil.* 13.74–78, gives the five lines as
a summary of E'.s view of god, as well as lines 4–5 at *Chil.* 7.517–18,
which are prefaced with 'Ε. τῷ τρίτῳ τε τῶν Φυσικῶν δεικνύων. The
defense of Tzetzes against Diels here (and Diels's assignation of the
fragment to the *Katharmoi*) has been taken up by Wilamowitz, *Kleine
Schriften* p. 498; Bignone, *Empédocle* pp. 631–49; Zuntz, *Persephone* pp.
214–18; van der Ben, *Proem* pp. 44–46; and see chap. 3. The first line is
given by Olympiodorus on E.'s anticipation of Plato's denial of anything
σωματικόν to god, and the whole fragment without line 2 is in the margin.

Following the marginalia I would write the fragment without the
second line. It does not fit grammatically after the first, the point is made
without including shoulders and arms with the other parts mentioned,

and the fragment has elegance and balance as a quatrain. The line comes from 22(29/28).1 (and little rests on whether the active or middle form of the verb is read), where it starts a similar quatrain—two lines of denial of anthropomorphic organs and two of positive definition. The rhythm and details of the first couplet of this fragment recall Hephaestos wiping his face, hands, neck, and shaggy chest at *Il.* 18.413–14 (which probably accounts for the variants χέρες for πόδες, and στήθεα for μήδεα in line 3).

4 ἔπλετο: for the aorist of the verb with present sense, cf. *Il.* 2.480, 6.434, 7.31, *Od.* 21.397.

5 φροντίσι: the Homeric use of the dative with ἀΐσσων and compounds is for rushing with a sword or spear, *Il.* 8.88, 10.348, 11.361, or with horses, 17.460. E. here gives a striking adaptation of the epic construction, combined with the Homeric recognition of the speed of thought, cf. *Od.* 7.36.

Ammonius and Tzetzes emphasize that the fragment is E.'s definition of god, and his own recognition of innovation here is seen in 3(131) and 95(132). He is giving an ἀγαθὸς λόγος of the gods to counteract the dark *doxa* which makes men miserable. The true gods are earth, air, fire, and water, and Philia and Neikos, cf. 7(6), 51(59), 8(17).24, 11(16); traditional gods are combinations of the four roots formed in the same way as plants, animals, and men. But the sphere is a god, comprising the four roots, which have been brought together by Philia in balance, joy, and stillness, cf. 21(27), 22(29/28), 24(31). The φρὴν ἱερή is surely to be connected with it, as the similarities between this fragment and 22(29/28) show. The four roots in proportion give thought; for man the best mixture is achieved in the blood, which is consequently the instrument of thought (cf. 94(105) and Theophrastus *Sens.* 10), but for the god the mixture is exact, a one-to-one proportion of the elements throughout. This means that the φρήν is physical (cf. καταΐσσεται used of the intake of air, 91(100).7) but inaccessible to the senses, for perfect mixture has no perceptible qualities, cf. chap. 3, pp. 73–74. The φρὴν ἱερή would be that which now remains of the sphere-god after the shattering of its unity and rest by Strife—holding at the circumference and, in the form of swift thoughts, darting through the whole. The new sense of κόσμος (cf. Heraclitus fr. 30), emphasized by ἅπας, broadens traditional views of god and opens the way to a new theology based on the denial of anthropomorphic features, the positive connection with thought, and the world dimension that has been adumbrated by Xenophanes, frs. 23–26. For the connection of this fragment with the daimons, cf. the commentary on 107(115).

Ammonius indicates that E. specifically criticized the traditional view of Apollo. Apart from a *Proem* to Apollo attributed to E. (D.L. 8.57; see chap. 1 and the context of 35[41]), a connection between E. and Apollo is lacking, and an introduction of the Pythagoreans is unhelpful (cf. Guthrie *HGP* vol. 2, p. 256, n. 1). If Ammonius is correct, two explanations for a connection may tentatively be put forward: (1) as prophets, minstrels, and healers instantiate the highest type of life on earth (132(146).1), the patron of these ways of life would be held in highest regard; (2) Apollo is to be explained as the intelligent source of heavenly fire and so accounts for Hippolytus' notice that E. identified ὁ θεός with νοερὸν πῦρ, . . . καὶ (ἔφη) συνεστάναι ἐκ πυρὸς τὰ πάντα καὶ εἰς πῦρ ἀναλυθήσεσθαι (*RH* 1.3, DK 31 A31). The basic idea here (in spite of confusion with Heraclitus and the Stoics), that everything has its origin and end in an intellectual but physically based principle of world dimensions, supports the contention that φρὴν ἱερή is derived from and will again identify with the god of 22(29/28). (S.M. Darcus, "Daimon Parallels the Holy Phren in E.," *Phronesis* 22, pp. 175–90, analyzes the meaning of φρήν in terms of activity and shape and of the cognates φρόντις and φρονεῖν. The conclusions that the "sphere of Love" is one of the stages of the Holy Phren's activity and that the spherical shape persists are in agreement with the above argument, but the suggestion that the Phren has only two *phrontides*—Love and Hate—is without foundation. Some clarification of *phrontides*, or at least a dual, is needed to support such a basic identification, but there is no hint in E. or the doxography that νεῖκος, described as οὐλόμενον and μαινόμενον, is a *phrontis* of god, and that half his thinking is concerned with hate. Aristotle expressly denies it, *Metaph.* 1000b5, and cf. further the commentary on 107[115].)

98(27a)
no discord or unseemly warring in the limbs

Bergk attributed the line, quoted anonymously in Plutarch, to E. The attribution is justified, for Δῆρις is contrasted with Ἁρμονίη in 116(122).2, ἐν μελέεσσιν repeats the phrase at 23(30).1, and Plutarch's context of φιλία and φιλοφροσύνη is Empedoclean, cf. 119(130).2.

All editors accept without question the reference of this fragment to the description of the sphere in 21(27) and 22(29/28). The "limbs" are said to be those of the sphere given in 23(30).1 and 24(31), and when the roots come together in Love, Strife obviously is absent. But Plutarch has no hint of such a cosmic explanation. He is speaking of the man who comes to virtue through philosophy by means of "the speech in the mind" (ὁ ἐνδιάθετος λόγος), which aims at *philia*. Such a man is σύμφωνος ἑαυτῷ, full of φιλοφροσύνη; the absence of *stasis* and *dēris* is explained as the absence of conflict between πάθος and λόγος—all his parts are εὐμενῆ (cf. the use of εὐμενέως, 100(110).2) and φίλα (cf. the description of the wise man in Horace *Sat.* 2.7.86, "in se totus, teres atque rotundus"). The line therefore probably belongs with the contrast, given in 100(110), between following E.'s philosophy and yielding to human desires, and with the example of the wise man in 99(129)—i.e., one who instantiates, as far as possible, divine intelligence in man. The observed behavior of earth, air, fire, and water, and of Love and Strife, reflects their cosmic activity, cf. the commentary on 25(22); divinity and holy thought are explained in terms of the harmonious mixture of constituent parts (cf. the commentary on the previous fragment), and it would be observed in man that attention to the right kind of thinking results in the physical constitution of the individual being balanced and strifeless, cf. the commentaries on the next two fragments. To this extent the individual is a microcosm.

99(129)

And there was among them a man knowing an immense amount, who had acquired a great treasure of thoughts, master especially of all kinds of wise works; for whenever he reached out with all his thoughts, easily he saw each of the things that there are, in ten and even twenty generations of men.

A reference to Pythagoras here is given in the source common to Iamblichus and Porphyry, and also in Diogenes Laertius (from Timaeus), who adds that some say that Parmenides is meant. This suggests that the person was anonymous in E. but easily assumed to be Pythagoras because of his proverbial wisdom, cf. Heraclitus frs. 40, 129, Herodotus 4.95. Parmenides is an attractive suggestion for the reference, and his influence on E. is pervasive, but the recognition of plurality and time implicit in the last two lines requires explanation.

The meaning of ἐν κείνοισιν, and so the context of the whole fragment, is in dispute. Editors after Stein assign it to the "Golden Age" of 118(128).1 because of the repetition of ἐν κείνοισιν. But the reason is insufficient. Pythagoras did not live in the distant past, and if the refer-

ence is anonymous, what is the significance of an exceptionally wise but unknown person living then? Nor is it a solution to put Pythagoras in an
age of heroes preceding the present age of iron (as Zuntz does, *Persephone* p.
209), for E. surely would not have believed in a distinctive heroic age only
fifty years before his own time. Van der Ben sees the τις as a netherworld
guide, *Proem* p. 181. But these interpretations create unnecessary difficulties. In 95(132) the man who has a treasure of thoughts is congratulated,
and in 100(110) Pausanias is exhorted to increase his wisdom by his own
effort and concentration. Between the two it would be appropriate to cite
as a model the example of a man, perhaps Pythagoras, who did have a
treasure of thoughts and wide-ranging wisdom (cf. the exercises in
concentration which aimed to enhance the strength of the soul, Burkert
Lore and Science in Ancient Pythagoreanism p. 213).

3 σοφῶν ἐπιήρανος ἔργων: cf. καλῶν ἐ. ἔργων, Ion *Eleg.* 1.15, where
the καλὰ ἔργα of which Dionysus is master are drinking, playing, and
thinking just thoughts. The phrase here covers understanding of different
matters, and also perhaps the practical application of this understanding,
especially in medicine, music, and prophecy, cf. 102(112).9–12 and
132(146).1–2. An exaggeration of the skills that come from increased understanding is given in 101(111). Zuntz, following Stein, transposes
lines 2 and 3, although 1 and 2 are quoted as a couplet in Diogenes.

4 πραπίδεσσιν: πραπίδες, recurring in this last group of fragments
in the *Physics* at 95(132).1, 100(110).1, and 2 and 4 here, like φρήν and
φρένες (cf. 96(133).3, 103(114).3, 8(17).14), is a reminder of the physical
basis of thought. The verb ὀρέξαιτο also has a physical connotation, and
it is picked up by ἐπορέξεαι in line 6 of the next fragment, which further
anchors this fragment to its present position.

5 ῥεῖά γε: a comparison with ἀργαλέη γε, 103(114).2, tells against
emendation here. For the metaphor in λεύσσεσκεν cf. Parmenides fr.
4.1.

6: for the reading of the line cf. Denniston *Greek Particles* p. 530 and
van der Ben *Proem* p. 185. Ten and twenty are alternatives, and the numbers are not to be taken precisely, cf. the gifts ten and twenty times as
great that Achilles would disdain, *Il.* 9.379, 22.349. It would be unwarranted to suppose that this line refers to Pythagoras remembering twenty,
or an indefinite number, of incarnations, as has been understood by the
commentators, e.g., Sturz ad loc., O'Brien *ECC* p. 335, n. 1, Burkert
Lore and Science p. 213, Guthrie *HGP* vol. 2, p. 251, and if αἰών has only
human connotations, the memory is of twenty incarnations as a man.

This is unlikely. The fragment sets out to describe a wise man, to be an example, I would suggest, for Pausanias. The wealth of wisdom acquired is emphasized in each of the first three lines; the last three show that when this wisdom is applied there is understanding of a comprehensive range of topics, covering a considerable extent of time. The last line could refer to the future rather than the past, and more plausibly so, given 132(146). The line is an adaptation of the assumed range of the prophet's wisdom, ὃς ᾔδη τά τ᾽ ἐόντα τά τ᾽ ἐσσόμενα πρό τ᾽ ἐόντα, *Il.* 1.70, and cf. Parmenides 4.1, 1.28.

100(110)

If you push them firmly under your crowded thoughts, and contemplate them favorably with unsullied and constant attention, assuredly all these will be with you through life, and you will gain much else from them, for of themselves they will cause each thing to grow into the character, according to the nature of each. But if you yourself should reach out for things of a different kind, for the countless trivialities which come among men and dull their meditations, straightaway these will leave you as the time comes round, longing to reach their own familiar kind; for know that all things have intelligence and a share of thought.

This important fragment is given by Hippolytus, who significantly links it with 107(115) and sees in it a reference to νοητὴ τρίτη τις δύναμις other than Love and Strife. He gives the last line after 77(109) and applies it to parts of fire engaged in thought. This line is also quoted by Sextus, who takes it to include plants and animals. The fragment is discussed by H. Schwabl, *WS* 1956, pp. 49–56; A. A. Long *CQ* 1966, pp. 268–73; and Bollack, *Empédocle* vol. 3, pp. 576–85, who prints it as the last fragment of the poem.

1: σφαδίνῃσιν is unknown, hence the correction to σφ᾽ ἀδινῇσιν (ὑπὸ πραπίδεσσιν)—the throbbing, crowded thoughts in the thorax under which "they" are to be pushed (cf. 9(12).3 for the meaning of ἐρείσας) and then contemplated. (So Penelope speaks of πυκιναί . . . ἀμφ᾽ ἀδινὸν κῆρ / ὀξεῖαι μελεδῶναι, *Od.* 19.516–17.) What does σφε, the object of ἐρείσας and ἐποπτεύσῃς, refer to? Answers include: "die Gründkraften der Natur," Schwabl *WS* p. 54; "die Lehren des Meisters," Diels *Vors.* 31 B110, "true statements about the world (conceived in physical terms)," Long *CQ* 1966, p. 269; "les puissances . . . sans doute les six," Bollack *Empédocle* vol. 3, p. 577. These suggestions are all to some extent correct.

In Homer words are winged (*Il.* 1.201, 2.7, 4.69, etc.), go past the barrier of the teeth (*Il.* 4.350, 14.83, etc.), and are put by the listener into his or her θυμός—μῦθον πεπνυμένον ἔνθετο θυμῷ (*Od.* 1.361, 21.355); cf. Hesiod *Erga* 274. So here. Pausanias is being urged to take the words that E. has spoken on the nature and activity of the four roots and Love and Strife, words which are themselves well constituted of the four roots, to put them deep down under his other thoughts, and in the language of initiation rites, to contemplate them with the correct disposition, and with assiduous and uncontaminated attention. Such a physical representation of words and thoughts, found in Homer, continues through the work of other Presocratics (Heraclitus is an obvious example) to Plato (in such passages as *Tim.* 71b, where thoughts are said to have reflections on the liver's surface), Aristotle (e.g., *Metaph.* 1072b20 νοητὸς γίγνεται θιγγάνων καὶ νοῶν, ὥστε ταὐτὸν νοῦς καὶ νοητόν), and the Stoics' assumption of φωναί as σώματα (cf. S. E. *adv. math.* 8.12).

2: the initiation vocabulary of the line expresses Pausanias' meditation on E.'s words in terms of his being granted the final revelation after purificatory rituals, but this is to add solemnity to the poem's epilogue rather than to indicate "Orphic" or Pythagorean affiliations on E.'s part. (The language of the exordium is similar, cf. ἐκ δ' ὁσίων στομάτων καθαρὴν ὀχετεύσατε πηγήν, 2(3).2.) μελέται indicates constant practice and effort, as in athletic training, military duty, or rehearsing, cf. LSJ s.v.

3 ταῦτα: the same reference as σφε in line 1. The thoughts, with their physical basis, if rightly regarded, will stay with Pausanias through life; the additional bonus is given in line 5. The verse is Homeric, cf. *Od.* 2.306.

4: τῶνδε κτήσεαι seems the best interpretation of a corrupt text, preferable to a future perfect form or a future middle with passive sense, for which LSJ gives only Plotinus as an example.

4-5: as with ταῦτα in line 3, αὔξει is probably transitive (cf. Long *CQ* 1966, p. 270, n. 1), and its object ἕκαστον, i.e., each appropriate thought within the body. The words and thoughts of E. are combinations of earth, air, fire, and water, and, being wise words, are well-blended combinations. If Pausanias takes them in and studies them, he will find that they will increase his like pieces of knowledge in the appropriate way—ὅπη φύσις ἐστὶν ἑκάστῳ. The process is cumulative, and so this increase in turn makes Pausanias more receptive to additional knowledge. εἰς ἦθος: the noun is ambiguous. It might refer to the individual constituent parts of earth, air, fire, and water as at 8(17).28, and is so taken by Long, *CQ* 1966, p. 269: "the ἦθος of fire would be fieriness"; but taking in E.'s words is not going to increase the fieriness of the fire in Pausanias. Moreover, the thought is composite, and its activity as separate elements is the result of rejection, not assimilation. The ἦθος could be that of each thought which is stimulated to grow in the appropriate way, but this is covered by the clause ὅπη φύσις ἐστὶν ἑκάστῳ. Most probably ἦθος refers to Pausanias' own character, i.e., his thinking self. The knowledge conveyed by E.'s thoughts and words, after being admitted and contemplated, becomes embedded in the heart area; it thus brings Pausanias closer to the condition of being a wise man both by causing the amount of right thoughts in the constitution to grow and by increasing his receptiveness to such thoughts. The basic idea was put forward by Parmenides in fr. 16 and was used previously by E. in 8(17).14, 79(106), and 80(108). Pausanias' control of the process brings lines 4–5 close to fr. 119 of Heraclitus, and also to passages like Sophocles' *Ajax* 595, where Ajax refuses to allow his ἦθος to be educated. ἦθος also may well be the specific reference for νοητὴ τρίτη τις δύναμις in the Hippolytus context, i.e., the well-blended combination of elements that has cognitive powers, observed in the cosmos as φρὴν ἱερή and in the individual as the thinking self, cf. the commentary on the daimons, 107(115).

6–7: the lines deliberately recall 1(2).1–2 in expression and content. At the beginning of the poem E. contrasts men of blunt thoughts and limited experience who claim knowledge of the whole with Pausanias, who will achieve genuine understanding. Now, on completion of his explanation, E. promises Pausanias that the understanding will be permanent, given good will and assiduous concentration, but if Pausanias allows himself to be distracted, the wise thoughts will leave and each of the constituent parts will become separate and drawn to its own elemental mass. ἀλλοῖα and μυρία δειλά refer to the variety of particulars around us with which men busy themselves, but which, when they divert or intrude, impede our understanding of the real nature of the world. περιπλομένοιο χρόνοιο: cf. the similar phrasing in 8(17).29 and 16(26).1 for the time of the domination of the elements. The resolution of a well-blended combination of elements, which comprises a thought, into its parts, is a microcosm of the perfect mixture of the sphere separating into individual elemental masses. The χρόνος for the individual must be his so-called death, and it contrasts with the αἰών of line 3 (cf. *Il.* 16.453). If therefore Pausanias heeds E.'s teaching there will be a sense in which he survives death, cf. the commentaries on 107(115) and 132(146).

9 φίλην ἐπὶ γένναν ἱκέσθαι: the basic φρόνησις (cf. line 10) exhibited by earth, air, fire, and water is an awareness of another part like itself

and a tendency to move toward it when not held in a compound by Love.

10 γάρ: the particle shows that the elements are to be included in the πάντα that have φρόνησις; for the form of primitive awareness that is the "intelligence" of the roots, cf. the commentary on line 9. In plant and animal life the thinking becomes more sophisticated as elements in combinations are involved. Men, because of the special character of the heart-blood, are able to comprehend the simple and the complex. With E. (and with Pausanias if his disposition and attention are as they should be) the blending of the mixture in the organ of thought becomes exact, and the real nature of the world intelligible. At the highest level the individual would communicate with the φρὴν ἱερή, which itself is constituted of elements arranged in the same way, cf. Long *CQ* 1966, pp. 270–71, the commentaries on 80(108), 81(103), and 97(134).4, and chap. 3.

101(111)

You will learn remedies for ills and help against old age, since for you alone shall I accomplish all these things. You will check the force of tireless winds, which sweep over land and destroy fields with their blasts; and again, if you wish, you will restore compensating breezes. After black rain you will bring dry weather in season for men, and too after summer dryness you will bring tree-nourishing showers (which live in air), and you will lead from Hades the life-force of a dead man.

The fragment is quoted by Diogenes from Satyrus. E. is called a doctor, but Gorgias' claim to have witnessed E.'s "wonder-working" is added. The lines are given in support of this claim and are followed by an account from Timaeus of E. checking winds (and consequently being called κωλυσάνεμος), and from Heraclides of E. curing the woman who was *apnous*. Both accounts are in the *Suda* in the context of the whole fragment, with κωλυσάνεμος and γόης repeated. Clement has the wind-checking story as the basis for lines 3–5, and he connects it with 102(112).12; the wind is described as noxious and causing sterility, whereas in Timaeus' account it is merely violent and damages the crops. It is checked by stretching asses' skins along hill (or possibly cliff) tops or, in Plutarch's account (*curios.* 515c), by blocking a gorge. It is likely that the various accounts go back to Timaeus, who made up the story from E.'s lines, using the connection between skins and weather magic (cf. *Od.* 10.19 and Guthrie's comments, *HGP* vol. 2, p. 134, n. 2); and perhaps there was some play on Pausanias' name. There is, however, a slight possibility that E. made a practical attempt at constructing a windbreak, in the same enterprising spirit in which he is said to have diverted a river; see chap. 1. The main point is that E. expects that an understanding of the nature of earth, air, fire, and water alone and in combinations will bring with it the ability to manipulate them. This may well have been thought to extend to medicine, where a knowledge of respiration could lead to the restoration of the breathing mechanism, cf. the commentary on line 9. Bollack puts the fragment at the beginning of the *Physics* between 1(2) and 2(3). This makes the promise of "wonder-working" the purpose of the exposition rather than some benefits added after the exposition has been grasped. Karsten and Mullach take it as a fragment ἐκ τῶν 'Ιατρικῶν.

1: that two items are mentioned here, (1) remedies for illnesses and (2) means of keeping off old age, is supported by the similar phrasing in *Hom. Hym. Apoll.* 193. E. confirms his success in (1) at 102(112).11–12, and (2) is an obvious extension of (1) in the practical application of the knowledge acquired.

2: in the singular address, emphatic here as at the beginning of the poem, E. is in the tradition of Hesiod and Theognis. In assuming a very limited audience capable of appreciating a complex philosophical argument E. follows Heraclitus and Parmenides. There is no need to suppose (from Plutarch *quaest. conv.* 728e) that E. is being particularly Pythagorean.

3–8: these six lines are devoted to showing how the balance of the elemental natural states should be maintained, with the expectation of eventually controlling the elements and achieving that balance. παλίντιτα (line 5) is found elsewhere only at *Od.* 1.379, and in an active sense; δενδρεόθρεπτα is ἅπ. λεγ.

8 †τάτ' αἰθέρι ναιήσονται†: the future form of the verb, adopted with a query by DK, is unacceptable in form and sense. The ῥεύματα come after summer drought, and this rules out versions with ἐν θέρει. Bollack suggests τά τ'αἰθέρι ναιετάουσι and sees a reference to "fleuves du ciel," comparable to the fires in the earth of 32(52), as an example of the present composite nature of the elements (*Empédocle* vol. 3, p. 25). E. seems to be adapting the Homeric αἰθέρι ναίων (of Zeus, *Il.* 2.412) as well as indicating that the ῥεύματα are rainfalls rather than floods.

9: as with the account of wind checking, that of the *apnous* may have been fabricated from these lines, or E. may have been emboldened to write them as a result of some success on a particular occasion. The interest in respiration shown in 91(100) and a confidence in understanding the process may have encouraged E. to try to restore the breathing mechanism in the *apnous*, and resuscitation could look like bringing the dead to life. For the details in Heraclides and an assessment, see chap. 1. The linking of medical practice to philosophical theory is condemned by the author of *Ancient Medicine* (20.1); the particular mention of E. there suggests that he did expect his knowledge to have practical application.

11. *Katharmoi*

102(112)

My friends who live in the great town of the tawny Acragas, on the city's citadel, who care for good deeds (havens of kindness for strangers, men ignorant of misfortune), greetings! I tell you I travel up and down as an immortal god, mortal no longer, honored by all as it seems, crowned with ribbons and fresh garlands. Whenever I enter prospering towns I am revered by both men and women. They follow me in countless numbers, to ask where their advantage lies, some seeking prophecies, others, long pierced by harsh pains, ask to hear the word of healing for all kinds of illnesses.

From Diogenes' quotation of the first two lines at 8.54 (αὐτὸς ἐναρχόμενος τῶν Καθαρμῶν φησιν) it is clear that this is the beginning of the *Katharmoi*. At 8.61 Diogenes connects the fragment with the story of the *apnous* (cf. 101(111).9) and gives it as Heraclides' evidence for E. being ἰατρός and μάντις. At 8.66, lines 4–5 (χαίρετε . . . πωλεῦμαι) are said to be Timaeus' evidence for E. being ἀλαζὼν καὶ φίλαυτος. The connection with 101(111) is found again in Clement, specifically lines 3–5 of that fragment with 10 and 12 here. In *Anth. Gr.* 9.569, *Suda*, and Philostratus, line 4 is taken closely with 108(117). The line is explained by Sextus (*adv. math.* 1.302), not, according to the obvious assumption, as a boast but as arising from the conviction that E. had kept free from evil, and so, by means of the god within, apprehended the god without (τῷ ἐν ἑαυτῷ θεῷ τὸν ἐκτὸς κατείληφεν); this interpretation is supported by Plotinus, 4.7.10.38. The line commonly accepted as the third of this fragment is given only by Diodorus, to illustrate, in his context, the hospitality of the citizens of Acragas.

1–4 ὦ φίλοι . . . χαίρετε: E. greets his peers in Acragas from abroad (as the present tenses in lines 5–8 show). He was perhaps on a tour of southern Italy (cf. D.L. 8.52), and while on his travels dedicates his poem and sends its message to his friends in his home town. Diels gratuitously understands him as being in exile and hoping for a recall through flattery and the account of his triumphs (*SPAW* 1898, pp. 396–99). The exile is supported by Tucker (*CR* 1931, pp. 49–50), who argues somewhat perversely, because of difficulties with 123(145), that E. is ironically addressing his enemies, and he emphasizes Lucian's rendering of χαίρετε as "farewell" (*laps.* 2). But Lucian quotes the whole line as a parting consequent on apotheosis, comparable to the farewell to life of Euripides *Phoen.* 1453; this may be because the line was well known as an independent unit (cf. the sources for the fragment), and so used by Lucian for his own purposes. On a possible conflict with 123(145) cf. the commentary on that fragment.

1 κάτα: with ἄστυ, cf. *Il.* 12.318, *Od.* 17.246, 21.346. The citadel, named after its river below, was built on the natural fortification of a cliff overlooking the harbor, and the city wall followed the contours of the slope, cf. the map and description in Freeman *Sicily* vol. 2, pp. 222–32; according to Diodorus there were over 20,000 citizens (13.84). ξανθὸς ᾿Ακράγας is the river Acragas, which gave the name to the city and which was colored the brownish yellow of lions, horses, and honey (cf. 118(128).7)—a color epitomized in the name of the Trojan river Xanthos, cf. Zuntz *Persephone*, pp. 181–82, 186, Bruno *Form and Colour in Greek Painting*, p. 90.

3: Diodorus gives the line on its own as a description by E. of the people of Acragas. Sturz and subsequent editors insert it here, but it was deleted by H. Fränkel; Zuntz puts it later, in the second book of the *Katharmoi*, on the grounds that it is superfluous in this position and postpones the greeting to the fourth line. It does, however, make explicit the description ἀγαθῶν μελεδήμονες ἔργων. The particular good work that the men of Acragas practice and are well known for is their hospitality, αἰδοῖοι being active here—"showing kindness," as in Aeschylus *Supp.* 28. Diodorus gives the example of Tallias, who kept open house and once fed and clothed 500 cavalry (13.83). In the adjacent chapters he elaborates on the wealth of the citizens and the scale of their buildings— εὐδαιμονίας πλήρη is his description of the city, another way of saying that the citizens were κακότητος ἄπειροι. They could afford to be generous because they were untouched (as yet) by life's misery. (Guthrie, *HGP* vol. 2, p. 246, n. 3, quotes a similar phrase from the Orphic *Lithica*, line 15.)

4 ὑμῖν: the dative is probably "ethic" (cf. Hdt. 5.30), not limiting, with the narrator and listener juxtaposed, cf. Zuntz on Wilamowitz, *Persephone*, p. 190. Help in explaining θεὸς ἄμβροτος οὐκέτι θνητός comes from 132(146). The four top lives which precede joining the ranks of the gods are combined in E. as prophet, minstrel, healer, and leader, and the apparent unanimous recognition of his qualifications by people of different towns confirms his expectation. Sextus' interpretation of the line as the apprehension by pure *nous*—the god within—of the god without, and Plotinus' description of E. in the same context as εἰς τὴν πρὸς αὐτὸ (τὸ θεῖον) ὁμοιότητα ἀτενίσας, point to a connection with the end of the *Physics*, where it is suggested that pure mind, in contemplating wise thoughts, can approximate to the φρὴν ἱερή. E., like the Homeric heroes but in a new kind of way, is ἰσόθεος.

5 ὥσπερ ἔοικεν: the *Anth. Gr.* reading is preferable to the personal form, which is not normally used parenthetically or without an infinitive expressed. And ἔοικε meaning "it is fitting" is "mostly with neg. and followed by inf.," LSJ s.v. The obvious translation therefore is "as it seems," to be taken with the previous phrase. E.'s status as ἰσόθεος (cf. the previous note) is confirmed by the apparently unanimous acclamation accorded him.

6: the people show how they honor E. by crowning him with ribbons (a sign of victory, celebration, or honor generally, cf. Alcibiades transferring them from his own head to that of Socrates, Plato *Symp.* 212e) and fresh garlands (Alcibiades, *Symp.* loc. cit., has them of ivy and violets; olive, myrtle, and laurel are other possibilities). ταινίαις *metris causa*, cf. LSJ s.v.

7–8: for the crux I suggest πᾶσι δ' ἄμ' εὖτ' ἄν, translating, "by all, by both men and women, I am revered, whenever I enter prospering towns." E. is not saying that an entourage accompanies him from town to town, but that when he approaches a populous town its inhabitants flock to greet him and put their questions to him.

9: the thousands who greet him and walk with him want answers from him in his roles of *mantis* and healer. The πρὸς κέρδος ἀταρπός does not refer to a particular, separate request—"how can I make money?"— but to a general one—"what is the best way to proceed?"—subdivided into the areas of prophecy and medicine. E. presents himself here in the

Katharmoi as giving a practical application to the wisdom which in the *Physics* he promised was in Pausanias' power to achieve, frs. 100(110) and 101(111). In particular, knowledge of the structure and functioning of the human body, a key interest in the *Physics*, will help in effecting cures.

11 εὐηκέα βάξιν: the phrasing is ambiguous, cf. chap 1, p. 10. It would seem, however, to be less likely to mean an incantation than an instant diagnosis and suggestion for a remedy, which would be all that the conditions of a crowded street surgery would allow.

12: the line was retrieved and completed by Bergk, for the noun comparing *Il.* 5.399.

103(114)

My friends, I know that there is truth in the words which I shall speak, but indeed it comes hard to men, and the onrush of conviction to the mind is unwelcome.

Clement sees the fragment as praise for *pistis*, mentioning in the context Numa's temple to Fides as well as 1 Cor. 11: 5, Heraclitus fr. 28, and Plato *Tim.* 22c–e. The address sets the fragment in the *Katharmoi*, and the promise of truth puts it near the beginning of the poem. The language of cognition, however, is that of the *Physics*. The words which E. speaks enter, as they are heard, into the mind of the listener as a "stream" (ὁρμή here, πηγή at 2(3).2, and cf. 96(133).2–3), and because they are true they bring with them conviction. So in 6(4) Pausanias is urged to learn by analyzing in his σπλάγχνα the πιστώματα of the Muse, and in 100(110) to contemplate and assimilate them. E. compliments his friends in expecting them to be, like Pausanias, receptive to and appreciative of the truth. Most men have "narrow" perceptions, impeded by distractions, and so find it hard to admit truth and be convinced, cf. 1(2).1–5, 6(4).1, 100(110).6–8.

2 ἀργαλέη: the adjective goes with ἀληθείη, rather than being held in suspense until ὁρμή. The Homeric adjective for war, death, illness, fire, and *eris* (used in connection with the workings of Strife at 107(115).8) is applied by E. to the "hard" attainment of truth.

3 δύσζηλος: according to LSJ, the prefix δυσ- "destroys the good sense of a word or increases the bad," but the adjective δύσζηλος is translated as "eager." The word, however, continues the sense of ἀργαλέη, meaning "disagreeable," "troublesome," "invidious," cf.

Hesiod *Erga* 195. That the ordinary man resents new truths and does not want to be convinced is a commonplace, cf. Heraclitus fr. 97 and the outstanding example in Plato *Rep.* 515c–516e of the pain and vexation felt by the prisoner when first turned to the light.

104(11)

Fools, for their meditations are not far-reaching thoughts, men who suppose that what formerly did not exist comes into existence, or that something dies and is completely destroyed.

This fragment and 106(15) come close together in Plutarch, and although they are quoted from E. in support of the interpretation of 13(9) as a factual denial of generation from and destruction into the nonexistent, there is no indication of which poem they are from. They have been here transferred to the *Katharmoi* on the grounds that their emphatic affirmation of continuous existence, and for men in particular of life and experience before birth and after death, suits the subject matter of the *Katharmoi* and is appropriate as an introduction to 107(115). And the impatience with common belief sounded in the first word of this fragment follows easily on the difficulties the ordinary man has with the truth, as described in the previous fragment. The denial of absolute genesis and destruction is in Parmenidean language (cf. fr. 8.5–14) and reiterates the basic argument of E.'s *Physics*, cf. 8(17).30, 9(12), 11(16), 12(8), and 13(9).

1 νήπιοι: for the condemnation of thoughtless naiveté cf. 124(137).2. δολιχόφρονες: ἅπ. λεγ. δολιχαίων, 14(21).12, 15(23).8, is a similar coinage. For μέριμναι being blunted, cf. 1(2).2 and 100(110).7.

105(113)

But why do I lay stress on this, as if it were some great achievement of mine, if I am superior to many-times-dying mortal men?

The lines are quoted by Sextus after 102(112).4–5 as a further instance of E. claiming to be a god, not, says Sextus, from boastfulness, but because he has been able to apprehend the god without by means of the god within, i.e., by pure *nous*. To this could be added the specific superiority E. has in that, now possessing perfected *nous* and enjoying the highest form of life on earth, he is soon to join the gods and be free of death. All this is to be explained in the poem that follows.

2: πολυφθερέων is ἅπ. λεγ. and ambiguous. It could mean that men are liable to death in many forms or that individual men die many times. Although editors adopt the former sense, the latter is preferable. Instead of a cliché, superfluous after θνητῶν, there is a pointed contrast between men, who go through many lives and deaths ("exchanging one hard way of life for another," cf. 107(115).8), and E., who no longer has to do so; cf. the commentaries on 108(117) and 133(147).

106(15)

A man who is wise in such matters would not surmise in his mind that men are, and good and ill befall them, for as long as they live, for a lifetime as they call it, and that before they were formed, and after they have disintegrated, they do not exist at all.

For the context in Plutarch cf. the commentary on 104(11). An appropriate place for these lines is before 107(115), which explains how it is that men exist and good and ill happen to them both before and after the life known here. As Plutarch says, E. affirms that those who have not yet been born, and the already dead, *are* in some way. According to the *Physics* birth and death are arrangements and rearrangements of parts of eternally existing roots, and this groundwork helps toward the understanding of this fragment and the next.

1 φρεσί: cf. the index s.v. φρήν. Wisdom comes with the assimilation, analysis, and contemplation of statements of truth in the heart region; for the complete phrase, cf. *Il.* 1.107.

2: the subject of the verbs is, as in line 4, men; they use inaccurate terms, as at 13(19).5.

3: δειλά is symmetrically superior to δεινά with ἐσθλά, cf. Hesiod fr. 164(DK 2B7).

4 πάγεν: for the verb as an almost technical term in E. for the formation of organs and organisms from the elements, cf. 70(75).1, 78(107).1, and 85(86).

FRAGMENTS 107–108 THE DECREE OF NECESSITY

107(115)

There is a decree of necessity, ratified long ago by gods, eternal and sealed by broad oaths, that whenever one in error, from fear, (defiles) his own limbs, having by his error made false the oath he swore—daimons to whom life long-lasting is apportioned—he wanders from the blessed ones for three times countless years, being born throughout the time as all kinds of mortal forms, exchanging one hard way of life for another. For the force of air pursues him into sea, and sea spits him out onto earth's surface, earth casts him into the rays of blazing sun, and sun into the eddies of air; one takes him from another, and all abhor him. I too am now one of these, an exile from the gods and a wanderer, having put my trust in raving strife.

These lines are among the most crucial for an understanding of E., but they are fraught with difficulties. Before coming to details of text and meaning, there are basic questions of how many lines make up the fragment, in what order they belong, to which poem they should be assigned, what they are in the most general way concerned with, and what the basic context might be.

As can be seen from the text printed here, the fragment is an amalgam of Plutarch *exil*. 607c, where 5 lines out of 14 are given without any indication that there are omissions, and Hippolytus (*RH* 7.29.14–23), who quotes 13 lines and in a different order (the last is first and the first two last), interspersed with commentary. The last line and a half, however, was well known as an independent quotation (called τὸ πολυθρύλητον ἐκεῖνο περὶ ψυχῆς by Philoponus) but in three different versions.

On the strength of the phrase with which Plutarch introduces his selection of lines, ἐν ἀρχῇ τῆς φιλοσοφίας προαναφωνήσας, van der Ben reverts to the edition of Karsten and prints part of the fragment as the opening lines of the *Physics*; and then, because of their connection with this fragment, he moves 27 more fragments to the so-called *Proem* of the *Physics*. But Plutarch's phrase should not be given the strict meaning, "E. set out as the first lines of the *Physics* . . .," for the following reasons: (1) ἐν ἀρχῇ would need the article to mean unambiguously "at the very beginning of"; without it the sense could well be "as a starting point." (2) τῆς φιλοσοφίας may refer either to the *Katharmoi* or the *Physics*; Plutarch could have taken either the account of the elements or that of the *psychē* (as he paraphrased the context here) as E.'s "philosophy" par excellence, and either could have been read before the other in separate rolls. (3) προαναφωνήσας does not have to refer "not only to the proem but to the very first words of it" (van der Ben *Proem* p. 19), as Plutarch's phrase προανακρούσασθαι καὶ προαναφωνῆναι (*esu. carn.* 996b) shows. Plutarch discusses for the length of nine Teubner pages the prohibition against meat eating before he hesitatingly makes a start on the principle underlying it. (4) We know Plutarch is not giving verbatim the opening of the *Physics*, as he promptly drops lines 2, 4, and 7–12. (5) The first topic of the *Physics* is the four roots, cf. πρῶτον ἄκουε, 7(6).1, after an exhortation to Pausanias to listen, 4(1); according to van der Ben's ordering these both come inexplicably late. (6) A prohibition against eating meat was one of the themes of the *Katharmoi* (cf. Hippol. *RH* 7.30.3–4), and the explanation for it surely belongs with it in the same poem (cf. chap. 4). The openings of the poems are more likely to be: *Physics*—remarks on limited human knowledge, prayer to Muse, address to Pausanias, and major theme, fr. 7(6); *Katharmoi*—address to friends, remarks on limited human knowledge, and major theme, fr. 107(115).

After moving 28 fragments from their traditional position in the *Katharmoi* to the beginning of the *Physics*, van der Ben then interprets them as a *katabasis* myth. The first-person expositor is not, however, E. but "the 'I' of the myth," who tells of a visit he made while still alive to the realm of the dead in the far west of a flat (!) earth, to a meadow where the dead wait for a return to life. There a "perfect man" acted as a guide and led "the 'I' of the myth" to a cave where the dead put on flesh and blood and were addressed in a "prebirth speech" on the kinship of living creatures. Zuntz, in book 2 of *Persephone*, also interpreted fr. 107(115) as the introduction to a *katabasis* myth, which he claimed was the subject of the first book of the *Katharmoi*. In his version the daimon E., being guilty of murder, was led, probably by Hermes, to a place of horror in the Netherworld, the abode of Furies and monsters and the reception ground for exiles awaiting incarnation. From there he came to a cave and was addressed by a deity, probably Persephone, in a long speech explaining the law governing incarnations. However, the account given here of this and the next fragment rejects their incorporation into a *katabasis* myth of any kind as being unsupported by ancient testimony and requiring a biased reading of the text. The fragments are comprehensible on their own and in relation to the theories of the *Physics*, and they do not need any such imaginative framework.

All the main sources for the lines of this fragment—Plutarch, Hippolytus, Philoponus, Asclepius, and Plotinus—agree that E. is here talking περὶ ψυχῆς. Hippolytus and Philoponus in their contexts explain the ψυχή in terms of the four roots and as being influenced by Love and Strife; Asclepius adds to this that the language of "path up" and "path down" of the soul is used συμβολικῶς (in Metaph. 197.17). The purport is that the thinking soul, which in the Physics was shown to consist of elements in a good ratio instantiated in the heart-blood and, in the best ratio, characterless and akin to the φρὴν ἱερή, in the Katharmoi is spoken of in terms of a daimon who, because of the inevitable workings of necessity, is cut off from his origins. Hippolytus further explains the daimons as united by Love, then scattered by Strife, and the scattered parts brought together by Love: τὰ ἀπεσπασμένα τοῦ παντός . . . (τὴν φιλίαν) προσάγειν καὶ ἓν ποιεῖν (RH 7.29.24). The whole account is finally related to the Physics by an explicit connection with 100(110).

1 ἔστιν: ἔστι τι is metrically inadmissible, cf. the commentary on 8(17).30, and unnecessarily dilutes the sense. ἀνάγκης χρῆμα: comparable to the θεσμὸς Ἀδραστείας of Plato's Phdr. 248c, the logos of the daughter of Anankē, Rep. 617d, and the Vergilian "fata deum." χρῆμα from χράω is unique here; the sense is "proclamation," "decree," the content of which is given in lines 3–8. ψήφισμα: a ratification long ago by gods who are represented as voting to accept and swearing to abide by what must inevitably happen. For the gods here cf. the commentaries on 3(131).4, 14(21).12, 15(23).8, 95(132).2, 132(146).3, and on line 5 below.

2 πλατέεσσι . . . ὅρκοις: the unusual adjective recalls immediately the "broad oath" of 23(30).3. The oath is the mark in both poems of the entry of Strife, the disruption of a state of unity and harmony, and the consequent generation of thnēta. It is here reinforced by the "seal" metaphor of authenticity and approval.

3: φόβῳ φίλα γυῖα μιν is the reading of the Plutarch MSS; the line is not in Hippolytus. The emendation φόνῳ . . . μιήνη is that of Stephanus in 1572; Xylander's text (1574) and translation are innocent of it. Wyttenbach has Stephanus' text and Xylander's translation without noting the discrepancy, and from then on Stephanus' reading has been unquestioningly adopted, and with it the melodramatic picture of a bloodstained spirit, epitomized in Jaeger's translation, "Whenever a demon . . . shall sinfully soil his hands with murderous blood" (TEGP p. 145); cf. van der Ben Proem p. 56, "[Strife is] fed as it were with the blood on the god's hands like an Erinys." The moral for men from the account of the daimon is prohibition against bloodshed, but the explicit mention of gore on a god in this solemn first exposition can be discarded; the daimon is said to make a mistake from fear. (For ἀμπλακίῃσι cf. 122(136).2.) If μιήνῃ is the correct verb to deduce from μιν, then φίλα γυῖα μιήνῃ is comparable to the phrase μιαίνειν τὸ θεῖον of Plato *Tim.* 69d, which refers to pollution of the divine (i.e., thinking) part of the soul, cf. also Sophocles *Ant.* 1044. Separation from one's fellows is widely recognized as the consequence of *miasma*, and so it would be in these terms that the isolation of the daimon is expressed. Fear is an adequate motive, but if the noun is corrupt Panzerbieter's ἀμπλακίῃσι φρενῶν (as Pindar *Pyth.* 3.24) would be a welcome reading.

4 ὃς καί: Diels's νείκει θ' ὃς κ(ε) with ἁμαρτήσας as ὁμαρτήσας (and so printed by Kirk-Raven *PP* p. 351) is quite unacceptable; Strife enters with panache in line 14, and there is no justification in text or sense for an earlier intrusion. Zuntz, following Knatz and Wilamowitz, rejects the line outright, cf. the discussion by Hershbell, *Phronesis* 1973, pp. 191–93. But a clause on perjury is most appropriate here, for like *miasma*, perjury brought with it exile from one's peers; the outstanding precedent is Hesiod, *Theog.* 793–806, and cf. *Erga* 282–85. The daimon, involved in *miasma*, is represented as having broken the oath with which necessity's decree was ratified; on both counts alienation and exile follow. From Hesiod *Theog.* 793, Homer *Il.* 3.279, and the full formula for perjury given in Aristophanes *Ran.* 150, I suggest for the line ὅρκον ὅτις κ' ἐπίορκον ἁμαρτήσας ἐπομόσσῃ. The participle ἁμαρτήσας is admissible, given E.'s preference for a weak aorist for βλαστάνειν, 14(21).10, 50(57).1, and his occasional flexibility with forms, cf. λελάχασι in the following line; and the participle picks up ἀμπλακίῃσι in line 3. The daimon is alienated when there is a deviation, but this does not mean that "culpable sin" or even choice or free will is attributable to the daimon.

5 δαίμονες: antecedent to the relative clause and in apposition to the indefinite τις of line 3; the anacoluthon is unexceptional, given that δαιμόνων is metrically impossible. The daimons are the gods of line 1, of 132(146).3, and in the *Physics* of 14(21).12 and 15(23).8, "long-lived" but not immortal, being composed, like all other forms of life, of earth, air, fire, and water in combination. Their excellence is in the harmony of the combination. In the *Physics* the rejoicing god, which is the whole cosmos brought into unity, is infiltrated by Strife; the consequent spoiling of the proportion and rearrangement of the roots bring with it a world of mortal things. In the *Katharmoi* the process is seen as individual gods cut off from their peers and born as a series of forms of mortal life. None of this implies that the daimon is an immortal soul persisting as an

identifiable individual, and it is not so taken by the sources, even by those who give the content of the fragment as περὶ ψυχῆς, cf. the commentary on the next fragment. λελάχασι· τετεύχασι, Hesychius; E. has the orthodox form at 93(100).1.

6: the time during which the daimon is represented as separated from his fellows is not an exact ten or thirty thousand years (ὥρα can be taken as a year or a season—a third of a year, cf. LSJ s.v.) but is indefinitely expressed, for the individual, when constituted as a man, has some control over the length of the process, cf. the commentaries on 100(110) and 122(136) ff. For related times cf. Aeschylus *PV* 94, Herodotus 2.123, Pindar *Ol.* 2.58–91 and fr. 127 (and the commentary on them by von Fritz, *Phronesis* 1957, pp. 85–94), Plato *Rep.* 546b, 615b, *Tim.* 39d, *Phdr.* 248e, *Pol.* 272d–e, and the varying terms of banishment for different kinds of homicide, Plato *Leg.* 866–69; in the Hesiod passage (*Theog.* 793–804) the period of banishment by the Styx for perjury is nine years (after one year's "coma"), cf. Homer *Il.* 18.400 (on Hephaistos) and 8.404. On the Ibscher papyrus for line 6 see M. L. West *CR* 1962, p. 120.

7: φυόμενον refers back to τις in line 3 and agrees with the participle in the following line, giving a particular description of what an indefinite number of daimons suffer; the plural reading is Hippolytus' adaptation of the line to his commentary. εἴδεα θνητῶν: for the immortal taking on mortal form, cf. 25(22).3, 47(35).14, and for εἴδεα as the consequent (temporary) structures of arrangements of parts of earth, air, fire, and water, cf. 60(71).3 and 62(73).2. διὰ χρόνου: cf. West on Hesiod *Theog.* 190. There is no call for an attempt to synchronize the time with that of the return of the elements to the unity of the sphere, as, for example, do Kirk-Raven, *PP* p. 352, and O'Brien, *ECC* p. 89. The "blessed god" survives through those vicissitudes of Strife which the *Katharmoi* describes in terms of daimons separated from and rejoining their peers.

8: the line is explained in 9–12. The daimon exchanges one hard way of life for another when the "roots" of which he is constituted are rearranged over a period of time to be parts of different forms of mortal life in different elements.

9–11: the terms for the individual masses in which the daimon takes on different forms of life deliberately recall the *Physics*, cf. the table of terms in chap. 2. The daimon, i.e., his physical structure, is spoken of as cast from one element to another because the conditions do not allow the parts to become properly constituted or settled, cf. chap. 3. The following fragment fills in some details but without exact correspondence. A form of life in air (as a bird) can be followed by that of a fish in the sea, then plant life on land, then a life in fire, and in air again, which with earth is likely to include animals and humans; on this cf. Aristotle *Resp.* 477a26–31 and *GA* 761b13. Life in fire (the meaning of ἥλιος here, for which φαέθων is the more appropriate epithet) was recognized, e.g., the salamander, the "flies" in the furnace, Aristotle *HA* 552b16–18, and perhaps forms of life seen on Etna. (Aristotle's notice, *GA* 761b18–23, that life in fire can be only on the moon is due to his own cosmology, cf. Jaeger *Aristotle* pp. 144–48, A. L. Peck's note in the Loeb *GA*, p. 312, and W. Lameere *L'Antiquité classique* 1949, pp. 287–301.)

12: the line is an adaptation of Hesiod *Theog.* 800. The strong language of the attitude of each elemental mass to the living things in it has its explanation in the *Physics*, where the differentiation of the elements is shown as the work of Strife, and each is attracted only to its own like parts, cf. 100(110).9; as such they could be looked on as the agents of Strife. So Hippolytus' commentary on the lines shows that the living things are hated and harassed by Strife and prevented from settling, but are pitied by Love, who tries to bring them back into their former unity.

13: Zuntz, *Persephone* p. 198, defends Plutarch's reading and translates, "this way I myself am now going"; but which way? Hippolytus' note is more appropriate (with νῦν supplied from Plutarch); the sense is that E. is one of the wanderers estranged from the gods now (but he expects soon to return). Proclus' paraphrase of the line in the context of 1(2), *in Tim.* 175c, supports the connection of the daimon's nature with the quality of thought.

14: E.'s "trust in raving strife" does not imply deliberate choice or the availability and rejection of an alternative "trust in Love." "Trust in Strife" is a stage in the necessary course of events preceding the generation of *thnēta*.

108(117)

For before now I have been at some time boy and girl, bush, bird, and a mute fish in the sea.

The fragment is widely quoted in late authors, which points to its survival in a compendium, independently of its context. This accounts too for the connection with Pythagoreanism found in many of the sources. Hippolytus has a more interesting confusion with the Stoics: the god that is the unity of all things is a thinking god (cf. φρὴν ἱερή, 97(134).4), but the separating from the god and returning to it is explained in terms of the Stoic *ekpyrōsis*. This indicates that the *egō* of this fragment and of line

13 in 107(115) is to be understood as a part that has come from and will be reassimilated into the νοερὸς θεός rather than as an individual surviving as such (e.g., as the "separate bundle of Love," Kirk-Raven *PP* p. 359, following Cornford *CAH* vol. 4, pp. 563–69, H. S. Long *AJPh* 1949, pp. 142–48, and amplified by O'Brien, *ECC* p. 329, or as a "divine potency stripped, for an aeon, of his divine identity," Zuntz *Persephone* p. 271, or as a "separate entity, divine in nature, that expressed Love and Strife," S. Darcus *Phronesis* 1977, p. 187; for a point of view explaining daimons in terms of elements cf. H. E. Barnes *CJ* 1967, pp. 18–23, and C. H. Kahn in *AGPh* 1960, pp. 3–35). This fragment does not imply a remembrance of the previous lives described, but it is an inference from the decree that the daimon be born in different elements as different kinds of living things. E. looks back and recognizes that the parts that now make up himself, a properly constituted *egō*, have been used for different kinds of lives in different elements, none of which was satisfactory or settled, cf. chap. 3.

1: boy and girl cover both sexes (without any of the implications, common in reincarnation theories, that the female is inferior), but they are also examples of lives that are not properly settled, because they are cut off before maturity.

2: the sources, although numerous, are interrelated, and the text of the end of the line is uncertain. θήρ in some form is an obvious omission (cf. 13(9).2, 14(21).11, 26(20).7), and attempts have been made to insert it, e.g., van der Ben suggests θὴρ καὶ ἀλίσπορος ἰχθύς. Exact correspondence is not necessary; and bush, bird, and fish are examples of lives in earth, air, and water. With reservation I accept ἔξαλος ἔλλοπος ἰχθύς as "in (or on) the sea (the noun indicating the bitterness of the environment, cf. Homer *Od.* 12.27) a mute fish" (with ἔλλοπος as an alternative form of ἔλλοψ—"unable to make articulate sound," the second disadvantage of life as a fish; cf. the use of this adjective for Echo, Theocritus *Syr.* 18).

FRAGMENTS 109–117 FROM GOOD FORTUNE TO THE ILL FORTUNE OF LIFE ON EARTH

109(116)
(she) abhors necessity, hard to bear.

Ananke here must surely have the same reference as 107(115).1 (rather than being one of a pair of opposites following 116(122), as Zuntz maintains, *Persephone* bk. 2, p. 256). Ammonius (in Plutarch's context), in reply to the Peripatetic, fixes the reference by denying that "the necessity among the gods" is hard to bear. The other well-known instance of the adjective, at Aeschylus *Ag.* 1571, is similarly applied to acceptance of a course of events that is "hard to bear," but Clytemnestra is willing to accept it on oath to the daimon of the house. Charis (who is Philia under another name, cf. Gēthosunē, 8(17).24, and the other titles, Plu. *de Is. et Os.* 370d) "abhors necessity"—in terms of the *Physics*, because of the inevitable completion of a time (marked by an oath) when the one has to become many, and in terms of the *Katharmoi*, because of necessity's decree (marked by an oath), which requires the inevitable separation of daimons from their fellows, and these, as Hippolytus explains, she pities and tries to restore to their former unity (*RH* 7.29.21).

110(126)
clothing (?the daimon) in an unfamiliar garment of flesh

The only appropriate feminine candidate for the participle is Ananke, interpreted by the sources as *physis*, i.e., what has to happen in the natural course of events. δαίμονα would provide the obvious accusative, perhaps being the first word of the line following the fragment. σαρκῶν χιτών is a mortal body, σάρκες being a composite term for skin and tissues, and χιτών an anatomical metaphor (cf. LSJ s.v., IV), used again as such in the context of E.'s fr. 142(70). Necessity or nature "putting around a mortal body" is a particular description of the way in which the daimon is born, i.e., his substance reconstituted as a form of living creature, cf. 107(115).7. The garment is "unfamiliar" ("unrecognized" or "unrecognizable," cf. Hdt. 1.85) because an alien and hard way of life is taken up by one who was represented as being previously a happy god, cf. the commentary on the "unfamiliar place" of 112(118).

111(119)
from what honor and from what great extent of happiness

Clement quotes the line as words spoken directly by E. on coming among mortals, Plutarch, on his being an exile and wanderer according to divine laws, exchanging "sky and moon" for earth. Hippolytus has no attribution, and the line occurs in the discussion of a heresy of souls coming from a primal man or Adam, to be born here of clay. The disagreement between the soul "remembering" a former state in Hippolytus and "forgetting" it in Plutarch is due to the quite different contexts, the Naasene heresy in the former and the Platonic reference in the latter. It is not significant except in suggesting that neither context gave supporting evidence for E. speaking of the daimon in such terms. The main point to be deduced from the sources is that E. is speaking of himself as having been in a happy state previously, but now an exile, born in mortal form on earth as a consequence of the working of cosmic laws.

112(118)

I wept and wailed on seeing an unfamiliar place

Plutarch (*soll. an.* 964d) has a comparison similar to Clement's between Heraclitus and E. on their railing at nature. Sextus preserves a fragment of Epicurus relating the line to a baby's first cry upon exposure to air (*adv. math.* 11.96). The fragment continues in the context of the previous one—the contrast between the earlier happiness and the grief at being born as a mortal creature. The "unfamiliar place" is this world, as Plutarch stated emphatically on 111(119); the former life has been exchanged for γῇ καὶ ὁ ἐπὶ γῆς βίος. (The wording of the fragment looks like an adaptation of Penelope's grief for her geese, *Od.* 19.541.)

113(121)

(a joyless place) where (there are) slaughter and hatred and hordes of other violent deaths (and parching fevers and consumptions and ?dropsy) . . . they wander in darkness over the field of Atē.

1 ἀτερπέα χῶρον: apparently a variation on ἀσυνήθεα χῶρον of the previous fragment. This suggests that the line beginning ἔνθα φόνος follows immediately on that fragment as part of a description of life on earth (cf. τὰ περὶ γῆν in Hierocles' context) and in some measure explains it. The line recalls 14(21).7 of the *Physics* and also 26(20).4–5. In those fragments, in the process of one becoming many, Strife keeps men apart and is the cause of hatred and death among them; here too the world is presented as a place where hatred and violent death are rife.

3: I indicate my suspicions about the authenticity of the line by parentheses. It is not in Hierocles; Proclus has it with the previous line in connection with the healing powers of Apollo, but without attribution; for a possible home for it as part of a Chaldean oracle, cf. H. Saffrey *RPh* 1969, pp. 64–67. Its meaning is obscure, but if it is genuine it would seem to be a list of diseases characterized by the excess of an element— fever by fire (cf. 101(111).6–7), and consumption and dropsy (if that is the correct interpretation) by water.

4: the change of subject in Hierocles points to a lacuna. Some editors suggest further lists, but we have them in 116(122) and 117(123), cf. the commentaries on them. Ἄτης ἀν λειμῶνα: those who wander in the field are, in Hierocles' language, the "fallen," i.e., daimons who are born as mortal creatures. They move over the face of the earth, living out their hard way of life here, not in some mythical area located in Hades, so Themistius, *Or.* 178: τὸν ἐπίγειον τόπον καὶ Ἄτης λειμῶνα ἐπονομάζον-τα. Dodds, *Plato: Gorgias* p. 375, has shown that the "asphodel meadow" of *Od.* 11.539 is the common source for fields that are (1) the home of blessed souls, as in Pindar fr. 114; Aristophanes *Ran.* 326; "Orpheus," Diod. Sic. 1.96.2; the "Gold Leaf" poem, DK 1 B20.6; (2) the place of judgment in Plato's myths, *Gorg.* 524a2, *Rep.* 614e2. The "field of Atē" is E.'s deviation from the Homeric tradition. Whatever the exact meaning of Atē (cf. Dodds *GI* pp. 2–8, 17–18, 37–41), it is an associate of νεῖκος μαινόμενον, bringing catastrophe and ruin, and characterizing, with darkness, a world coming under the domination of Strife.

114(124)

Alas, poor unhappy race of mortal creatures, from what strifes and lamentations were you born.

The lines are from Clement, quoted after 112(118) and 130(125) and fol-lowed by well-known lines from Theognis (*Eleg.* 1. 425–27), Euripides (frs. 452 and 638), Homer (*Il.* 6.146), and others who take a pessimistic view of mortal life. Porphyry quotes the second line anonymously, and Eusebius includes it in a pastiche of satirical lines by Timon. The general sense of the previous three fragments—the pity for mortal creatures—is continued (for θνητά as an almost technical term in E. to cover plant, animal, and human life, cf. 8(17).3; 12(8).2; 15(23).10; 25(22).3; 47(35). 7, 16; 60(71).3). They are born of ἔριδες inasmuch as it is the power of Strife that brings about the generation of *thnēta*, cf. 26(20).4; Porphyry's reading of νεικέων for στοναχῶν reinforces the link with the Strife of the *Physics*.

115(120)
We have come under this roofed cave.

Porphyry and Plotinus, the sources for the line, refer the cave mentioned here to this world, and so it should be understood. Although Zuntz assigns the cave to Hades, he admits that he "knows of no Greek instance" of a cave in the underworld, *Persephone* p. 255; for this world as a cave, though without any necessarily "Orphic" connotations, cf. Proclus *in Tim.* 29c, τῶν παλαιῶν ἄντρον καλούντων τὸν κόσμον, the discussions by Jaeger, *TEGP* p. 149; Bignone, *Empedocle* p. 493; Millerd, *Empedocles* p. 93; Dodds, *GI* p. 174, n. 114; and in detail J. H. Wright, "The Origin of Plato's Cave," *HSPh* 1906, 131–42. "A 'Cave' is not a 'Field'," as Zuntz says, p. 204, but this is not an argument against a highly metaphorical poet like E., who can speak of "funnels" in the earth (48(96).1) and the "seashore of life" (26(20).5), describing life here both as on a gloomy field of Atē (he had already used "field" metaphorically in 55[66]) and as in a (gloomy) cave. The life of the gods compared to ours in brightness and joy is as this one compared to underground living, which gives the sources an obvious comparison with Plato *Rep.* 7. Little can be deduced from the anonymous and anachronistic ψυχοπομποὶ δυνάμεις mentioned by Porphyry, especially since any connecting verb has to be supplied.

116(122)
There were Earth and far-seeing Sun, bloody Discord and serene Harmony, Beauty and Ugliness, Speed and Slowness, lovely Truth and blind Uncertainty.

With the next fragment, which probably follows this, there is a list of pairs of feminine personifications, many of them unusual adjectival forms, and some perhaps coined by E. The Index Verborum shows ten words from the two fragments as ἅπ. λεγ. In the introductory ἔνθα and in the formation of the nouns and compound adjectives the list is closely modeled on the catalogue of the Nereids in Homer *Il.* 18.39–49 and in Hesiod *Theog.* 240–64, and cf. the Oceanids, 346–61. Plutarch contrasts the personifications as spirits of good and evil accompanying men through life (*tranq.*

an. 474b), and at *de Is. et Os.* 370d the second pair given here are identified with Philia and Neikos; the members of each pair, however, especially in the next fragment, are not all opposed as obviously good and bad. ἔνθα indicates the same provenance as frs. 112(118), 113(121), and 115(120), namely this world, the area for the interplay of a number of opposite conditions. There is no "impossible" conflict with 113(121), as claimed by van der Ben, *Proem* p. 159. The existence of oppositions within an overall structure of the domination of strife is Heraclitean.

1: the "nymphs" of Earth and far-seeing Sun give the setting for mortal life, which is on the earth and under the sun. (Zuntz, *Persephone* p. 256, claims yet another mythical region in the underworld, where these personages "condition the daimon's impending incarnate existence.")

2: Plutarch identifies this pair with the Love and Strife of the *Physics*. It would be appropriate for them to be given prior mention here, after the basic scene of earth and sun, as the overwhelming influences in mortal life.

3 Θόωσα: the mother of Polyphemus, *Od.* 1.71. E. seems to be using an etymological link with θέω and θόος. The point of contrast with the feminine of δηναιός—"long-lived," "long-lasting"—is not clear; perhaps it is "swift youth" versus "slow old age" rather than the conventional "Haste and Tarrying."

4 Νημερτής: the name occurs in the Homeric and Hesiodic list of Nereids, and it is an epithet of Proteus and Nereus. Truth contrasts with obscurity, certainty with "dark opinion," cf. 95(132).2. The color of the latter's hair is irrelevant, even if the derivation from κείρω can be justified; μελάγκουρος is with black, i.e., sightless pupils, so Mullach, *FPG* vol. 3, p. 22, and cf. δόξαι τυφλαί of Plato *Rep.* 506c and van der Ben's discussion, *Proem* p. 162.

117(123)

Birth and Death, Sleep and Wakefulness, Movement and Rest, much-crowned Splendor and ?Vileness, Silence and Speech.

The lines continue the catalogue of female personifications in the previous fragment, which as Cornutus says, are "riddles" for ἡ ποικιλία τῶν ὄντων.

1: "Birth and Death" are probably the first pair, rather than the

conventional "Growth and Decay," cf. 12(18).4. Φυσώ (with ῡ), like
Κινώ and Μεγιστώ in line 2, is ἅπ. λεγ., coined on the model of Δωτώ
τε Πρωτώ τε, Il. 18.43, Hesiod Theog. 248.

2–3 Μεγιστώ: the "Splendor" of the prosperous man in his prime.
†φορίη† is difficult. Φορύη is usually read, presumably connecting with
the root of φορύνω and -ύσσω. If this could give a contrast of wretched
poverty with prosperity, it would be an obvious and appropriate one.

3 Σωπή: Bergk's reading here gives the needed opposite to 'Ομφαίη,
from ὀμφή—any speech, but especially one that is pleasing or, in Homer,
divine.

FRAGMENTS 118–125 MISFORTUNE INTENSIFIED BY
THE SHEDDING OF BLOOD

118(128)

*They did not have Ares as god or Kydoimos, nor king Zeus nor Kronos nor Poseidon,
but queen Kypris. Her they propitiated with holy images and painted animal
figures, with perfumes of subtle fragrance and offerings of distilled myrrh and
sweet-smelling frankincense, and pouring on the earth libations of golden honey.
Their altar was not drenched by the (? unspeakable) slaughter of bulls, but this
was the greatest defilement among men—to bereave of life and eat noble limbs.*

The passage from Porphyry occurs in an extract from Theophrastus on
early sacrifices. The first libations were of water, then of honey, oil, and
wine; E.'s lines are given in support. The whole is set in the early history
of man: "When friendship and a proper sense of the duties pertaining to
kindred natures were possessed by all men, no one slaughtered any living
being, in consequence of thinking that other animals were allied to him.
But when strife and tumult (Ares and Kydoimos), every kind of contention, and the principle of war, invaded mankind, then, for the first time,
no one in reality spared any one of his kindred natures" (*abst.* 2.21, trans.
T. Taylor, 1823). The connection with the *Physics*, reinforced by the
identification of Kypris with Philia, is clear. There is here a particular
description of the life of men (ἐν ἀνθρώποισι in line 9 is unambiguous)
at the beginning of their generation, when Love was dominant over
Strife, but now the positions are being reversed. It need not be assumed
from the introductory phrase περὶ τῆς θεογονίας διεξιών that E. inserted

a complete Hesiodic-type theogony into his poem; the description may cover just the first three lines of this fragment.

1 κείνοισιν: the first generations of men. Kydoimos accompanies Ares and Enyo, *Il.* 5.593, and is personified with Eris on Achilles' shield, 18.535; he is the attendant of Polemos in Aristophanes' *Pax*.

2: βασιλεύς, like the feminine in the next line, is attributive rather than predicative, cf. *Hom. Hym. Cer.* 358. The denial of a reign of Kronos counters Hesiod's golden race of men, *Erga* 111. ·

3 Κύπρις: for the identification with Philia in the *Physics* cf. 62(73), 70(75).2, 83(98).3, 87(95). The polemic in these three lines directed against traditional theology would be particularly scathing to the people of Acragas, where the line of new and magnificent temples to various deities stretched along the south wall, chief of them being the (unfinished) one to Zeus. (It is interesting to speculate whether the additional temple, attributed to Concordia and built some 50 years after the Olympeion, i.e., ca. 430, could have been due to E.'s influence; on the details of the temples cf. K. H. Waters, *Anc. Soc.* 1974, pp. 8–10.)

4–7: Kypris is offered (1) *agalmata*—presumably representations of the goddess, (2) painted animal figures (as she would be the patroness of living creatures when they lived in friendship, cf. the commentary on the next fragment), (3) perfumes, frankincense, and myrrh (Matt. 2:11 is a striking parallel), (4) honey. For bloodless offerings generally as belonging to the early history of man, cf. Porphyry's context here, Plato *Laws* 782, and Pausanias 8.2.3. For the anecdote, obviously fabricated from this fragment, of a bull of meal and honey offered by E. at Olympia, see chap. 1.

8–10: cf. "the men of old who thought it unholy to stain the altars of the gods with blood," Plato *Laws* 782c, and the early Athenians, Pausanias 8.2.3. †ἀκρίτοισι† φόνοις: "unmixed blood" looks like a confusion with line 6; in support of ἀρρήτοισι cf. δείπνων ἀρρήτων, Sophocles *El.* 203. For the violent language of line 10, cf. 124(137).6; φίλας σάρκας there confirms ἠέα γυῖα here and an infinitive of ἔδουσιν. ἐέδμεναι is a unique form but perhaps admissible for E.

119(130)

All creatures, both animals and birds, were tame and gentle to men, and bright was the flame of their friendship.

The fragment, preserved only in the *Schol.*, complements the previous one and perhaps followed it. Under the sway of Kypris men did not kill, sacrifice, or eat animals, and they in turn were gentle to men. The tameness of animals is a traditional feature of "Golden Age" literature, cf. Isaiah 11:6, Vergil *Ecl.* 4.22, *Orac. Sib.* 3.791–93; for the opposite view, of the cruelty of animals to primitive man, cf. the ghoulish description by Lucretius, 5.990–98.

2: ἄνθρωποι is obvious dittography, hence Sturz's emendation; the enmity of (some) birds to men is illustrated at Aeschylus *Sept.* 1020 and Sophocles *Ant.* 1082. For φιλοφροσύνη as the work of Love, cf. her introduction at 8(17).23, and for the contrast with Strife, cf. Homer *Il.* 9.256–57. The commonplace metaphor of fire for the feelings aroused by Aphrodite has in this context a striking beauty.

120(139)
Alas that the pitiless day did not destroy me first, before I devised for my lips the cruel deed of eating flesh.

The heinous crime of eating meat is tantamount, in E.'s theory, to cannibalism, because of the kinship of living things, which is a consequence of their common structures and the way in which these structures are separated and re-formed into different kinds of mortal life. One of the most abominable of all acts in myth and tragedy, the eating of one's kin, E. sees perpetrated in the sacrificial meal, cf. 122(136). E. represents himself as having been guilty of this, not, I think, as a god (as if he had been tempted by steak after a diet of ambrosia, in H. E. Barnes's vivid wording, *CJ* 1967, p. 22), but in human form. It is what he interprets as appalling human action that gives point to his warning to his fellow men.

2: Fränkel's reordering of the line is to be commended, as it removes the unlikely σχέτλια and eliminates the problem of the meaning of the preposition here. χείλεσι is then dative either of instrument with βορᾶς (in an active sense "of eating flesh") or of indirect object with the infinitive. For σχέτλια ἔργα cf. *Od.* 9.295 of Polyphemus' cannibalism.

121(135)
but the law for all extends throughout wide-ruling air and measureless sunlight.

Aristotle quotes the fragment with Sophocles *Ant.* 456–57 to illustrate universal law, a natural justice binding on all, the content of which for E. is a prohibition against killing living creatures. The lines are therefore an introduction to 122(136) and 124(137). The law recalls that of Heraclitus (fr. 114) and also that of Hesiod *Erga* 276–78, which has, however, a specifically human application: fish, animals, and birds devour each other because, unlike men, they have no *dikē*.

1 ἀλλά . . . μέν: "a stereotyped opening formula," Denniston, *Greek Particles* p. 366, in a discussion of Xenophon, and cf. the Homeric uses, p. 378. It is unnecessary and confusing to suppose that the particles indicate a contrast between a law in the sky and one on earth (as DK vol. 1, p. 366, and others). There is a single universal law, the range of which extends from the surface of the earth to the boundary of the cosmos, that is applicable to all who breathe the air and live in the light of the sun. εὐρυμέδων: rare as an adjective but used of the sea, personified in Poseidon at Pindar *Ol.* 8.31.

2 αἰθέρος: E.'s word for the element of air, see the table in chap. 2. ἀπλέτου: applied to the extent of air, 8(17).18, and here to the light of the sun; not "boundless" (cf. 33[39]) but "measureless," cf. Hesychius ἄπλετον· ἀμέτρητον.

122(136)

Will you not cease from the din of slaughter? Do you not see that you are devouring one another because of your careless way of thinking?

In Sextus this fragment is followed by its elaboration in 124(137). According to his context, E. as well as Pythagoras and the other Italians believed in a kinship of man with the gods and with animals. The slaying and eating of animals is therefore the destruction of one's own family; for a contemporary philosophical defense of animal rights on similar lines cf. R. Knowles Morris and M. W. Fox, eds., *On the Fifth Day: Animal Rights and Human Ethics.* The "law" of the previous fragment is interpreted as a *pneuma* pervading the whole cosmos, and this looks like a Stoic version of the φρὴν ἱερή of 97(134).4.

1 δυσηχέος: the Homeric epithet for war is deliberately recalled, cf. *Il.* 7.395 and 11.590; killing an animal is comparable to killing a man in battle.

2 *ἀκηδείῃσι νόοιο*: a variant on the Homeric *ἀφραδίῃσι νόοιο, Il.* 10.122, where Agamemnon denies that Menelaus is lazy or careless. The deficiency of the understanding of the ordinary man is a standard complaint with E., as with Heraclitus and Parmenides. As in 107(115).3 the wrong action may be due to ignorance or carelessness, but this does not exempt one from the consequences.

123(145)

That is why, being distraught with bitter misfortunes, you will never lighten your hearts of grievous sorrows.

1 *τοιγάρτοι*: "approximating in force to *διὰ ταῦτα καί*," Denniston, *Greek Particles* p. 566, and cf. Aeschylus *Supp.* 654. This gives the connection with the previous fragment: "you do not stop slaughtering and devouring each other, and that is why your sufferings do not cease." The main difficulty in the fragment is the apparent inconsistency with 102(112).3, which, wherever it belongs, has the phrase *κακότητος ἄπειροι* of the men of Acragas (cf. the commentary on the line), who are here spoken of as distraught *χαλεπῇσι κακότησιν* and never free of grievous sorrows. But it is a standard sermonizing tactic to show that apparent prosperity is built on shifting sands. The overall view of life in the *Physics* and the *Katharmoi* is one of Hesiodic pessimism as the domination by Strife increases, cf. *Erga.* 200–01 for phrasing similar to that here, and also the commentary on 114(124); a respite can be won only if there is a concerted refusal to further the work of Strife. The individual can by intellectual effort revert to his former status where he will be free of human sorrows, cf. 100(110) and 133(147). A warning to the men of Acragas that despite their show of wealth and security they were not immune to misfortune may well have struck home, if they looked back into the past to the tyranny of Phalaris, reflected on the contemporary political unrest, and saw in the future a lethal threat from Carthage.

124(137)

The father will lift up his dear son in a changed form, and, blind fool, as he prays he will slay him, and those who take part in the sacrifice ?bring (the victim) as he pleads. But the father, deaf to his cries, slays him in his house and prepares an evil feast. In the same way son seizes father, and children their mother, and having bereaved them of life devour the flesh of those they love.

Sextus adds the fragment to 122(136) with καί, but Chalcidius puts it "alio loco." Plutarch's quotation, to illustrate those who unwittingly slay their kin, stops at νήπιος. The whole fragment is a horrifying account of what the theory of the kinship of life implies in practice (Xenophanes made a joke of it in fr. 7). It is a description that recalls the great family murders of tragedy, and in particular is in the opening lines strongly reminiscent of Agamemnon's sacrifice of his daughter as told by the chorus in Aeschylus *Ag.* 218–47. E. shows the father engaged in the ritual of raising a victim at an altar and, after the customary prayer, slaying, carving, and eating it in a family meal. The outwardly pious act is most impious. (Heraclitus, without E.'s motivation, had felt revulsion at the proceedings, fr. 5.) However, even in E.'s terms, it would be a rare coincidence for the prematurely dead son to take on immediately the form of a sacrificial animal, but the extreme example is taken to reinforce the exhortation against any slaying of living creatures (and so furthering the work of Strife).

2–3: for a comprehensive list of suggestions for the text of these lines cf. van der Ben *Proem* pp. 201–02, and for a detailed discussion cf. Zuntz *Persephone* pp. 220–26. It is clear that no definitive conclusion can be reached. I suggest Origen's future, σφάξει, which gives the following stages of the narrative: (1) The father stands at the altar ready to carry out the sacrifice, but he is μέγα νήπιος, totally and tragically unaware of disaster, as are Patroclus, *Il.* 16.46, and Andromache, *Il.* 22.445 (and cf. 122(136).2). (2) The attendants bring on the remonstrating victim; for λισσόμενον cf. Iphigenia's pleas λιτὰς δὲ καὶ κληδόνας πατρῴους, *Ag.* 228. With a large animal, perhaps a calf (cf. line 4), and a formal ceremony there would obviously be attendants, and so for the unacceptable πορεῦνται a verb like φέρονται is needed. (The line has an unusual lengthening, θύοντες, cf. ἀλύοντες in the previous fragment.) (3) The father kills the victim, deaf in his turn to its cries (accepting Diels's ὁ δ' αὖ νήκουστος), and prepares the meat.

6 ἀπορραίσαντε: for the dual cf. 15(23).2, 4, 6; it may be due here to the juxtaposition μητέρα παῖδες, recalling the matricide by Orestes and Electra. The line contrasts with the practice in the early history of man, 118(128).9–10.

125(138)

drawing off life with bronze

The fragment comes with 129(143) in Aristotle as two citations from the same poet, and that this is E. is confirmed by Theon's quotation of the latter fragment and attribution to him. Both fragments seem to be concerned with ritual sacrifice and so are placed here in the *Katharmoi*. Aristotle is discussing metaphor in general and gives the two quotations as examples of that from species to species, for ἀρύσαι is used for ταμεῖν and ταμεῖν for ἀρύσαι, the prosaic word for both being ἀφελεῖν. ψυχή, the only instance of the word in the fragments, is the principle of life and thought concentrated, in E.'s theory, in the blood around the heart. The official "takes away" the life, i.e., metaphorically "draws it off" or, nonmetaphorically, "severs" it with the sharp bronze sacrificial knife. The victim is bled to death by having its throat cut, and it is this wastage that E. emphasizes as both the ruination of the work of Love and the furtherance of that of Strife.

FRAGMENTS 126–129 FURTHER ADVICE

126(144)
to be empty of misfortune

Plutarch has high praise for this phrase, and it looks like a tag that he found appropriate to attach to his discussion of the restraining of anger, along with sex, wine, and lies. But this is not sufficient to give it a moral connotation in E. κακότης for him is human misery generally, cf. the commentaries on the other instances at 102(112).3 and 123(145).1. νηστεῦσαι seems to mean "not to eat," "to be empty" of food; van der Ben, *Proem* p. 211, quotes Callimachus fr. 191.61–63 for another example of the verb with a genitive—νηστεύειν τῶν ἐμπνεόντων—but this may be a parody of E. There is no reason to assume that there is an imperative here. "To be free of ill" is a description of the state that might be achieved if E.'s words are heeded (cf. the last two fragments of the *Physics*), and it is in fact achieved by those who join the gods, cf. 133(147).2.

127(140)
to keep completely from leaves of laurel

Plutarch in his context extends E.'s prohibition against picking laurel leaves to picking the leaves of all trees, because of the injury to them. In E.'s catalogues of living things (related because they share a common structure, cf. 13(9).2, 26(20).6, and also 12(8).2), θάμνος, which refers to the larger forms of plant life such as bushes and trees, is included, and of these the laurel, or bay, is chief, cf. 131(127).2. The preservation of the tree unharmed, as with an animal, allows its constitution to become properly arranged and settled, and so a re-formation as a higher type of life is expedited. The selection of the laurel does not of itself imply a particular interest on E.'s part in Apollo (cf. the commentary on 97[134]) but would rather be a criticism of a cult involving leaves plucked from the tree.

ἔχεσθαι: I doubt that the infinitive is for the imperative and that E. is giving curt instructions to his friends. The context suggests χρή with the infinitive, and the recommendation probably belonged with the passages warning against harming animals (rather than being one of a hypothetical list of rules supposed necessary to justify the title *Katharmoi*).

128(141)
wretches, utter wretches, keep your hands from beans

This appalling line should be rejected as a genuine quotation from E. In Geoponica it is attributed to Orpheus, and a similar phrase is ascribed to Pythagoras in Callimachus fr. 128. Gellius, who gives the Callimachus fragment as well as the attribution to E. here, is late and unreliable. The line is a parody of E.—a pastiche of *Od.* 22.316 and fragments 127(140) and 114(124). πάνδειλος does not appear again until the third century A.D.; it would have been unacceptable to the addressees. A list of possible explanations for the Pythagorean taboo on beans is given by Guthrie, *HGP*, vol. 1, pp. 184–85; they (with the exception of the political interpretation) connect beans with sex, life or soul, or the dead. If E. did accept such a taboo, the most reasonable one is the medical one— that an excessive amount of beans is bad for the heart and blood.

129(143)
cutting from five streams with a long bronze blade

For the context in Aristotle cf. the commentary on 125(138); Theon gives the attribution, and the first hand of the MS confirms the reading, cf. P. Maas *Byz* $\mathcal{Z}$ 1936, p. 456. As van der Ben shows (*Proem* pp. 203–08), the phrase is not concerned with some unknown ritual of collecting water in a container from five springs but, like 125(138), with drawing blood with a knife. ταναήκεῖ χαλκῷ is Homeric for the blade of a sword or ax or the point of a spear; ταμών according to Aristotle would be, less metaphorically, ἀρύσας. The object therefore can only be a liquid, and the obvious liquid one "draws" with a long bronze blade is blood. The "springs" therefore must be metaphorical, and van der Ben suggests that "streams of blood" from five sacrificial animals are intended. Perhaps, rather, the "springs" are the five senses, the sources of sensation, which cease to function as the victim is bled. This may all be connected, as Theon's context suggests, with a ritual of purification by blood (which E. would inveigh against), cf. Heraclitus fr. 5.

FRAGMENTS 130–133 THE HIERARCHY OF LIVES

130(125)
for from living creatures it set out dead bodies, changing the form

Clement quotes the line as a unit with 112(118), and with other famous lines of an extremely pessimistic nature, illustrating the misery and brevity of human life; for the list see the commentary on 112(118). The missing masculine subject is therefore probably something like πόλεμος, and the context not a piece of mythical mysticism but a straightforward reminder that the living die and their structure decomposes, cf. from the *Physics* 14(21).13–14. If the death is abrupt or violent, the result of the work of Strife, then the reconstitution of the parts would be into inferior and even more temporary forms of life; the consequences when the opposite state of affairs prevails are given in the next three fragments.

131(127)
Among animals they are born as lions that make their lairs in the hills and bed on the ground, and among fair-leafed trees as laurels.

Aelian explains the fragment as a ranking of forms of mortal life. Best of all is human life, but among ζῷα that of the lion is best, and among plants that of the laurel. ζῷον is a comprehensive term, and there is no reason to suppose that E. gave a more explicit and pedestrian list, including, for example, the dolphin as the best form among fish, the snake among reptiles, and the eagle among birds. (The late Roman *Kore Kosmou* fragment, Herm. ap. Stob. fr. xxiii, Nock-Festugière iv, pp. 13–14, enthusiastically adopted by Zuntz, *Persephone* pp. 232–33, is too remote and confused to be helpful for an elaboration of the lines here. The λῆξις in Aelian's context is an anachronistic intrusion from Plato *Rep.* 10, 617e.)

1 ὀρειλεχέες: the adjective occurs in the *Physics* at 26(20).7 (if the reading is correct) in the list of different forms of life, but apparently nowhere else. There is an interesting discussion of lions in chapter 12 of Aelian, including an account of their deification in Egypt, their connection with fire, with dreams and prophecies, and with the punishing of perjury. They are carnivorous but, unlike men, cannot change their ways.

2 γίγνονται: the subject would be "mortals," i.e., those who have lived and died as temporary combinations of elements. ἠυκόμοισιν: a reminder from *Physics* 71(82) that hair and leaves are analogous parts. The choice of laurel would be particularly appropriate for its supposedly prophetic properties (cf. Hesiod *Theog.* 30), without implying any particular honor to Apollo, cf. the commentaries on 97(134) and 127(140).

132(146)

And at the end they come among men on earth as prophets, minstrels, physicians, and leaders, and from these they arise as gods, highest in honor.

A list of the best types of human life starts with Homer, *Od.* 17.384–86. Hesiod singles out wise kings who are like gods among men, *Theog.* 91–93. Pindar, fr. 133, has kings, athletes, and wise men, and in *Ol.* 2 the favored are instantiated in Peleus, Cadmus, and Achilles and include those who abide by their oaths, *Ol.* 2.120 and cf. 107(115).4. For Plato, philosophers are preeminent (*Phaedo* 114c), for Cicero statesmen (*Somn. Scip.* passim, but musicians and astronomers also qualify, chap 18), and for Vergil the number includes heroes, priests, and prophets headed by the priest/minstrel Orpheus and the minstrel/physician Musaeus, *Aen.* 6.642–68. And ἰατρόμαντις is a traditional title for Apollo and Asclepius, cf. Aeschylus *Eum.* 62, *Supp.* 263. It is probable that E. supposed all four types of life to be united in himself.

2 πρόμοι: not the Homeric πρόμαχοι but the statesman and leader in peace; on E.'s political leadership see chap. 1.

3 θεοὶ τιμῆσι φέριστοι: the description of the gods in *Physics* 14(21).12 and 15(23).8 is a reminder of the common basis of the two poems and of the status of gods as beings not totally different from men but as having the same origin and constitution as them, superior only in the longer term to their existence; and these gods at the culmination of the types of lives are again the δαίμονες given at the beginning of the *Katharmoi*, see chap. 3.

133(147)

With other immortals they share hearth and table, having no part in human sorrows, unwearied.

The lines follow closely if not immediately on the previous fragment as a more detailed description of the daimons, both before they are born as the different types of mortal life and again when the mortal becomes immortal. But "immortal" for E. is not an unending and unchanging state, as it is in Clement's Christian adaptation of the fragment, but one that alternates with "mortal"; there is no incompatibility with 107(115). 5. The description is not to be taken literally, but it puts into more comprehensible human terms that unity with divine thought proffered to Pausanias at the end of the *Physics*, in much the same way as the separation is described in terms of the wrongdoing which among men results in exile.

1 αὐτοτράπεζοι: ἄπ. λεγ., if the reading is correct, cf. ὁμοτράπεζοι καὶ ὁμέστιοι, Plutarch *quaest. conv.* 703e. The most famous mortal to join the banquet of the gods was Herakles, cf. Homer *Od.* 11.602–04, Horace *Carm.* 4.30, and in general Hesiod *Theog.* 796, 802, Plato *Phdr.* 247a, Vergil *Ecl.* 4.62–63.

2 †ἐόντες†: postponing the participle until after ἀπόκληροι saves the meter; for the phrase cf. ἀποκλάρος πόνων, Pindar *Pyth.* 5.71. The "human sorrows" that the gods escape have been elaborated throughout the *Katharmoi*, e.g., 107(115).8, 112(118), and 123(145).

12. Addenda

The group of quotations in this section contains single words from E., phrases that are too meager to be treated as separate fragments, and lines in which the text is so corrupt that nothing positive can be said.

134(5)   The question under discussion is Pythagorean abstention from fish. One of the speakers in the dialogue, another Empedocles, puts forward a secondhand etymology as a reason for respecting fish as keepers of silence. He adds that his namesake was speaking Πυθαγορικῶς to Pausanias in his exhortation to cover the teaching in his ?silent heart. Both ἔλλοπας and ἔλλοπος here are conjectures, and the form itself is uncertain, cf. the commentary on 108(117).2. Even if Wyttenbach's emendation is accepted, and the translation "silent heart" along the right lines, Plutarch's Pythagorean implications are unjustified. An exhortation to take in E.'s words well and meditate on them is in the same tone as 6(4).3 and 100(11).1–2.

135(7)   It is unlikely that ἀγένητα (or ἀγέννητα, the Hesychius reading) was used by E. as a noun. The singular as an adjective is in Parmenides fr. 8.3 contrasting with ἀνώλεθρον, and Hippolytus (not Heraclitus, *pace* LSJ) has the adjective in the introduction to Heraclitus fr. 50. Elsewhere in fifth-century authors the word means "not having happened" (e.g., Soph. *Trach.* 743), "baseless," "low-born," and at Sophocles

OC 973, "not yet born." E. could well have adopted the adjective in the Eleatic sense of "without birth or beginning" for the four roots and/or Love and Strife, cf. 8(17).30–34 and 11(16).

136(10)   The quotation comes immediately after 13(9) and is a comment on it. φῶτας, θῆρας, θάμνους, and οἰωνούς are repeated from the fragment, and for μιγνυμένων τῶν στοιχείων cf. 47(35).7, 16, and also 51(59).1, 15(23).5, 12(8).3, and 13(9).1. φύσις is the controversial word from 12(8).1, which Plutarch here too clearly takes as "birth," a σύγκρισις of the roots, as opposed to "death," their διάκρισις. πότμος δυσδαίμων is from line 4 of 13(9) and θάνατος ἀλοίτης a variant on it and on the θάνατος οὐλόμενος of 12(8).2. It is uncertain whether ἀλοίτης is E.'s adjective or Plutarch's alternative for οὐλόμενος, but the sense "wicked" holds in either case, as ἀλείτης is used of Paris, *Il.* 3.28, and of the suitors, *Od.* 20.121. Death, in a conventional sense, is a "wrongdoer" but hardly, in E.'s terms, an "avenger." A comparison with Ἀθηνᾶ Ἀλοῖτις (Lyc. *Alex.* 936) is misleading, cf. Bollack *Empédocle* vol. 3, p. 100.

137(19)   νεῖκος οὐλόμενον occurs at 8(17).19, and for the adjective cf. 77(109).3 and 107(115).14. σχεδύνη is ἅπ. λεγ. The context provides the sense of "binding" for the adherence of the parts of the compounds formed by Love, in contrast to the destructive function of Strife, cf. κολλητικόν here and 48(96).4, 49(34). Plutarch wants to identify Strife with fire and Love with water, despite E.'s regarding fire as a hardening or setting agent for the roots. That Plutarch did not suppose that E. identified Strife with fire and Love with water but found the opposition of Strife and Love as destructive and unifying forces useful for his own contrast between fire and water is shown by his earlier quotation of 14(21).3–4 at 949f; there fire and water have their obvious identification with sun and rain as elements.

138(32)   The phrase and its context in *lin. insec.*, listing differences between "joint" and "pivot," are corrupt. Even if Diels's Heraclitean reading of δύω δέει ἄρθρον is acceptable, it does not fit the context, for it gives no reason for the joint being διαφορά πως. The phrase may have been part of a medical simile for the work of Aphrodite on the elements, but E.'s use of ἄρθρον at 8(17).22 does not have any technical sense. There is little to be extracted from this passage.

139(58)   The sentence comes between the quotation of lines 10–13 of 47(35) and fr. 51(59). The *katastasis* that features the μουνομελῆ is designated by Simplicius as that in which Strife is retreating before the advance of Love. Examples of the μουνομελῆ, called by Simplicius τὰ ἄμικτα καὶ μονόγυια, are given in 50(57); the word is ἅπ. λεγ. and probably E.'s coinage. ἐπλανᾶτο occurs also at 50(57).3.

140(60)   βουγενῆ ἀνδρόπρῳρα is from 52(61).2 and εἰλίποδ' ἀκριτόχειρα a cognate phrase. εἰλίπους is an epithet of oxen—"with rolling walk," "lumbering." ἀκριτόχειρος is ἅπ. λεγ., defined in LSJ as "with countless hands," a bizarre picture even in the present context. A more appropriate sense would be "with hands not properly articulated or distinguishable"; as the other phrase shows, the creatures are oxlike, with some crude human features. Both phrases belong in the general context of 52(61); Plutarch is using such creatures along with the Furies as absurd nightmare visions which the Epicureans are compelled to accept as true impressions. This is some confirmation that E. does not have such creatures in the present *katastasis*, cf. the commentary on 52(61).3.

141(69)   διγόνους: elsewhere "twin-born," "double," "twin-bearing," but here, from the Proclus context, "capable of two terms of childbearing," i.e., after pregnancies of seven or nine months' duration. Proclus elaborates E.'s observation of a gynecological detail in terms of Pythagorean/Platonic number symbolism, based on 35 as the sum of the numbers 2–8, 45 of 1–9, and their respective multiplication by 6.

142(70)   ἀμνίον: the fine inner membrane enclosing the fetus, which breaks with the waters at birth. The word, with its ovine connection, is a typically Empedoclean combination of observation and analogy and has survived as the technical medical term; for the sense cf. the φλοιός which Anaximander thought enveloped early man, Aetius 5.19.4, and the χιτών of 110(126). The general context of frs. 141–42 is with 55–59, but cf. the commentary on 151(153a).

143(92)   The notice from Aristotle on E.'s theory of the sterility of mules may come either from the section of the *Physics* on reproduction or later, from that on types of mixture, cf. the commentary on 74(91). E.'s explanation, which Aristotle rejects, is that as the combination of two soft substances (copper and tin) produces a hard alloy (bronze), so the mixing of the soft secretions in the coupling of horse and ass results in a "hard" offspring, the infertile mule. In both cases, and as with water and wine, the process is a fitting together of κοῖλα and στερεά in the two substances, the sexual connotation of μειγνύναι probably also being involved here. The original phrase may have been χαλκὸν κασσιτέρῳ μιγέντα.

144(97) A fragment can hardly be extracted from the word ῥάχιν here, but the point, that the backbone is divided into vertebrae because it was broken originally by its twisted position in the womb, is significant for the interpretation of 52(61). The explanation is incompatible with teleology and the consequent immutability of species, and is therefore rejected outright by Aristotle.

145(99) ὄζος deliberately links plant and animal organs, cf. the commentary on 71(82).1–2. E.'s theory of hearing, probably coming after the section on sight (frs. 84–89), is given enigmatically in Theophrastus *Sens.* 9 and 21, and in Aetius 4.16.1. According to Aetius and *Sens.* 21 a sound like that of a bell is heard within, and this suggests that *Sens.* 9 here is an abbreviated version—the κώδων mentioned is an inner extension of the "sprig of flesh" of the auricle. With the MS ἔξωθεν in the first line retained, and τῶν ἴσων ἤχων taken as echoes "equal to," i.e., "reproducing" the original sound, the theory might be reconstructed as follows: external sounds, which are emanations of air particles, enter the channel of the outer ear and, presumably because they fit the pores of the organ, reverberate as in a trumpet bell in what is now called the middle ear. (A modern general account of the process also uses a simile: "the central portion of the drum-membrane vibrates as a stiff cone in response to sound," *Enc. Brit. Macr.* 5.1120–28, esp. 1125.) Theophrastus' question at *Sens.* 21, "How can we hear the internal sound?" is crucial, but E.'s failure to answer it should not be held against him. He is on the right track, and exactly how we hear the inner sound, i.e., how the mechanical vibrations are turned into nerve impulses, is still not fully understood.

146(142) These two lines are quoted for the grammatical point of a singular verb having both plural and singular subject. The reading of the first line can be accepted. For the second there are, among others, the following suggestions: οὔτε ποτ᾽ ᾿Αΐδεω δέχεται ἠδ᾽ οἰκτρῆς τέγος αὐδῆς

(Diels); τέρποι ἂν οὐδ(ὲ) αἰνῆς Ἑκάτης τέγος ἠλιτόποινον (Bignone); οὔτ' ἄρα πως 'Αίδεω δέχεται κατὰ γῆς τέγος ἔνδον (van der Ben). δέχεται seems preferable for the common verb, and the line scans if it starts with οὔτ' 'Αίδεω δέχεται. Little can be done with the end. The overall sense is, "the house of aegis-bearing Zeus does not receive him, nor that of Hades." The context is probably the *Katharmoi*, the "him" being the daimon, and the meaning similar to the rejection of the daimon by the elements at 107(115).9–12. From 7(6).2 we know that Zeus is fire (especially and appropriately the fire in the heavens) and Aidoneus/Hades earth.

147(148–50) Plutarch praises a point of E.'s style, that his adjectives are not merely decorative but give essential information, and he quotes three disconnected examples; their contexts can only be hazarded. ἀμφιβρότην χθόνα—"man-enclosing earth"—perhaps connects with the χιτών of 110(126) or with the τύποι sent up from earth, 53(62).4, or with the formation of living things by Kypris; whatever its placing, the Homeric adjective for a shield has been put to a new use. Some straightforward meteorological reference is perhaps behind the transference of Zeus' Homeric adjective νεφεληγερέτην to air. πολυαίματον τὸ ἧπαρ suggests that the physiological section was quite detailed. After the heart the liver is the most important organ, a repository of the lifeblood, with an essential part to play in digestion and embryology, and the source of blood and *pneuma* for the fetus, cf. Soranus, DK 31 A79.

148(151) ζείδωρος: the Homeric epithet for the earth, usually interpreted as "grain-giving," with an etymological twist means "life-giving" here (from ζάω rather than ζεῖα) and is applied to Philia/Aphrodite, cf. 14(21).8–11. Plutarch again commends E.'s choice of adjective.

149(152) The reference is to types of metaphor, and, in the same context as 129(143), Aristotle is describing metaphor by analogy; his second example is of old age being to life as evening is to day. Evening will then be called the old age of day (of which we have no examples), and old age the evening or sunset of life (which became a cliché, cf. Plato *Laws* 770a and other examples cited by A. Gudeman, *Aristoteles Poetik* p. 359). The text adopted here is that of P² (Gudeman), which quotes the last example as being from E.; elsewhere ἢ ὥσπερ 'E. comes after ἡμέρας, giving a reference to a phrase of E. well known to Aristotle but unknown to us.

150(153) βαυβώ: an obscure word, connected probably with "sleeping" or "rocking to sleep" as βαυβάω. The appropriate "cavity" would be where the unborn sleeps before birth, i.e., the womb, either that of the individual mother or, metaphorically, of the earth, cf. 48(96).1 and 53(62).4–6. For the likely connection of a figurine of the womb with the cult of Demeter cf. Bollack, *Empédocle* vol. 3, pp. 401–02.

151(153a) A notice on the formation of the embryo would be expected to come from the *Physics* in the context of frs. 55–59. There is, however, no reason to doubt the attribution to the *Katharmoi* because of the subject matter (as Zuntz does, *Persephone* p. 235, n. 1, and Bollack, *Empédocle* vol. 3, p. 539, following Wilamowitz). αἰνίττεται shows that there is not a detailed exposition, and a brief mention of the growth of the embryo could belong with the putting on of the χιτών of flesh, 110(126), or the birth cry of 112(118). Whatever number theory may be involved here (cf. the commentaries on 59[68] and 141[69]), the time given happens to be correct. By the end of the seventh week internal and external organs are articulated, "the stage of the embryo ends and 'fetus' is the preferred term." *Enc. Brit. Macr.* 6.74.

152 This fragment, published by H. Hunger in 1967 (*Jahrbuch der Österreichischen Byzantinischen Gesellschaft* 1967, pp. 1–33) and discussed by M. L. West (*Maia* 1968, p. 199), F. Lasserre (*MH* 1969, p. 82), and van der Ben (*Proem* pp. 15–16, 18) is important for showing that there were two books of the *Katharmoi*. It also breaks down further the long-held view that the *Physics* is concerned only with "nature" and the *Katharmoi* with "religion," which led to one of only two other fragments explicitly assigned to the *Katharmoi* being transferred (cf. the previous note). The quotation is given to illustrate an unexciting lengthening of alpha. τῶν γὰρ ὅσα ῥίζαις (or ῥίζῃς) μὲν ἐπασσοντέρα . . . μανοτέροις ὅρπηξιν . . . τηλεθάοντα seems clear, and the gaps are here filled according to Lasserre. The sense is, "of those thriving with roots closer set and branches spaced farther apart"—a mundane arboreal allusion. Perhaps it belongs toward the end of the *Katharmoi* in the account of the different forms of life and their highest exemplars. The contrast between compact and rare parts, as well as the actual wording, recalls 70(75).1: τῶν δ' ὅσ' ἔσω μὲν πυκνά, τὰ δ' ἔκτοθι μανὰ πέπηγεν.

Bibliography

Journal abbreviations are as in *L'Année Philologique*

Anton, J. P., and Kustas, G. L., eds. *Essays in Ancient Greek Philosophy.* Albany, N.Y.: S.U.N.Y. Press, 1971.

Arundel, M. R. (=Wright) "Empedocles fr. 35, 12–15." *CR* 12 (1962): 109–11.

———. "An Interpretation of Empedocles." B. Litt. diss., University of Oxford, 1963.

———. "*Principio Caelum.*" *PVS* 3 (1964): 27–34.

Barnes, H. E. "Unity in the Thought of Empedocles." *CJ* 63 (1967): 18–23.

Beare, J. I. *Greek Theories of Elementary Cognition.* Oxford: Clarendon Press, 1906.

Bennett, J. "Empedocles the Poet: His Style and Metre." Ph. D. diss., Trinity College Dublin, 1940.

Bergk, T. *Commentatio de Prooemio Empedoclis.* Berlin: Königlichen Akademie der Wissenschaften, 1839. Reprinted as "Commentatio de Empedoclis Prooemio" in his *Kleine Philologische Schriften*, edited by R. Peppmüller, vol. 2, pp. 8–43. Halle am Saale: Waisenhaus, 1886.

Bidez, J. *La Biographie d'Empédocle.* Ghent: Clemm, 1894.

Bignone, E. *Empedocle: studio critico.* Turin: Bocca, 1916.

Bluck, R. S. "The *Phaedrus* and Reincarnation." *AJPh* 79(1958): 156–64.

Blumenthal, H. J. "Empedocles fr. 17.19–20." *GB* 3(1975): 21–29.

Bodrero, E. *Il principio fondamentale del sistema di Empedocle.* Rome: E. Loescher, 1904.

Bollack, J. "Die Metaphysik des Empedokles." *Philologus* 101(1957): 30–54.

———. "Le Proème du Περὶ φύσεως d'Empédocle." *REG* 72(1959): 15–16.

———. "Les Zones de la Cosmogonie d'Empédocle." *Hermes* 96(1968): 239–40.

———. *Empédocle.* Vol. 1: *Introduction à l'ancienne physique.* Vol. 2: *Les Origines, édition et traduction des fragments et des témoignages.* Vol. 3, pts. 1 and 2: *Les Origines, commentaire.* Paris: Les Éditions de Minuit, 1965, 1969.

Booth, N. B. "Empedocles' Account of Breathing." *JHS* 80(1960): 10–15.

———. "Aristotle on Empedocles B100." *Hermes* 103 (1975): 373–75.

Brown, T. S. *Timaeus of Tauromenium.* Berkeley: University of California Press, 1958.

Brun, J. *Empédocle ou le Philosophe de l'amour et de la haine.* Paris: Seghers, 1966.

Bruno, V. J. *Form and Colour in Greek Painting.* London: Thames & Hudson, 1977.

Burkert, W. *Lore and Science in Ancient Pythagoreanism.* Translated by E. Minar. Cambridge, Mass.: Harvard University Press, 1972.

Burnet, J. *Early Greek Philosophy.* 4th ed. London: A. & C. Black, 1930.

Burton, A. *Diodorus Siculus Book I.* Leiden: E. J. Brill, 1972.

Calhoun, G. M. *The Growth of Criminal Law in Ancient Greece.* Berkeley: University of California Press, 1927.

Cardini, M. T. "Respirazione e clessidra." *PP* 12 (1957): 250–70.

———. "La zoogonie di Empedocle." *Physis* 2 (1960): 5–13.

Chantraine, P. *Grammaire Homérique.* Paris: C. Klincksieck, 1948.

Cherniss, H. *Aristotle's Criticism of Presocratic Philosophy.* Baltimore: The Johns Hopkins Press, 1935.

Classen, C. J. s.v. Empedokles, *Pauly-Wissowa* Suppl., vol. 12, pp. 241–47. Stuttgart: A. Druckenmüller, 1970.

Cleve, F. M. *The Giants of Pre-Sophistic Greek Philosophy.* The Hague: M. Nijhoff, 1965.

Cornford, F. M. *From Religion to Philosophy.* London: E. Arnold, 1912.

———. "Mystery Religions and Pre-Socratic Philosophy." *Cambridge Ancient History,* vol. 4, pp. 522–78. Cambridge: Cambridge University Press, 1930.

Cumont, F. *Astrology and Religion among the Greeks and Romans.* New York: G. P. Putnam's Sons, 1912.

————. *After Life in Roman Paganism*. New Haven: Yale University Press, 1922.

Darcus, S. M. "Daimon Parallels the Holy Phren in Empedocles." *Phronesis* 22 (1977): 175–90.

Daube, D. *Roman Law: Linguistic, Social and Philosophical Aspects*. Edinburgh: Edinburgh University Press, 1969.

Davison, J. A. "Protagoras, Democritus and Anaxagoras." *CQ* 3 (1953): 33–45.

Denniston, J. D. *The Greek Particles*. 2nd ed. Oxford: Clarendon Press, 1954.

Détienne, M. "La Démonologie d'Empédocle." *REG* 72 (1959): 1–17.

Devambez, P. *Greek Painting*. Translated by J. Stewart. London: Weidenfield & Nicolson, 1962.

Diels, H. *Doxographi Graeci*. Berlin: de Gruyter, 1879. Reprinted 1958.

————. "*Studia Empedoclea*." *Hermes* 15 (1880): 161–79.

————. "Gorgias und Empedokles." *SPAW* 49 (1884): 343–68.

————. "Über ein Fragment des Empedokles." *SPAW* 62 (1897): 1062–73.

————. "Über die Gedichte des Empedokles." *SPAW* 63(1898): 396–415. (The last three articles are reprinted in *Hermann Diels, Kleine Schriften*, ed. W. Burkert. Darmstadt: Wissenschaftliche Buchgesellschaft, 1969.)

————. "Symbola Empedoclea." In *Mélanges H. Weil*, pp. 125–30, Paris: A. Fontemoing, 1898.

————. *Poetarum Philosophorum Fragmenta*, pp. 74–168. Berlin: Weidmann, 1901.

————. *Die Fragmente der Vorsokratiker*. 3rd ed., vol. 1, pp. 193–283. Berlin: Weidmann, 1912.

Diels, H., and Kranz, W. *Die Fragmente der Vorsokratiker*. 10th ed., vols. 1 and 2. Berlin: Weidmann, 1961.

Dietrich, B. C. "Peak Cults and Their Place in Minoan Religion." *Historia* 18 (1969): 257–75.

Dodds, E. R. *The Greeks and the Irrational*. Berkeley: University of California Press, 1951.

————. "On Misunderstanding the *Oedipus Rex*." *G&R* 13 (1966): 37–49.

————. *Plato: Gorgias*. Oxford: Clarendon Press, 1959.

Dümmler, F. *Akademika*. Giessen: J. Ricker, 1889.

Ellis, R. "Some Suggestions on Diels' *Poetarum Philosophorum Fragmenta*." *CR* 16 (1902): 269–70.

Ferrari, S. *Empedocle*. Rome: G. Balbi, 1891.

Fraenkel, E. "Der Zeushymnus in Agamemnon des Aischylos." *Philologus* 86 (1931): 1–17.

Freeman, E. A. *The History of Sicily from the Earliest Times*. 4 vols. Oxford: Clarendon Press, 1891–94.

Furley, D. J. "Empedocles and the Clepsydra." *JHS* 77 (1957):31–34.

Gallavotti, C. *Poema fisico e lustrale: Empedocle*. N.p.: Fondazione Lorenzo Valla, 1975.

Gildersleeve, B. L. *Syntax of Classical Greek from Homer to Demosthenes*. New York: American Book Co., 1900.

Glotz, G. *La Solidarité de la famille dans le droit criminel en Grèce*. Paris: A. Fontemoing, 1904. Reprinted, New York: Arno Press, 1973.

Gomperz, T. *Greek Thinkers*. Translated by L. Magnus. Vol. 1, pp. 227–54. London: J. Murray, 1901.

Goodwin, W. W. *Syntax of the Moods and Tenses of the Greek Verb*. London: Macmillan, 1889. Reissued 1965.

Gow, A. S. F. *Theocritus*. 2 vols. Cambridge: Cambridge University Press, 1950.

Gray, Asa. *Gray's Manual of Botany*. 8th ed. New York: Van Nostrand Reinhold, 1970.

Gray, Henry. *Gray's Anatomy*. 35th ed. London: Longman, 1973.

Gudeman, A. *Aristoteles Poetik*. Berlin: de Gruyter, 1934.

Guthrie, W. K. C. *History of Greek Philosophy*, vol. 2. Cambridge: Cambridge University Press, 1965.

Harris, C. R. S. *The Heart and the Vascular System in Ancient Greek Medicine*. London: Oxford University Press, 1973.

Head, B. V. *Historia Numorum*. Oxford: Clarendon Press, 1911.

Heidel, W. A. "Qualitative Change in Presocratic Philosophy." *AGPh* 19 (1906):333–79.

———. " Περὶ φύσεως: A Study of the Conception of Nature among the Pre-Socratics." *Proceedings of the American Academy* 45 (1910): 77–133.

———. "On Certain Fragments of the Pre-Socratics." *Proceedings of the American Academy* 48 (1913):725–29.

———. *The Frame of the Ancient Greek Maps, with a Discussion of the Discovery of the Sphericity of the Earth*. New York: American Geographical Society, 1937.

Hershbell, J. P. "Empedocles' Oral Style." *CJ* 63 (1968): 352–57.

———. "Plutarch as a Source for Empedocles Re-examined." *AJPh* 92 (1971): 156–84.

———. "Hippolytus' *Elenchos* as a Source for Empedocles Re-examined."
   Phronesis 18 (1973): 97–114, 187–203.

———. "Empedoclean Influences on the *Timaeus*." *Phoenix* 28 (1974):
   145–66.

———. "The Idea of Strife in Early Greek Thought." *The Personalist*
   55 (1974): 205–15.

Hölscher, U. "Weltzeiten und Lebenzyklus: eine Nachprüfung der
   Empedokles-Doxographie." *Hermes* 93 (1965): 7–33.

Horna, C. "Empedocleum." *WS* 48 (1930): 3–11.

Hunger, H. "Palimpsest-Fragmente aus Herodians 'Καθολικὴ προσῳδία'."
   Jahrbuch der Österreichischen Byzantinischen Gesellschaft 16 (1967):1–33.

Hussey, E. *The Presocratics*. London: Duckworth, 1972.

Jacoby, F. *Apollodors Chronik*. Berlin: Weidmann, 1902. Reprinted New
   York: Arno Press, 1973.

Jaeger, W. *The Theology of the Early Greek Philosophers*. Oxford: Clarendon
   Press, 1947.

———. *Aristotle: Fundamentals of the History of His Development*. Translated
   by R. Robinson. 2nd ed. Oxford: Clarendon Press, 1948.

Joachim, H. H. *Aristotle: On Coming-to-Be and Passing-Away*. Oxford:
   Clarendon Press, 1922.

Jones, J. W. *The Law and Legal Theory of the Greeks*. Oxford: Clarendon
   Press, 1956.

Jones, W. H. S. *Philosophy and Medicine in Ancient Greece*. Suppl. *Bulletin
   of the History of Medicine* 8. Baltimore: The Johns Hopkins Press, 1946.

———. *The Medical Writings of Anonymus Londinensis*. Cambridge: Cambridge University Press, 1947.

Jouanna, J. "Présence d'Empédocle dans la Collection Hippocratique."
   BAGB 20 (1961): 452–63.

Kahn, C. H. *Anaximander and the Origins of Greek Cosmology*. New York:
   Columbia University Press, 1960.

———. "Religion and Natural Philosophy in Empedocles' Doctrine of
   the Soul." *AGPh* 42 (1960): 3–35. Reprinted in Anton and Kustas,
   Essays, and in Mourelatos, *The Pre-Socratics*.

———. Review of J. Bollack, *Empédocle* vol. 1. *Gnomon* 41 (1969): 439–47.

Karsten, S. *Empedoclis Agrigentini carminum reliquiae, de vita et studiis dis-
   seruit, fragmenta explicuit, philosophiam illustravit*. Amsterdam: J. Müller,
   1838.

Kirk, G. S. *Heraclitus: The Cosmic Fragments*. Cambridge: Cambridge
   University Press, 1954.

Kirk, G. S., and Raven, J. E. *The Presocratic Philosophers,* pp. 320–61. Cambridge: Cambridge University Press, 1957.

Knatz, F. "Empedoclea." In *Schedae philologae H. Usener oblatae,* pp. 1–9. Bonn: F. Cohen, 1891.

Knox, B. M. W. *Oedipus at Thebes.* London: Oxford University Press, and New Haven: Yale University Press, 1957.

Kranz, W. "Empedokles und die Atomistik." *Hermes* 47 (1912):18–42.

———. "Die ältesten Farbenlehren der Griechen." *Hermes* 47 (1912): 126–40.

———. "Die *Katharmoi* und die *Physika* des Empedokles." *Hermes* 70 (1935):111–19.

Lambridis, H. *Empedocles: A Philosophical Investigation.* University: University of Alabama Press, 1976.

Lameere, W. "Au temps ou Franz Cumont s'interrogeait sur Aristote." *L'Antiquité Classique* 18 (1949): 279–324.

Lasserre, F. "Trois nouvelles citations poétiques." *MH* 26 (1969): 80–83.

Last, H. "Empedokles and His Klepsydra Again." *CQ* 18 (1924):169–73.

Leonard, W. E. *The Fragments of Empedocles Translated into English Verse.* Chicago: Open Court, 1908.

Lloyd, A. H. "The Coin Types of Selinus and the Legend of Empedocles." *NC* 15 (1935):73–93.

Lloyd, G. E. R. "Right and Left in Greek Philosophy." *JHS* 82 (1962): 56–66.

———. "The Hot and the Cold, the Dry and the Wet in Greek Philosophy." *JHS* 84 (1964):92–106.

———. *Polarity and Analogy.* Cambridge: Cambridge University Press, 1966.

Lloyd-Jones, H. "The Guilt of Agamemnon." *CQ* 12 (1962):187–99.

———. "The Seal of Posidippus." *JHS* 83 (1963):75–99.

Lodge, R. C. *Plato's Theory of Education.* London: Kegan Paul, 1947.

Long, A. A. "Thinking and Sense-Perception in Empedocles: Mysticism or Materialism?" *CQ* 16 (1966): 256–76.

———. "Empedocles' Cosmic Cycle in the Sixties." In *The Pre-Socratics,* edited by A. P. D. Mourelatos, pp. 397–425. Garden City, N. Y.: Anchor Press/Doubleday, 1974.

Long, H. S. "A Study of the Doctrine of Metempsychosis in Greece from Pythagoras to Plato." Ph. D. diss., Princeton University, 1948.

———. "The Unity of Empedocles' Thought." *AJPh* 70 (1949):142–58.

Longrigg, J. "Galen on Empedocles (fr. 67)." *Philologus* 108 (1964): 297–300.

———. "Empedocles' Fiery Fish." *JWI* 28 (1965): 314–15.

———. " *Κρυσταλλοειδῶς.*" *CQ* 15 (1965):249–51.

———. "Roots." *CR* 17 (1967):1–4.

———. "Empedocles' Fertile Fish." *JHS* 94 (1974):173.

———. "The 'Roots of All Things'." *Isis* 67 (1976):420–38.

Lovejoy, A. O. "The Meaning of *φύσις* in the Greek Physiologers." *PhR* 18 (1909): 369–83.

Lüth, J. C. *Die Struktur des Wirklichen im empedokleischen System.* Meisenheim: Hain, 1970.

Maas, P. "Eustathios als Konjekturalkritiker." *ByzZ* 36 (1936):27–31.

———. *Greek Metre.* Translated by H. Lloyd-Jones. Oxford: Clarendon Press, 1962.

MacDowell, D. M. *Athenian Homicide Law in the Age of the Orators.* Manchester: Manchester University Press, 1963.

Mansfeld, J. "Ambiguity in Empedocles B 17.3–5." *Phronesis* 17 (1972): 17–39.

Millerd, C. E. *On the Interpretation of Empedocles.* Chicago: University of Chicago Press, 1908.

Minar, E. L. "Cosmic Periods in the Philosophy of Empedocles." *Phronesis* 8 (1963): 127–45.

Morris, R. K., and Fox, M. W., eds. *On the Fifth Day: Animal Rights and Human Ethics.* Fontwell, Arundel, Sussex: Centaur Press, 1978.

Mourelatos, A. P. D., ed. *The Pre-Socratics.* Garden City, N.Y.: Anchor Press/Doubleday, 1974.

Mugler, C. "Sur quelques fragments d'Empédocle." *RPh* 25 (1951): 33–65.

Mullach, F. G. A. *Fragmenta Philosophorum Graecorum,* vol. 3, pp. xii–xxvii, 1–80. Paris: A. Didor, 1883.

Müller, C. W. *Gleiches zu Gleichem.* Wiesbaden: O. Harrassowitz, 1965.

Munding, H. "Zur Beweisführung des Empedokles." *Hermes* 82 (1954): 129–45.

Nélod, G. *Empédocle d'Agrigente.* Brussels: S. A. Éditeurs, 1959.

Nestlé, W. "Der Dualismus des Empedokles." *Philologus* 65 (1906): 545–57.

O'Brien, D. "Empedocles fr. 35.14–15." *CR* 15 (1965): 1–4.

———. "Empedocles' Cosmic Cycle." *CQ* 17 (1967): 29–40.

———. "The Relation of Empedocles and Anaxagoras." *JHS* 88 (1968): 93–113.

———. *Empedocles' Cosmic Cycle.* Cambridge: Cambridge University Press, 1969.

————. "The Effect of a Simile: Empedocles' Theories of Seeing and Breathing." *JHS* 90 (1970): 140–79.

Onians, R. B. *The Origins of European Thought.* Cambridge: Cambridge University Press, 1951.

Owen, G. E. L. "Eleatic Questions." *CQ* 10 (1960): 84–102.

Owens, J. "Aristotle on Empedocles Fr. 8." *Canadian Journal of Philosophy*, suppl. vol. 2 (1976): 87–100.

Page, D. *Sappho and Alcaeus.* Oxford: Clarendon Press, 1955.

Panzerbieter, F. "Zu Empedokles." *ZATW* 111 (1845):883–87, 889–93.

Pease, A. S. *M.Tulli Ciceronis De Natura Deorum.* Cambridge, Mass.: Harvard University Press, 1955.

Peyron, A. *Empedoclis et Parmenidis fragmenta ex codice Taurinensis Bibliothecae restituta*, pp. 27–55. Leipzig: I. A. G. Weigel, 1810.

Powell, J. U. "The Simile of the Clepsydra in Empedocles." *CQ* 17 (1923): 172–74.

Rathmann, W. *Quaestiones Pythagorae Orphicae Empedocleae.* Halle: E. Klinz, 1933.

Reiche, H. *Empedocles' Mixture, Eudoxan Astronomy and Aristotle's "connate pneuma."* Amsterdam: A. M. Hakkert, 1960.

Richter, G. M. A. "Polychromy in Greek Sculpture." *AJA* suppl. 1944: 322–33.

————. *A Handbook of Greek Art.* 6th ed. London: Phaidon, 1969.

Robertson, M. *Greek Painting.* Geneva: Skira, 1959.

Rohde, E. *Psyche.* Translated by W. B. Hillis. London: Routledge & Kegan Paul, 1925.

Ross, W. D. *Aristotle's Metaphysics.* 2 vols. Oxford: Clarendon Press, 1924.

————. *Aristotle's Physics.* Oxford: Clarendon Press, 1936.

Rostagni, A. "Il poema sacro di Empedocle." *RF* 1 (1923): 7–39.

Rudberg, G. "Empedokles und Evolution." *Eranos* 50 (1952): 23–30.

Saffrey, H. O. "Nouveaux oracles chaldaïques dans les scholies du *Paris. gr.* 1853." *RPh* 43 (1969): 59–72.

Schmalzriedt, E. *Peri Physeos, zur Frühgeschichte der Buchtitel.* Munich: Wilhelm Fink, 1970.

Schneidewin, F. W. "Neue Verse des Empedokles." *Philologus* 6 (1851): 155–67.

Schwabl, H. "Empedokles, fr. B 110." *WS* 69 (1956): 49–56.

————. "Zur 'Theogonie' bei Parmenides und Empedokles." *WS* 70 (1957): 278–89.

Schwyzer, E., and Debrunner, A. *Griechische Grammatik*, vol. 2. Munich: C. H. Beck'sche, 1950.

Seeck, G. A. "Empedokles B17.9–13, B 8, B100 bei Aristoteles." *Hermes* 95 (1967): 28–53.

Segal, C. "The Embassy and the Duals of *Iliad* 9.182–98." *GRBS* (1968): 101–14.

Sigerist, H. E. *History of Medicine*, vol. 2. New York: Oxford University Press, 1961.

Solmsen, F. "Aristotle and Presocratic Cosmogony." *HSPh* 63 (1958): 265–82.

———. *Aristotle's System of the Physical World.* Ithaca, N.Y.: Cornell University Press, 1960.

———. "Nature as Craftsman in Greek Thought." *JHI* 24 (1963):473–96.

———. "Love and Strife in Empedocles' Cosmogony." *Phronesis* 10 (1965):109–48.

———. "ζωρός in Empedocles." *CR* 17 (1967):245–46.

———. "Eternal and Temporary Beings in Empedocles' Physical Poem." *AGPh* 57 (1975):123–45.

Souilhé, J. "L'énigme d'Empédocle." *APhilos* 9 (1932):1–23.

Stein, H. *Empedocles Agrigentinus, Fragmenta disposuit, recensuit, adnotavit.* Bonn: A. Marcus, 1852.

Stephanus (= Estienne), H. *Poesis Philosophica*, pp. 17–31. Geneva: H. Stephanus, 1573.

Stokes, M. C. *One and Many in Presocratic Philosophy.* Washington, D.C.: Center for Hellenic Studies/Harvard University Press, 1971.

Stratton, G. M. *Theophrastus and the Greek Physiological Psychology before Aristotle.* London: George Allen & Unwin; New York: Macmillan, 1917.

Sturz, F. G. *Empedocles Agrigentinus, de vita et philosophia eius exposuit, carminum reliquias ex antiquis scriptoribus collegit, recensuit.* 2 vols. Leipzig: Goeschen, 1805.

Susemihl, F. *Geschichte der Griechischen Litteratur.* 2 vols. Leipzig: B. G. Teubner, 1891.

Taillardat, J. "Le sens d' 'amorgos' et les lanternes dans l'antiquité." *REG* 72 (1959):11–12.

Tannery, P. *Pour l'Histoire de la science hellène.* 2nd ed. Edited by A. Diès. Paris: Gauthier-Villars, 1930.

Taylor, A. E. "On the Date of the Trial of Anaxagoras." *CQ* 11 (1917): 81–87.

Taylor, C. C. W. "Pleasure, Knowledge and Sensation in Democritus." *Phronesis* 12 (1967): 6–27.

Thiele. G. "Zu den vier Elemente des Empedokles." *Hermes* 32 (1897): 68–78.

Traglia, A. *Studi sulla lingua di Empedocle.* Bari: Adriatica, 1952.

Tucker, G. M. "Empedocles in Exile." *CR* 45 (1931):49–51.

van der Ben, N. *The Proem of Empedocles' Peri Physios.* Amsterdam: B. R. Grüner, 1975.

———. "Empedocles' Fragments 8, 9, 10 DK." *Phronesis* 23 (1978): 197–215.

van Groningen, B. A. "Trois notes sur Empédocle." *Mnemosyne* 9 (1956): 221–24.

———. "Le fragment 111 d'Empédocle." *C&M* 17 (1956):47–61.

———. "Empédocle, poète." *Mnemosyne* 24 (1971):169–88.

Veazie, W. *Empedocles: His Psychological Doctrine in Its Original and Traditional Setting.* New York: Columbia University Press, 1922.

Verdenius, W. J. *Parmenides: Some Comments on His Poem.* Groningen: J. B. Wolters, 1942.

———. "Empedocles' Doctrine of Sight." In *Studia Vollgraff oblata*, pp. 155–64. Amsterdam: North-Holland, 1948.

———. "Notes on the Presocratics." *Mnemosyne* 4 (1948):10–14.

Vlastos, G. "Parmenides' Theory of Knowledge." *TAPhA* 77 (1946): 66–74.

———. "Equality and Justice in the Early Greek Cosmologies." *CPh* 42 (1947):156–78.

———. "Theology and Philosophy in Early Greek Thought." *PhilosQ* 2 (1952):97–123.

———. *Plato's Universe.* Oxford: Clarendon Press, 1975.

von Arnim, H. "Die Weltperioden bei Empedokles." *Festschrift Gomperz*, pp. 16–27. Vienna: A. Hölder, 1902.

von Fritz, K. "Νοῦς, νοεῖν, and Their Derivatives in Pre-Socratic Philosophy." *CPh* 41 (1946):12–34.

———. "Ἐστρὶς ἑκατέρωθι in Pindar's Second *Olympian* and Pythagoras' Theory of Metempsychosis." *Phronesis* 2 (1957):85–94.

Wackernagel, J. *Vorlesungen über Syntax*, vol. 1. Basel: Emil Birkhaüser, 1920.

———. "Orthographica und Verwandtes." *Philologus* 86 (1931):133–40.

Waters, K. H. "The Rise and Decline of Some Greek Colonies in Sicily." *AncSoc* 5 (1974):1–19.

Wellmann, E. s.v. Empedokles (3), *Pauly-Wissowa*, vol. 5, cols. 2507–12. Stuttgart: J. B. Metzler, 1905.

Wellmann, M. *Die Fragmente der sikelischen Ärzte.* Berlin: Weidmann, 1901.

West, M. L. "Empedocles on Papyrus." *CR* 12 (1962):120.

————. "ζωρός in Empedocles." *CR* 16 (1966):135–36.

————. "Notes on Newly-Discovered Fragments of Greek Authors."
    Maia 20 (1968):199–200.

Wilamowitz-Moellendorff, U. von. "Lesefrüchte." *Hermes* 37 (1902):
    326–27; 40 (1905):165–70; 65 (1930):245–50.

————. "Die *Katharmoi* des Empedokles." *SPAW* 94 (1929):626–61.
    Reprinted in his *Kleine Schriften*, pp. 473–521. Berlin: Weidmann,
    1935.

Wilford, P. A. "Embryological Analogies in Empedocles' Cosmogony."
    Phronesis 13 (1968):108–18.

Wilkens, K. "Wie hat Empedokles die Vorgänge in der Klepsydra
    erklärt?" *Hermes* 95 (1967):129–40.

Wiśniewski, B. "Quaestiones empedoclea." *PP* 29 (1974):158–71.

Witton, W. F. "The Word *O-PE-TE-RE-U.*" *AJPh* 79 (1958):414–15.

Worthen, T. "Pneumatic Action in the Klepsydra and Empedocles'
    Account of Breathing." *Isis* 61 (1970):520–30.

Wright, J. H. "The Origin of Plato's Cave." *HSPh* 17 (1906):131–42.

Zafiropulo, J. *Empédocle d'Agrigente.* Paris: Budé ("Les Belles Lettres"),
    1953.

Zeller, E. *Die Philosophie der Griechen.* Edited by W. Nestlé. Vol. 1, pt. 2,
    pp. 939–1038. Leipzig: O. R. Reisland, 1920.

Zuntz, G. "De Empedoclis librorum numero coniectura." *Mnemosyne*
    18 (1965):365.

————. "Empedokles fr. 137." *WS* 79 (1966):38–44.

————. *Persephone.* Bk. 2: *Empedokles' Katharmoi*, pp. 181–276. Oxford:
    Clarendon Press, 1971.

Bibliographical Afterword

Since 1981 the study of the Presocratics has flourished, and Empedocles has shared in this prosperity. The comprehensive studies published in this period include the revised Kirk and Raven, *The Presocratic Philosophers*, with Schofield in 1983, and a century bibliography by Paquet and others (1988). Dumont gave the Greek text of Diels/Kranz with a French translation (1988), while Mansfeld had a similar presentation with Greek and facing German translation in the Reclam series (1986), as well as his background volume on the historiography (1990). A selection of the fragments in Greek with commentary appeared in Wright (1985), a comprehensive English translation of contexts and fragments in the Penguin Classics by Barnes (1987), and more recently a substantial *Introduction* to the Presocratics by McKirahan for Hackett (1994), which contains an essay on each individual, preceded by a translation of the main texts.

Specifically on Empedocles there is a verse translation by Lombardo (1982), the thin Bryn Mawr commentary by Johnston (1985), and the rather disappointing *Phoenix* volume by Inwood (1992). This gives the fragments in Greek, a translation of them with their contexts and the Diels-Kranz (A) Testimonia, but very little in the way of commentary on particular or general issues. Inwood put all the fragments into one poem called *Katharmoi* with *Physika* 'as a kind of alternative title', taking to extremes a tendency that first began with Van der Ben (1975, in the main bibliography) to remove 107(115) with some related fragments to the beginning of the *Physics*; this was answered among others by Calzolari (1984), who supported the present stand with B2 and 3 as the openers. Sedley (1989) favoured Van der Ben's ordering, but for different reasons, and reduced *Katharmoi* to a set of purificatory oracles and 'healing utterances', using some evidence from Lucretius to bolster his case. He argued cogently, although I still find the transition then necessary, from a popular address for the citizens of Acragas to a more technical account for a favoured student, too abrupt (see pp. 81-2 above). Inwood's more drastic move, as well as his complicated use of contexts with double translations, was apparently influenced by Osborne (1987a). A new home was found for fr. 49(34) by Sider (1982) in Empedocles' *Persika* as an account of food supplies for the Persian army, and Solmsen earlier (1980) had suggested ascribing frs. 95-7(132-4) to the *Hymn to Apollo*.

The two volume *Index Empedocleus* (1991) by Imbraguglia and others is a mixed compilation. One volume is devoted to reproducing Wright's Index

Verborum, expanded by some words which might be direct quotations from the
(A) Testimonia; the other gives a text (in a poor Greek font) with 'Commento
alle *variae lectiones* e riferimenti bibliografici', but prefaced by some useful
essays, especially on the language, style and vocabulary of Empedocles. This
is a topic on which there is still much work to be done, although it was touched
on by Edwards (1991); a particular example was examined by Slings (1991),
and Robb (1983) produced an important collection of related general essays.

There was also surprisingly little textual analysis of individual fragments.
The six main notes are on 12(8) by Nilles (1989) which accuses Aristotle of
some sharp practice here, Janko (1986) on the difficult reading of 14(21).6,
Meriani (1991) on *anaesimos* at 96(27a), Sider (1984) on 48(96), Rösler (1983)
on the opening of *Katharmoi* at 102(112) and Janssen's contrast in 1984 of
Nemertēs and *Asapheia* at 116(122).4; Mansfeld also has a note on the manuscript tradition of *Katharmoi* (1994).

An important new volume by Kingsley (1995b) re-examines Empedocles'
involvement in the Pythagorean tradition and the practitioners of magic, but
without shunting him out of the history of Presocratic philosophy; Kingsley's
work is particularly noteworthy in that he introduces virtually unknown
Arabic and Armenian texts. Less controversially, Kerferd (1986) discusses the connection of Empedocles and Gorgias; Castner (1987), Edwards
(1989) and Mesturini (1989), along with Sedley, trace the influence of
Empedocles on Lucretius on various topics; Obbink (1988) is interested in
the title of Hermachus' polemic against Empedocles, whereas Kohlschitter
(1991) studies his place in Porphyry's *History of Philosophy*. Kyriakou (1994)
finds Empedoclean echoes in Apollonius of Rhodes; Sedley (1992) looks at
Theophrastus and Empedocles on vision, but Gallavotti (1985) tackles the
range of the diffusion of Empedocles' work from Aristotle to Averroes.

It is encouraging that the controversy about the interpretation of Empedocles'
cosmology, and in particular the cycle of phases involved, has moved from the
undue prominence it had centre stage, and is settling into the main lines
accepted in the present volume. Van der Ben (1984) argued for 8(17).3-5
referring to cycles of life, and Brown (1984) opted for a linear rather than a
cyclic development, but he is in a minority. Graham (1988) on 8(17) supported
the double creation view as does Stevens (1989), who comes to the problem from
her analysis of Simplicius, and Steiger (1986) from a comparison of the cosmologies of Empedocles and Parmenides; Osborne too (1987b) supports the cycle of
daimons linked to the elements and the motive forces, albeit in the one poem.

Taking *Katharmoi* still as giving some account of the life of the *daimon* and
the achievement of wisdom, Karin Alt has two thoughtful articles in *Hermes* on
the complex themes involved (1987/8), and Ruocco (1987) links the concepts of
Daimon, Sphairos and Ananke. Panagiotou (1984) and Demoulie (1993) pursued
the theme as directly related to Empedocles, and Chitwood (1986) found the
anecdote of the leap into Etna a logical and poetically appropriate end for him.

Perhaps the most profitable way forward in work on Empedocles will come from a study of his place in the history of science. The topic of the four elements is obviously relevant here, and is the subject of articles by Moriani (1990), by Gemelli Marciano (1991) in comparisons with atomism, and, with an enlightening reconsideration of the doxography, by Kingsley (1994), who also has a piece on Empedocles' solar theory (1995a). There is more to be done on the themes of perception and epistemology, on the linking of biological structures and functions in the various forms of life, on the working of force and matter in individual and cosmos, and on the general search for a 'theory of everything'. This optimism for the future is encouraged by the recent discovery (reported in *The Times*, 16 April 1994, p.3) of small fragments of an early Greek papyrus in the University of Strasbourg from a site in upper Egypt; they have been identified as Empedoclean.

M. R. Wright
Lampeter, 1995.

Additional Bibliography

Alt, Karin "Wenige Fragen zu den *Katharmoi* des Empedokles." *Hermes* 115 (1987): 385-411; 116 (1988): 264-71.

Barnes, J. *Early Greek Philosophy*, Harmondsworth: Penguin Classics, 1987.

Brown, G. "The cosmological theory of Empedocles." *Apeiron* 18 (1984): 97-101.

Calzolari, A. "Empedocles, frr. 2 and 3 Diels-Kranz." *Studi Classici e Orientale* 34 (1984): 7-81.

Castner, C. J. "Lucretius' application of Empedoclean language to Epicurean doctrine." *Phoenix* 41 (1987): 40-49.

Chitwood, A. "The Death of Empedocles." *American Journal of Philology* 107 (1986): 175-91.

Demoulie, C. "Empedocles on the Pathos of Harmony." *Critique* 49 (1993): 357-71.

Dumont, Jean-Paul *Les Présocratiques*, Paris: Gallimard, 1988.

Edwards, M. J. "Lucretius, Empedocles and Epicurean politics." *Antike und Abendland* 35 (1989): 104-15.

———. "Being and Seeming – Empedocles' Reply." *Hermes* 119 (1991): 282-93.

Gallavotti, C. "Nuove appunti sul testo di Empedocle." *Bollettino dei classici* 6 (1985): 3-27.

Gemelli Marciano, M. L. "L'atomismo e il corpuscolarismo empedocleo." *Elenchos* 12 (1991): 5-37.

Graham, D. W. "Symmetry in the Empedoclean Cycle." *Classical Quarterly* 38 (1988): 297-312.

Imbraguglia, G. et al. *Index Empedocleus*. 2 vols, Genoa: Erga, 1991.

Inwood, Brad. *The Poem of Empedocles*. (*Phoenix* suppl. 29), Toronto: University of Toronto Press, 1992.

Janko, R. "Hesychius 216 and Empedocles fr. 21.6." *Classical Philology* 81 (1986): 308-9.

Janssen, T. H. "Nemertēs and Asapheia." *Journal of Hellenic Studies* 104 (1984): 107-08.

Johnston, H. W. *Empedocles: Fragments*. Bryn Mawr: Bryn Mawr College, 1985.

Kerferd, G. B. "Gorgias and Empedocles." *Siculorum Gymnasium Catania* 38 (1986): 595-605.

Kingsley, Peter. "Empedocles and his Interpreters – the Four-Element Doxography." *Phronesis* 39 (1994): 235-54.

———."Empedocles' Sun." *Classical Quarterly* 44 (1995): 316-24.

———. *Ancient Philosophy, Mystery and Magic*: Empedocles and the Pythagorean Tradition. Oxford: Clarendon Press, 1995.

Kirk, G. S., Raven, J . E. and Schofield, M. *The Presocratic Philosophers*. 2nd ed., Cambridge: Cambridge University Press, 1983.

Kohlschitter, Silke. "Parmenides and Empedocles in Porphyry's *History of Philosophy*." *Hermathena* 150 (1991): 43-54.

Kyriakou, P. "Empedoclean Echoes in Apollonius Rhodius' *Argonautica*." *Hermes* 122 (1994): 309-19.

Lombardo, S. *Parmenides and Empedocles: the fragments in verse translation*. San Francisco: Grey Fox Press, 1982.

Mansfeld, J. *Die Vorsokratiker* II. Stuttgart: Reclam, 1986.

———. *Studies in the Historiography of Greek Philosophy*. Assen and Maastricht: Van Gorcum, 1990.

———. "A Lost Manuscript of Empedocles' 'Katharmoi'." *Mnemosyne* 47 (1994): 77-82.

Marciano, G. "L'atomismo e il corpuscolorismo empedecleo: frammenti di interpretazioni nel mondo antico." *Elenchus* 12 (1991): 5-37.

McKirahan, R. D. *Philosophy before Socrates: an Introduction with Texts and Commentary*. Indianapolis: Hackett, 1994.

Meriani, A. "*Anaesimos* de Plutarco ad Empedocle (B 27a)." in *Contributi di Filologia greca*, ed I. Gallo, vol 1, Naples: Studi di Salerno (1991): 121-5.

Mesturini, A. M. "L'eclissi di sole in Empedocle e in Lucrezio." *Studi Italiani di Filologia classica* 5 (1989): 173-80.

Moriani, F. "Materia comune e generazione degli elementi in Aristotele."

Elenchos 9 (1990): 329-51.

Nilles, J. "Le fragment 8 d' Empédocle selon la perspective de Plutarque et d' Aristote." *Mnemosyne* 42 (1989): 365-79.

Obbink, D. "Hermachus *Against Empedocles.*" *Classical Quarterly* 32 (1988): 428-35.

Osborne, C. *Rethinking Early Greek Philosophy: Hippolytus of Rome and the Presocratics.* Ithaca N.Y.: Cornell University Press, 1987.

———. "Empedocles Recycled." *Classical Quarterly* 37(1987): 24-50.

Paquet, L., Roussel M. and Lafrance Y. *Les Présocratiques: Bibliographie analytique, 1879-1980.* Montreal: Bellarmin, 1988/9.

Panagiotou, S. "Empedocles on his own divinity." *Mnemosyne* 36 (1984): 276-85.

Robb, Kevin *Language and Thought in Early Greek Philosophy.* La Salle, Illinois: The Hegeler Institute, 1983.

Rösler, W. "Der Anfang der *Katharmoi* bei Empedokles." *Hermes* 111 (1983): 170-79.

Ruocco, E. "Daimon, Sphairos, Ananke: Psicologia e Teologia in Empedocle" in *Forme del sapere nei presocratici*, edited by A. Capizzi, Roma: Ed. della Ateneo, 1987: 187-21

Sedley, D. "The Proems of Empedocles and Lucretius." *Greek, Roman and Byzantine Studies* 30 (1989): 269-96.

———. "Empedocles' Theory of Vision and Theophrastus' *De Sensibus*" in W.W. Fortenbaugh (ed) *Theophrastus: His Psychological, Doxographical and Scientific Writings.* Rutgers: Rutgers University Studies in Classical Humanities, 1992: 10-31.

Sider, D. "Empedocles' *Persika*", *Ancient Philosophy* 2 (1982): 76-78.

———. "Empedocles B 96 and the poetry of adhesion." *Mnemosyne* 37 (1984): 14-24.

Slings, S. R. "Moniē in Empedocles and a Rule of Greek Words Formation." *Mnemosyne* 44 (1991): 413-15.

Solmsen, F. "Empedocles' *Hymn to Apollo.*" *Phronesis* 35 (1980): 219-27.

Steiger, K. "Die Kosmologie des Parmenides und Empedokles." *Oikumene* 5 (1986): 173-236.

Stevens, A. "La physique d' Empédocle selon Simplicius." *Revue Belge de Philologie* 67 (1989): 65-74.

Van der Ben, N. "Empedocles' cycle and fragment 17.3-5." *Hermes* 18 (1984): 97-101.

Wright, M. R. *The Presocratics.* London: Duckworth (Bristol Classical Press), 1985: 27-33, 107-21.

Index Fontium

315

	334a5	30(54)
Mete.	357a25	46(55)
	382a1	49(34)
	387b4	71(82)
De An.	404b13	77(109)
	410a4	48(96).1–3
	427a23	79(106)
	427a24	80(108)
	430a29	50(57).1
Sens.	437b26	88(84)
Resp.	473b9	91(100)
Part. Anim.	640a21	144(97)
GA	722b12	56(63)
	722b20	50(57).1
	723a24	57(65)
	731a5	65(79)
	747b3	143(92)
	764a1	57(65)
	764b17	56(63)
	777a10	59(68)
Metaph.	1000a29	14(21).9–12
	1000b2	20(36)
	1000b6	77(109)
	1000b14	23(30)
	1009b18	79(106)
	1009b20	80(108)
	1015a1	12(8).1, 3–4
Rhet.	1373b16	121(135)
Poet.	1457b13	125(138)
	1457b14	129(143)
	1457b25	149(152)
	1458a5	89(88)
	1461a24	47(35).14–15
(mund.)	399b26	14(21).9–11
(probl.)	929b16	49(34)
(lin. insec.)	972b30	138(32)
(MXG)	975b1	9(12)
	975b7	12(8).3–4
	975b11	8(17).32
	976a35	33(39)
	976b25	8(17).32
	976b26	10(13)

Asclepius: *Comm. in Aristotelem Graeca* ed. M. Hayduck, Berlin 1888

in Metaph.	112.1	48(96).1–3
	197.20	107(115).13–14
	197.33	14(21).10–13
	198.1	20(36)
	198.11	77(109).1–2
	198.33	23(30).3

277.9	79(106)
277.17	80(108)
311.33	12(8).4

Athenaeus: *Deipnosophistae* ed. G. Kaibel, Leipzig (Tb) 1887

8.334b	63(74)
8.365e	108(117)
10.423f	47(35).14–15
12.510c	118(128).1–7

Athenagoras: *Libellus pro Christianis* ed. E. Schwartz, Leipzig 1891

| 22 | 7(6).2–3 |
| 22 | 8(17).18,20 |

Clemens Alexandrinus: *Opera* ed. O. Stählin, Berlin 1960, 1972

Protrept.	2.27.3	123(145)
Strom.	3.14.2	112(118)
	3.14.2	130(125)
	3.14.2	114(124)
	4.13.1	111(119)
	4.150.1	132(146)
	5.9.1	103(114)
	5.15.4	8(17).21
	5.18.4	6(4)
	5.48.3	27(38)
	5.59.3	5(3).1–2
	5.81.2	96(133)
	5.85.3	8(17).14
	5.122.3	133(147)
	5.140.5	95(132)
	6.17.4	7(6).1
	6.17.4	8(17).18
	6.17.4	14(21).9
	6.24.3	108(117)
	6.30.2	101(111).3–5
	6.30.3	102(112).10,12
	6.149.1	33(39).2–3

Cornutus: *Theologiae Graecae Compendium* ed. C. Lang, Leipzig (Tb) 1881

| 17(30.3) | 117(123) |

Cyrillus: *adversus Julianum* ed. J. Aubert, Paris 1863

| 872c | 108(117) |
| 972d | 118(128).8–10 |

Diodorus Siculus: *Bibliotheca Historica* ed. F. Vogel, Leipzig (Tb) 1895

| 13.83.2 | 102(112).3 |

Theodoretus: *Graecorum Affectionum Curatio*
ed. J. Raeder, Leipzig (Tb) 1907

1.71	6(4).1–2
1.74	96(133)
4.14	10(13)
8.36	132(146)

Theon Smyrnaeus: *Expositio Rerum Mathematicarum* ed. E. Hiller, Leipzig (Tb) 1878

15.10	129(143)
104.1	151(153a)
149.6	113(121).2

Theophrastus: *De causis plantarum* ed. F. Wimmer, Leipzig (Tb) 1854, *De sensibus* ed. H. Diels, *Doxographi Graeci* Berlin 1958

Sens.		
	9	145(99)
	10	78(107)
	16	25(22).6–7
	22	93(102)

caus. plant.	1.7.1	65(79)
	1.13.2	64(77,78)

Tzetzes: *Exegesis in Iliadem* ed. G. Hermann, Leipzig 1812, *Alleg. Iliadis, ad Alleg. Iliadis* ed. P. Matranga, Rome 1850, *Chiliades* ed. P. A. M. Leone, Naples 1968, *ad Lycophronem* ed. E. Scheer, Berlin 1881

ex. Il.	29.24	102(112).4
	53.23	7(6)
	54.25	12(8).4
Alleg. Il.	15.86	44(50)
ad. Alleg. Il.	4.33	50(57).1
Chil.	2.909	101(111)
	7.517	97(134).4–5
	12.569	116(122).4
	13.74	97(134)
ad Lyc.	507,711	50(57).1

Index Verborum

Words in the quotations under *Addenda* are not included.
Asterisked words are found only in Empedocles.

323

ἀλλότριος. ἀλλότριον φῶς 39(45).1
ἀλοξ. πυχναῖς τέτρηνται ἀλοξιν 91(100).3
ἀλς. ἄλς ἐπάγη ῥιπῇσιν ἐωσμένος ἠελίοιο
    45(56).1
ἀλύειν. χαλεπῇσιν ἀλύοντες κακότησιν 123
    (145).1
ἄλφιτον. ἄλφιτον ὕδατι κολλήσας 49(34).1
ἄμα. 102(112).†7, 8
ἀμαξιτός. πειθοῦς ἀνθρώποισιν ἀμαξιτός
    96(133).3
ἀμαρτάνειν. ἐπίορκον ἀμαρτήσας ἐπομό-
    σσῃ 107(115).4
ἀμβλύνειν. ἀμβλύνουσι μερίμνας 1(2).2,
    100(110).7
ἄμβροτος. φιλότητος ἀμεμφέος ἄμβροτος
    ὁρμή 47(35).13; ἐγὼ δ' ὑμῖν θεὸς ἄμβ-
    ροτος ... πωλεῦμαι 102(112).4; ἄμβρ-
    οτε Μοῦσα 3(131).1; ἄμβροτα δ' ὅσσ'
    †ἐδεῖτο† καὶ ἀργέτι δεύεται αὐγῇ 14
    (21).4
ἀμείβειν. εἶδε' ἀμείβων 130(125).1
ἀμεμφής. φιλότητος ἀμεμφέος ἄμβροτος
    ὁρμή 47(35).13; οὐ γὰρ ἀμεμφέως /
    πω πᾶν ἐξέστηκεν ἐπ' ἔσχατα τέρματα
    κύκλου 47(35).9
ἀμήχανος. ἐκ γὰρ τοῦ μὴ ἐόντος ἀμήχανόν
    ἐστι γενέσθαι 9(12).1
ἄμικτος. πολλὰ δ' ἄμικτ' ἔστηκε 47(35).8
ἀμοιβαῖος. ὅς σφιν ἀμοιβαῖος πλατέος
    παρ' ἐλήλαται ὅρκου 23(30).3
ἀμοργός. ἄψας ... ἀνέμων λαμπτῆρας
    ἀμοργούς 88(84).3
ἄμουσος. φῦλον ἄμουσον ... καμασήνων
    68(74).1
ἀμπλακία. ἀμπλακίῃσι φόβῳ φίλα γυῖα
    μιήνῃ 107(115).3
ἀμφί. 3(131).4, 15(23).2, 91(100).19, †102
    (112).12
*ἀμφινάειν. ὕδατος ἀμφινάοντος 88(84).9
ἀμφιπολεύειν. μέγαν οὐρανὸν ἀμφιπολεύει
    35(41).1
ἀμφιπρόσωπος. ἀμφιπρόσωπα καὶ ἀμφίστ-
    ερνα 52(61).1
*ἀμφίστερνος. ἀμφιπρόσωπα καὶ ἀμφίστε-
    ρνα 52(61).1
ἀμφότερος. οὐδέ ποτ' οἴω / τούτων ἀμφοτ-
    έρων κενεώσεται ἄσπετος αἰών 11(16).
    2; ἀμφοτέρων ὕδατός τε καὶ εἴδεος
    53(62).5; μία γίγνεται ἀμφοτέρων ὄψ
    89(88).1
ἄν. 8(17).31, 102(112).7, 106(15).1
ἀνά. ἀν' ἄκρα πόλεος 102(112).2; ἀμ

βροτέων μελέων 26(20).1; ἀν λειμῶνα
    ("Ἄτης) 113(121).4
*ἀναβλαστεῖν. ἔνθεν ἀναβλαστοῦσι θεοί
    132(146).3
ἀνάγειν. ἐννυχίους ὄρπηκας ἀνήγαγε κριν-
    όμενον πῦρ 53(62).2
ἀνάγκη. στυγέει δύστλητον 'Ανάγκην
    109(116).1; ἔστιν ἀνάγκης χρῆμα
    107(115).1
ἀνάθημα. ἀναθήματα ποικίλλωσιν 15(23).
    1
ἀναθρώσκειν. αἰθήρ ... εὖτε δ' ἀναθρ-
    ώσκῃ 91(100).8; αἷμα ... εὖτε δ' ἀν-
    αθρώσκῃ 91(100).25
ἀναιρεῖν. ἄνθεα τιμῆς ... ἀνελέσθαι
    5(3).2
*ἀναίσιμος. οὐδέ τε δῆρις ἀναίσιμος ἐν
    μελέεσσιν 98(27a).1
ἄναξ. ἄνακτος ... ἀγέα κύκλον 37(47).1
ἀναπέμπειν. τοὺς μὲν πῦρ ἀνέπεμπε 53
    (62).6
ἀναπνεῖν. ὧδε δ' ἀναπνεῖ πάντα καὶ ἐκ-
    πνεῖ 91(100).1
*ἀναύχην. κόρσαι ἀναύχενες 50(57).1
ἀνδάνειν. ἡμετέρας μελέτας ⟨ἄδε τοι⟩ διὰ
    φροντίδος ἐλθεῖν 3(131).2
ἄνδιχα. 14(21).7, 26(20).5
ἀνδρεῖος. ἀνδρείων ἀχέων ἀπόκληροι
    133(147).2
ἀνδρόμεος. οὐδὲ γὰρ ἀνδρομέῃ κεφαλῇ
    κατὰ γυῖα κέκασται 97(134).1
*ἀνδρόπρωρος. βουγενῆ ἀνδρόπρωρα 52
    (61).2
*ἀνδροφυής. ἀνδροφυῆ βούκρανα 52(61).3
ἀνελίσσειν. ἅρματος ὥσπερ †ἂν ἴχνος ἑλί-
    σσεται† 40(46).1
ἄνεμος. Ἶρις δ' ἐκ πελάγους ἄνεμον φέρει
    44(50).1; ἄψας ... ἀνέμων λαμπτῆρας
    ἀμοργούς, οἵ τ' ἀνέμων μὲν πνεῦμα
    διασκιδνᾶσιν 88(84).3, 4; παύσεις ἀκα-
    μάτων ἀνέμων μένος 101(111).3
ἀνήκουστος. †ὁ δ' ἀνήκουστος† ... κακὴν
    ἀλεγύνατο δαῖτα 124(137).3
ἀνήνυστος. ἐὸν ἐξαπόλεσθαι ἀνήνυστον 9
    (12).2
ἀνήρ. 8(17).26, 99(129).1, 106(15).1; ἀν-
    δρός 56(63).1, 101(111).9; ἀνέρες
    14(21).10, 15(23).2, ἄνδρες 58(67).2;
    ἀνέρας 15(23).6, ἄνδρας 100(110).6;
    ἀνδρῶν 52(61).3, 53(62).1; ἀνδράσι
    1(2).7, 53(62).8, 102(112).8, 103(114).3
ἄνθος. ἄνθεα τιμῆς 5(3).1

γλαυκῶπις. εὖρος γλαυκώπιδος ... μήνης 41(42).3

γλυκύς. ὡς γλυκὺ μὲν γλυκὺ μάρπτε 75 (90).1

γλῶσσα. μανίην ἀποτρέψατε γλώσσης 2 (3).1; τρανώματα γλώσσης 5(3).6; ὡς διὰ πολλῶν δὴ γλώσσης ἐλθόντα ματαίως / ἐκκέχυται στομάτων 33(39).2

γόμφος. γόμφοις ἀσκήσασα καταστόργοις Ἀφροδίτη 86(87).1

γομφοῦν. ὡς δ' ὅτ' ὀπὸς γάλα λευκὸν ἐγόμφωσεν 61(33).1

γόνυ. οὐ πόδες, οὐ θοὰ γοῦνα 22(29).2, 97 (134).3

γραπτός. ἱλάσκοντο / γραπτοῖς τε ζώοισι 118(128).5

γραφεύς. ὡς δ' ὁπόταν γραφέες ἀναθήματα ποικίλλωσιν 15(23).1

γυῖον. ἐπιχώριον ἀνδράσι γυῖον 53(62).8; κατὰ γυῖα 1(2).1, 97(134).1; ἠελίοιο... ὠκέα γυῖα 21(27).1; γυῖα θεοῖο 24(31). 1; γυῖα, τὰ σῶμα λέλογχε 26(20).3; φίλα γυῖα 107(115).3; ἠέα γυῖα 118 (128).10; γυίων πίστιν ἔρυκε 5(3).8; διὰ γυίων 91(100).22; †σκιεροῖς† ἠσκημένα γυίοις 52(61).4

γυμνός. γυμνοὶ δ' ἐπλάζοντο βραχίονες 50 (57).2

*γυναικοφυής. μεμιγμένα τῇ μὲν ἀπ' ἀνδρῶν / τῇ δὲ γυναικοφυῆ 52(61).4

γυνή. ἀνέρες ἠδὲ γυναῖκες 14(21).10; ἀνέρας ἠδὲ γυναῖκας 15(23).6; τὰ μὲν τελέθουσι γυναῖκες / ψύχεος ἀντιάσαντα 57(65).1; πολυκλαύτων τε γυναικῶν 53 (62).1; ἀνδράσιν ἠδὲ γυναιξί 102(112).8

*δαιδαλέοδμος. μύροισί τε δαιδαλεόδμοις 118(128).5

δαίειν. φιλοφροσύνη τε δεδήει 119(130).2

δαίμων. ἐπεὶ κατὰ μεῖζον ἐμίσγετο δαίμονι δαίμων 51(59).1; δαίμονες οἵτε μακραίωνος λελάχασι βίοιο 107(115).5

δαίς. κακὴν ἀλεγύνατο δαῖτα 124(137).4

δαΐφρων. δαΐφρονος Ἀγχίτεω υἱε 4(1).1

δάκρυον. Νῆστίς θ' ἣ δακρύοις τέγγει κρούνωμα βρότειον 7(6).3

δάπτειν. οὐκ ἐσορᾶτε / ἀλλήλους δάπτοντες 122(136).2

δάφνη. δάφνης φύλλων ἄπο πάμπαν ἔχεσθαι 127(140).1; (γίγνονται) δάφναι δ' ἐνὶ δένδρεσιν 131(127).2

*δαψιλός. δαψιλὸς αἰθήρ 33(39).1

δέ. 1(2).2, 3, 6, †8; 2(3).2; 4(1).1; 5(3). 8; 6(4).2; 8(17).2, 3(bis), 5, 8, 12, 13, 17, 26, 28(bis) 29, 32, 33, 34; 12(8). 1, 4; 13(9).1, 4(bis), 5; 14(21).4, 5, 6, 7, 8, 13; 15(23).1, 4; 16(26).1, 3, 6, 11, 12; 20(36).1; 25(22).4; 26(20).4, 6; 27(38).1; 28(51).1; 29(53).1; 31(37).1 (bis); 32(52).1; 41(42).1, 2; 42(48).1; 44(50).1; 47(35).4, 7, 8, 11, 12, 14, 16; 48(96).1, 3(bis); 50(57).2; 52(61).2, 4; 57(65).1; 60(71).1; 61(33).1; 62(73).1; 65(79).1; 70(75).1(bis); 75(90)1, 2; 76 (93).1; 77(109).1, 2, 3(bis); †80(108).1; 83(98).1; 84(85).1; 88(84).1, 5, 7, 9, 10; 91(100).1, 5, 8, 16, 18, 20, 22, 25; 95 (132).2; 99(129).1; 100(110).6; 101 (111).1, 3, 6, 7, 9; 102(112).4, 8, 10; 103 (114).2; 106(15).4; 107(115).10(bis), 11, 12(bis); 118(128).8; 119(130).1; 124 (137).1, 2, 3, 5; 131(127).2; 132(146).1

δεδαηκέναι. τὴν οὔ τις μετὰ τοῖσιν ἑλισσομένην δεδάηκε 8(17).25; ἀνέρες ἀμφὶ τέχνης ὑπὸ μήτιος εὖ δεδαῶτε 15(23).2

δεδιέναι. ἔνθ' οὔτ' ἠελίοιο †δεδίσσεται† ἀγλαὸν εἶδος 19(27).1

δείλαιος. δειλαίων ἀχέων 123(145).2

δειλός. δειλὸς δ' ᾧ σκοτόεσσα θεῶν πέρι δόξα μέμηλεν 95(132).2; ὦ δειλὸν θνητῶν γένος 114(124).1; δειλοί, πάνδειλοι 128(141).1; πολλὰ δειλ' ἔμπαια 1(2). 2; μυρία δειλά 100(110).7; δειλὰ καὶ ἐσθλά 106(15).3

δεῖν. καὶ δὶς γάρ, ὃ δεῖ, καλόν ἐστιν ἐνισπεῖν 17(25).1

δεῖν. ὡς δ' ὅτ' ὀπὸς γάλα λευκὸν ἐγόμφωσεν καὶ ἔδησε 61(33).1

δέκα. δέκ' ἀνθρώπων καί τ' εἴκοσιν αἰώνεσσιν 99(129).6

δέκατος. μηνὸς ἐν ὀγδοάτου δεκάτῃ 59 (68).1

δέμας. αὔξει δὲ χθὼν μὲν σφέτερον δέμας 31(37).1; μελέων ἐρατῶν δέμας 53(62). 7; ὕδατος ... τέρεν δέμας 91(100).11

*δενδρεόθρεπτος. ῥεύματα δενδρεόθρεπτα 101(111).8

δένδρεον. δένδρεα 14(21).10, 15(23).6, 63(72).1, †64(77).1, 65(79).1; ἐν δένδρεσιν ἠυκόμοισιν 131(127).2

δέρκεσθαι. νόῳ δέρκευ 8(17).21; ἐπιμάρτυρα δέρκευ 14(21).1

δεύειν. ἄμβροτα δ' ὅσσ' †ἐδεῖτο† καὶ ἀργέτι δεύεται αὐγῇ 14(21).4; ταύρων ...

Ἔγερσις. καὶ Εὐναίη καὶ Ἔγερσις 117 (123).1

ἐγχεῖν. ἐν δ᾽ ἐχύθη καθαροῖσι 57(65).1

ἐγώ. 47(35).1, 101(111).2, 102(112).4, 103(114).2, 107(115).13, 108(117).1; με 120(139).1

ἔδειν. φίλας κατὰ σάρκας ἔδουσιν 124 (137).6; ἐέδμεναι ἠέα γυῖα 118(128).10

ἐθέλειν. (ὕδωρ) ἐλαίῳ οὐκ ἐθέλει 74(91).2; ἢν ἐθέλησθα 101(111).5, cf. s.v. θέλειν

ἔθνος. ἄλλων ἔθνεα θῆρων 16(26).4; ἔθνεα μυρία θνητῶν 47(35).7, 16; ἔθνεα κηρῶν 113(121).2

εἰ. 3(131).1; 14(21).2; 27(38).1; 60(71).1; 100(110).1, 6; 105(113).2; ἢν 101(115).5

εἰδέναι. οἶδα μὲν οὔνεκ᾽ ἀληθείη πάρα μύθοις / οὓς ἐγὼ ἐξερέω 103(114).1; ἴσθι 15(23).11, 100(110).10; ἀνὴρ περιώσια εἰδώς 99(129).1

εἶδος (form). ἠελίοιο ... ἀγλαὸν εἶδος 19(27).1; εἴδη τε ... χροιά τε θνητῶν 60(71).3; εἴδεα πᾶσιν ἀλίγκια 15(23).5; (Κύπρις) εἴδεα ποιπνύουσα 62(73).2; ἄλλης εἴδεα σαρκός 83(98).5; παντοῖα ... εἴδεα θνητῶν 107(115).7; εἴδε᾽ ἀμείβων 130(125).1; ἀπ᾽ ἀλλήλων διέχουσι... εἴδεσιν ἐκμάκτοισι 25(22).7

εἶδος (heat). †εἶδει τετ καὶ ἀργέτι δεύεται αὐγῇ 14(21).4; εἴδεος αἶσαν ἔχοντες 53(62).5

εἴκοσι. δέκ᾽ ἀνθρώπων καί τ᾽ εἴκοσιν αἰώνεσσιν 99(129).6

εἶναι. τῶν καὶ ἐγὼ νῦν εἰμι 107(115).12; ὧν θέμις ἐστίν ... ἀκούειν 2(3).4; ὁπόσῃ πόρος ἐστὶ νοῆσαι 5(3).7; ἐκ γὰρ τοῦ μὴ ἐόντος ἀμήχανόν ἐστι γενέσθαι, / καί τ᾽ ἐὸν ἐξαπόλεσθαι ἀνήνυστον ... αἰεὶ γὰρ †τῇ γ᾽ ἔσται† 9(12).13; δίς ... καλόν ἐστιν ἐνισπεῖν 17(25).1; αἷμα γὰρ ἀνθρώποις περικάρδιόν ἐστι νόημα 94(105).3; ὅπῃ φύσις ἐστὶν ἑκάστῳ 100(110).5; αὐτ᾽ ἔστιν ταῦτα 8(17).34, 16(26).3; φύσις οὐδενός ἐστιν ἁπάντων / θνητῶν ... ἀλλὰ μόνον μίξις τε διάλλαξίς τε μιγέντων / ἐστί 12 (8).1, 4; ἐκ τῶν πάνθ᾽ ὅσα τ᾽ ἦν ὅσα τ᾽ ἔστι καὶ ἔσται ... αὐτὰ γὰρ ἔστιν ταῦτα 14(21).9, 13; οὐκ ἔστιν πελάσασθαι ἐν ὀφθαλμοῖσιν ἐφικτόν 96(133).1; ἔστιν ἀνάγκης χρῆμα 107(115).1; ταύτῃ δ᾽ αἰὲν ἔασιν ἀκίνητοι κατὰ κύκλον 8 (17).13, 16(26).12; ἤλικα γένναν ἔασι

8(17).27; ὅσα κρῆσιν ἐπαρκέα μᾶλλον ἔασιν 25(22).4; πάντων εἰσὶν ἀπορροαί 73(89).1; οὐ γάρ σφιν δολιχόφρονές εἰσι μέριμναι 104(11).1; τόφρα μὲν οὖν εἰσίν 106(15).3; οὐδὲν ἄρ᾽ εἰσίν 106(15).4; οὐκέτ᾽ ἂν ἦσαν 8(17).31; ἔ⟨στ⟩ι γὰρ ὡς πάρος ἦν τε καὶ ἔσσεται 11(16).1; ὅσον ταναώτερον ἦεν 88(84).5, 10; ἢν δε τις ἐν κείνοισιν ἀνήρ 99(129).1; ἔνθ᾽ ἦσαν Χθονίη τε καὶ Ἡλιόπη 116(122).1; οὐδέ τις ἦν κείνοισιν Ἄρης θεός 118(128).1; ἀλλὰ μύσος τοῦτ᾽ ἔσκεν 118(128).9; ἦσαν δὲ κτίλα πάντα 119(130).1; τῶν ὄντων πάντων λεύσσεσκεν ἕκαστον 99 (129).5; οἳ δὴ γίγνεσθαι πάρος οὐκ ἐὸν ἐλπίζουσιν 104(11).2; αὐτοτράπεζοι / †ἐόντες 133(147).2; ἐν μόνον εἶναι ἐκ πλεόνων ... πλέον᾽ ἐξ ἑνὸς εἶναι 8 (17).1, 2, 16, 17; ἄλλοθεν εἶναι θνητῶν ... πηγήν 15(23).10; ἐν μόνον εἶναι ... τὰ πρὶν μάθον ἀθάνατ᾽ εἶναι 47 (35).5, 14

εἰνάλιος. εἰνάλιοι καμασῆνες 63(72).1

εἴπερ. 33(39).1

εἴργειν. εἴργει / ἀέρος ὄγκος 91(100).12; ἐεργμένον ὠγύγιον πῦρ 88(84).7

εἰς. 8(17)7; 13(9).1; 16(26).2, 5; 23(30).2; 26(20).2; 91(100).11, †12; 96(133).3; 100(110).5; 132(146).1; ἐς †41(42).2; 47(35).1; 102(112).7; 107(115).10(bis); 118(128).7

εἷς. μία γίγνεται ἀμφοτέρων ὄψ 89(88).1; εἰς ἕνα κόσμον 16(26).5; μύθων ... ἀτραπὸν μίαν 18(24).2; ἐν μόνον εἶναι 8(17).1, 16; 47(35).5; εἰς ἐν ἅπαντα 8(17).7, 26(20).2; ἐν ἐκ πλεόνων 8(17). 9, 16(26).8; †ἐν†τ συμφύντα 16(26).7; πλέον᾽ ἐξ ἑνὸς εἶναι 8(17).2, 17; ἑνὸς διαφύντος 8(17).10, 16(26).9

εἰσέρχεσθαι. ἄγγοσδ᾽ ὄμβρος ἐσέρχεται... ἐσέρχεται αἴσιμον ὕδωρ 91(100).12,15

εἰσόκε. 16(26).7, 91(100).14, 20

εἰσορᾶν. τὰ νῦν ἐσορῶμεν ἅπαντα 27 (38).2; οὐκ ἐσορᾶτε / ἀλλήλους δάπτοντες 122(136).1

εἴτε. 8(17).31, 83(98).4(bis)

ἐκ. 2(3).2; 8(17).2(bis), 9, 17(bis); 9(12). 1; 14(21).6, 9; 15(23).5; 16(26).8; 27 (38).1; 44(50).1; 78(107).1; 83(98).5; 85(86)1; 101(111).6, 7, 9; 107(115).12; 111(119).1; 114(124).2(bis); 130(125).1

ἕκαστος. 1(2).5; ἕκαστον 5(3).4, 8; 99

βάξιν 102(112).11
εὐήνιος. ἐλάουσ' εὐήνιον ἄρμα 2(3).5
εὐθύς. 91(100).24
εὔκομος. δένδρεσιν ἠυκόμοισιν 131(127).2
εὐμενής. εἰ ... εὐμενέως καθαρῇσιν ἐποπτεύσῃς μελέτῃσιν 100(110).2
Εὐναίη. καὶ Εὐναίη καὶ Ἔγερσις 117(123).1
εὖνις. βραχίονες εὔνιδες ὤμων 50(57).2
εὐπορία. εὐπορίην διόδοισι τετμῆσθαι 91
(100).5
εὑρίσκειν. τὸ δ' ὅλον ⟨πᾶς⟩ εὔχεται εὑρεῖν
1(2).6
εὖρος. εὖρος γλαυκώπιδος ... μήνης 41
(42).3
εὐρυμέδων. διά τ' εὐρυμέδοντος / αἰθέρος
121(135).1
εὐρύς. σεληναίης κύκλον εὐρύν 38(43).1
εὐσεβής. εὐσεβέεσσιν ἀγάλμασιν ἱλάσκοντο
118(128).4
εὐσεβία. πέμπε παρ' Εὐσεβίης 2(3).5
εὔστερνος. ἐν εὐστέρνοις χοάνοισι 48(96).1
εὖτε. 13(9).4; 91(100).8, 10, 25; †102
(112).7†; 107(115).3
εὔχεσθαι. τὸ δ' ὅλον ⟨πᾶς⟩ εὔχεται εὑρεῖν
1(2).6; εὐχομένῳ ... παρίστασο 3(131).3
ἐφημέριος. ἐφημερίων ἕνεκέν τινος 3(131).
1; ὧν θέμις ἐστὶν ἐφημερίοισιν ἀκούειν
2(3).4
ἐφικνεῖσθαι. οὐκ ἔστιν πελάσασθαι ἐν
ὀφθαλμοῖσιν ἐφικτόν 96(133).1
ἔχειν. ὅθ' ὕδωρ μὲν ἔχει κατὰ βένθεα
χαλκοῦ 91(100).16; πάντα γὰρ ἴσθι
φρόνησιν ἔχειν 100(110).10; μήτε τιν'
ὄψιν ἔχων †πίστει† πλέον ἢ κατ' ἀκουήν 5(3).5; ὕδατός τε καὶ εἴδεος αἶσαν
ἔχοντες 53(62).5
ἐχῖνος. ἐχίνοις / ὀξυβελεῖς χαῖται νώτοις
72(83).1
ἔχθος. νείκεος ἔχθει 8(17).8, 16(26).6
ἐχθρός. ἐχθρά ... ⟨ὅσα⟩ πλεῖστον ἀπ'
ἀλλήλων διέχουσι 25(22).7

Ζεύς. Ζεὺς ἀργής 7(6).2; οὐδὲ Ζεὺς βασιλεὺς οὐδὲ Κρόνος 118(128).2
ζωή. †ἐν ζωῇσι† βίου μέρος ἀθρήσαντες
1(2).3
ζῷον. ἐκ μὲν γὰρ ζωῶν ἐτίθει νέκρα 130
(125).1; ἱλάσκοντο / γραπτοῖς τε ζῴοισι
118(128).5
ζωρός. ζωρά τε πρὶν κέκρητο 47(35).15

ἤ. 5(3).5, 6; 13(9).2(bis); 44(50).1; 91

(100).20; 96(133).2; 104(11).3; ἠέ
†1(2).9; 13(9).3
ἤ. ἦ σ' ἄφαρ ἐκλείψουσι 100(110).8
ἤ. 5(3).8; 8(17).9, 12; †13(9).5; 16(26).
8, 11; 50(57).1
ἠδέ. 7(6).2; 8(17).10, 24; 14(21).10; 15
(23).6; 16(26).9; 25(22).2; 27(38).3, 4;
34(40).1; 78(107).2; 91(100).17; 102
(112).8
ἤδειν. καὶ τούτοις φρονέουσι καὶ ἥδοντ'
ἠδ' ἀνιῶνται 78(107).2
ἤδη. 108(117).1
ἠθμός. ἀμφὶ πύλας ἠθμοῖο δυσηχέος 91
(100).19
ἦθος. πάρα δ' ἦθος ἑκάστῳ 8(17).28; αὐτὰ
γὰρ αὔξει / ταῦτ' εἰς ἦθος ἕκαστον 100
(110).5
ἠλάσκειν. Ἄτης ἂν λειμῶνα κατὰ σκότος
ἠλάσκουσιν 113(121).4
ἠλέκτωρ. ἠλέκτωρ τε χθών τε καὶ οὐρανὸς
ἠδὲ θάλασσα 25(22).2
*Ἡλιόπη. Χθονίη τε καί Ἡλιόπη τανα-
ῶπις 116(122).1
ἥλιος. ἐξ ὧν ἥλιος ἀρχήν / ⟨τἆλλα τε⟩
δῆλ' ἐγένοντο 27(38).1; ἥλιος ὀξυβελής
34(40).1; ἠέλιον μὲν λευκὸν ὁρᾶν καὶ
θερμὸν ἀπάντῃ 14(21).3; ἔνθ' οὔτ' ἠελίοιο †δεδίσσεται† ἀγλαὸν εἶδος 19(27).
1; ἠελίοιο ... ὠκέα γυῖα 21(27).1; ἅλς
ἐπάγη ῥιπῇσιν ἐωσμένος ἠελίοιο 45(56).
1; ὕδατος γαίης τε καὶ αἰθέρος ἠελίου
τε / κιρναμένων 60(71).2; γαῖα δ' ἐς
αὐγάς / ἠελίου φαέθοντος 107(115)11
ἤλιξ. ἥλικα γένναν ἔασι 8(17).27
ἦμαρ. οἴμοι, ὅτ' οὐ πρόσθεν με διώλεσε
νηλεὲς ἦμαρ 120(139).1
ἡμέτερος. παρ' ἡμετέρης ... Μούσης 6
(4).2; ἡμετέρας μελέτας 3(131).2; ἐν
ὀφθαλμοῖσιν ἐφικτόν / ἡμετέροις 96
(133).2
ἠνεκής. ἠνεκὲς αἰὲν ὁμοῖα 8(17).35; διά
... αἰθέρος ἠνεκέως τέταται 121(135).2
ἤπερ. 96(133).2
*ἠπιόφρων. ἠπιόφρων φιλότητος ... ὁρμή
47(35)13
Ἥρα. Ἥρη φερέσβιος 7(6).2
ἧσθαι. μηδ' ὄμμασιν ἧσο τεθηπώς 8(17).
21
ἠΰς. ἐέδμεναι ἠέα γυῖα 118(128).10
Ἥφαιστος. τῶν ὀκτὼ μερέων ... τέσσαρα
δ' Ἡφαίστοιο 48(96).3; Ἡφαίστῳ τ'
ὄμβρῳ τε καὶ αἰθέρι 83(98).2

ἱκνεῖσθαι. εὖτ' ἂν ἵκωμαι ἐς ἄστεα
102(112).7; ὅτε μὲν κατὰ φῶτα μιγέντ'
εἰς αἰθέρ' ἵ⟨κωνται⟩ 13(9).1; ἐπεὶ νεῖκος
μὲν ἐνέρτατον ἵκετο βένθος / δίνης
47(35).3; πῦρ ... θέλον πρὸς ὁμοῖον
ἱκέσθαι 53(62).6; ποθέοντα φίλην ἐπὶ
γένναν ἱκέσθαι 100(110).9
*ἱλάειρα. ἱλάειρα σελήνη 34(40).1; φλὸξ
ἱλάειρα 84(85).1
ἱλάσκειν. τὴν οἵ γ' εὐσεβέεσσιν ἀγάλμασιν
ἱλάσκοντο 118(128).4
ἰότης. ἰότητι τύχης πεφρόνηκεν ἄπαντα
81(103).1
Ἶρις. Ἶρις δ' ἐκ πελάγους ἄνεμον φέρει
ἢ μέγαν ὄμβρον 44(50).1
ἴσος. ὅ γε πάντοθεν ἴσος ⟨ἑοῖ⟩ καὶ πάμπαν ἀπείρων 22(28).3; ἡ δὲ χθὼν τούτοισιν ἴση συνέκυρσε μάλιστα 83(98).1;
ἴση μῆκός τε πλάτος τε 8(17).20; ταῦτα
γὰρ ἰσά τε πάντα 8(17).27; πάλιν ἐκπνέει ἴσον ὀπίσσω 91(100).25
ἰχθύς. ἤδη γάρ ποτ' ἐγὼ γενόμην ... ἔξαλος ἔλλοπος ἰχθύς 108(117).2; ὑδατοθρέμμονες ἰχθῦς 14(21).11; ὑδατοθρέμμονας ἰχθῦς 15(23).7; ἰχθύσιν ὑδρομελάθροις 26(20).6
ἴχνος. ἅρματος ὥσπερ ἂν ἴχνος ἑλίσσεται
40(46).1

καθαρός. ἐκ δ' ὁσίων στομάτων καθαρὴν
ὀχετεύσατε πηγήν 2(3).2; ἐν δ' ἐχύθη
καθαροῖσι 57(65).1; καθαρῇσιν ἐποπτεύσεις μελέτῃσιν 100(110).2
καθύπερθεν. 41(42).2
καί. 2(3).3; 5(3).3; 8(17).6, 11, 15,
18(ter), 20, 22, 23, 27, 30, 32, †33, 35;
9(12).2(bis); 11(16).1; 13(9).5; 14(21).2,
3, 4, 6, 7, 8, 9, 10, 11, 12; 15(23).6,
7, 8; 16(26).2(bis), 4, 10; 17(25).1;
22(28).3; 25(22).2, 7, 8; 26(20).6;
27(38).3; 33(39).1; 52(61).1; 53(62).5;
54(64).1; 58(67).2(bis), 3; 60(71).2;
61(33).1; 63(72).1(bis); 64(77).1; 66(80).
1; 71(82).1(bis), 2; 78(107).2(bis); 80
(108).2; 82(104).1; 83(98).2, 5; 91(100).
1, 3; 93(102).1; 97(134).4; 99(129).6
(bis); 100(110).1, 10; 101(111).1, 5, 7;
103(114).3; 104(11).3; 106(15).3(bis),
4; 107(115).†4, 13(bis); 108(117).2; 111
(119).1; 112(118).1; 113(121).2, 3; 116
(122).1, 2; 117(123).1(bis), 3(bis); 119
(130).1; 124(137).5; 132(146).1(bis), 2

καίειν. ἔνερθ' οὔδεος πυρὰ καίεται
32(52).1
καινύναι. οὐδὲ γὰρ ἀνδρομέη κεφαλῇ κατὰ
γυῖα κέκασται 97(134).1; μή σ' ἀπάτη
φρένα καινύτω ἄλλοθεν εἶναι θνητῶν
... πηγήν 15(23).9
καίριος. καίριον αὐχμόν 101(111).6
κακός. κακὴν ἀλεγύνατο δαῖτα 124(137).
4; φάρμακα ... κακῶν καὶ γήραος ἄλκαρ 101(111).1; κακοῖς μὲν κάρτα
πέλει κρατέουσιν ἀπιστεῖν 6(4).1; κακῇσι διατμηθέντ' ἐρίδεσσι 26(20).4
κακότης. κακότητος ἄπειροι 102(112).3;
νηστεῦσαι κακότητος 126(144).1; χαλεπῇσιν ἀλύοντες κακότησιν 123(145).1
καλεῖν. †ῇ θέμις† καλέουσι 13(9).5; ὡς
ὄφρα μέν τε βιῶσι, τὸ δὴ βίοτον καλέουσι
106(15).2; Γηθοσύνην καλέοντες ἐπώνυμον 8(17).24
Καλλιόπεια. εὐχομένῳ νῦν αὖτε παρίστασο
Καλλιόπεια 3(131).3
Καλλιστώ. Καλλιστώ τ' Αἰσχρή τε
116(122).3
καλός. δὶς γάρ, ὃ δεῖ, καλόν ἐστιν ἐνισπεῖν
17(25).1
καμασήν. εἰνάλιοι καμασῆνες 63(72).1;
φῦλον ... πολυσπερέων καμασήνων
68(74).1
καπνός. ὠκύμοροι καπνοῖο δίκην 1(2).4
καρπάλιμος. καρπαλίμως δ' ἀνόπαιον
28(51).1
καρπός. καρπῶν ἀφθονίῃσι 64(78).2
κάρτα. κάρτα πέλει 6(4).1
κατά. κατὰ γυῖα 1(2).1, 97(134).1; κατ'
ἀκουήν 5(3).5; κατὰ κύκλον 8(17).13,
16(26).12; κατὰ φῶτα ... ἢ κατὰ
θηρῶν ἀγροτέρων γένος ἢ κατὰ θάμ-
νων / ἠὲ κατ' οἰωνῶν 13(9).1, 2(bis),3;
κατὰ χθόνα 30(54).1; κατὰ μεῖζον
51(59).1; κατ' ἄρρενα 58(67).1; κατ'
ἠέρα 64(78).2; καθ' ὅσον 82(104).1;
κατὰ σῶμα 91(100).2; κατὰ βένθεα
91(100).16; κατ' ἄνδρας 100(110).6;
κατὰ σκότος 113(121).4; κατὰ βηλόν
88(84).6; κατὰ ξανθοῦ Ἀκράγαντος 102
(112).1
καταθνῄσκειν. ἤ τι καταθνῄσκειν τε καὶ
ἐξόλλυσθαι ἀπάντῃ 104(11).3
καταΐσσειν. αἰθὴρ παφλάζων καταΐσσεται
οἴδματι μάργῳ 91(100).7; φρὴν ἱερὴ
... φροντίσι κόσμον ἅπαντα καταΐσσουσα θοῇσιν 97(134).5

καταλέγειν. τὸν πρότερον κατέλεξα
47(35).2
καταμίσγειν. βύσσῳ ... κρόκου καταμίσγεται ἀκτίς 76(93).1
*κατάστοργος. γόμφοις ἀσκήσασα κατασ-
τόργοις 'Αφροδίτη 86(87).1
κατασφραγίζειν. πλατέεσσι κατεσφρηγισμένον ὅρκοις 107(115).2
καταφθίνειν. καταφθιμένου μένος ἀνδρός
101(111).9
καταφθινύθειν. (ἄνεμοι) καταφθινύθουσιν
ἀρούρας 101(111).4
κατέδειν. s.v. ἔδειν
κατέρχεσθαι. αἰθέρος εὐθὺς ῥεῦμα κατέρχεται οἴδματι θῦον 91(100).24
κε. 8(17).32, 33; 9(12).3
κελαινός. ἐξ ὄμβροιο κελαινοῦ 101(111).6
κέλεσθαι. ὡς δὲ παρ' ἡμετέρης κέλεται
πιστώματα Μούσης 6(4).2
κέλευθος. διαλλάξαντα κελεύθους 47(35).
15; ἀργαλέας βιότοιο μεταλλάσσοντα
κελεύθους 107(115).8
κενοῦν. οὐδέ ποτ' οἴω / τούτων ἀμφοτέρων
κενεώσεται ἄσπετος αἰών 11(16).2
κενός. οὐδέ τι τοῦ παντὸς κενεὸν πέλει
οὐδὲ περισσόν 10(13).1
κεραννύναι. ζωρά τε πρὶν κέκρητο 47(35).
15; πολλὰ δ' ἄμικτ' ἔστηκε κεραιομένοισιν ἐναλλάξ 47(35).8
κέρδος. ἐξερέοντες ὅπη πρὸς κέρδος ἀταρπός 102(112).9
κέρμα. κέρματα θηρείων μελέων 92(101).1
κεύθειν. ὥστε φόνον μέν / κεύθειν 91(100).
5
κεφαλή. οὐδὲ γὰρ ἀνδρομέη κεφαλῇ κατὰ
γυῖα κέκασται 97(134).1
κήρ. ἄλλων ἔθνεα κηρῶν 113(121).2
κῆρυξ. κηρύκων τε λιθορρίνων χελύων τε
69(76).2
κικλήσκειν. τῇ τε νόημα μάλιστα κικλήσκεται ἀνθρώποισιν 94(105).2
Κινώ. Κινώ τ' 'Αστεμφής τε 117(123).2
κιρνάναι. ὕδατος γαίης τε καὶ αἰθέρος
ἠελίου τε / κιρναμένων 60(71).3
*κλαδάσσειν. τέρεν αἷμα κλαδασσόμενον
διὰ γυίων 91(100).22
κλάδος. οὐ γὰρ ἀπὸ νώτοιο δύο κλάδοι
ἀΐσσονται 22(29).1, [97(134).2]
κλαίειν. κλαῦσά τε καὶ κώκυσα ἰδὼν
ἀσυνήθεα χῶρον 112(118).1
κλεψύδρα. κλεψύδρη παίζουσα διειπετέος
χαλκοῖο 91(100).9

κλύειν. κλῦθι 4(1).1, 8(17).14; κλύε
53(62).3; ἐπύθοντο κλύειν εὐηκέα
βάξιν 102(112).11
κόγχη. ἐν κόγχαισι θαλασσονόμοις βαρυν-
ώτοις 69(76).1
κόλλα. ἁρμονίης κόλλησιν ἀρηρότα θεσπεσίηθεν 48(96).4
κολλᾶν. ἄλφιτον ὕδατι κολλήσας 49(34).1
κόρη. πῦρ ... λοχάζετο κύκλοπα κούρην
88(84).8; ἤδη γάρ ποτ' ἐγὼ γενόμην
κοῦρός τε κόρη τε 108(117).1
κόρση. κόρσαι ἀναύχενες ἐβλάστησαν
50(57).1
κορυφή. κορυφὰς ἑτέρας ἑτέρῃσι προσάπτων 18(24).1
κόσμος. ἄλλοτε μὲν φιλότητι συνερχόμεν'
εἰς ἕνα κόσμον 16(26).5; φροντίσι
κόσμον ἅπαντα καταΐσσουσα θοῇσιν
97(134).5
κότος. ἔνθα φόνος τε κότος τε καὶ ἄλλων
ἔθνεα κηρῶν 113(121).2; ἐν δὲ κότῳ
διάμορφα ... πέλονται 14(21).7
κοῦρος. ἤδη γάρ ποτ' ἐγὼ γενόμην κοῦρός
τε κόρη τε 108(117).1
κραίνειν. ἐπεὶ μούνῳ σοι ἐγὼ κρανέω τάδε
πάντα 101(111).2
κρᾶσις. †τὰ γὰρ διὰ κρῆσις† ἀμείβει
14(21).14; ὅσα κρῆσιν ἐπαρκέα μᾶλλον
ἔασιν 25(22).4; ἀπ' ἀλλήλων διέχουσι
... γέννῃ τε κρήσει 25(22).7
κρατεῖν. ἐν δὲ μέρει κρατέουσι 8(17).29,
16(26).1; κρατέουσιν ἀπιστεῖν 6(4).1
κρατύνειν. ἄκρα κρατύνων 91(100).19;
χθόνα Κύπρις ... θοῷ πυρὶ δῶκε κρατῦναι 62(73).1
κρήνη. κρηνάων ἄπο πέντε 129(143).1
κρίνειν. ἐννυχίους ὀρπηκας ἀνήγαγε κρινόμενον πῦρ 53(62).2
κρόκος. βύσσῳ ... κρόκου καταμίσγεται
ἀκτίς 76(93).1
Κρόνος. οὐδὲ Ζεὺς βασιλεὺς οὐδὲ Κρόνος
118(128).2
*κρούνωμα. κρούνωμα βρότειον 7(6).3
κρυφός. ἁρμονίης πυκινῷ κρυφῷ ἐστήρικται 21(27).2
κτᾶσθαι. ὄλβιος ὃς θείων πραπίδων ἐκτήσατο πλοῦτον 95(132).1; πραπίδων ἐκτήσατο πλοῦτον 99(129).2; ἄλλα τε πόλλ'
ἀπὸ τῶνδε κτ⟨ήσε⟩αι 100(110).4
κτίζειν. δένδρεά τε κτίζοντε καὶ ἀνέρας
ἠδὲ γυναῖκας 15(23).6
κτίλος. ἦσαν δὲ κτίλα πάντα 119(130).1

μακρὰ δένδρεα ... ἐλαίας 65(79).1;
αἰθήρ ... μακρῇσι κατὰ χθόνα δύετο
ῥίζαις 30(54).1; μήκιστον πραπίδων
πλοῦτον 99(129).2
μάλα. 25(22).8, 100(110).3, 103(114).2;
μᾶλλον 25(22).4, 58(67).3, 74(91).1;
μάλιστα 25(22).6, 83(98).1, 94(105).2,
99(129).3
μανθάνειν. ἐν ἐκ πλεόνων μεμάθηκε φύεσθαι 8(17).9, 16(26).8; τὰ πρὶν μάθον
ἀθάνατ' εἶναι 47(35).14
μανίη. τῶν μὲν μανίην ἀποτρέψατε γλώσσης 2(3).1
μανός. τὰ δ' ἔκτοθι μανὰ πέπηγεν 70
(75).1
μαντεύεσθαι. οὐκ ἂν ἀνήρ ... φρεσὶ
μαντεύσαιτο / ὡς ... 106(15).1
μάντις. εἰς δὲ τέλος μάντεις τε καὶ ὑμνοπόλοι 132(146).1
μαντοσύνη. οἱ μὲν μαντοσυνέων κεχρημ-
ένοι 102(112).10
μάργος. οἴδματι μάργῳ 91(100).7
μάρπτειν. ὣς γλυκὺ μὲν γλυκὺ μάρπτε 75
(90).1; ἐπεὶ οὖν μάρψωσι πολύχροα
φάρμακα χερσίν 15(23).3
μάταιος. ἐλθόντα ματαίως 33(39).2
μέγαρον. ἐν μεγάροισι 124(137).4
μέγας. μέγα νεῖκος 23(30).1; μέγα νήπιος
124(137).2; μέγαν οὐρανόν 35(41).1;
μέγαν ὄμβρον 44(50).1; μέγα ἄστυ 102
(112).1; μέγα χρῆμα 105(113).1; ὀλίγον
μείζων 83(98).4; κατὰ μεῖζον 51(59).1;
μεγίστη / πειθοῦς ἀνθρώποισιν ἁμαξιτός
96(133).2; μύσος ... μέγιστον 118
(128).9
*Μεγιστώ. πολυστέφανός τε Μεγιστώ 117
(123).2
μέδειν. τιμῆς δ' ἄλλης ἄλλο μέδει 8(17).
28
μεθιέναι. εἰσόκε χειρὶ μεθῇ 91(100).20
μειγνύναι. ἐπεὶ κατὰ μεῖζον ἐμίσγετο
δαίμονι δαίμων 51(59).1; ἁρμονίῃ μίξαντε 15(23).4; κατὰ φῶτα μιγέντα 13
(9).1; μεμιγμένα τῇ μὲν ἀπ' ἀνδρῶν /
τῇ δὲ γυναικοφυῆ 52(61).3; τῶν δέ τε
μισγομένων χεῖτ' ἔθνεα μυρία θνητῶν
47(35).7, 16; μόνον μίξις τε διάλλαξίς
τε μιγέντων 12(8).3
*μελάγκουρος. μελάγκουρός τ' Ἀσάφεια
116(122).4
μέλας. καὶ μέλανες διὰ τοῦτο ... ἄνδρες
58(67).2

μελεδήμων. ἀγαθῶν μελεδήμονες ἔργων
102(112).2
μέλειν. δειλὸς δ' ᾧ σκοτόεσσα θεῶν πέρι
δόξα μέμηλεν 95(132).2
μελέτη. ἡμετέρας μελέτας ... διὰ φροντίδος ἐλθεῖν 3(131).2; καθαρῇσιν ἐποπτεύσεις μελέτῃσιν 100(110).2
μέλι. ξανθῶν τε σπονδὰς μελίτων ῥίπτοντες 118(128).7
μέλος. μελέων φύσις 56(63).1; μελέων
ἐρατὸν δέμας 53(62).7; βροτέων μελέων
ὄγκον 26(20).1; κέρματα θηρείων μελέων
92(101).1; τὰ μέν τ' ἐνέμιμνε μελέων τὰ
δέ τ' ἐξεβεβήκει 47(35).11; λεπίδες ...
ἐπὶ στιβαροῖσι μέλεσσιν 71(82).2; ἐπεὶ
... μέγα νεῖκος ἐνὶ μελέεσσιν ἐθρέφθη
23(30).1; οὐ στάσις οὐδέ τε δῆρις ...
ἐν μελέεσσιν 98(27a).1
μέν. 1(2).1; 2(3).1; 6(4).1; 8(17).1, 4. 7,
9, 11, 16; 13(9).1, 3; 14(21).3; 15(23).4;
16(26).5, 8, 10; 19(27).2; 25(22).1;
26(20).1, 2; 31(37).1; 35(41).1; 37(47).1;
47(35).3, 11; 50(57).1; 52(61).1, 3;
53(62).4, 6; 56(63).1; 57(65).1; 69(76).1;
70(75).1; 75(90).1; 77(109).1; 81(103).
1; 82(104).1; 88(84).4, 9; 91(100).4,
6, 10, 16, 23; 93(102).1; [97(134).2];
102(112).10; 103(114).1; 106(15).2, 3;
107(115).9; 121(135).1; 130(125).1
μένος. αἰης λάσιον μένος 19(27).2; ἀνέμων
μένος 101(111).3; καταφθιμένου μένος
ἀνδρός 101(111).9; αἰθέριον μένος
107(115).9
μέριμνα. οὐ γὰρ σφιν δολιχόφρονές εἰσι
μέριμναι 104(11).1; δείλ' ... ἀμβλύνουσι μερίμνας 1(2).2, 100(110).7
μέρος. βίου μέρος 1(2).3; ἐν δὲ μέρει κρατέουσι 8(17).29, 16(26).1; ἐν μέρει
αἴσης 16(26).2; τὰ δύο τῶν ὀκτὼ μερέων 48(96).2; ἄρθμια μέρεσσιν 25(22).1
μέσος. ἐν δὲ μέσῃ ... στροφάλιγγι
47(35).4
μετά. μετὰ τοῖσιν 8(17).25; μετὰ πᾶσι
102(112).5
μεταλλάσσειν. μεταλλάσσοντα κελεύθους
107(115).8
μετάρσιος. ὅσσ' ἔτι νεῖκος ἔρυκε μετάρσιον
47(35).9
μεταφύειν. ὅσσον ἀλλοῖοι μετέφυν 80(108).
1
μέτωπον. ὄμματα ... πενητεύοντα μετώπων 50(57).3

μή. 9(12).1, 15(23).9, 18(24).2

μηδέ. 5(3).1, 8(17).21

μῆδος. μήδεα γεννήεντα 22(29).2; μήδεα
λαχνήεντα 97(134).3

μῆκος. ἴση μῆκός τε πλάτος τε 8(17).20;
μήκεος ὄλβου 111(119).1

μῆλον. ὑπέρφλοα μῆλα 66(80).1

μήν (particle). 69(76).2

μήν (month). μηνὸς ἐν ὀγδοάτου δεκάτῃ
59(68).1

μήνη. εὖρος γλαυκώπιδος . . . μήνης
41(42).3

μῆνιγξ. ἐν μήνιγξιν ἐεργμένον ὠγύγιον πῦρ
88(84).7

μήτε. 5(3).5, 7

μήτηρ. πατέρ' υἱὸς ἑλὼν καὶ μητέρα
παῖδες 124(137).5

μητίειν. πρὶν σχέτλι' ἔργα βορᾶς περὶ
χείλεσι μητίσασθαι 120(139).2

μῆτις. βροτείη μῆτις 1(2).9; πρὸς παρεὸν
γὰρ μῆτις ἀέξεται ἀνθρώποισιν 79(106).
1; ὑπὸ μήτιος εὖ δεδαῶτε 15(23).2

μαίνειν. εὖτέ τις . . . φόβῳ φίλα γυῖα
†μήνῃ† 107(115).3

μιν. 91(100).12, 107(115).6

μινυνθάδιος. ἡ δὲ φλὸξ ἱλάειρα μινυνθαδίης τύχε γαίης 84(85).1

μίξις. μόνον μίξις τε διάλλαξίς τε μιγέντων 12(8).3

μονίη. σφαῖρος κυκλοτερὴς μονίῃ περιηγέι
γαίων 21(27).3, 22(28).4

μόνος. αὐτὸ μόνον πεισθέντες 1(2).5; ἐν
ηὐξήθη μόνον εἶναι 8(17).1,16; ἀλλὰ
μόνον μίξις τε διάλλαξίς τε μιγέντων
12(8).3; συνέρχεται ἐν μόνον εἶναι
47(35).5; ἀλλὰ φρὴν ἱερὴ καὶ ἀθέσ-
φατος ἔπλετο μοῦνον 97(134).4; ἐπεὶ
μούνῳ σοι ἐγὼ κρανέω τάδε πάντα
101(111).2

μορφή. εἰ τι . . . λιπόξυλον ἔπλετο μορφῇ
14(21).2; μορφὴν δ' ἀλλάξαντα 124(137).
1

Μοῦσα. πολυμνήστη λευκώλενε παρθένε
Μοῦσα 2(3).3; ἄμβροτε Μοῦσα 3(131).
1; ὡς δὲ παρ' ἡμετέρης κέλεται πιστώματα Μούσης 6(4).2

μῦθος. οὐ γὰρ μῦθος ἀπόσκοπος 53(62).3;
θεοῦ πάρα μῦθον ἀκούσας 15(23).11;
ἀλλ' ἄγε μύθων κλῦθι . . . πιφαύσκων
πείρατα μύθων 8(17).14, 15; μύθων
. . . ἀτραπὸν μίαν 18(24).2; ἀληθείῃ
πάρα μύθοις / οὓς ἐγὼ ἐξερέω 103(114).1

μυκτήρ. μυκτῆρσιν ἐρευνῶν 92(101).1

μυρίος. οἱ δ' ἄμ' ἕπονται / μυρίοι ἐξερέοντες
102(112).9; τρίς μιν μυρίας ὥρας ἀπὸ
μακάρων ἀλάλησθαι 107(115).6; ἔθνεα
μυρία θνητῶν 47(35).7, 16; μυρία δειλά
100(110).7

μύρον. ἱλάσκοντο . . . μύροισί τε δαιδαλεόδμοις 118(128).5

μύσος. μύσος τοῦτ' ἔσκεν ἐν ἀνθρώποισι
μέγιστον 118(128).9

μυχός. παλίνορσον ἐπαΐξειε μυχόνδε
91(100).23

ναί. 69(76).2

ναίειν. †τάτ' αἰθέρι ναιήσονται† 101
(111).8; ναίετ' ἀν' ἄκρα πόλεος 102
(112).2

ναιετᾶν. ὄψει χθόνα χρωτὸς ὑπέρτατα
ναιετάουσαν 69(76).3

νεῖκος. νεῖκος οὐλόμενον 8(17).19; τῶν δὲ
συνερχομένων ἐξ ἔσχατον ἵστατο νεῖκος
20(36).1; ἐπεὶ . . . μέγα νεῖκος ἐνὶ
μελέεσσιν ἐθρέφθη 23(30).1; ἐπεὶ νεῖκος
μὲν ἐνέρτατον ἵκετο βένθος / δίνης 47
(35).3; πολλὰ δ' ἄμικτ' ἔστηκε . . . ὅσσ'
ἔτι νεῖκος ἔρυκε μετάρσιον 47(35).9;
ὀπώπαμεν . . . νεῖκος δέ τε νείκεϊ λυγρῷ 77(109).3; δίχ' ἕκαστα φορεύμενα
νείκεος ἔχθει 8(17).8, 16(26).6; μάλα
λυγρά / †νείκεος ἐννεσίῃσιν† 25(22).9;
νείκεϊ μαινομένῳ πίσυνος 107(115).14

νεκρός. ἐκ μὲν γὰρ ζωῶν ἐτίθει νέκρ'
εἴδε' ἀμείβων 130(125).1

νηλής. νηλεὲς ἦμαρ 120(139).1

Νημερτής. Νημερτής τ' ἐρόεσσα 116(122).
4

νήπιος. μέγα νήπιος 124(137).2; νήπιοι
104(11).1

νηστεύειν. νηστεῦσαι κακότητος 126(144).1

Νῆστις. Νῆστίς θ' ἣ δακρύοις τέγγει κρούνωμα βρότειον 7(6).3; τὼ δύο τῶν ὀκτὼ
μερέων λάχε Νήστιδος αἴγλης 48(96).2

νοεῖν. ὁπόση πόρος ἐστὶ νοῆσαι 5(3).7;
νόει δ' ᾗ δῆλον ἕκαστον 5(3).8; ὅτε τις
πρόοδον νοέων 88(84).1

νόημα. τῇ τε νόημα μάλιστα κικλήσκεται
ἀνθρώποισιν, / αἷμα γὰρ ἀνθρώποις
περικαρδιόν ἐστι νόημα 94(105). πάντα
γὰρ ἴσθι φρόνησιν ἔχειν καὶ νώματος
αἶσαν 100(110).10

νομίζειν. ἥτις καὶ θνητοῖσι νομίζεται
ἔμφυτος ἄρθροις 8(17).22

341   INDEX VERBORUM

νόμιμος. τὸ μὲν πάντων νόμιμον διά ...
αἰθέρος ἠνεκέως τέταται 121(135).1
νόμος. νόμῳ δ' ἐπίφημι καὶ αὐτός 13(9).5
νόσος. ἐπὶ νούσων παντοίων ... εὐηκέα
βάξιν 102(112).10; αὐχμηραὶ νόσοι
113(121).3
νοῦς. ἀλλήλους δάπτοντες ἀκηδείῃσι νόοιο
122(136).2; οὔτε νόῳ περιληπτά 1(2).8;
τὴν σὺ νόῳ δέρκευ 8(17).21
νῦν. 3(131).3, 27(38).2, 53(62).1, 60(71).4,
107(115).13
νύξ. νύκτα δὲ γαῖα τίθησιν 42(48).1; χειμερίην διὰ νύκτα 88(84).2; νυκτός ἐρημαίης ἀλαώπιδος 43(49).1
νῶτον. ἀπὸ νώτοιο δύο κλάδοι ἀΐσσονται
22(29).1, [97(134).2]; ἐχίνοις / ὀξυβελεῖς
χαῖται νώτοις ἐπιπεφρίκασιν 72(83).2

ξανθός. κατὰ ξανθοῦ 'Ακράγαντος 102
(112).1; ξανθῶν τε σπονδὰς μελίτων
ῥίπτοντες 118(128).7
ξένος. ξείνων αἰδοῖοι λιμένες 102(112).3
ξύλον. οἶνος ... σαπὲν ἐν ξύλῳ ὕδωρ
67(81).1

ὁ. (article) ἡ 48(96).1, 83(98).1, 84(85).1;
τό 1(2).6, 8(17).32, 16(26).7, 58(67).1,
80(108).2, 121(135).1; τοῦ †9(12).1, 10
(13).1, 33(39).3; τῷ 48(96).2; τῶν 5(3).
7, 48(96).2, 99(129).5
(demonstrative) ἡ περὶ ἄκρην 40(46).2;
τήν ... δέρκευ 8(17).21; τὴν οὔ τις
... δεδάηκε 8(17).25; τὴν οἵ γ'ἰλάσκ-
οντο 118(128).4; ἐν τῇ 47(35).5; †τά
14(21).14; δίχα τῶν 8(17).19; ἐκ τῶν
14(21).9, 15(23).5, 83(98).5; ἐν τοῖσιν
8(17).20; μετὰ τοῖσιν 8(17).25; πρὸς
τοῖς 8(17).30, 51(59).3; ἐπὶ τοῖς 12(8).
4; οἱ μέν ... οἱ δέ 102(112).10; τὰ
μέν ... τὰ δέ 47(35).11; τὴν μέν ...
ἡ δέ 8(17).4, 5; ὁ μὲν 35(41).1; ἡ μὲν
56(63).1; τοὺς μὲν 53(62).6; τὰ μὲν
15(23).4, 57(65).1; τῶν μέν 2(3).1; ὁ δέ
107(115).11, †124(137).3; τὸ δέ 13(9).4;
τῷ δέ 54(64).1; οἱ δέ 13(9).1, 102
(112).8, †124(137).2; αἱ δέ 88(84).9;
τὰ δέ 48(96).3, 52(61).2; τῶν δέ ...
τὰ δέ 70(75).1; τῶν δέ 20(36).1,
47(35).7, 16; τῶν γὰρ ἐγὼ νῦν εἰμί
107(115).13
(relative) τὸν πρότερον κατέλεξα 47
(35).2; τό ⟨γέ φασι⟩ γενέσθαι 13(9).3;

τὸ δή βίοτον καλέουσι 106(15).2; τῇ τε
φίλα φρονέουσι 8(17).23; τά τ' ἀμβλύνουσι μερίμνας 1(2).2; τὰ σῶμα λέλογχε
26(20).3; τὰ νῦν ἐσορῶμεν 27(38).2; τὰ
πρὶν μάθον 47(35).14; †τά 101(111).8
δαρος. τῶνδ' δάρων προτέρων ἐπιμάρτυρα
δέρκευ 14(21).1
ὀγδόατος. μηνὸς ἐν ὀγδοάτου δεκάτῃ
59(68).1
ὄγκος. ἀέρος ὄγκος 91(100).13; ἀμ βροτέων
μελέων ... ὄγκον 26(20).1
ὅδε. τόδε 115(120).1; τάδε 1(2).7, 16(26).
11, 47(35).5, 101(111).2; τῶνδε 8(17).
33, 14(21).1, 53(62)3, 60(71).1, 100
(110).4; τοῖσδε 105(113).1
ὀδύνη. χαλεπῇσι πεπαρμένοι ⟨ἀμφ' ὀδύν-
ῃσιν⟩ 102(112).12
ὀθόνη. πῦρ / λεπτῇσίν ⟨τ'⟩ ὀθόνῃσι λοχάζετο κύκλοπα κούρην 88(84).8
οἶδμα. αἰθήρ ... καταΐσσεται οἴδματι
μάργῳ 91(100).7; αἰθέρος εὐθὺς ῥεῦμα
κατέρχεται οἴδματι θῦον 91(100).24
οἴειν. οἴω 11(16).1
οἴμοι. οἴμοι, ὅτ' οὐ πρόσθεν με διώλεσε
νηλεὲς ἦμαρ 120(139).1
οἶνος. οἶνος ἀπὸ φλοιοῦ πέλεται σαπὲν ἐν
ξύλῳ ὕδωρ 67(81).1; ⟨ὕδωρ⟩ οἴνῳ μᾶλλον
ἐνάρθμιον 74(91).1
οἷος. οἷα 100(110).6; ἐξ οἵης τιμῆς 111
(119).1; οἵων ἐξ ἐρίδων 114(124).2
οἷος. ὄμματά τ' οἵ' ἐπλανᾶτο 50(57).3
οἰωνός. ἤδη γάρ ποτ' ἐγὼ γενόμην ...
θάμνος τ' οἰωνός τε 108(117).2; θῆρές
τ' οἰωνοί τε 14(21).11, 119(130).2;
θῆράς τ' οἰωνούς τε 15(23).7; γένος
... κατ' οἰωνῶν 13(9).3; οἰωνῶν πτερὰ
πυκνά 71(82).1
ὀκτώ. τὼ δύο τῶν ὀκτὼν μερέων 48(96).2
ὄλβιος. ὄλβιος ὃς θείων πραπίδων ἐκτήσατο πλοῦτον 95(132).1
ὄλβος. ἐξ ... ὅσσου μήκεος ὄλβου 111(119).1
ὀλέκειν. τὴν μὲν γὰρ πάντων σύνοδος
τίκτει τ' ὀλέκει τε 8(17).4
ὀλίγος. ὀλίγον τοῦ παντὸς ἰδόντων 33(39).
3; εἴτ' ὀλίγον μείζων 83(98).4
ὅλος. τὸ δ' ὅλον ⟨πᾶς⟩ εὔχεται εὑρεῖν
1(2).6
'Όλυμπος. ἀνταυγεῖ πρὸς 'Όλυμπον
36(44).1
ὄμβρος. ἄγγοσθ' ὄμβρος ἐσέρχεται ... αἰθήρ δ' ἐκτός ... ὄμβρον ἐρύκει 91(100).
12, 18; ὄμβρον δ' ἐν πᾶσι δνοφόεντα

τε ῥιγαλέον τε 14(21).5; Ἶρις δ᾽ ἐκ
πελάγους ἄνεμον φέρει ἢ μέγαν ὄμβρον
44(50).1; θήσεις δ᾽ ἐξ ὄμβροιο κελαινοῦ
καίριον αὐχμόν 101(111).6; χθόνα Κύπρις ἐπεί τ᾽ ἐδίηνεν ἐν ὄμβρῳ 62(73).1;
Ἡφαίστῳ τ᾽ ὄμβρῳ τε καὶ αἰθέρι
83(98).2
ὀμέστιος. ἀθανάτοις ἄλλοισιν ὀμέστιοι
133(147).1
ὄμμα. μηδ᾽ ὄμμασιν ἧσο τεθηπώς 8(17).
21; ὄμματά τ᾽ οἳ ἐπλανᾶτο πενητεύοντα μετώπων 50(57).3; ὄμματ᾽ ἔπηξεν
ἀτειρέα δι᾽ Ἀφροδίτῃ 85(86).1
ὁμοῖος. ἠνεκὲς αἰὲν ὁμοῖα 8(17).35; πῦρ
. . . θέλον πρὸς ὁμοῖον ἱκέσθαι 53(62).6
ὁμοιοῦν. ἀλλήλοις ἔστερκται ὁμοιωθέντ᾽
Ἀφροδίτῃ 25(22).5
ὁμοκλή. †ὁ δ᾽ ἀνήκουστος† ὁμοκλέων
124(137).3
Ὀμφαίη. Σωπῇ τε καὶ Ὀμφαίη 117(123).
3
ὀνομάζειν. φύσις δ᾽ ἐπὶ τοῖς ὀνομάζεται
ἀνθρώποισιν 12(8).4
ὀξυβελής. ἥλιος ὀξυβελής 34(40).1; ἐχίνοις
/ ὀξυβελεῖς χαῖται νώτοις ἐπιπεφρίκασι
72(83).2
ὀξύς. ὀξὺ δ᾽ ἐπ᾽ ὀξὺ ἔβη 75(90).2
ὄπῃ. 9(12).3, 51(59).2, 100(110).5, 102
(112).9
ὀπίσσω. 14(21).9, 91(100).25
ὁπλίζειν· ὡς δ᾽ ὅτε τις πρόοδον νοέων
ὡπλίσσατο λύχνον 88(84).1
ὀπός. ὡς δ᾽ ὅτ᾽ ὀπὸς γάλα λευκὸν ἐγόμφωσεν 61(33).1
ὁπόσος. ὁπόσῃ 5(3).7
ὁπόταν. 15(23).1, 91(100).6
ὁπότε. ὁππότε 91(100).23, 99(129).4
ὅπως. 53(62).1
ὁρᾶν. γαίῃ μὲν γὰρ γαῖαν ὀπώπαμεν 77
(109).1; ἠέλιον μὲν λευκὸν ὁρᾶν 14(21).
3; θαῦμα ἰδέσθαι 47(35).17; ἔνθ᾽ ὄψει
χθόνα 69(76).3; ἰδὼν ἀσυνήθεα χῶρον
112(118).1; ὀλίγον τοῦ παντὸς ἰδόντων
33(39).3
ὀργή. ὅτι σφίσι †γέννᾳι ἐν ὀργῇ† 25(22).9
ὀρέγειν. ὁππότε γὰρ πάσῃσιν ὀρέξαιτο
πραπίδεσσιν 99(129).4
*ὀρειλεχής. θηρσί τ᾽ ὀρειλεχέεσσιν 26(20).
7; λέοντες ὀρειλεχέες 131(127).1
ὅρκος. πλατέος παρ᾽ ἐλήλαται ὅρκου 23
(30).3; ἀνάγκης χρῆμα . . . πλατέεσσι
κατεσφρηγισμένον ὅρκοις 107(115).2

ὁρμή. φιλότητος ἀμεμφέος ἄμβροτος ὁρμή
47(35).13; δύσζηλος ἐπὶ φρένα πίστιος
ὁρμή 103(114).3
ὁρμίζειν. ἡ δὲ χθών . . . Κύπριδος ὁρμισθεῖσα τελείοις ἐν λιμένεσσιν 83(98).3
ὀρνύναι. βροτείη μῆτις ὄρωρεν 1(2).9;
(ἄνεμοι) ἐπὶ γαῖαν / ὀρνύμενοι 101
(111).4
ὀρούειν. πικρὸν δ᾽ ἐπὶ πικρὸν ὄρουσεν
75(90).1
ὄρπηξ. ἐννυχίους ὄρπηκας ἀνήγαγε κρινόμενον πῦρ 53(62).2
ὅς. ὅς 95(132).1, 99(129).2, †107(115).4;
ἤ 7(6).3; ὃ 17(25).1, 22(28).3; ᾧ 95(132).
2; ἐφ᾽ ᾧ 5(3).2; οἳ 15(23).3, 88(84).
4, 101(111).3, 104(11).2, 107(115).5; αἳ
88(84).9; ἃ 100(110).7; οὓς 103(114).2;
ὧν 2(3).4, 27(38).1, 85(86).1
ὀσία. ὀσίης πλέον εἰπεῖν 5(3).2
ὅσιος. ἐκ . . . ὁσίων στομάτων 2(3).2
ὀσμή. πνοίης τε λελόγχασι πάντα καὶ
ὀσμῶν 93(102).1
ὅσος. ὅσον 41(42).3, 82(104).1, 88(84).5,
10; ὅσσον 47(35)12, 80(108).1; ὅσσου
111(119).1; ὅσα 14(21).9(bis), 25(22).
4, 60(71).4, 70(75).1; ὅσσα 14(21).4,
15(23).10, 25(22).3, 47(35).9, 73(89).1,
101(111).1
ὅστις. ἥτις 8(17).22; ὅτῳ 1(2).5
ὀστοῦν. τὰ δ᾽ ὀστέα λευκὰ γένοντο 48(96).3
ὅταν. 91(100).8
ὅτε. 13(9).1, 61(33).1, 87(95).1, 88(84).1,
91(100).16
ὅτι. 25(22).9, 120(139).1
οὐ. 1(2).9; 8(17).11, 26; †13(9).5; 16(26).
10; 22(29).1, 2(ter); 47(35).6; 53(62).3;
74(91).2; 96(133).1; 97(134).[2], 3(ter);
98(27a).1; 104(11).1, 2; 106(15).1; 118
(128).8; 120(139).1; 122(136).1(bis)
οὖ. †ἑοῖ 22(29).2; οἷ 41(42).1
οὐδαμά. 8(17).6, 12; 16(26).11
οὖδας. ἔνερθ᾽ οὖδεος 32(52).1; πόντος δ᾽
ἐς χθονὸς οὖδας ἀπέπτυσε 107(115).10;
ῥίπτοντες ἐς οὖδας 118(128).7
οὐδέ. 8(17).30(bis), 10(13).1(bis), 12(8).2,
19(27).2(ter), 53(62).3, 97(134).1,
98(27a).1, 118(128).1(bis), 2(ter)
οὐδείς. οὐδέν 8(17).33, 106(15).4; οὐδενός
12(8).1
οὐδέτι. †91(100).12
οὐδέποτε. οὐδὲ ποτ᾽ οἴω 11(16).1
οὐκέτι. 8(17).31, 102(112).4

οὐλόμενος. νεῖκος οὐλόμενον 8(17).19; οὐλομένου θανάτοιο τελευτή 12(8).2
*οὐλοφυής. οὐλοφυεῖς τύποι 53(62).4
οὖν. 1(2).8, 15(23).3, 81(103).1, 93(102).1,
106(15).3
οὕνεκα. 103(114).1; οὕνεκεν 66(80).1
οὕποτε. 123(145).2
οὕπω. οὐ γὰρ ἀμεμφέως / πω πᾶν ἐξέστηκεν 47(35).9-10
οὐρανός. ἠλέκτωρ τε χθών τε καὶ οὐρανὸς
ἠδὲ θάλασσα 25(22).2; μέγαν οὐρανὸν
ἀμφιπολεύει 35(41).1
οὔτε. 1(2).7(bis), 8; 19(27).1; 21(27).1;
53(62).7, 8(bis)
οὔτις. 8(17).25
οὗτος. τοῦτο 8(17).32, †26(20).1, 58(67).
2, 69(76).1, 118(128).9; ταῦτα 8(17).6,
27, 34; 14(21).13; 15(23).11; 16(26).3;
†25(22).1; 51(59).2; 100(110).3,5;
τούτων 11(16).2, 78(107).1; τούτοις
78(107).2; τούτοισιν 83(98).1
οὕτως. 1(2).7, 8(17).9, 16(26).8, 21(27).
2; οὕτω 15(23).9, 29(53).1, 65(79).1
ὀφθαλμός. οὐκ ἔστιν πελάσασθαι ἐν ὀφθαλμοῖσιν ἐφικτόν 96(133).1
ὄφρα. 106(15).2
ὀχετεύειν. ἐκ δ' ὁσίων στομάτων καθαρήν
ὀχετεύσατε πηγήν 2(3).2
ὄψ. μία γίγνεται ἀμφοτέρων ὄψ 89(88).1
ὀψίγονος. ὀψίγονοί τε σίδαι 66(80).1
ὄψις. μήτε τιν' ὄψιν ἔχων †πίστει† πλέον
ἢ κατ' ἀκουήν 5(3).5; †δι' ὄψιος†
54(64).1

παίζειν.   παῖς / κλεψύδρη   παίζουσα
91(100).9
παῖς. παῖς / κλεψύδρη παίζουσα 91(100).
8; ὡς δ' αὕτως πατέρ' υἱὸς ἑλὼν καὶ
μητέρα παῖδες 124(137).5
παλαιός. θεῶν ψήφισμα παλαιόν 107(115).
1
παλάμη. στεινωποί ... παλάμαι κατὰ
γυῖα κέχυνται 1(2).1; ἄθρει πάσῃ παλάμῃ πῇ δῆλον ἕκαστον 5(3).4; Κύπριδος
ἐν παλάμῃσι 70(75).2; 87(95).1
πάλιν. 8(17).5, 10; 16(26)9; 91(100).8,
20; 101(111).5
παλίνορσος. παλίνορσος ἐλεύσομαι 47(35).
1; αἷμα ... ὁππότε μὲν παλίνορσον
ἐπάιξειε μυχόνδε 91(100).23
παλίντιτος. παλίντιτα πνεύματ' ἐπάξεις
101(111).5

πάμπαν. πάμπαν ἀπείρων 22(28).3; δάφνης φύλλων ἄπο πάμπαν ἔχεσθαι
127(140).1
παμφανόων. αἰθέρι παμφανόωντι 83(98).2
πάνδειλος. δειλοὶ πάνδειλοι 128(141).1
πάντῃ. πάντῃ συγγίγνεσθαι ἀήθεα 25(22).
8
πάντοθεν. πάντοθεν ἶσος ⟨ἐοῖ⟩ 22(28).3
παντοῖος. παντοῖα ... εἴδεα θνητῶν
107(115).7; παντοίων ἀνέμων 88(84).3;
παντοίων ... σοφῶν ἐπιήρανος ἔργων
99(129).3; ἐπὶ νούσων / παντοίων 102
(112).11; παντοίαις ἰδέῃσιν ἀρηρότα
47(35).17
πάντοσε. πάντοσ' ἐλαυνόμενοι 1(2).6
παρά. παρ' Εὐσεβίης 2(3).5; παρ' ἡμετέρης ... Μούσης 6(4).2; πάρα δ' ἦθος
ἑκάστῳ 8(17).28; θεοῦ πάρα 15(23).11;
παρ' ἐλήλαται ὅρκου 23(30).3; πάρα
μύθοις 103(114).1; σφιν πάρα 106(15).3
παρεῖναι. δι' αἰῶνος παρέσονται 100(110).
3; πρὸς παρεὸν γὰρ μῆτις ἀέξεται
79(106).1
παρθένος. παρθένε Μοῦσα 2(3).3
παριστάναι. καὶ τὸ φρονεῖν ἀλλοῖα παρίσταται 80(108).2; εὐχομένῳ νῦν αὖτε
παρίστασο 3(131).3
πάρος. ὡς πάρος ἦν τε καὶ ἔσσεται
11(16).1; γίγνεσθαι πάρος οὐκ ἐὸν ἐλπίζουσιν 104(11).2
πᾶς. †1(2).6; τὸ πᾶν 8(17).32, 16(26).7;
πᾶν ἐξέστηκεν 47(35).10; τοῦ παντός
10(13).1, 33(39).3; πάσῃ παλάμῃ 5(3).
4; πάντες 107(115).12; πάντα 8(17).
27; 14(21).7, 9; 24(31).1; 25(22).1; 47
(35).5; 64(78).2; 78(107).1; 93(102).1;
100(110).3, 10; 101(111).2; 119(130).1;
πάντα ... πᾶσι 91(100).1; πάντων
7(6).1, 8(17).4, 73(89).1, 99(129).5,
121(135).1; πᾶσι 14(21).5, 15(23).5,
102(112).5; πάσῃσιν 121(135).1
πατήρ. πατὴρ φίλον υἱὸν ἀείρας ...
αὕτως πατέρ' υἱὸς ἑλὼν 124(137).1, 5
παύειν. παύσεις δ' ἀκαμάτων ἀνέμων
μένος 101(111).3; οὐ παύσεσθε φόνοιο
δυσηχέος 122(136).1
παῦρος. παῦρον ... βίου μέρος 1(2).3
Παυσανίας. Παυσανίη, σὺ δὲ κλῦθι 4(1).1
παφλάζειν. αἰθὴρ παφλάζων 91(100).7
πείθειν. αὐτὸ μόνον πεισθέντες, ὅτῳ προ-
σέκυρσεν ἕκαστος 1(2).5
πειθώ. ἠπύει τε μεγίστη / πειθοῦς ἀνθρώ-

ρεῖα. ρεῖα ... λεύσσεσκεν ἕκαστον 99 (129).5

ρεῦμα. αἰθέρος ... ρεῦμα 91(100).24; ρεύματα δενδρεόθρεπτα 101(111).8

ρευστός. ἔργα τε ρευστά 113(121).3

ρηγμίν. περὶ ρηγμῖνι βίοιο 26(20).5

*ριγαλέος. ὄμβρον δ' ἐν πᾶσι δνοφόεντά τε ριγαλέον τε 14(21).5

ρίζα. αἰθήρ ... μακρῆσι κατὰ χθόνα δύετο ρίζαις 30(54).1

ρίζωμα. τέσσαρα γὰρ πάντων ριζώματα πρῶτον ἄκουε 7(6).1

ριπή. ριπῆσιν ... ἠελίοιο 45(56).1

ρίπτειν. σπονδὰς μελίτων ρίπτοντες ἐς οὖδας 118(128).7

ρίς. ρινῶν ἔσχατα τέρθρα 91(100).4

ρόος. πυκινὸν ρόον 91(100).14

σάρξ. αἷμα ... καὶ ἄλλης εἴδεα σαρκός 83(98).5; φίλας κατὰ σάρκας ἔδουσιν 124(137).6; σαρκῶν σύριγγες 91(100). 2; σαρκῶν ἀλλογνῶτι περιστέλλουσα χιτῶνι 110(126).1

σεβίζειν. εὖτ' ἂν ἴκωμαι ἐς ἄστεα τηλεθάοντα ... σεβίζομαι 102(112).8

σέλας. πυρὸς σέλας αἰθομένοιο 88(84).2

σελήνη. ἱλάειρα σελήνη 34(40).1; ὡς αὐγὴ τύψασα σεληναίης κύκλον εὐρύν 38(43). 1

σήπειν. οἶνος ἀπὸ φλοιοῦ πέλεται σαπὲν ἐν ξύλῳ ὕδωρ 67(81).1

σῆψις. αὐχμηραί τε νόσοι καὶ σήψιες 113(121).3

σίδη. ὀψίγονοί τε σίδαι 66(80).1

σκιερός. †σκιεροῖς† ἠσκημένα γυίοις 52 (61).4

σκοτόεις. σκοτόεσσα θεῶν πέρι δόξα 95 (132).2

σκότος. κατὰ σκότος ἠλάσκουσιν 113(121). 4

σμύρνα. ἱλάσκοντο ... σμύρνης τ' ἀκρήτου θυσίαις 118(128).6

σοφία. σοφίης ἐπ' ἄκροισι †θοάζει† 5(3).3

σοφός. ἀνὴρ τοιαῦτα σοφός 106(15).1; σοφῶν ἐπιήρανος ἔργων 99(129).3

σπλάγχνον. διατμηθέντος ἐνὶ σπλάγχνοισι λόγοιο 6(4).3

σπονδή. ξανθῶν τε σπονδὰς μελίτων ρίπτοντες 118(128).7

στάσις. οὐ στάσις οὐδέ τε δῆρις ... ἐν μελέεσσιν 98(27a).1

στεινωπός. στεινωποί ... παλάμαι 1(2).1

στέργειν. ἀλλήλοις ἔστερκται ὁμοιωθέντ' 'Αφροδίτη 25(22).5

*στερεωπός. ἐκ δ' αἴης προρέουσι ... στερεωπά 14(21).6

στέφος. ταινίαις τε περίστεπτος στέφεσίν τε θαλείοις 102(112).6

στήκειν. πολλὰ δ' ἄμικτ' ἔστηκε 47(35).8

στηρίζειν. ἁρμονίης πυκινῷ κρυφῷ ἐστήρικται / σφαῖρος κυκλοτερής 21(27).2

στιβαρός. ἐπὶ στιβαροῖσι μέλεσσιν 71 (82).2

στόλος. λόγου στόλον οὐκ ἀπατηλόν 8(17). 26

στόμα. ἐκ δ' ὁσίων στομάτων ... ὀχετεύσατε πηγήν 2(3).2; διὰ πολλῶν δὴ γλώσσης ἐλθόντα ματαίως / ἐκκέχυται στομάτων 33(39).3

στόμιον. καί σφιν ἐπὶ στομίοις πυκναῖς τέτρηνται ἄλοξιν 91(100).3

στοναχή. ἔκ τε στοναχῶν ἐγένεσθε 114 (124).2

στοργή. στοργὴν δὲ στοργῇ (ὀπώπαμεν) 77 (109).3

στροφάλιγξ. ἐν δὲ μέσῃ φιλότης στροφάλιγγι γένηται 47(35).4

στυγεῖν. στυγέουσι δὲ πάντες 107(115).12; στυγέει δύστλητον ἀνάγκην 109(116).1

σύ. σύ 1(2).8; 4(1).1; 8(17).21, 26; 100 (110).6; σέ 5(3).1, 15(23).9, 100(110). 8; σοί 60(71).1, 100(110).3, 101(111).2 (Παυσανίας); σέ 2(3).3 (Μοῦσα)

συγγίνεσθαι. πάντῃ συγγίνεσθαι ἀήθεα 25 (22).8

συγκυρεῖν. συνέκυρσε 29(53).1, 51(59).2, 83(98).1; ξυνέκυρσεν 82(104).1

συμβαίνειν. σὺν δ' ἔβη ἐν φιλότητι 14 (21).8

συμπίπτειν. ταῦτά τε συμπίπτεσκον, ὅπῃ συνέκυρσεν ἕκαστα 51(59).2

συμφύειν. †ἐν† συμφύεται 16(26).7; ὅτε ξὺμ πρῶτ' ἐφύοντο 87(95).1

συναρμόζειν. συναρμοσθέντ' 'Αφροδίτῃ 60 (71).4

συνέρχεσθαι. συνέρχεται ἓν μόνον εἶναι 47 (35).5; συνερχόμεν' εἰς ἓν ἅπαντα 8 (17).7, 26(20).2; εἰς ἕνα κόσμον 16(26). 5; τῶν δὲ συνερχομένων ἐξ ἔσχατον ἵστατο νεῖκος 20(36).1

συνιστάναι. συνιστάμεν' ἄλλοθεν ἄλλα 47 (35).6

σύνοδος. τὴν μὲν γὰρ πάντων σύνοδος τίκτει τ' ὀλέκει τε 8(17).4

οἵης τιμῆς 111(119).1; (νεῖκος) εἰς
τιμάς τ' ἀνόρουσε 23(30).2; (θεοί)
τιμῇσι φέριστοι 14(21).12, 15(23).8,
132(146).3
τίς. τοῦτο δ' ἐπαυξήσειε τὸ πᾶν τί κε 8
(17).32; τί τοῖσδ' ἐπίκειμαι 105(113).1
τις. τις 9(12).3, 12(8).2, 88(84).1, 99
(129).1, 107(115).3, 118(128).1; τινα
5(3).5; τι 5(3).7, †8(17).30, 10(13).1,
14(21).2, 53(62).7, 60(71).1, 104(11).
3, 105(113).1; τινος 3(131).1
Τιτάν. Τιτὰν ἠδ' αἰθήρ 27(38).4
τοι. †3(131).2, 8(17).14, 12(8).1, 27(38).1
τοιγάρτοι. 123(145).1
τοιόσδε. πλάδης τοιῆσδε 70(75).2
τοιοῦτο. τοιαῦτα σοφός 106(15).1
τορός. τορῶς ταῦτ' ἴσθι 15(23).11
τόσος. τόσον 47(35).12, 80(108).1; τόσσον
41(42).3; τόσσα 60(71).4
τότε. 5(3).3, 13(9).3, 29(53).1, 62(73).1,
88(84).7, 91(100).20
τοτέ. τοτὲ μέν . . . τοτὲ δέ 8(17).1, 2,
16, 17
τόφρα. ὄφρα μέν τε βιῶσι . . . τόφρα μὲν
οὖν εἰσίν 106(15).3
*τράνωμα. ὑπὲρ τρανώματα γλώσσης 5
(3).6
τρέφειν. αὐτὰρ ἐπεὶ μέγα νεῖκος ἐνὶ μελέεσσιν ἐθρέφθη 23(30).1; ἡ δὲ πάλιν
διαφυομένων θρεφθεῖσα διέπτη 8(17).5;
αἵματος ἐν πελάγεσσι †τεθραμμένη
ἀντιθορόντος† 94(105).1
τρῆμα. ἀέρος ὄγκος ἔσωθε πεσὼν ἐπὶ τρή-
ματα πυκνά 91(100).13
τρίς. τρὶς μιν μυρίας ὥρας 107(115).6
τυγχάνειν. ἡ δὲ φλὸξ ἱλάειρα μινυνθαδίης
τύχε γαίης 84(85).1; μάλα δ' ἀργαλέη
τέτυκται / ἀνδράσι (ἀληθείη) 103(114).
2; πλάδης τοιῆσδε τυχόντα 70(75).2
τύπος. οὐλοφυεῖς . . . τύποι 53(62).4
τύπτειν. αὐγὴ τύψασα σεληναίης κύκλον
38(43).1
τύχη. ἰότητι τύχης πεφρόνηκεν ἅπαντα
81(103).1

ὑγρός. ὑγρὸς ἀήρ 27(38).3
*ὑδατοθρέμμων. ὑδατοθρέμμονες ἰχθῦς 14
(21).11; ὑδατοθρέμμονας ἰχθῦς 15(23).7
*ὑδρομέλαθρος. ἰχθύσιν ὑδρομελάθροις 26
(20).6
ὕδωρ. πῦρ καὶ ὕδωρ καὶ γαῖα καὶ ἠέρος
ἄπλετον ὕψος 8(17).18; οἶνος . . . σαπὲν

ἐν ξύλῳ ὕδωρ 67(81).1; αἴσιμον ὕδωρ
91(100).15, 21; ὅθ' ὕδωρ μὲν ἔχει κατὰ
βένθεα χαλκοῦ 91(100).16; (ὕδωρ) οἴνῳ
μᾶλλον ἐνάρθμιον 74(91).1; (ὀπώπαμεν)
ὕδατι δ' ὕδωρ 77(109).1; ὕδατός τε καὶ
εἴδεος αἶσαν ἔχοντες 53(62).5; ὕδατος
γαίης τε καὶ αἰθέρος ἠελίου τε / κιρναμένων 60(71).2; αἱ δ' ὕδατος μὲν
βένθος ἀπέστεγον ἀμφινάοντος 88(84).9;
ὕδατος . . . τέρεν δέμας ἀργυφέοιο 91
(100).11; ἄλφιτον ὕδατι κολλήσας 49
(34).1
υἱός. δαΐφρονος Ἀγχίτεω υἱέ 4(1).1; πατὴρ φίλον υἱὸν ἀείρας . . . αὔτως πατέρ' υἱὸς ἑλών 124(137).1, 5
ὑμεῖς. ἐγὼ δ' ὑμῖν θεὸς ἄμβροτος . . .
πωλεῦμαι 102(112).4
ὑμνοπόλος. εἰς δὲ τέλος μάντεις τε καὶ
ὑμνοπόλοι καὶ ἰητροί / καὶ πρόμοι . . .
πέλονται 132(146).1
ὕμνος. ἐς πόρον ὕμνων 47(35).1
ὑπεκθεῖν. ὑπεκθέει αἴσιμον ὕδωρ 91(100).
21
ὑπεκπροθεῖν. ὅσσον δ' αἰὲν ὑπεκπροθέοι,
τόσον αἰὲν ἐπήει 47(35).12
ὑπένερθε. εἰσόκεν †ἓν† συμφύντα τὸ πᾶν
ὑπένερθε γένηται 16(26).7
ὑπέρ. ὑπὲρ τρανώματα γλώσσης 5(3).6
ὑπέρτατος. χθόνα χρωτὸς ὑπέρτατα ναιετάουσαν 69(76).3
*ὑπέρφλοος. ὑπέρφλοα μῆλα 66(80).1
ὑπό. ἠλύθομεν τόδ' ὑπ' ἄντρον 115(120).
1; ἀνέρες ἀμφὶ τέχνης ὑπὸ μήτιος εὖ
δεδαῶτε 15(23).2; ὑπὸ πραπίδεσσιν ἐρείσας 100(110).1
ὑπόστεγος. ἠλύθομεν τόδ' ὑπ' ἄντρον ὑπ-
όστεγον 115(120).1
ὑφιστάναι. νύκτα δὲ γαῖα τίθησιν, ὑφισταμένη φαέεσσι 42(48).1
ὕψος. ἠέρος ἄπλετον ὕψος 8(17).18

φαέθων. ἐς αὐγάς / ἠελίου φαέθοντος 107
(115).11
φάναι. τότε μὲν τὸ ⟨γέ φασι⟩ γενέσθαι
13(9).3
φάρμακον. πολύχροα φάρμακα 15(23).3;
φάρμακα δ' ὅσσα γεγᾶσι κακῶν 101
(111).1
φέρειν. Ἶρις δ' ἐκ πελάγους ἄνεμον φέρει
44(50).1
φερέσβιος. Ἥρη τε φερέσβιος 7(6).2
φέριστος. θεοὶ τιμῇσι φέριστοι 14(21).12,

132(146).3; θεοὺς τιμῆσι φερίστους 15 (23).8

φθείρειν. εἴτε γὰρ ἐφθείροντο διαμπερές, οὐκέτ' ἂν ἦσαν 8(17).31

Φθιμένη. Φυσώ τε Φθιμένη τε 117(123).1

φθίνειν. καὶ φθίνει εἰς ἄλληλα καὶ αὔξεται ἐν μέρει αἴσης 16(26).2

φίλος. ὦ φίλοι 102(112).1, 103(114).1; φίλον υἱὸν ἀείρας 124(137).1; ποθέοντα φίλην ἐπὶ γένναν ἱκέσθαι 100(110).9; φίλας κατὰ σάρκας ἔδουσιν 124(137).6; τῇ τε φίλα φρονέουσι 8(17).23; φίλα γυῖα 107(115).3

φιλότης. φιλότης ἐν τοῖσιν, ἴση μῆκός τε πλάτος τε 8(17).20; ἐν δὲ μέσῃ φιλότης στροφάλιγγι γένηται ... τόσον αἰὲν ἐπήει / ἠπιόφρων φιλότητος ἀμεμφέος ἄμβροτος ὁρμή 47(35).4, 13; ἄλλοτε μὲν φιλότητι συνερχόμεν' εἰς ἓν ἅπαντα 8 (17).7, 26(20).2; εἰς ἕνα κόσμον 16(26). 5; σὺν δ' ἔβη ἐν φιλότητι καὶ ἀλλήλοισι ποθεῖται 14(21).8

φιλοφροσύνη. φιλοφροσύνη τε δεδήει 119 (130).2

φλοιός. οἶνος ἀπὸ φλοιοῦ πέλεται σαπὲν ἐν ξύλῳ ὕδωρ 67(81).1

φλόξ. ἡ δὲ φλὸξ ἱλάειρα μινυνθαδίης τύχε γαίης 84(85).1

φόβος. φόβῳ φίλα γυῖα †μήνητ† 107(115).3

φόνος. ἔνθα φόνος τε κότος τε 113(121). 2; ὥστε φόνον μὲν κεύθειν 91(100).4; οὐ παύσεσθε φόνοιο δυσηχέος 122(136). 1; ταύρων δ' †ἀκριτοισι† φόνοις οὐ δεύετο βωμός 118(128).8

φορεύειν. δίχ' ἕκαστα φορεύμενα νείκεος ἔχθει 8(17).8, 16(26).6

*Φορύη. Μεγιστώ / καὶ Φορύη 117(123).3

φρήν. φρὴν ἱερή 97(134).4; μή σ' ἀπάτη φρένα καινύτω 15(23).9; πειθοῦς ἀνθρώποισιν ἁμαξιτὸς εἰς φρένα πίπτει 96 (133).3; δύσζηλος ἐπὶ φρένα πίστιος ὁρμή 103(114).3; μάθη γάρ τοι φρένας αὔξει 8(17).14; οὐκ ἂν ἀνὴρ τοιαῦτα σοφὸς φρεσὶ μαντεύσαιτο 106(15).1

φρονεῖν. φίλα φρονέουσι 8(17).23; τούτοις φρονέουσι 78(107).2; ἰότητι τύχης πεφρόνηκεν ἅπαντα 81(103).1; καὶ τὸ φρονεῖν ἀλλοῖα παρίσταται 80(108).2

φρόνησις. πάντα γὰρ ἴσθι φρόνησιν ἔχειν 100(110).10

φροντίς. ἡμετέρας μελέτας ... διὰ φροντίδος ἐλθεῖν 3(131).2; φρὴν ἱερή ...

φροντίσι κόσμον ἅπαντα καταΐσσουσα θοῇσιν 97(134).5

φυγάς. φυγὰς θεόθεν καὶ ἀλήτης 107(115). 13

φύειν. θνήτ' ἐφύοντο 47(35).14; ἀμφίστερν' ἐφύοντο 52(61).1; ὅσσα φιν ἐν θνητοῖσιν ἀποπλαχθέντα πέφυκε 25 (22).3; ἐν ἐκ πλεόνων μεμάθηκε φύεσθαι 8(17).9, 16(26).8; φυόμενον παντοῖα διὰ χρόνου εἴδεα θνητῶν 107(115).7

φύλλον. ταὐτὰ τρίχες καὶ φύλλα 71(82).1; δάφνης φύλλων ἀπο πάμπαν ἔχεσθαι 127(140).1

φῦλον. φῦλον ἄμουσον ἄγουσα πολυσπερέων καμασήνων 68(74).1

φύσις. φύσις οὐδενὸς ἐστιν ἀπάντων / θνητῶν ... ἀλλὰ μόνον μίξις τε διάλλαξίς τε μιγέντων / ἐστί, φύσις δ' ἐπὶ τοῖς ὀνομάζεται ἀνθρώποισιν 12(8).1, 4; διέσπασται μελέων φύσις 56(63).1; αὔξει / ταῦτ' εἰς ἦθος ἕκαστον, ὅπη φύσις ἐστὶν ἑκάστῳ 100(110).5

*Φυσώ. Φυσώ τε Φθιμένη τε 117(123).1

φῶς. κατὰ φῶτα μιγέντα 13(9).1

φῶς. ἀλλότριον φῶς 39(45).1; φῶς δ' ἔξω διαθρῷσκον 88(84).5; νύκτα δὲ γαῖα τίθησιν, ὑφισταμένη φαέεσσι 42(48).1

χαίρειν. ὦ φίλοι ... χαίρετε 102(112).4

χαίτη. ἐχίνοις / ὀξυβελεῖς χαῖται νώτοις ἐπιπεφρίκασιν 72(83).1

χαλεπός. χαλεπῇσι πεπαρμένοι ⟨ἀμφ' ὀδύνῃσιν⟩ 102(112).12; χαλεπῇσιν ἀλύοντες κακότησιν 123(145).1

χαλκός. κλεψύδρῃ ... διειπετέος χαλκοῖο ... κατὰ βένθεα χαλκοῦ 91(100).9, 16; χαλκῷ ἀπὸ ψυχὴν ἀρύσας 125(138).1; ταναήκεϊ χαλκῷ 129(143).1

χαμαιεύνης. λέοντες ὀρειλεχέες χαμαιεῦναι 131(127).1

χεῖλος. ἔργα βορᾶς περὶ χείλεσι μητίσασθαι 120(139).2

χειμέριος. χειμερίην διὰ νύκτα 88(84).2

χεῖν. στεινωποί ... παλάμαι κατὰ γυῖα κέχυνται 1(2).1; χεῖτ' ἔθνεα μυρία θνητῶν 47(35).7, 16

χείρ. ἐπ' εἰειδεῖ χερὶ ... εἰσόκε χειρὶ μεθῇ 91(100).10, 20; κυάμων ἀπο χείρας ἔχεσθαι 128(141).1; μάρψωσι ... φάρμακα χερσίν 15(23).3; οὐκ ἔστιν ... χερσὶ λαβεῖν 96(133).2

χέλυς. λιθορρίνων χελύων 69(76).2

Index Locorum

Index Nominum et Rerum